Zohl dé Ishtar, an Irish-Australian Lesbian who, since 1983, has travelled to twenty-seven countries, some of them more than once, raising people's awareness of the Pacific or in the Pacific learning from the women. During the 1980s she organised tours to Britain for Indigenous Pacific women.

Daughters of the Pacific contains stories given to her by Indigenous Pacific and Aboriginal women during a 1986–87 journey through the Pacific. While living at Greenham Common Women's Peace Camp (Britain, 1983–88), she initiated a national network, Women Working for a Nuclear Free and Independent Pacific. Zohl established the bulletin, *Be Active for a Nuclear Free and Independent Pacific*, and coedited the booklet, *Pacific Women Speak: "Why Haven't You Known?"*.

Zohl co-edited *Connecting Cultures*, with Chris Sitka, for the National Lesbian Conference, Sydney, 1991. She worked with Hilda Halkyard-Harawira and Katie Boanas, on "Women and the Peace Movement in Aotearoa" in Rosemary De Plessis (Ed.) *Feminist Voices. Women's Studies Texts for Aotearoa/New Zealand*, Auckland: Oxford University Press, 1992.

Zohl is the initiator and convenor of the Lesbian Cancer Foundation which has recently produced *Strategies of Care: A Study into Lesbian Experiences of Cancer*. She is presently working on her second book, *Keepers of the Fire: Stories from the Common*, which reflects the experiences of women who have lived at Greenham Common during the thirteen years of its continuing empowerment of women.

T0159867

DAUGHTERS

OF

THE PACIFIC

Zohl dé Ishtar

Spinifex Press Pty Ltd,
504 Queensberry Street,
North Melbourne, Vic. 3051
Australia

First published by Spinifex Press, 1994

Typeset in 11/14 pt Times
   by Claire Warren, Melbourne
Printed in Australia by Australian Print Group, Maryborough
Cover photograph by Zohl dé Ishtar
Cover design by Lin Tobias

National Library of Australia
Cataloguing-in-Publication entry:

CIP

dé Ishtar, Zohl, 1953–   .
   Daughters of the Pacific

   ISBN 1 875559 32 9

   1. Women – Islands of the Pacific. 2. Women – Australasia.
   3. Oral history. I. Title.

305.4099

Oz C'cil
logo

This publication is assisted by the Australia Council, the
Australian Government's arts funding and advisory body.

This book is dedicated to
Abiko Ralpho
Daughter of the Rongelap People
and to all
Daughters of the Pacific.

At the young age of six
Abiko held the future still
long enough for me to see.
She encouraged me to believe in justice.
The love she shared with me
has guided my work over long years.
I salute her spirit.

The spirit of resistance is strong.

Her photo on the cover
reminds us that we work for a Pacific
that is safe for our children.

In memory of my mother
Patricia O'Donoghue Hanlon
my own matriarch.

Foreword I

To most people of the world, we ... who are called "Pacific Islanders" ... are not real.

We are thought of as people of the past; people who come from small island states; people who live in the sun by sky blue oceans.

We are thought of romantically ... by the Western world ... with images of beautiful women thinly clad in cloth with hibiscus patterns, flowers in our hair, hips swaying under the coconut palm trees, beckoning the Western world into a world of magic and romance.

Our traditions and cultures are thought of as entertainment, some seventh wonder of the world, as a show to visit and see, but for the most part to be left on the storybook shelves, or in the natural history section of the museums of the world, alongside the fossils, the dinosaurs and other dead things.

WE are alive, equipped by the Gods and Goddesses to share with you once again that piece of the puzzle which is uniquely ours, by virtue of our unique history and the gifts that have evolved from our unique experiences of tradition and culture.

WE are alive, with our traditional scientific data that offers solutions to the problems caused by Western scientists and researchers.

WE are alive with a body of wisdom, made up of many parts, which have been developed, collected, preserved and passed on to us from our ancestors of many Pacific Ocean Nations, from ancient times. True democracy has been practised by Indigenous peoples for thousands of years.

WE have a genius for government. WE have a genius for human relations. WE know how to protect Mother Earth, Father Sky, Mother Ocean/Father Ocean.

WE, the Indigenous peoples of the Pacific Ocean, who live on our huge oceans and land mass, see the destruction first because most of us live on the nuclear front line – but you will see it soon.

WE are alive because Zohl dé Ishtar keeps our stories alive, because this woman and her friend Bridget travelled and stayed on our lands, and experienced the realities of our struggle to survive. Committed women of the Western Hemisphere are strong –

thank you Zohl in your continued effort to put to print our stories, our songs: songs that will be sung forever; our plight which will benefit the world. Thank you. We support the writing of these stories. We support you in this effort.

WE are alive because Women Working for a Nuclear Free and Independent Pacific are working, because Greenham Common women are working. Because women all over the Pacific Ocean are working. In many different organisations: Maori women in the forefront of struggle, writing their own histories; Micronesian women; matrilineal women; Melanesian women; Polynesian women; Indigenous women of Australia and of Great Turtle [North Americas]. Women, in their organizations, are talking and sharing their struggles.

WE are alive, because we fight for our rights to a safe environment for the future of our children. Our elders, our young mothers, our children, our menfolk are all fighting for our survival, and we will never die. The struggle will be kept alive in our children.

WE are alive, because this book will continue to tell the stories, and though it is eight years of compilation, it will always be the same until the Western culture understands the losses they faced many thousands of years ago; until they connect themselves to the traditions of their people; until they connect themselves to an understanding that the future for their children also is bleak.

WAKE UP WORLD! When the headlines show Indigenous people resisting governments' so-called "development", destructions of our Mother Earth, our forests, our oceans, our rivers, this is not some tug-of-war over a real estate deal: it is a matter of life and death, for we are part of the environment. It's all happening far from your eyes, but it's in our backyards, and we are dead serious.

For we know that Mother Earth does not belong to us: but that we belong to Mother Earth.

Hinewirangi Kohu
Ngati Kahungungu Ngati Ranginui (Maori)
Aotearoa, 1994

Foreword II

I first really heard about the Pacific in 1984 at Greenham Common. This wild Australian woman called Zohl just wouldn't shut up about Ebeye, Bikini, Maralinga, Belau. I joined up with her to raise money so that Pacific women could come to Britain and tell their stories directly. The women who came opened my eyes and my heart.

We started networking, nationally and internationally, joining threads, spinning new ones, contacting women and men far and wide to extend a web – however fragile – which would trap and weaken oppression and break the patterns of silences and disinformation.

Then I travelled through parts of the Pacific. What did I learn from the women I met? Endurance, humour, compassion, a sense of connection to elders and to future generations, the value of story-telling.

This book is about tiny communities and global issues. The truth of these women's stories is both their own and every woman's. I hope that reading them will bring under-standing and, beyond understanding, action.

Bridget Roberts
Australia, 1994

Contents

Acknowledgements

This book is the product of many people, all of whom I want to acknowledge and thank.

I am deeply indebted to the women and men whose stories fill these pages. It can truly be said that without them there could be no book. I want to thank them for sharing their lives, their struggles, their visions, their strength, their defiance with me. I want to thank them for "talking story" the Pacific way, for having patience with the limitations of my perceptions and understanding of their worlds, for inspiring me with their spirit.

From the Marshall Islands: Renam Anjain, Betty Edmond, Lijon Eknilang, Alvin Jacklick, Katrine Jelij, Giff Johnson, Darlene Keju-Johnson, Admini Koon, Roko Laninvelik, Julian Riklon, Aisen Tima and Solang.

From Belau: Roman Bedor, Lilana Isao, Bernie Keldermans, Xavier Maech, Cita Morei, Maech Ngirakedrang, Gabriela Ngirmang, Balerio Pedro, Lorenza Pedro, Ubad Rehetaoch, Bena Sakuma, and Isabella Sumang.

From Guam: Hope Cristobal, Angel Santos, Laura Souder and Melissa Taitano.

From the Northern Marianas: Chailang Palacios, Maria Pangelinan, Margarita Sarapao and Jacoba Seman.

From Hawai'i: Noa Emmett Aluli, Sharkal Aweau, Puanani Burgess, Luana Busby, Ho'oipo De Cambra, Ku'umea'aloha Gomez, Poka Laenui (Hayden Burgess), Alohawaina Makanani, Earnestine Marfil, Sister Anna McAnany and the Wai'anae Women's Association.

From Fiji: Shamima Ali, Rusula Buretini, Judith Denaro, Vanessa Griffen, Ruth Lechte, Vijay Naidu, Suliana Sitwatibau and Claire Slatter.

From Australia: Faith Bandler, Joan Clifton, Helen Corbett, Cathy Craige, Rachael Cummins, Barbara Flick, Karen Flick, Pauline Nola Gordon, Robyn Greco, Erica Kyle, Tjama Napanangka, Gwen Rathman, Joan Wingfield and Elaine Yasseril.

From Aotearoa: Sue Culling, Lenis Davidson, Hilda Halkyard-Harawira, Titewhai Harawira, Mona Lisa Johnson, Hinewirangi Kohu, Moana Kohu, Nganeko Kaihau Minhinnick, Lynx and Kiri Potaka-Dewes.

From Tahiti-Polynesia: Charlie Ching, Marie-Therese Danielsson, Myron Mataoa, Pomaré Brothers, William Tcheng, Oscar Temaru and Maea Tematua.

Also: Theresa Minitong (Bougainville); Jean Florence (Britain); Lola Reis (East Timor); Manami Suzuki (Japan); Bertha Nare, Susanna Ounei and Louis Uregei (Kanaky/New Caledonia); Binatia Iakobo (Kiribati); Lenora Hill and Tawna Sanchez (Native America); Louise Aitsi and Elizabeth Yamanson (Papua New Guinea) and Hilda Lini (Vanuatu).

I especially want to thank Abiko Ralpho, Lijon Eknilang's daughter, for her permission to use a photo taken when she was six years old as the cover of this book. Her strength and her love, reflected in that photo, have sustained and inspired me over many years. This book is dedicated to her, and her spirit. She is now a young woman of fourteen years and I thank her for her lasting friendship.

For their poems: Puanani Burgess (Hawai'i) Lynx and Hinewirangi Kohu (Aotearoa). (The copyright on poems remain with their authors.)

To all the people who opened their homes and their hearts to Bridget and myself as we passed through their lives in our Pacific Journey, and without whom it would never have been possible. They sheltered us, showed us around, educated us in their local struggles and cultures, shared their visions, made sure we caught planes and boats on time, and generally took care of us. And to all the women and men whom I have worked beside in our common striving to re-create an independent and nuclear free Pacific and to restore to Indigenous peoples their inalienable rights. And most especially those Indigenous people who have offered me a glimpse of their knowledge of what it is to be Indigenous in this distorted and unjust world.

To Bridget Roberts who, with myself, co-founded the British network Women Working for a Nuclear Free and Independent Pacific. We travelled the Pacific and forged lasting friendships with many of the Indigenous women whose lives are reflected in this book. The story of the Pacific Journey is also Bridget's – her voice has found a place amongst its pages.

My thanks must go to my mother, Patricia O'Donoghue Hanlon, who organised things; my sister, Tricia Hanlon, for her insistence that I write this book, for the computer(s), for help with the maps, and for interrupting her own work to assist me with mine; my other sister, Margaret Hanlon Dunn for her advice and help; and to my niece, Tristan Hanlon for her assistance.

To Chloe Bardsley who encouraged me when finishing and publishing this book seemed impossible, who lent her wisdom to its pages and who was there when I most needed her.

To the thousands of Greenham Common women who, listening to Indigenous Pacific and Aboriginal women "talk story", took those stories into their hearts and acted upon them, taking up the challenge – thank you particularly those women who formed Women Working for a Nuclear Free and Independent Pacific, to the countless others who have worked beside women of South Africa, Nicaragua, former-Yugoslavia, Ireland, Black women in Britain, and all the other campaigns to which Greenham women have contributed. And to all the women and men who joined them, too numerous to mention but never forgotten. To the women of the Maypole Foundation (Britain) for the word processor.

I want to thank Susan Hawthorne and Renate Klein of Spinifex Press for believing in the necessity of this book and giving it a home, and for their support and assistance. To Maori Powhiri Rika-Heke for her wonderful artwork that cradles these stories. To Christine Gillespie: as editor her creative talent with words is hidden in the pages; Claire Warren for the typesetting, and Lin Tobias for the cover design. And to the other women of Spinifex Press for their support and assistance.

My thanks also to the following for their interpreting assistance: Lijon Eknilang with the interviews with Admini Koon and Katrine Jelij on Mejatto; Lorenza Pedro with the 1986 interview with Gabriela Ngirmang of Belau, and similarly, Cita Morei and Isabella Sumang in 1992. Vanessa Griffen was interviewed in 1988 by Stephanie Mills on my behalf, while the interview with Maea Tematua of Tahiti-Polynesia was arranged by Marie-Therese Danielsson and translated by Bronwyn Winters.

To the following for their comments on the text: Katie Boanas, Sue Culling, Pauline Gordon, Vanessa Griffen, Hilda Halkyard-Harawira, Giff Johnson, Nic McLellan, Nangeko Minhinnick, Cita Morei, Vijay Naidu, Susanna Ounei, Balerio Pedro, Lorenza Pedro, Helen Printer, Bridget Roberts, Claire Slatter, and Zane.

For permission to publish extracts my thanks go to: John Carter of *Pacific Islands Monthly* for permission to reprint from *Story of the Solomon Islands*, by Charles E. Fox (Pacific Publications, 1967); Jane Dibblin for her book *Day of Two Suns. US Nuclear Testing and the Pacific Islanders* (Virago, 1988); Sister Anna McAnany and the Wai'anae Women's Association for a story from *A Time for Sharing. Women's Stories for the Waianae Coast* (Wai'anae Women's Association, 1982); and Stephanie Mills for Toimata's story "My baby became rigid, like wood", which appeared in *Testimonies. Witnesses of French Nuclear Testing in the South Pacific* (Greenpeace International, 1990).

There are many others involved in the creation of this book who have not been mentioned. I remain forever indebted to them for their contributions in getting it into your hands.

Thank you.

Zohl dé Ishtar

Notes

"European" is used throughout to mean those of European heritage and descent, and includes the settler communities in Australia and Aotearoa (New Zealand), as well as those in other countries mentioned in the text. This is not to deny the heterogeneity of European cultures, but refers to a group of peoples bonded by their historical relationship to the Indigenous peoples of the Pacific and Australian region.

"Pacific" refers to that region defined by the Charter of the Indigenous Peoples of the Pacific as incorporating Australia, Great Turtle Island (US and Canada), East Timor and West Papua (claimed by Indonesia), Japan and the Philippines, and all the nations between.

Pronunciation

There is no space to provide a full description of the phonetics of each main language covered in the text. What follows are some of the key points in pronunciation.

In Hawai'ian "w" is pronounced "v", hence "Hawai'i" sounds like "Havai'i" and "Kaho'olawe" sounds like "Kaho'olave".

In Fijian the "b" is pronounced "mb" so that "Rabuka" sounds like "Rambuka" and "d" is pronounced "nd", so that "Dr Bavadra" is sounded like "Dr Bavandra".

In Maori the "wh" is pronounced "f", so that "whanau" (family) is pronounced "fanau" and "whenua" (land) is pronounced "fenua".

In Kukatja the "k" is pronounced "g" and "tj" is pronounced "dj" so that "Kukatja" is pronounced "Gugadja", "Kartiya" (white person) sounds like "Gardiya", and "karnti" (yam) sounds like "garndi".

In I'Kiribati the "ti" in "Kiribati" is pronounced "s" as "Kiribas".

Preface

This is a book of stories. Stories of survival, of strength, determination and compassion. Stories of violence and of shame. They are stories told by Indigenous women and men who have guided their peoples through long years of colonisation and exploitation by foreign nations.

When Europeans first ventured into the world's greatest ocean four hundred years ago they wrought devastation ·far beyond anything comprehensible to the peoples to whom the ocean waves and the ancestral lands were home. In that short time Indigenous peoples have been decimated and many forced into poverty; their lands and waters stolen for military bases, tourism and other corporate interests; their lives contaminated by nuclear testing, uranium mining and nuclear waste dumping.

But Indigenous peoples have not been victims. They have a long history of resistance – when possible through peaceful means, when necessary through armed struggle. It has been a struggle against the greatest violence perpetrated against any peoples, and while the obstacles at times have seemed insurmountable there have been many successes – the greatest being that they have survived and have maintained their cultures.

The strength of that defiance, the compassion of the insistence on another more just way to live with this planet, is held within the voices of the women.

The giving of stories is not a mundane, haphazard event. Indigenous peoples have a strong oral tradition. It is by stories that they convey and maintain the wisdom of their ancestors. Their songs and chants, and the tales they tell their children, contain the seeds of knowledge upon which they base their purpose and existence in the world.

In the re-telling I have tried to present these stories as they were told to me – in the same spirit. I have attempted to reflect the women's lives: their strength, their determination, their concerns through their own voices. As such I have kept as true to the oral word as is possible in written text. This endeavour is important for, as Puanani Burgess of Hawai'i (1986) has written, "language is believed to be a gift of the gods, the spirits of the gods live within the word". Thus, these words contain not only the meaning of the women, but their spirit. Their cultures, transmitted through the centuries by the oral tongue of their ancestors, have been kept alive because when peoples speak they remember. Indigenous peoples did not create a written language, asserts Native American, Tawna Sanchez (1987), because "we never wanted to have one. We know that it is important to keep our religion, our ways, our history, oral so that our minds would never become weak, and we would never forget".

There have been few attempts to listen to the stories, to the actual voices, of Indigenous women. Indigenous women's lives have been ignored, erased, in a world that increasingly gives power to the written word. And in that we are all disadvantaged. Europeans need to hear the stories of Indigenous women. We are being invited to work beside Indigenous people against our nations' violations of the Pacific lands and waters. We must accept that challenge! The future depends upon it.

My journey amongst Pacific and Aboriginal women began in 1982 when I left Australia, with the World Bike Ride for Peace, to ride around the world on a bicycle to talk of colonisation and justice. It was an experience that awoke in me the consciousness that we live on one very small shared planet. I quickly realised that very few people knew that there were islands in the Pacific, let alone that they were the homes of people who had been colonised by European nations for hundreds of years. Later, finding myself at Greenham Common Women's Peace Camp, outside a US military base in southern England, I began to "talk story" about the impact of European colonisation. I was not alone in this – other women from Australia and Aotearoa (New Zealand), and from Britain, shared their knowledge also. Very soon women had united to form the network Women Working for a Nuclear Free and Independent Pacific, which hosted tours by Indigenous Pacific and Aboriginal women to tell their stories themselves. Those Indigenous women gave birth to a national network that still flourishes today.

During that time I met Bridget Roberts and, for twelve months in 1986 and 1987, we travelled throughout the Pacific. In a journey that involved over thirty plane flights and half as many boat rides, we visited Indigenous women in the Marshall Islands, Belau, the Northern Marianas, Guam, Hawai'i, Fiji, Australia, Aotearoa (New Zealand) and Tahiti-Polynesia. Our journey finished with a speaking tour of the west coast of Great Turtle Island (North Americas). And as we visited them in their homes women welcomed us, sharing their visions and dreams, their hopes and their problems. They inspired us with their spirit, their courage, determination and strength. They gave us their stories.

Woven into the book are the voices of other women, some of whom I had met before my Pacific journey, some whom I've met since, all of whom I have worked beside in a common goal of an independent and therefore nuclear free Pacific. There are also stories told by some men whose experiences complement those of the women of their communities, for Indigenous men also suffer from colonisation and, together with women, they are acting to reassert their sovereignty and bring an end to the abuses of colonising nations.

When Bridget and I were given these stories we were given them as gifts. They provided glimpses into the personal and collective lives, experiences, worries and dreams of the tellers. With the receiving came responsibility: it is our obligation to hold and share these stories. They were told to us in the trust that we would retell them to others who also needed to hear.

Through the years as I have worked alongside Indigenous women I have consistently questioned what right I, who am not Indigenous, had to tell these stories. During that process I oscillated in my answers but finally came to an understanding that I do not have a right to retell them – I have an obligation! The colonisation of the Pacific is, to my shame, as much part of my history as an Irish-Australian woman as it is that of any Indigenous person. When it is Europeans who are responsible for the atrocities perpetrated against Indigenous peoples then, surely, it is necessary for Europeans to participate in the educating of our own peoples so that the violations may come to an end the sooner with our assistance. I began writing to fulfil that obligation – I consider myself an activist not a writer. It was only in the process of writing that I became aware that, for me, to write is to be an activist.

This book does not present the full picture of the colonisation of the Pacific. Many countries have not been touched upon, and much more remains to be told of those that have. Every story must have a beginning, which inspires the listener to dive deeper. This is my intention – to alert you, the reader, to what is occurring in the region and to inspire you towards wanting to know more – and to act! This book has been written not only because Europeans need to hear these stories, but because we need to act on them.

In writing I have gained much, but possibly the most significant has been to be able to immerse myself in these women's stories, in their lives. As I cried in fury and pain and laughed in joy and defiance with these women – and for that I am privileged – I hoped that this book might be a way to give back some of what I have received. It is my hope that it will aid Indigenous peoples in their campaigns to bring an end to the colonisation of their lands and waters and that it will encourage you to act towards the creation of a just Pacific.

Zohl dé Ishtar, Sydney, May 1994.

"The Pacific Is Our Home"

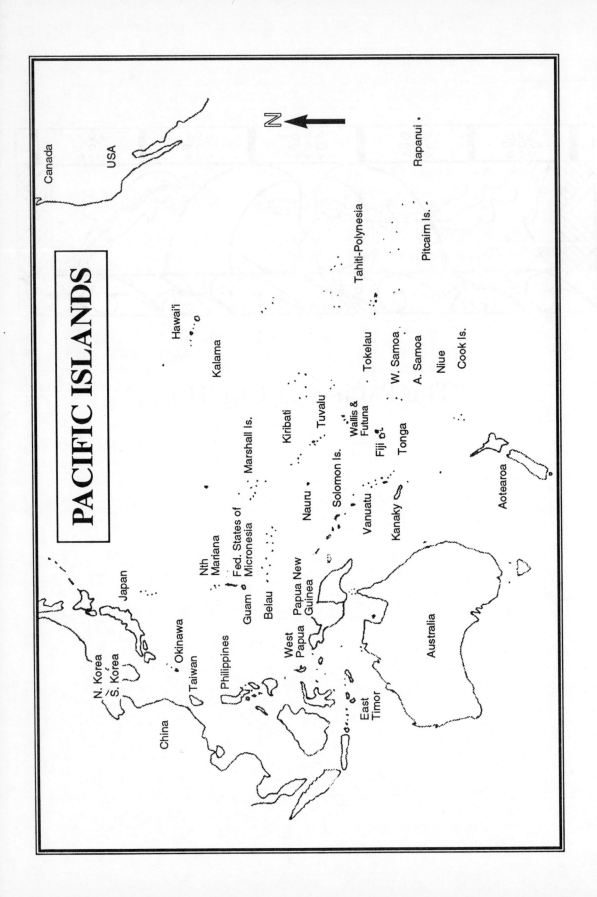

PACIFIC ISLANDS

Listen to the voices of Indigenous Pacific women . . .

Women talk, men have always had their say, so it is about time women talked about their lives.
> Binatia Iakobo. Kiribati.[1] (Iakobo, 1989)

Our spirit is beginning to grow up, become very strong. That's why we are here to tell you this nuclear madness will not just stop in the Pacific.
> Chailang Palacios. Northern Marianas. (Women Working for a Nuclear Free and Independent Pacific (WWNFIP), 1987: p. 14)

Our thing is to tell the people our experience – to make sure that what we have gone through so that you make the decision of not having it again.
> Darlene Keju-Johnson. Marshall Islands. (Chin, 1983)

The Pacific is wrapped in a veneer of silence that has masked the Pacific peoples from those of us who live outside the region, and for most of us who live on its edges. Relegated to the far corners of our minds we assume "nothing ever happens" there. It is forgotten and ignored. The world's media focuses our attention on North America and Europe and, at best, on Africa, Asia or Central and South America. Pacific peoples, such a small proportion of the world's population, are not accorded serious consideration in global terms. For tourist companies, the Pacific is a tropical paradise of endless golden beaches adorned with smiling women with swaying hips. For military planners, it is a strategically important arena essential to their concepts of "national security". For the corporate elite, it is an economic goldmine in the "Ocean of the Future". For the majority of the world's people, it is simply forgotten. But for Pacific peoples, this ocean and its lands are "home".

Covering over one-third of the planet, its waters stretching from Alaska to the Antarctic and sweeping the shores of Asia and the far reaches of the Americas, the Pacific is home to almost six million Indigenous people. It is a world of contrasts and diversity. Thousands of emerald islands preside over the world's largest ocean, seemingly mere specks beside their huge neighbour, the Australian continent. These are homes of distinct peoples each with their own culture, custom, way of life. The Islanders alone (including Papuans) speak 1,200 languages between them (Crocombe, 1976: p. 1), while 700 Aboriginal languages indicate the numerous peoples that populate the many "countries" to be found on the world's largest island. This diversity is mirrored in the differing landscapes – the high fertile lands of Papua New Guinea,

---

1. The countries covered in this book relate directly to those considered by the Nuclear Free and Independent Pacific movement to be within its parameters. The list is contained within the Peoples' Charter for a Nuclear Free and Independent Pacific, as created and adopted by the Indigenous peoples themselves networking within the region. They include all the island nations of the Pacific Basin, Australia, the Philippines, Japan, East Timor, West Papua (aka Irian Jaya) and the west coast of Great Turtle Island (the Native North American continent).

the small scattered atolls of the Marshall Islands, the damp, tropical islands of Fiji and the vast deserts of central Australia.

The heterogeneity is reflected in the political status of the region. While there are thirteen independent states, many nations remain heavily colonised. To the North are the Marshalls, Belau, the Northern Marianas and the Federated States of Micronesia, all bound to the United States (US). These are joined by the US territories of Guam, American Samoa and Hawai'i. The French have their domain – Kanaky (New Caledonia), Tahiti-Polynesia (French Polynesia) and Wallis and Futuna. Rapa Nui, also known as Easter Island, is governed by Chile. Other nations, like Tokelau and Niue, have special arrangements with Aotearoa (New Zealand) or Australia, both lands where the Indigenous peoples have become minorities under a dominant European culture.[2]

And yet, while these nations have experienced colonialism to differing degrees there are also patterns of similarity: the dispossession of land, the decimation of a people, the distortion of culture, as Maori, Hilda Halkyard-Harawira (1986a) writes:

> Our histories of colonisation match almost exactly those of our Indigenous brothers and sisters throughout the world. We too have suffered from the sham of the Treaty process. We too have been subjected to genocide. We too have been victims of land alienation. We too have been decimated by the diseases of Europe. We too have had to pay dearly for our hospitality. We too have been forced to carry our cultures within our hearts and wear the culture of the European like a second skin.

Some nations have been colonised by two or more powers. The Micronesian islands have the dubious distinction of having had more colonising powers imposing their will than any other colony in the world. The lands of the Indigenous peoples of Aotearoa and Australia have been overrun by European settlers. East Timor and West Papua have been annexed by Indonesia.[3] Pacific nations which are independent – Papua New Guinea, Vanuatu, and Kiribati, to name a few – have had to strive to reclaim their inalienable rights to self-determination, and yet even they remain trapped under the economic control of neo-colonial governments.

It has not always been this way. The era of colonisation is minute in comparison to the period that Indigenous peoples have lived in this ocean and its lands. A mere 400 years beside the 80,000 to 100,000 years of the Australian Aboriginal peoples, or even

---

2. Colonisation has occurred within the region. Indonesia has colonised and maintains control over East Timor and West Papua, and both countries are in armed struggle against their common oppressor. Papua New Guinea refuses to consider self-government for the people of Bougainville despite five years of armed resistance by the Bougainvilleans.

3. Indonesia invaded East Timor in 1975 when it was on the brink of becoming fully independent from Portugal. Under a regime that denies basic human rights, over a third of Timorese have died through famine, torture, bombing, disappearance, or massacre. In 1991 Indonesian troops killed over 270 Timorese peacefully demonstrating in Dili. Similarly, in 1963 Indonesia annexed West Papua. A transmigration policy has resulted in the immigration of vast numbers of Javanese peasants into the half-island, rapidly making the Indigenous people a minority in their own lands. The Timorese and the West Papuans have maintained armed resistance against their oppressor since the invasions.

the thousands of years of other Pacific peoples. The agelessness of the Pacific peoples is reflected in the stone remnants of ancient civilisations that adorn such dispersed nations as Belau (Palau), Rapa Nui (Easter Island) and Pohnpei.

When Europeans first sailed the Pacific in the early 1500s they were late comers. David Lewis (1977) claims that long before the "flowering of Greece", the so-called source of civilisation, the Pacific had been populated by the ancestors of today's Indigenous people. The Aboriginal peoples lived in Australia, developing a highly spiritual and egalitarian culture, when Europeans were still neanderthal. Al Grassby and Marji Hill (1988) record that Aboriginal people, having lived on the Australian continent for over 2,000 generations, were among the first people to develop a sophisticated technology. They are recognised as the Earth's oldest living culture. David Lewis (1977) argues that a millennium before Europeans first put to sea the "Malayo-Polynesians" had navigated by the stars, wind, waves and birds and travelled over two-thirds of the Earth, taking humanity to the immensity that lay between Madagascar and Rapa Nui (Easter Island). Women participated in these voyages as much as men, maintaining the cultures and establishing communities. The stories of Paintapu – an I'Kiribati woman navigator of a great war fleet – and other heroic Polynesian chieftainnesses are preserved in oral heritage (Lewis, 1977).

The early Pacific peoples, living at one with the ocean, traded widely amongst themselves and with their closest neighbours, the Asians. David Lewis (1977) documents that the Chinese and Malaccans traded with the Aboriginal peoples, as did the peoples of Papua New Guinea. Northern Aboriginal stories and songs speak of the Baijini, a lighter skinned people, who came in search of trepang (sea slug) and set up temporary agricultural settlements across the northern coast of Australia, a practice that was halted only in 1906 under pressure from the European settler government. The people of what is now northern Queensland traded, intermarried and exchanged cultural values and technology with the Papuans although each developed separately, adapting to their unique environments. Aboriginal people travelled to and lived in the islands around Australia's shores even in recent times, sometimes under adverse conditions. A man of Aboriginal descent in Tahiti told me that his ancestors had fled when the Europeans arrived in northern Queensland and, after drifting in a small boat, arrived and settled in Vanuatu, only to move on to Kanaky (New Caledonia), and later Tahiti, under French colonialism.

It was not until 1513 that the first European, the Spaniard, Vasco N'nez de Balboa, sighted the Pacific. He was closely followed by Fernao de Magalhaes (Ferdinand Magellan), the first European to circumnavigate the world. With their crews, they heralded the colonial age into the world's largest ocean. The European attitude to the Indigenous peoples was one of conquest and exploitation. Hilda Halkyard-Harawira asserts:

The colonisers had many faces. They were British, French, German, American, Spanish, Japanese, and Dutch. They all came into the Pacific. They had many faces and many tongues but they had one purpose: to uproot the existing lifestyle and implant their own societies in order to acquire the land. That basically is the bottom dollar of colonialism – the acquisition of land by any means possible (Hanly, 1986: p. 27).

Flag-raising became a favourite preoccupation as European nations competed with each other to attain control of the Pacific's rich resources. There have been three stages of colonisation in the Pacific: the early period of the Spanish and Portuguese, then, later, the Dutch; the English-French-German period, with Japan taking over where Germany left off; and the latest, the strategic period under the US and the French military coupled with renewed economic influence by the Japanese.

The Spanish and Portuguese, having divided the world between themselves under the 1493 Treaty of Tordesillas, were joined by other European governments – all vying for dominance in the region. In the rush to claim land, islands were named and renamed, and the Indigenous inhabitants violated. Often local inhabitants welcomed the European visitors only to be fired on by nervous sailors, even when the presence of women and children indicated that it was not a war party. Lewis records that the Spanish explorer Quiro, visiting the Marquesas under Mendana in 1567, reported that the soldiers opened fire to establish proper relationships of "respect". He cites an incident when a Marquesan jumped overboard from his canoe with a child in his arms, a soldier killed them both with a single shot "lest he should lose his reputation as a good marksman" (Lewis, 1977: p. 101). Stories abound of bloody first meetings between the Indigenous people and the newcomers.

These early explorers were followed by stranded sailors, survivors of shipwrecks. Adopted into the local community, they were often the first to introduce European customs and technology. They were followed by the early missionaries, the gun runners who profited by local tensions, and those who came to exploit the region economically.

In the short period of 400 years that Europeans have been in the region, Indigenous peoples have become disadvantaged citizens in their own lands, asserts Hilda Halkyard-Harawira (1986a):

Today we are but second class citizens in our own homelands. Today we suffer the classic effects of colonisation: endemic drug and alcohol problems, high mortality and suicide rates, apathy, self-hatred and identity crises. And now, as if that weren't enough to cope with, an even greater and more deadly monster looms – nuclear death. The super powers have invested in a new war game. The Pacific is the battlefield. Pacific peoples are the pawns.

Charles E. Fox, a Solomon Islander, describes the disruption of the Indigenous way of life:

In one way or another our people lived without hope. European diseases, we felt would destroy us. European customs would take the place of our own. Our arts and crafts would be forgotten. We would buy European things instead of making our own. Our dancing and feasting and ceremonies would pass away ... And worst of all we could do nothing about it;

we were helpless. Women were then saying, "We don't want to have babies. We don't want them to grow up in the whiteman's Solomon Islands". They felt hopeless about the future.

. . . Every year an epidemic of dysentery went through the islands. In 1910 there were five small villages, about two hundred people, when the epidemic of that year was over no one was left alive in those villages. There were epidemics of whooping cough; in one of these a hundred children died in one island. After the First World War a great sickness followed in many countries [islands]. In San Cristobal the people left their village when it reached them, built small leaf shelters in the bush and died in large numbers. Polio, measles, whooping cough and other sicknesses went through our islands as there was little medical knowledge among the people and very little medical help for them (Fox, 1967: pp. 45–6).

From the earliest arrival of the Europeans, whole populations have been decimated so that today, wherever one looks, once flourishing nations struggle to regain their numbers. Communities estimated to have been in hundreds of thousands now stand at fifteen to twenty thousand. The violence was so extreme on the great continent that many Aboriginal nations no longer exist.

Centuries after colonisation began, Indigenous peoples are still being removed from their ancestral lands to make way for tourist complexes, military bases, mines and plantations. As Sue Culling (1988), of Aotearoa, asserts:

The Pacific has been colonised by successive countries for the last 400 years. They have all been at it – and they're all still there, they're all still implicated. And the legacy of their alien way of life, their alien culture, is that [Indigenous people] have lost access to their lands.

The nuclearisation of the region, from uranium mining to nuclear testing, is simply the latest instrument of genocide, explains Maori, Titewhai Harawira:

It is the same colonial powers who colonised our lands, . . . who have come back into the Pacific to test their nuclear bombs on us, to store them, to bring warships and uranium mining (Connelly *et al.*, 1987: p. 6).

Indigenous peoples have experienced the nuclear age to an extent beyond anything imaginable in Europe. The US, France, Britain and Japan have pushed onto the Pacific the political, social and economic programs of the nuclear industry which were unacceptable at home.

As people all over the world rejoice in the "new era" in Europe, the pressure against Pacific Island nations to surrender their lands for military bases continues. The US Pentagon's demand for two-thirds of Belau's precious land for military bases has not subsided despite the declaration of the "end of the nuclear era". What the world is witnessing is not the hoped-for awakening from madness but a simple shift of terror. But Indigenous people, particularly the Micronesians, have already paid a heavy price for the luxury of the superpowers to declare each other "enemy" and then "friend":

Our islands have been essential in the development of American military might and their names should be familiar to you. Bikini in the 1940s and 50s was the site of atomic and nuclear tests. So was Enewetak. The people of Rongelap became human guinea pigs in 1954 when radiation from a hydrogen bomb test "accidentally" reached their island. Kwajalein is still in the hands of the US military and provides the biggest missile testing base. Saipan, for eleven years, was a CIA training base for Asian guerrilla forces. Our people from a number of these islands are still living in exile and long to return home (Friends of Micronesia, 1972: p. 24).

Although this was written in the early 1970s, very much to our shame, it remains true over twenty years later. The signing away of a few nuclear weapons has not rid the world of the bombs capable of destroying the planet. It will never return to the Marshallese or to the I'Kiribati, the Tahitian Maohi, the Kokatha and Pitjantjatjara of Australia – to name but a few – their homelands and their health.

We are the people of the land and the ocean and we are struggling for survival. The ocean is our spirit.

Chailang Palacios. Northern Marianas. (WWNFIP, 1987: p. 14)

The Pacific story is also a story of resistance.

Since the arrival of Europeans and their abuses of local hospitality, Indigenous peoples have resisted the European presence in their homelands. That refusal to submit to oppression continues today. Sharing common attitudes to life, and bound by a common historical experience, they are uniting in an effort to reclaim control over their own destinies.

They share a common vision: the inalienable right to live by the dictates of their own cultures in a just Pacific – as Gamalroi (Aboriginal), Karen Flick (1987) asserts:

Aboriginal people see a connection with the struggles of the Indigenous and oppressed groups in the Pacific. Like them we want recognition of our sovereignty, of our right to control our own country, our own land, and to determine the way that we want to live. We don't want European colonising powers coming here and telling us what to do.

At the centre of the Indigenous determination to end oppression in the Pacific struggle is their strong affinity with the land and ocean that surrounds them, a connection expressed by Chamorro, Chailang Palacios (1985):

Our only resources are the ocean and the land. Our spirituality is the water, nature, the land, the stones, and this beautiful nature under the sea. That's what keeps us alive today. It gives us strength to keep on living while the Japanese, the US, the English and the French are destroying it.

For Indigenous people, identity is inextricably linked with the land and the ocean that cradles it. This is the spiritual basis of their reality. Pauline Gordon (1990) speaks from a Bundjalung perspective:

Our whole being is tied up with the land. She is our mother, she feeds us, she protects and shelters us. She looks after you and you look after her, then you'll never want. Our Dreaming time, Creation time, that's when the whole world was created – how the rocks and the streams and the rivers were formed – in our culture we are a part of that, spiritually and physically. Aboriginal people dance the corroboree – that's not just dancing mad, they're doing a traditional thing – they're making something happen. So they dance and sing, and as they dance their powers dance up. The spirit of the land replenishes the land, all the animals. Each tribe has a different speciality: I've seen them call up the rain. They can do it. And it comes from the land, that power.

That's why our people are nomadic – they moved with the bush and the seasons. And that's why for Aboriginal people its our obligation to protect the land, those sacred sites – it's our life. And our Law. We have a very real fear of breaking the Law – the Law of the land. For Aboriginal people we need land, each community needs land – to identify with, for access to their Creation time, to revitalise their soul, their spirit. With Aboriginal people, land is not for commercial use. It is for the regeneration of the people after two hundred years of cultural breakdown. We've got to get our people out of the twilight zone where they don't know if they're Black or White. We've been here since the first sunrise, put here by our creator spirit, and we aren't going to forget that.

Diné (Navajo)[4] woman, Lenora Hill (1987) expresses the depth of her people's connection with the land:

It's our teaching that our spiritual way of living keeps the balance of the universe. We are constantly healed by making our offerings, by praying to the earth. It is our understanding that the animals pray to the land. They greet the land, they greet the plant life. And that ensures the continuation of life. And that's how they maintain the balance in this world. We know that. Why don't the whites know that?

Land is the bond that Indigenous peoples hold in common. Maori, Hinewirangi Kohu (1987) asserts her relationship with the Native American nations:

We Maori come from a long, long way back and I know that the Indian nations belong to me too. I am Indian. I am Indian of Aotearoa [New Zealand]. When we look at a lot of the legends and stories that are told, they are the same. Yesterday I heard how they believe in

---

4. The Diné (Navajo) people are members of the Nuclear Free and Independent Pacific movement and their struggle is recognised within the mandate of the movement. The largest coal strip mine on Native American land, operated by Peabody Coal Company, at Black Mesa, only 30 miles from the community of Big Mountain, has heavily polluted their land.

burying the umbilical cord. We do too. It is the privilege of the mother to offer it back to the Earth Mother. That is so that we belong. We also have the same feeling about not being able to sell the land. The land is not ours, it belongs to the Earth Mother. She is our Mother. And it is not just the knowledge in our heads but practice in our hearts and in our bodies.

That the land belongs to the people and the people everlastingly to the land is clearly depicted in the Maori language where "*te whenua*" means both land and afterbirth. And again in Belauan, where ''beluu'' translates as ''our land'', the land and the people are one. Indigenous peoples are united by their conception of themselves as custodians of the earth for future generations.

The land is not for sale, but it has been taken, stolen, by Europeans and used for military bases, nuclear testing, tourism, and corporate enterprise. Maori, Hilda Halkyard-Harawira (1986b) explains:

For the nuclear cycle to survive it needs land and water. The superpowers need someone else's land and water. The French do not wish to test their bombs in Paris, they practise on Tahiti. The Americans do not test their MX missiles on Washington, they practise on the Marshall Islands.

Kokatha, Joan Wingfield's (1988d) story of the Aboriginal people is an example:

A lot our people were forced to live in reserves and missions as we were pushed off our land by the pastoralists and mining companies, by atomic bomb testing and rocket testing.

Theresa Minitong (1990) of Bougainville,[5] explains the problems that arise when land is taken, in this case by a major Australian mining company:

Even though I come from an island that has the world's largest copper mine, it doesn't benefit us. Imagine the impact of the mine when it was built in the middle of a remote mountain village in central Bougainville. Soon there were mining towns, supermarkets, international schools and a huge influx of foreign workers from all over Papua New Guinea, Australia and elsewhere. We suddenly had all sorts of people on the island. Out of this developed a wealthy, western-style modern town, but in the villages, especially in the remote mountain villages around the mine, there was little material change. Yet people felt the social disturbances and destructions around them. Modern western ways conflicted with traditional ways. The old people could not understand the modern ways of the young restless people. These changes took place so rapidly.

Landowners were aware of the destruction to their land and felt hopeless, poor and without any security. One woman, who was a leader of the militant landowners, said, "We

---

5. Although culturally part of the Solomon Islands, Bougainville has been politically grouped with Papua New Guinea as a result of its colonial legacy. Rich in minerals, it has the world's largest copper mine, owned by Australian mining corporation, CRA, a subsidiary of Rio Tinto Zinc, Britain's largest mining corporation. The mine has disrupted lives, poisoned and irreparably damaged the land. The Bougainvilleans organised local protests which the PNG government responded to with military force. This developed into armed resistance and demands for secession from PNG.

weep for our land because it has been damaged. We know it will never be revived to its natural state again". And she cried when she said that. This led to demonstrations by the landowners demanding adequate compensation for the use of their land. Although other Bougainvilleans thought that the landowners were well off with the compensation money, they were in reality poorer than us. I saw this often. For example, they did not have enough money to send their children to school. I could not understand it. I thought they would be the richest people on the island, but they weren't. Why? They didn't have their land. To us land is our birthright. It is land that provides our spiritual and physical needs. It is the regeneration of our ancestor stories. Without land we cannot go and say, "This is where my father built his house", or "This is where my mother had her garden", or "This is where we do initiation". Therefore those whose land was taken for mining felt that they had no future, no past and no ancestral stories. This led directly to the [Papua New Guinea-Bougainvillean] crisis.

Loss of access to resource and heritage-rich land has led to increased health and social problems, which are intertwined with environmental degradation. This is a major concern to Indigenous people, as Maori, Nganeko Minhinnick (1988) expresses:

We are at one with nature in all its forms, be it waterways, lands, forests, animals and bird life. We are the natural scientists, the true conservationists and environmentalists in every sense of the word. We were created by Papatuanuku, Mother Earth, herself, and in our custom and traditions we return the placenta from our childbirth to her. And when we pass away we are returned to Mother Earth. Because we are so close to Papatuanuku we feel the crushing torment as industrial, hazardous chemical and nuclear wastes are disposed into her womb and other wastes dispersed into the waterways and atmosphere. And we wonder at man's sanity and the global outcome of such irresponsible actions.

Pacific peoples are united in their determination to reclaim and care for their land. And women play an important role in that initiative, as Theresa Minitong (1990) recalls happened in the Bougainvillean people's campaign against the Australian mine:

We women protested against the mine in the early 1970s. Bare-breasted women lay in front of the surveyor's pegs, often with their babies, to stop the bulldozers. They were beaten with batons by the police. All along, women have been fighting because we know that our children must have land. Because it is a matrilineal society, it falls to the women to allocate the land to the child, it is our responsibility. If we don't have the land how can we give it to our children?

Diné, Lenora Hill (1987) stresses the unique role of women in the protection of the land:

We see that the destruction of Mother Earth is the destruction of women. We have the responsibility as women, the givers of life, to make sure that that destruction does not continue.

It is this connection with the land that has led Pacific peoples to muster their strength behind a move to be independent and nuclear free. Fijian, Claire Slatter (1988) explains:

Pacific peoples have been involved in a struggle to end colonial rule. We believe that it is because these major powers continue to exercise colonial control over our islands that they are able to use these islands for their strategic purposes. We have been engaged in the campaign for the right of Pacific peoples to say "No" to the continued use of our region and our islands for the purpose of preparing for war.

The Indigenous resistance has been long and enduring. In 1767, having experienced the violence of visiting Europeans, the Tahitians put to sea with 300 war canoes to blockade the arrival of the British explorer Samuel Wallis. The Chamorro of the Northern Marianas and Guam fought for twenty-three years against the Jesuit priests who killed thousands while imposing Christianity. Maori, Hilda Halkyard-Harawira (1986b) echoes Indigenous histories throughout the region when she asserts:

> The Maori people are the tangata whenua [people of the land] of Aotearoa [New Zealand] … We have a history of resistance against the uninvited guests who invaded our lands and who systematically worked to destroy the foundations and morale of Maoridom.

That this refusal to submit continues into the present era is witnessed by the ability of the Marshallese people to recover from the atrocities perpetrated against them by the US through its nuclear testing program. The Marshallese spirit is reflected in Darlene Keju-Johnson's assertion:

> Now we realize we've got the power, we can do it together … Although it took us 35 years to really come out and say that we don't want be to part of this Nuclear Age, the important thing is: we did it (Smith, 1983, pp. 1–2).

The strength and determination of the Indigenous peoples, particularly the women, promises that the Pacific, and the world, will one day be free and just.

And the challenge is: why haven't you known what's been happening? Why haven't you known about nuclear testing by the US, Britain and France; about jelly-fish babies born to women who are exposed to the tests? Why haven't you known about the effects of alien colonial, political, and military domination of Indigenous peoples? Why haven't you known about uranium mining on Aboriginal land and nuclear waste dumping?
Titewhai Harawira. Aotearoa. (Harawira, 1985)

The Pacific has been ringed by a deafening silence, not only as an effect of distance from the heavily populated regions of the world, but also as a result of European racism. Focused upon ourselves, upon our "known world", our racism has fostered an ignorance that has allowed our governments to exploit and dominate the region. In the shadow of this ignorance the US, British, French, Japanese, Australian and other governments and corporate elites are getting away with murder.

As Indigenous peoples have increasingly spoken out, our limited awareness has begun to expand, but still it seems as if we cannot see. There is a story that runs something like this: when the Spanish arrived in the Northern Marianas, land of the Chamorros, they came in big ships with huge white sails. They sailed in to harbour near a well-populated village, yet the villagers, unable to comprehend what was hitherto unknown, could not see them. This is a common tale that Europeans tell each other about many different Pacific nations. But history would suggest that it has been the Europeans who have not seen what is evident before them. Bringing with them the baggage of a belief in their own cultural superiority and God-given right to conquer the world, they were unable to recognise or to respect the Indigenous civilisations already thriving in the region.

The silence is strongest in relation to women. In a world based upon male power, where men (predominantly European men) control the media and the governments and the guns, this is not surprising. But Indigenous women have been guiding their communities since the beginning of time. Now they are speaking out. In that process they discover that their stories and experiences are shared by women across the ocean, around the world. Wherever you turn on this planet women have been and are affected by a myriad oppressions – racism, sexism, heterosexism, classism. Indigenous women, European women. But we have not played victim. These challenges have been met with a strength that is all too often under-estimated. Women are strong, and as we move from a place which is uniquely our own, that arises directly from our life experiences and our cultural heritage, we find that we can reach across seeming chasm to find each other. But European women must listen to and act upon the stories of Indigenous women. As Sue Culling (1988) urges:

> Europe needs to hear the voices of the people who suffer from the priorities and programs of Europe and the West, especially the women. It is the women who can speak of their suffering and the suffering of their families. You should be listening to their stories.

It is time to break the silence. It is time for the world to listen to the voices of Indigenous Pacific Women.

HEAR US SISTERS

In the Hawai'ian tradition language is believed to be a gift of the gods. The spirits of the gods live within the word.

Words then become prayers when spoken with the knowledge of their spiritual content. As we speak to each other, Sisters, we are praying, and the god or gods to whom we thank for Life are with us.

We share these words, our prayers, with you, Sisters.

We hope they will reveal in you the pain and conflicts we as Native Hawai'ian women have felt in disowning our gods, our spirituality, our culture, our symbols, our languages and our dignity, replacing them with the Christian God.

It is significant that the Hawai'ian Experience is not an isolated one. It is the experience of other native peoples as well.

Our purpose is not to produce guilt, which paralyses, but to produce understanding which leads to change.

We ask for an end to the use of the Cross as a symbol of conquest or as a partner of any flag.

> Sister, Hear our prayer to you.
> In the Spirit of *Aloha* which our gods bequeathed to us,
>   and to you,
> We ask you to hear our words and feel our pain.
> Long before the Christian missionaries came upon our sacred *'Aina* (land)
>   bringing the Cross and the Flag,
> We were three hundred thousand strong,
> Strong in body, mind and spirit.
> Our gods, our ways, our *'Aina*, our sea and sky provided for us and
>   nourished us.
>
> But they came, and they offered,
> No, they demanded,
> That we accept the Cross and the Flag
>   (these Siamese twins of power).
> They said, "Here. With these you will prosper".
>
> And people came to our shores,
>   bringing disease and alcohol,
>   despair and greed,
>   and shame for what we were . . . "lowly heathens",
>   I think they said.

We tried to put into their hands our symbols:
The *Kalo*, (taro), from whose body we take sacred nourishment,
The *'Aina*, from whose body we take sacred nourishment,
The *Wai* and the *Kai* (the inland and sea waters) from
    whose body we take sacred nourishment.
But they scorned our symbols.
They said, "Here. With these you will prosper".

But look at us now, Sisters
We are the poorest in our own land.
We live in cars, tents, on benches and sidewalks.
We occupy more jail cells, more hospital beds,
    more morgue slabs and coffins
Than any other race in Hawai'i.

Our children are labelled 'DISADVANTAGED' and can't read,
    can't write,
    can't get a job,
    can't get an education.
We are beggars in our own homeland.

But no more!
We set aside the Cross
And we set aside the Flag
To search and to find those symbols which spring
    from this place,
    from this time,
    from this People.

In our hands we offer you a scoop of earth, the *'Aina*;
    a scoop of water, *Wai*, from the land, and *Kai*, from the sea . . .
Life!
Ke Anuenue, a rainbow . . .
Hope!
    and *Aloha*, Love!

We will continue to speak the truth of our history
    the truth of our pain
    the truth of our oppression
    the truth of our colonization.
And through this truth, we will be free.

This is our prayer to you, Sisters.
Listen to it with your soul, Sisters.

                        Puanani Burgess. Hawai'i. (Burgess, 1986b)

FIRE IN THE WATER

– *Marshall Islands* –

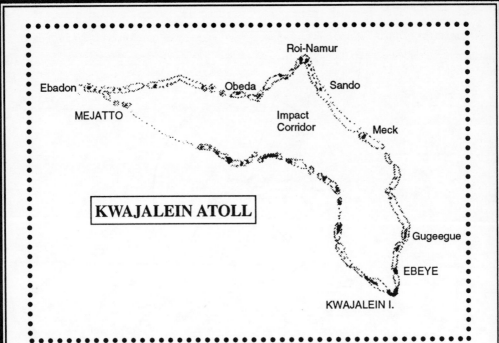

Roi-Namur

Ebadon

Obeda

Sando

MEJATTO

Impact
Corridor

Meck

KWAJALEIN ATOLL

Gugeegue

EBEYE

KWAJALEIN I.

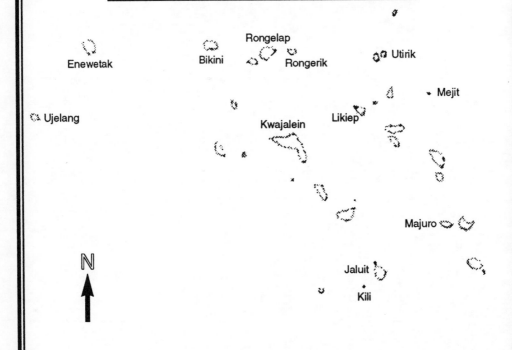

MARSHALL ISLANDS

Rongelap

Enewetak

Bikini

Rongerik

Utirik

Mejit

Ujelang

Kwajalein

Likiep

Majuro

Jaluit

N

Kili

The history of these islands over the last few centuries has not been the history of the Micronesian people. It has been the history of missionaries, colonizers, commercial exploiters, warring armies, atomic testing and a vast, unresponsive, indifferent bureaucracy.
Sen. Petrus Tun, Yap. (Friends of Micronesia, 1972: p. 1)

Micronesia consists of over 2,000 islands scattered across the Pacific like stepping stones flung between Hawai'i and Asia. It is politically divided into the Marshall Islands, Belau, the Northern Marianas, Guam, and the Federated States of Micronesia (Yap, Pohnpei, Truk and Kosrae). The high volcanic islands and coral atolls are the tips of vast mountain ranges with their valleys deep beneath the world's greatest ocean. Only ninety of these islands are inhabited by a people who, over a thousand years ago, travelled in outrigger canoes across three million square miles of ocean, guided by the stars and waves, to make a new home and to live in peace.

Their life was shattered by the arrival in the 1600s of the *Ribelli* (Marshallese for "strangers"). The Spanish, bringing disease and a violence that decimated the thriving and prosperous communities, were followed by German whalers, slavetraders, planters and missionaries. They introduced Christianity, the Protestant work ethic and a cash economy, further destroying cultural beliefs and a subsistence way of life. The Japanese took over from the Germans in 1921, using the islands as settlements to relieve their growing population problem and, in 1944, the Americans arrived to wrest control from the Japanese at the cost of much suffering by the Micronesians. In four successive eras, colonising nations imposed their own lifestyles upon the Indigenous people.

During the Second World War, the Micronesians were forced to live and die in a war that was not of their making. That war did not bring them liberation as the western world claims. Solang (1986) remembers:

It was really good when the war ended. You feel something good because you were so frightened during the war time. We were thinking about us Marshallese people, "Maybe after this fifteen years of Japanese we will, we Marshallese people will, be free, will be independent". Nothing wrong with that. But no, the Americans came.

In 1947, as the spoils of war were divided up amongst the victors, the United Nations handed the lives of the Micronesian people - without consultation, consideration or (it seems) conscience – into US control. Bound together as the "Trust Territory of the Pacific Islands" the Islanders were once again robbed of their autonomy. The US agreed to "promote the economic advancement and self-sufficiency of the [Islanders] … protect them against the loss of their lands and resources" and "promote [them] … towards self-government or independence" (Johnson, G., 1984: p. 6).

Instead, the members of the United Nations allowed the Pentagon free rein in the world's only strategic trust territory. Positioned on the sea routes to Africa and the Persian Gulf through the Indian Ocean, Micronesia is coveted for its strategic potential as a fall-back zone from the Asian mainland. The islands have been locked into the US plan to establish military facilities from Alaska to the Antarctic. The Micronesians became hostages to US hegemonic intentions.

At the time that the US arrived, the islands were prosperous; the Islanders provided for themselves and exported produce from the plantations developed under the Germans and Japanese. The townships thrived. But the US set about destroying all this, Chailang Palacios relates:

> After the war the Americans came ... I remember my parents shaking their heads and saying, "My God, because of America and Japan we have suffered so much". My beloved father couldn't understand the stupidity of the American soldiers. He saw his own home completely built of stone from the ocean and with just two holes from the bombs and the American soldiers coming with their bulldozers and destroying all the houses and all the roads. The Americans hated the Japanese so much that they had to destroy everything. They didn't want to be reminded of anything that had been in the possession of the Japanese (WWNFIP, 1987: p. 12).

The Marshallese, in particular, have paid a high price for the US's nuclear arms race. Even before the US gained administrative status over Micronesia, it had begun testing nuclear weapons in the Marshall Islands. The Marshallese have been forced to live in unsustainable communities, on small isolated islands. Their health has also been robbed. They now suffer from illnesses related to poverty, nuclear contamination and the devastation of their culture. However the Marshallese are a nation of survivors. What follows is the Marshall Islands story.

We are already dying from nuclear war while you are thinking how to prevent it.
Chailang Palacios. Northern Marianas. (Francke, 1985: p. 31)

Between 1946 and 1958, the US used the Marshall Islands as a testing site for their atmospheric nuclear program. The US has long acknowledged the detonating of sixty-six nuclear devices on Bikini and Enewetak atolls. Evidence came to light in December 1993 that indicated that an additional forty-eight tests had not been announced – an increase of seventy-five per cent (Pacific Concerns Resource Centre [PCRC], 12/1993: p. 4). Widespread radiation-related illnesses suggest that the tests have contaminated the majority of islands in the small nation.

Darlene Keju-Johnson describes the military misadventures in her people's islands:

> One important date that I never forget was 1946. In that year a navy official from the US government came to Bikini Island. He came and told the Chief Juda [Kessibuki], and I quote – "We are testing these bombs for the good of mankind, and to end all wars".

When the navy official came it was too late. There were already thousands of soldiers and scientists on the atoll and hundreds of airplanes and ships in the Bikini lagoon. They were ready to conduct the tests. The Bikinians had no choice but to leave their islands, and they have never returned. The navy official did not tell the chief that the Bikinians would not see their home again. Today Bikini is off-limits for thirty thousand years. In other words Bikini will not be safe for these Bikinian people ever again.

The Bikinians were promised that the US only wanted their islands for a short time. The chief thought maybe a short time is next week, maybe next month. So they moved to Rongerik.

Rongerik is a sandbar island. It is too poor to feed the people. We live on our oceans – it's like our supermarket – and from our land we get breadfruit and other foods. But on Rongerik there was nothing. The US put the Bikinians on this island and left them there. After a year they sent a military medical official to see how they were. When he got there he found out that they were starving. Imagine: move someone from their home, by your power. Dump them on a little sand and don't even bother to go back and see how they are doing for a year.

The people of Bikini have been moved three times. The people of Enewetak were also relocated. You cannot imagine the psychological problems they have to go through because of relocation.

In Enewetak Atoll there is one little island called Runit. It is off-limits forever. After the testing the US tried to clean up the radiation on Enewetak. It collected all the nuclear debris from the southern islands (the northern islands were too contaminated) and dumped it into a bomb crater on Runit [Island]. Then they covered it up with concrete. It is a huge dome. Now the scientists are saying that it is already leaking. But they say it doesn't matter because the lagoon that the dome is leaking into is already radioactive. There are people living only three or four miles from there. Runit Island will not be safe from contamination for 250,000 years.

In 1954 the United State exploded a hydrogen bomb, code named BRAVO, on Bikini. It was one thousand times stronger than the Hiroshima bomb. The Marshallese were not told about this bomb. We were never warned that this blast was about to happen on our islands. (WWNFIP, 1987: pp. 6, 8–9)

Lijon Eknilang, who was on Rongelap at the time of the "Bravo" blast, remembers:

I was seven years old at the time of the Bravo test on Bikini. I remember that it was very early in the morning that I woke up with a bright light in my eyes. I ran outside to see what had happened. I thought someone was burning the house. Soon after we heard a big loud noise, just like a big thunder and the earth started to move – the ground started to sway and sink. The loud noise hurt our ears. You can never imagine. We were very afraid because we didn't know what it was. Some people thought the war had started again. A little later we saw a big cloud moving to our islands. It covered the sky.

Maybe two or three hours later, about ten o'clock, we started to feel itchy in our eyes – it felt like we had sand in our eyes. Then came the fallout. It was white, and to us kids it was white soap powder. The kids were playing in the powder and having fun, but later on everyone was sick and we couldn't do anything. We wanted to drink water so bad we went to the water drums. The water was changing colour but we drank it anyway because we were very thirsty. For many hours, poison from the bomb kept falling on our islands. (WWNFIP, 1987: p. 15)

Hundreds of tons of material from Bikini's reef, islands and lagoon were lifted up into the air and carried as fallout over Rongelap, Utirik and other inhabited islands. US military personnel stationed on Rongelap were ordered to leave the atoll. Three US naval ships stationed nearby sailed away without evacuating the Islanders. Darlene Keju-Johnson continues:

> The people of Rongelap and Utirik were not picked up until three days after the explosion. It was horrible. Some American soldiers came and said, "Get ready. Jump in the ocean and get on the boat because we are leaving. Don't bring any belongings. Just go in the water." That's your home and you have to decide, with your husband and children, whether you are going to leave or not. But there is no time. People had to run fast. There was no boat to get the people, not even the children and the old people, to the ship. People had to swim with their children. It was very rough . . .
>
> They were taken to Kwajalein. They were not told what had happened, why it had happened, what was wrong with them. Their hair was falling out, finger nails were falling out but they were never told why.
>
> The people of Rongelap and Utirik were on Kwajalein for three months before they were moved again. The people of Utirik went back to their contaminated island. The people of Rongelap didn't return to Rongelap for three years: it was too contaminated. (WWNFIP, 1987: p. 7)

Marshallese living on other contaminated islands were not evacuated, nor have they been recognised by the US as having been affected by the testing.

Betty Edmond and Roko Laninvelik, Rongelap women now living on Majuro, the major island of the Marshalls, recall their experience of the "Bravo" blast of 1 March 1954.

Roko Laninvelik (1986):

> When the bomb exploded, I was twelve years old and I understood what was happening. I saw a very bright light all over Rongelap. In the afternoon the fallout came. In the evening I could not sleep, there was rash all over my body. The next morning I could not eat my food, I vomit, I could not eat. The rash was so itchy I could not bear. That day there was a plane come to Rongelap to see the drinking waters. They said it was poison. They didn't stay for even ten minutes. They didn't say anything to us so we just keep eating our food. Two days later the military men came to evacuate all the peoples to Kwajalein. They said not to take anything, just what we have on. Not the money or nothing. When we got to Kwajalein our hair fell out and burns started to show. We go to beach and take a bath that is all, the doctors did not treat us. After three months on Kwajalein we came to Majuro. We were there for three years. Then they say we can go back Rongelap, because it is safe. I stayed here to go to school. I married and had children, and stayed so they could go to school. But I went back to Rongelap every summer. Rongelap is my home and I want to go back. I want it cleaned up so that we can all go back and be together as one family and be happy.

Betty Edmond (1986):

> I was seven years old when the bomb exploded. I was so frightened. I kept running to everybody. There was a bright light all over Rongelap. I saw the coconut trees bending

down. I went into the coffee shop, the food was covered with white powder, fallout. It was everywhere. I was playing in the fallout with the other kids, throwing it everywhere. When the Americans came to the island they were wearing things like astronauts. They didn't say anything and left as quickly as they can. Maybe they knew it was really contaminated.

When they came to evacuate us, I was one of the really sick ones taken on the plane with the pregnant ones, the kids that vomited, the old ones. I was vomiting and itchy. I keep scratching and scratching. I still have rashes, I still scratch. Now I have scars on my legs, all over. I have had thyroid operation twice. When we arrive on Kwajalein they just put us on the runway, don't take us anywhere. We waiting for the people come in the boat. On Kwajalein we live in two storey barracks. The whole building was full of sick people. Every family in that house was sick and itching. The doctors told us we have radiation but they don't do nothing.

In 1957, I went back to Rongelap. My parents take me, I was young so I go where they go. I want Americans to clean up Rongelap. They are responsible for the poison. They must look after us until we die. They are the ones that gave us our sickness. I want to go home. Rongelap is my homeland where I was brought up, my homeland which I am used to. Where else can I go that is my home?

There is evidence which indicates that not only was the US aware before the detonation that the wind was blowing towards the inhabited islands but that it may have been an intentionally designed experiment (Johnson. G., 1984: pp. 12–13). Subsequent events indicated similar attitudes. For example, when the Rongelap people were returned to their contaminated atoll in 1957, the US Atomic Energy Commission stated: "the habitation of these people on the islands will afford most valuable ecological data on human beings" (Johnson, G., 1984: p. 13). Isolated from the rest of the world, the Marshallese were used as a human laboratory. Radiation-related illnesses resulted. According to Suliana Sitwatibau and B. David Williams (1982: p. 54), "In 1958 the rate of stillbirths (babies born dead) and miscarriages (babies born very early unable to survive) among Rongelap women rose to more than twice the rate of unexposed Marshallese women for the first four years following their exposure in 1954". They also report that, in 1966, 52 per cent of the exposed children on Rongelap who were under ten years old at the time of the Bravo test and 35 per cent of the total population had developed thyroid abnormalities.

In a study of Brookhaven Laboratory documents, Dr Rosalie Bertell, a world expert on low-level radiation and others, working on behalf of the Islanders, uncovered evidence that the US Department of Energy (DOE) was aware in 1973 that the Rongelap people had ingested plutonium into their blood system. Although the levels were ten times greater than that ingested by their neighbours the Bikinians, and five hundred times higher than the average readings in Europe or North America, the DOE did not inform the Rongelap people. The tests were repeated in 1976 and 1981, but the Islanders were still not alerted. The Rongelap however noticed inedible fish, mutant coconut trees and deformed fruits and vegetables – the food chain was irradiated (Bertell, 1985: pp. 70–76).

The full impact of the nuclear detonations will not be known for several generations but already the effects have been devastating. Darlene Keju-Johnson explains:

Since the testing there has been a tremendous increase in health problems. The biggest problem we have now, especially among women and children, is cancers. We have cancer in the breast. We have tumour cancers. The women have cancer in their private places. Children are being deformed. I saw a child from Rongelap. Its feet are like clubs. And another child whose hands are like nothing at all. It is mentally retarded. Some of the children suffer growth retardation. Now we have this problem, what we call "jellyfish babies". These babies are born like jellyfish. They have no eyes. They have no heads. They have no arms. They have no legs. They do not shape like human-beings at all. But they are being born on the labour table. The most colourful, ugly things you have ever seen. Some of them have hairs on them. And they breathe. This ugly thing only lives for a few hours. When they die they are buried right away. They do not allow the mother to see this kind of baby because she will go crazy. It is too inhumane. (WWNFIP, 1987: p. 8)

Many women are afraid that if they give birth their baby will be deformed. Lijon Eknilang tells her story:

Sometimes I feel that I have a baby inside me. I feel very happy that I will have a baby, but then I am afraid what kind of baby it is going to be. I live in two worlds: one part of me I want to have a baby but this other part of me is scared (WWNFIP, 1987: p. 17).

The Marshallese have continuously requested that their islands be made habitable once again. The Bikinians, the world's first "nuclear nomads", wanting to return home, have long pressured for a clean-up program similar to that undertaken in Enewetak. They now live on Kili Island, a small isolated island, where they are dependent upon US food aid. In 1967 the US Atomic Energy Commission declared Bikini Atoll "safe for human habitation". A four million dollar clean-up operation resulted in 150 Bikinians returning home in 1971. Rosalie Bertell writes of the homecoming:

The Bikinians old enough to remember the atoll before the bomb could hardly believe that some islands had evaporated in the blasts, leaving only blue water and sand bars. One of the leaders wept openly. The people said their island "had lost their bones" (Bertell, 1985: p. 74).

Although the Bikinians had been told that the atoll was now safe, they were increasingly advised not to eat local foods. By 1972, the US Department of the Interior was requesting a new environmental survey, but it was not conducted until 1978. It found that the Bikinians' blood carried a 75 per cent increase in cesium 137, the highest level of cesium 137 in any population. In September 1978, they were returned to Kili. Then in 1990, following consistent pressure from the Bikinians, the US allocated US$90 million to cleaning up the atoll. By 1992, there were plans to scrap the topsoil of the less contaminated islands in a bid to remove the bulk of the cesium 137. Clean topsoil would then be placed on Eneu island, the proposed site of the new settlement. Bikini Island (an atoll takes its name from the largest island) would still be too contaminated to return to, as are all the islands to the north of the atoll. Eneu Island has been covered with potassium phosphate in a bid to limit the cesium 137 taken up by the local plants, and therefore making it possible for the people to eat a 100 per cent local diet, including coconuts and breadfruit. It is still too early to tell to what extent those Bikinians who return to Eneu Island will be safe, or whether it will be a repeat of the 1970s disaster. The Rongelap people also want to return to their bountiful atoll. They are hoping that a clean-up program similar to that being undertaken on Bikini will free their land of contamination.

In 1986, the Rongelap people, responding to the increasing illnesses following their return to Rongelap, evacuated themselves, with Greenpeace assistance, from their ancestral islands to tiny Mejatto in Kwajalein Atoll (Toyosaki, 1986). Compelled by the contamination to move, they found themselves living in the midst of the next phase of the US nuclear program – Kwajalein Atoll.

We have no word in the Marshallese language for "enemy". So when the US says, "We are doing this to protect you", we say, "Protect who?".
Darlene Keju-Johnson. Marshall Islands. (Smith, 1983: p. 1)

In 1959, the US began using Kwajalein Atoll as the target for its testing program for ballistic missile delivery systems. Most US strategic missile systems have been fired from Vandenburg Airforce Base, California, over 7,500 kilometres, to splash down in the lagoon. Julian Riklon (1986) describes the experience of living at the receiving end of the incoming missiles:

At night, when the missiles come, you can see them, like shooting stars. Sometimes the missile breaks up, explodes, and pieces fall onto the islands. The only thing that protects us is a red flag that the US flies to tell us a missile is coming – then people know they cannot go fishing.

With no comparable technology anywhere in the world, the Kwajalein facilities remain essential to the development of the Pentagon's first-strike capability and space warfare technology. To quote Giff Johnson, "Kwajalein has probably contributed more to the arms race than any other spot on earth" (Smith, 1983: p. 1). Despite global nuclear disarmament, the US remains determined to attain its Strategic Defense Initiative (SDI) or Star Wars capability, and insists upon its right to test its missile systems. Accordingly its facilities on Kwajalein Atoll have recently been significantly expanded. The Pentagon is using Kwajalein to produce a deployable shield to ward off limited nuclear attack. If the Pentagon continues with its plan, the American scientific and technical population on Kwajalein will double to 6,000 by 1996 (PCRC, June 1993: p. 14).

As the program has developed, a rapidly growing, complex network of sensors and other paraphernalia has steadily pushed Kwajalein's traditional landowners off their home islands on to tiny Ebeye Island. Ebeye, once a serene Pacific island, was the home of sixteen people who lived a traditional life in close communication with the other Islanders scattered around the atoll. Under the US it became an overcrowded slum, its children dying from illnesses of malnutrition, its youth confused in their identity.

Jane Dibblin records in her book *Day of Two Suns. US Nuclear Testing and the Pacific Islanders* how Ebeye came to be so heavily populated:

> A US navy base had been established on the biggest island in the atoll immediately after the Second World War. Its population was dumped on to the tiny neighbouring island of Ebeye. Already an overcrowded labour camp, Ebeye's problems were to worsen dramatically as more and more people were cleared from the necklace of islands that make up Kwajalein atoll. There are now over 9,500 people living on Ebeye, on 66 acres or one-tenth of a square mile of land. Britain would have to accommodate twice the world's population to achieve the same density (Dibblin, 1988: p. 5).

Ebeye has been described as "the slum of slums", as a "biological time-bomb ready to go off" (Keju-Johnson, 1983: p. 3) but, in the words of Bridget Roberts (1986), "Ebeye is far more, much more, than that. It is a story of survival". She described the situation we found on Ebeye in 1986:

> There were plenty of slum conditions – fifteen people sharing a small plywood and tin shack; the streets for playspace; few community facilities; rubbish everywhere; increasing infant mortality and malnutrition; sexually transmitted diseases running rampant. Without land to grow food they are dependent on the five hundred plus people who work in low-paid, menial jobs on the base, the minimal rent paid to the 5,500 Kwajalein landowners, or the Islanders from Rongelap, Utirik, Bikini and Enewetak who receive some compensation for the effects of the nuclear testing program. Over 50 per cent are below fifteen years old and, as they become adults and have their own children, the problems will increase. But, although conditions were difficult, there were indications of determined survival: young fruit trees being protected and watered; spaces outside houses cleaned and the coral raked daily; new breeze-block houses being built around collapsing shacks; moves to reoccupy Kwajalein and other islands in a bid for better compensation, basic human rights and the return of their islands. We could see that conditions were improving under the dynamic local government (Cox, 1983: p. 1).

Since then the local government, encouraged and led by Ebeye's then Mayor, Alvin Jacklick, has instigated such vast changes on Ebeye that it has been paraded as a model of development (*Marshall Islands Journal*, April 1985). Ebeye has become a better place to live. There have been improvements in power and water, a new sewerage system and new roads have been installed. Ebeye is being transformed and the credit goes to its people. The spirit of Ebeye is strong.

Giff Johnson reports that the US has "launched a self-styled 'good-neighbour' policy towards Ebeye" (Johnson, G., 1990: p. 34). The military, he observes, seems more cooperative with the Islanders' initiatives. He suggests that this seems to be predominantly a result of the Marshallese acceptance of the US military presence and their decision to focus more on development than protest. The finances to improve conditions on Ebeye come directly from the US through the Compact of Free Association, a treaty which gives the US military control over Kwajalein in exchange for financial assistance. In a society where the traditional means of livelihood have been destroyed, particularly through the taking and abusing of land by the dominant power, and in a world that demands that so-called underdeveloped countries strive to keep abreast with over-developed countries, what real choice is there?

Even though they benefit little from the Pentagon's presence, many have accepted the American consumer society – although neither the goods portrayed on the US television beamed into Kwajalein Atoll from California, nor the means to buy them, are available. Most Islanders are dependent on their relatives. It is the Marshallese custom of sharing, the underlying principle of their culture, that enables these people to live on a small, resource-limited island in the midst of the US war machine. A society built on individualism would not have survived. But, with the imposition of American culture many of those traditional values are being displaced.

Alvin Jacklick (1986) considers the impact:

> We are losing some of the values of our country. There is a big difference in traditions. I can't be Marshallese and American at the same time. I have to decide what I want to be. Now I am in the middle – I have to serve as mayor and law-abiding citizen but I want to be a traditional leader. The Marshallese system is so complex that it can't be mixed with American or Japanese or Australian laws. There is a great distinction between the two worlds. That is why people are confused – they don't know what to do and they want to preserve the Marshallese customs. For example, if I go out to the bar, start dancing, maybe I dance with a girl who is maybe my relative, first or second cousin – that is, my sister. We might not realise we are closely related! Now we are living in mixed customs. If I go to Kwajalein and live like an American maybe I cope. But only here can I live like a Marshallese.

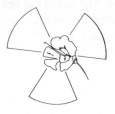

Kora lep jaltap ailin kein an kora.
Women are like a basket where you put what is precious . . . the Marshall Islands belong to women.
                    Marshallese proverb. (WWNFIP, February 1989: p. 1)

Women's power has been undermined as a consequence of colonisation. The Marshallese are traditionally matrilineal. Women have always been the keepers of the land which is passed down by the mother, but the male-dominated American community imposes an alien social structure upon the weave of traditional culture.

Lijon Eknilang (1986) explains the role women have traditionally played in decision making:

> Men don't have the power. They will talk about it and take it to the community and the women will make all the decisions. Without women nothing will happen. If women want men to do something they will tell them to do it. Women of Rongelap are more active than men, they always do things, and men are always waiting until something comes up, and the women say, "All the Islanders will do this". Then the men will do their part. But always women come up with the idea. Men will only sit around and have coffee and talk all day long, and then they will say, "We will go and play baseball". It has always been this way. Men will do the meetings. If there is a meeting with the Iroij [paramount chief] the men will go. If there is only one youngest brother in a family of women, the oldest woman will be the *alab* [land owner] but still her brother will go to the meeting for her. But then she will give the orders, give some word to the community, and will say, "Do that", and everyone will do it. The men will go to the meeting but nothing will happen because they don't have the power. It is the women who will decide what will happen in the community.

Traditionally, power, social and political status, is contained within the land. Identity stems from the land. And while both women and men possess land, in matrilineal custom it is inherited through the mother, a social structure that assures that women have equal status with men, albeit with different responsibilities. But male-dominated cultures (Japanese, German, now American) have imposed alien social structures upon the weave of traditional culture with severe consequences for the entire community. The balance between the genders is being eroded under the guise of adopting individual freedom proffered by the US. Culture and identity is distorted, and with that the connection with the land is lost.

There is a common saying: "Without land a Marshallese is nobody – it is land that makes a person Marshallese", as Lijon Eknilang (1986) explains:

> We own land because we are born. The island has belonged from generation to generation. That land is not really ours – it belongs to our next generations too. That means you cannot give it away. We have our way of sharing land with friends or someone who has done good to you, just like when you share your food. Just like a plate and you say, "You will eat this plate with me". The plate you will never have for your own. Just to share it. Your kids and my kids will share the land. But sometimes some people who you invite to eat with you like to take all the plate themselves. There will be problems then. That is why Marshallese are taking Marshallese to court – sometimes sisters and sisters, brothers and brothers. But it is not right for the court to decide what to do with your land. The Iroij [paramount chief], *alab* [clan-leader], *dri jerbal* [land owners] must make the decision but not the court. But the law says the court must decide. That is the American way.
>
> We don't buy land. Except, now, maybe some place in Majuro. But people are very poor and think they need something that Americans have, like a car, and they trade the land for the car. They think it's special because it's something they never had before. But the car will break down in two years. And what happens? They've lost their land. It's really sad. What about their children and grandchildren? They have given away their land. They have

forgotten that the great, great, great grandparents gave us this land. Forgotten that the land belongs to the generations. That happened to Likiep [Island] when the Germans came. They took all the land, traded with necklaces, guns and useless things. It's not different from when the Americans took over the US and what they did to the Indian [Native American] people.

We are only small – very few thousand people out there on tiny islands, but we are doing our part to stop this nuclear madness. And although we are few we have done it! Which means you can do it too! But we need your support. We must come together to save this world for our children and the future generation to come.
                                    Darlene Keju-Johnson. Marshall Islands. (WWNFIP, 1987: p. 10)

The Marshallese have resisted the taking of their precious lands and waters. For the sake of their children, they are determined to maintain their cultural ties with their ancestral lands.

The people of Kwajalein have fought a long and difficult struggle against the US, and often against their own government which rules their atoll. Julian Riklon has been involved in attempts to better life on Ebeye since the early sixties. He recalls the vital role played by women in the demand for improvements, human rights and access to the islands of Kwajalein Atoll (Riklon, 1986):

Kwajalein was used as a naval base to support the testing program until 1958. At that time the US didn't use the rest of the lagoon, just Kwajalein island. Then, in 1959, they switched command from navy to army and started using Kwajalein as a testing ground for long-range missiles. They took more and more land. By the early sixties they had evicted all the people in the mid-corridor islands and put them onto Ebeye. They've continued to use our islands for testing.

People always want to obey because that's our custom, that's the culture, the way people have been brought up. The same thing with the Bikini people. When they were told to move to another island to make way for the nuclear testing they got up and left. It's the same thing with the Kwajalein landowners.

The people couldn't stand the living conditions on Ebeye. It was unbearable. So, little by little, we try to tell the US government that they have to do something to alleviate the problems. But no response. That's why the landowners made several demonstrations, or re-occupations of their islands. The biggest one was the "Operation Homecoming" in 1982. It was really important. Because of the reoccupation we got a new Agreement that reduced the lease from fifty to thirty years and gave more money to the landowners and development projects on Ebeye. There were other things that we weren't satisfied with, but that was a good start.

That Agreement expired in September 1985. Still the landowners weren't happy with the way the US was treating them. The money wasn't enough to live on. Other people didn't want the US to use their land for testing weapons. But always the US says, "We want your land and we're going to stay. We will come up with some kind of agreement that will benefit both us and you". Unfortunately that has never been the case. They always win because our government is on their side.

So, on 30 September 1985, a group of landowners went into the restricted areas. Some of us to Meck and other islands in the Corridor [the in-atoll off-limits area] and others to Kwajalein Island. We stayed there for four months, men, women and children. There were more women than men. Always more women. That went on for four months. The US didn't have a lease so they didn't have a right to be there but they acted as if they did. They said, "We have an agreement with your government. This is a government to government matter. We cannot deal with you. The Marshall Islands government has signed an agreement of extension which gives us the right to stay on your land. If you have any problems go to your government and speak to them".

In February we had the big incident. We had the right to be on our land but people were arrested and handcuffed and brought back to Ebeye. Women and men. Some forty women. Old women. Some of the old men were badly beaten. It was very brutal. The missile range's private security staff shifted them. People were peaceful but they resisted and were dragged along the ground to the boat. The way they were handled was unreal. The protesters were charged with trespass but the court dismissed the charges and gave us the right to go back on our land. Well, actually we didn't really leave the island anyway. We continued the occupation.

Then in April another court order on Eminent Domain gave the government the right to take our land for the "national interest". That eviction was the most brutal one. They tried to move the women and children. All night they were fighting, trying to get the women on the boat. It was so brutal that four women almost got killed the way they were dragging them around. They were taken back to Ebeye, but by that time there was a lot of people on the pier. People were going to get on the boat and go back to Kwajalein when they heard what had happened. So, instead of landing at Ebeye, they were taken to the island north of Ebeye, and dumped. They just threw them off the boats. There was nothing on that island. They had to wait for low tide to walk the reef back to Ebeye. All night long. They were really hungry and thirsty. You can imagine how horrible it was for them. Women, old women, children and some old men.

When they got back to Ebeye they went immediately to the pier, and they continued to occupy the pier for two or three weeks. Mainly the women, just staying on the pier. It really was a good move. It stopped people going to work on Kwajalein. Some people walked to work along the reef to Kwajalein, but they couldn't come back because the moment they tried to land, people were ready to jump on the boat. So the Americans let them stay on Kwajalein for a while. But they couldn't stand having them there so they send them to another island across the lagoon, on the other side of Kwajalein island – there's a town there.

RepMar [Marshall Islands government] sent in their police and they dragged the old women, children and old men off the pier. It was not a good sight. The American police just stood back and probably laughed at Marshallese being pulled around by Marshallese. Finally the President of the Marshall Islands, Iroij Amata Kabua, came to Ebeye to negotiate. That's what stopped the people on the pier. He promised, as Iroij, that he would help and so people had to believe him. If he had spoken as the president we could have ignored him, but as Iroij he must be believed. But he lied, he didn't do anything.

We don't have any enemies so why should we give our land to the US government to test its weapons to kill other people? They're not our enemy. The Americans came and taught us Christianity, they said, "You should love your neighbour". Have they forgotten the Bible already?

Isolated in a world which seems not to even know that they exist, the people of Kwajalein have decided to focus for a while on improving their lifestyle. But the strength to fight back is not lost. The day is coming when the US will be forced to leave Kwajalein.

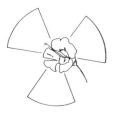

Please, let it be known, that the Children of Micronesia want to live in peace and security.
Micronesian Independence Advocates. (Friends of Micronesia, 1972: p. 24)

The Marshallese are caught in a net intentionally laid by the US to gain lasting control over Micronesia. The Pentagon has deliberately and carefully undermined the Marshallese economy forcing a dependency that has allowed them to use the islands as a testing ground for nuclear weapons, delivery systems and space warfare technology.

In 1963, faced with increasing international pressure to de-colonise and with no intention of relinquishing its military presence in the islands, the US government under President John F. Kennedy employed Harvard Business School professor Andrew Solomon to design a plan for the rapid Americanisation of Micronesia. Solomon's detailed instructions have been carried out to the fullest. The US has deliberately flooded the islands with money, technology and personnel, to disrupt the indigenous economy and make the Micronesians totally dependent on the US (Johnson, G., 1984: pp. 6–10).

In 1971, the US government, in keeping with Solomon's suggested pretence of a "reasonable appearance of self-government", offered commonwealth status to all the island states, up until then united as one political entity as the Trust Territory of the Pacific Islands. Although rejected by Micronesians as a whole, it was accepted by the Northern Marianas, dividing the Territory. Taking advantage of the situation the US then offered the other states individual treaties, called "Compacts of Free Association". The Marshall Islands and the Federated States of Micronesia (Pohnpei, Kosrae, Truk, and Yap), pressured by economic dependency, have accepted these agreements, which determine that the Marshallese may only control their own internal and external affairs as long as they do not conflict with US interests, particularly those of its military.

On 3 November 1986, US President Ronald Reagan proclaimed the compacts for the Marshall Islands and Federated States of Micronesia operational. The Northern

Marianas had earlier become linked to the US through a Commonwealth agreement. Belau, meanwhile, has continued to reject the Compact offered to them. Under international law the US remains obligated to the trusteeship agreement which has not been honoured. Despite the US's 1947 agreement with the nations of the world (acting for the United Nations) to lead the Micronesians to economic independence, the infrastructure required to enable true self-reliance has been deliberately restricted. The Marshalls and the Federated States, as well as the Northern Marianas, are tightly bound economically and politically to the US. Jane Dibblin explains:

> While the Compact promises independence ... it is in fact a virtual US annexation of the islands for military purposes, a denial of self-determination and a shrugging off of responsibility for past actions. The US has "full authority and responsibility for security and defence matters" ... the governments ... are required to "consult" the US over foreign affairs ... the US can veto any item of domestic or foreign policy or any business or trade agreement which it deems is threatening to its security ... US security interests overshadow every other consideration. Self-determination is a mere gloss (Dibblin, 1988: p. 180).

There has been, as Jane Dibblin reports, considerable opposition to the compact:

> Out of the 60 per cent of Islanders who voted 58 per cent were in favour; meaning that little over 32 per cent actually voted yes. Many ballot slips with a "yes" vote included a written opposition ... All the atolls most directly affected by US military activity ... voted overwhelmingly against: 70 per cent on Kwajalein, 90 per cent on Bikini/Kili and 85 per cent on Rongelap. In all 10 out of 24 [island communities] voted against (Dibblin, 1988: p. 180).

For the Marshalls, the Compact of Free Association also frees the US from any further responsibility for the effects, present or future, of their nuclear testing program. That responsibility is now to be carried by the Marshallese Government, although it was a colony at the time of the testing program. Compensation money, granted under the compact, was the ingredient by which the US secured the Marshallese vote – compensation was dependent upon the compact. Under the agreement, a fund has been set up to attempt to give some monetary recompense to those affected. Lijon Eknilang (1986) expressed her thoughts on the issue:

> Compact is an agreement, a treaty. It says the US will take care of our defence and foreign affairs but give us independence. I do not see how we can be independent if we cannot control our relations with other countries. If we can't control the US in our own land. It allows the US to have their base here at Kwajalein. That is a terrible place. In exchange they will give us money for fifteen years – for our government, for compensation. That is why people vote "Yes", because of the money. The US made it like this, they took our land, made us dependent on them. But many people vote "No". We, Rongelap people, we vote "No", because the money will not help us. The US says that they will no longer be responsible for compensation. It will not take its responsibility. It is in the compact. It says once the compact is approved people will not be able to take US to court for nuclear [compensation]. If anyone suffers in the future from radiation then that is just too bad. They know radiation's going to go on through the generations. Of course they know that. But the Americans don't

have to worry about it. It is unconstitutional – it is against the American Constitution. But it is in the compact approved by the United Nations.

It was a big mess from way, way back because even though there were all these problems no one seemed to understand the compact until we had already negotiated for a long time. We got so confused. People wanted to blame their own leaders. But I don't blame them because they didn't even know, didn't understand what they were reading in the papers [documents]. They might have been too embarrassed to mention that. If you really feel you want to be a smart person you don't want people to find out that you don't read things. It's really sad for us. There were only four or five men in the Marshalls who were much educated. In 1975, when they made the compact, they still don't understand English that much.

Right from the beginning when we started to negotiate, we wanted to have our own government but we didn't understand English that much to beat the US. No one understands English that much! They use the really big words, especially when they write it down for you to sign. You maybe know only one meaning, the good one, but there's another ten meanings. The negotiators were too embarrassed to mention that they couldn't understand the compact. Crazy! They only know one word – "mankind", that's the only one they understood, it came from the Bible. And so they said, "Okay, if that's what God wants then I will do it".

But now we realise we have to stand up and talk about it. We have tried to take the US to court to make them be responsible but it is not easy in their own justice system. There is so much the US has done to us that is so bad. Our lives and our land have been hurt. Seems to me all these people are fighting for the US to really recognise the things they have done to us, the cost to our lives. They agreed to protect us and lead us to independence but they haven't.

Many people don't really think that our tiny island of Rongelap is very important to us. But it is our home. We are meant to be there. Our land is everything, our medicine, our food, our houses, our everyday supply. Our land is everything and it has been ruined by the US government. It wasn't easy to leave Rongelap. We had to give up everything. Our land is our memory of those people we've lost. It's in the land – their spirit.

Lijon Eknilang. Marshall Islands. (WWNFIP, 1987: pp. 18–19)

Kwajalein Atoll, island after island, literally bristles with antennae and other paraphernalia – radomes, radio masts and more – essential to the US military. But these rich, lush islands are the ancestral homes of Islanders. They hold a promise of a life free of the problems of Ebeye. But their lands have been stolen so that Americans can, supposedly, live in safety from a non-existent enemy.

A few islands in Kwajalein Atoll are still inhabited. Sando is a dormitory island for Marshallese workers on Roi-Namur second only to Kwajalein island for military facilities. Fifty miles north of Ebeye it stands in sharp contrast. Each house is surrounded by plenty of coconut, pandanus, breadfruit and shade trees and lots of pigs and chickens. Then Obeda is a copra plantation with a population of six, where boats from Ebeye often stop to exchange rice and other dry groceries for coconuts, pandanus fruits, freshly killed and cooked pig and perhaps a great sea turtle and her babies or eggs.

And then there is Mejatto. I wrote in my journal:

> The sea was alive with dolphins dancing and leaping in perfect coordination about us. They led us to Mejatto. As we neared the island the church women [on whose ship we were travelling] festooned the ship with lengths of colourful dress materials, while a small boat, the "*boum boum*", came out from the island and buzzed around us. It was crowded with a party of women, who sang their welcome across the water only to be pelted with doughnuts and canned drinks by the women on the ship. Then they came aboard to crown us all with *wu'u*, garlands of sweet-smelling flowers, and ferried us to the island where we were warmly welcomed by the entire community. After we had settled into a hut with Lijon's relatives I took a few moments for quiet reflection and walked to the lagoon. The sun was setting. Wind sang in the coconut trees, while children laughed and played. Out beyond the trapped lagoon, waves pounded on the reef. So this is Mejatto. It's so beautiful! I find it difficult to remember that this is the rock of coral, isolated in the domain of the Pentagon, on which the Rongelap people have been exiled.

In May 1985, the Rongelap people engaged in one of the most inspirational and courageous actions of the nuclear age. They left their bountiful ancestral home, Rongelap Atoll, now contaminated by the "Bravo" detonation, to live on Mejatto, a mere rock of coral on the edge of the world's biggest missile range. The decision to leave Rongelap was infinitely painful; the daily living on Mejatto almost as difficult. These people have a strength that is borne from the love of their children and an urge for the safety of their people. When the Rongelap people had chosen to return home only three years after radioactive fallout had covered their islands, they had been told that it was safe to return. Increasing illnesses made them insist upon an inquiry which found that their islands were not safe. Faced with little choice, and concerned for the welfare of their people, they asked the US to find them another home. The US agreed, but the ships never came. Only after they had realised that they would not be assisted to flee their contaminated islands did they make the difficult decision to evacuate themselves, a task achieved through the goodwill of Greenpeace and the landowners of Mejatto Island.

Lijon Eknilang (1986) remembers:

> When they first decided they wanted to move from Rongelap I asked them questions. I said, "What happens if you are facing terrible, terrible things like you don't have no food and you don't have no clothes, and you don't have all these things. Would you look back and say, 'I was happy when I was on Rongelap' and start to blame somebody because of all these terrible things we are going to face?". And they said, "No matter what we must go". As long as they will move from Rongelap, they don't care where. They knew Mejatto was only a small place and nothing here. They wanted to move anywhere. They said only

temporarily, until the [radiological] survey [promised in the compact agreement] had finished. But now we don't know if we're going to be able to get back to Rongelap. It is very hard. Maybe we never be able to go home again.

A year after their exodus to Mejatto, Admini Koon (1986) recalled her experience of the return to Rongelap and the decision for exile:

Ever since we went back to Rongelap in 1957 we started feeling something wrong. Many people complaining. When I eat some fish my body really burning all over, just like high fever. We never had those problems before. People they very tired easily, and the body feel weak. They have terrible feeling. Heart problems. Very weak. Itching on our skin. I wasn't on Rongelap during the bomb. I went back in 1957. I had the itching all over.

In 1982 the US came and said the northern islands were too contaminated. We were very scared. We didn't know what to think. They told us to stay on the southern islands and not eat food from the northern islands. But the northern islands is where all the food is, just like a supermarket. The southern islands don't have much food. They said the southern islands was safe, only low level radiation. They said no damage will come to us because the fallout only go on the lagoon side, on the other side from where we lived. But we know. We were there when the fallout come. We know. Some Department of Agriculture food aid would come but not enough so we still go get the food from the north. We were very scared to know that it was too contaminated but we never have no other choice.

We complain to the US since before 1982. But they didn't do nothing. Then people begin thinking about leaving, to find another island. They been thinking about it and started to sit down together and talk about it maybe four years after we went back in 1957. They started talking about going somewhere else. Twenty-five years ago. But it is not easy to leave your home.

We tell the US, "We want to leave, you got to help us". That was in 1976. They said, "Okay, then we will help you move away from your island". But they are only words. We waited long time. They never help. We shift ourselves on the *Rainbow Warrior*, the Greenpeace.

I evacuated because I was afraid to let my kids stay on contaminated land. That was the first thing we ever think about, to bring our kids away from contaminated island.

I feel a little bit better, not much, just a little bit. I still have sickness. They told me I will probably go to Majuro for a checkup. They didn't tell me what is wrong.

People really want to go back to Rongelap, to their home. We are waiting for the survey [to determine to what extent Rongelap is contaminated]. We don't know how long it will take. But as long as Rongelap is not clean we cannot go back.

Aisen Tima (1986), a school teacher on Mejatto during the early days of settlement, recollected his people's painful passage:

It was hard leaving Rongelap, leaving our home. Really sad. When I left Rongelap it seem like one of my best friends die. I didn't show the people that I was crying. I just sit by the rail of the boat and look down. When we sail from there, the sunset, that's the best time in Rongelap. I can see all those people were really sad. Singing a song about leaving the homeland and going to a place they don't know what. People were crying. We really missing our island.

Those people they don't really know Mejatto. Some older people, they used to live in Kwajalein before the war, before the fallout. They know about this island. They say this is lousy place, not like Rongelap, really big difference. Rongelap is one of the most beautiful islands in the Marshalls. Beautiful. But what choice we have? We had to get away from the poison.

Some of the old people die when they got here. One lady she was really old, really weak. Two weeks after the evacuation she died. One old man died too. Really he was strong. He start hunger strike. They gave him food and he say, "No, I'm not hungry". Every time I go to him he say, "I want to stay on Rongelap, not coming to this island. At night I feel cold but on Rongelap my big house there I have my own mattress but here I just live on a mat on the sand and I don't have any door to close". He says, "I'd rather die". After two weeks he really weak. He die.

People are suffering. They are starving. They don't have anything to eat. What do you expect them to eat, keno [wood]? We depend on the US for food. It is not good food. It might give you some kind of diabetes, all those kinds of bad sickness. Doctors say our children are not growing. We ask them why. They say, "Because they don't eat fresh fruit, don't eat fresh vegetables, don't eat enough pandanus, papaya, coconut. They eat only rice, flour". On Rongelap, children were eating pandanus, drinking coconut and we were measuring how tall they were. But here on Mejatto they grow just little. This is cruel. And I believe those doctors. They say local food is much better than tourist food we import from outside world. The doctors say, "Give this food to the children". But here on Mejatto there is no panadanus, no coconut, no papaya, no breadfruit. And there is no water on Mejatto. Only a few water catchments. Most water is from the ground, brown water. We never drink this kind of water when we were on Rongelap. We came here to drink what? Soda water?

People are just waiting to go home. Waiting for the scientists to do their study on Rongelap. They have to really tell us. Honestly. And if they say we can't go back to Rongelap? Well, we will have to find another place to live. And if we can't then this is our second home.

Darlene Keju-Johnson has said of this immense courage:

By doing this the Rongelap people said that they don't want to be part of this whole nuclear craziness. And that their bottom line is: "We care about our children's future". Because they know that they are contaminated. They know that they'll be dying out soon. They are dying now – slowly (WWNFIP, 1987: p. 10).

"Kandrikdoik ken yokwe" – "what little we have we share".

Marshallese proverb

Mejatto was available for the Rongelap people because, although it was used as a camping site by fishermen, it was considered uninhabitable. It does not provide the basic essentials of life. Food does not grow there, the ground water is brackish, sharks infest the turbulent oceans making fishing a hazard. The Rongelap people have attempted to grow vegetable gardens and to keep chickens and pigs but their success has been limited by the scarcity of adequate top soil. Hence they are dependent upon US Department of Agriculture food aid brought to the island by ship. The Mejatto diet, consists of pancakes, doughnuts, white rice, corn-flour porridge, tinned fish (and a few fresh ones), tinned pears and sweet coffee. Renam Anjain (1986) described the difficulties of getting food on Mejatto:

> The fieldship only comes every three months and never brings enough food. This time it has only brought eighty-seven boxes of rice instead of two hundred. That is not good. It will not last three months. Usually they only bring rice, flour, some cans of meat, like tuna. Sometimes one family only has three cans of tuna, three cans of mackerel. Sometimes they only have one can of coffee.
>
> One time my family had to live on only one case, twenty four tins, of meat balls. No other meat. It only lasted two weeks. We are thirteen people so we were really hungry. All we had to eat was a little rice for the children. All us old people, we should eat only yew [coconut sprout]. Each night we sleep and in the morning we still eat some yew. But here on Mejatto we don't have any coconuts, so we got the yew from the other island, Ebadon. It's really hard to go there – low tide, we walk and then carry those things back. I don't know how many miles – really long. That time the *boum boum* [small motorboat] was not working. It was really hard. If we have the boum boum we can go to Ebeye and take some supplies from the DA [Department of Agriculture] store there. When we moved from Rongelap we were hungry that time. We don't have no food on the ship. No food on Mejatto. So our family from Ebeye they get together and said, "Okay, we got to help those people on Mejatto". Our people on Ebeye they sent some food to us.
>
> We get fresh food by going fishing. And we can go to the other islands. But it is very hard, because it is [open] ocean, not lagoon like Rongelap. Some men they go fishing but when they come back they don't have any fish. It's really harder than Rongelap. Too many fish there on Rongelap. When you go fishing there no other men will come and fish at that place – only you. Here there is no room. Everyone gotta fish same place.
>
> Here on Mejatto we are totally dependent on the outside world. But what can we do? I cannot think of anything. What projects could we do? We plant trees, coconut, panadanus, breadfruit, but they will take five maybe seven years to grow. Some pumpkin is growing now, not much. We started a garden, but it won't grow well. There is no soil. People can make things to sell but there's no pandanus for baskets, no *keno* [wood] for canoes. People think of different things. Like more pigs and chickens. But what can you feed the chicken and the pigs if you don't have anything to feed the people? People don't throw away scraps when there is no food. Many people think, "Why do anything? I don't want to stay here". We are waiting for the survey. Then we will know if we can go home. It is hard living on Mejatto. We were better off before the bombs. We took care of ourselves. We got fish, water, food. But the testing, it destroy the land, our lives, our custom.

Lijon Eknilang (1986) explains:

> No one goes hungry while there is any food left anywhere on the island. If the sharing [of the food brought by the fieldship] is wrong and a family runs low they will always feel free to ask their relatives. But the American food had damaged our custom. We don't work like

we used to. Once there was only one kitchen and the whole family would get together and prepare food and eat together. But now the American way separates the people into small families. That's not the old way, it's the American way. It started when we first went back to Rongelap [in 1957] and the fieldship started coming and we started to have American food. Then you didn't have to worry about taking food to that house over there because they have their own food. They cook it in their houses. So today there are two ways, Marshallese way and American way.

The generosity of these people cannot be overstated. Their hospitality displays their consideration for the stranger. While on Mejatto Bridget and I were treated to a *komolo*, a strongly maintained custom that involves the giving of food. I wrote in my journal:

> We were suddenly surrounded by dancing women, all singing. One by one they placed food and gifts before us, *leis* around our necks, *wu'u* (garlands) on our heads. Food mounted up before us – *yew* (coconut kernel), *biro* (breadfruit cake), fresh fish, arrowroot, pumpkin, tapioca, rice balls, tins of grape juice, fans, shells, money. It was amazing. These people had so little and yet they were giving us so much.

Ba-Eman Kabjere
– We Love the Future of Our Kids

Rongelap Placard

The burden of colonisation has invariably rested with the women. Australian, Robyn Greco (1986: p. 5) reported from Mejatto:

> The women seem to hold the whole thing together. The domestic chores that seem to be so downgrading and burdensome to Westerners have proved to be almost lifesaving for Marshallese women. By continuing this role they have been able to maintain their identity and some stability.

It is the women who are predominantly concerned about the impact of the American culture upon the lives of their people. Lijon Eknilang (1986) complains that:

> The Americans change everything. Life is harder for women now. They start having children really early. These days our kids go out and get drunk and smoke and things. They are young, thirteen. The videos change everything. Marshallese do what they see in the movies. It is something new to them. When we see teenagers make out on the movies we don't see the other half of it, we only see the make-out. So our kids go off and make out. And thirteen-year-old girls get pregnant. When I was a kid, mothers and fathers never slept together in one place, they weren't allowed to in front of the children. We waited twenty

years before we started seeing boys, we weren't allowed to be with boys after dark or where people couldn't see us. Now eleven year old girls are going out with boys. Here on Mejatto young girls and boys sleep together. Life has changed so fast. It causes big problems in the families. If parents don't like what their kids are doing, sooner or later the kids will run away to be with the ones who are free, just to enjoy themselves.

Women have less protection under the American culture than was inherent in Marshallese custom. Traditional laws, for example modes of behaviour governing male access to menstruating and pregnant women, were originally designed to protect women. Under colonisation these have been steadily eroded, initially by the missionaries, and later distorted as colonisers imposed their own moral standards. And it is women who pay the price. Modern forms of contraception, for example, have not adequately replaced age old systems. Renam Anjain (1986) is concerned for the welfare of the women:

Women are tired of having too many babies, too many children. They want some control, but the health worker doesn't agree. He's a Christian, and a man. It is hard for women to ask because he is a man. It is not a thing to talk with men. There's nothing here anyway, only some condoms. We have to go to Ebeye. I have had an injection [depo provera] but it made me really sick. Another woman has had an injection too and when she wanted to have a baby she couldn't.

Katrine Jelij (1986), the island midwife, is also worried:

Many women are having babies every year. That causes problems, because they don't have enough vitamins, not enough strength. They have infections in the uterus and sometimes cancers. Women are more likely to have that if they have many children. There are other problems too. Problems with "jellyfish" babies, miscarriages and still-births because of the poison [radiation]. There are women who can't have any babies. A lot of young girls have miscarriages. They are all scared to have babies. Even women born after the bomb. It is getting worse. Before 1954 we never had these kinds of problems – miscarriages, still-births, jelly-fish babies but then they began to be big problems for us. I had that kind of baby and I made more babies. They all made it but now they're all having problems like pneumonia, high fevers and all that kind of thing. And I was not there for the bomb. A lot of women who were there are suffering. Moving from Rongelap might help but it's too early to know.

Health is a major issue on Mejatto. Because of the nuclear testing many Rongelapese have been to hospitals in the US or Hawai'i to have thyroid cancers removed and are now dependent on tablets which must be taken daily. Lijon Eknilang (1986) expresses a common dissatisfaction with the Rongelaps' perception of the way they are treated by the US medical system:

Almost every person on this island have thyroid [problems]. That is why they are taking the lady on small boat. She have thyroid. But they don't know for sure which kind. They going to take her to mainland, to US, and check. They have another guy going next month. Same problem. There are other people but their thyroid is too small, they say, "not ripe, too small yet for operation", but it's growing. Those people they on Rongelap during bomb or went back in 1957, they also has thyroid. In 1960s was hardly any people have thyroid but now there are more. The number is growing.

And other cancers. Breast cancer and things. There are livers, kidney and bone, you know, cancer in the bone. Cataracts. I have cataract. Many miscarriages. All these women on the island have problems like this. If you talk to them you will find out how many and what diseases they have. Like Remeda. She might have leukaemia. She's in Hawai'i expecting some news from her doctor. Everybody really scared if she have leukaemia, everybody really cross their finger and wait for the word. She was one of the people there was emergency for after Rose died. Rose, she die of miscarriage, too much bleeding.

We know that we are dying out. There's no cure for these radiation problems.
Darlene Keju-Johnson. Marshall Islands. (Cox, 1983: p. 1)

The story of the Rongelap and Kwajalein peoples is echoed across the Pacific. The loss of land to military bases, the loss of health to radiation, the eternal exile. The French testing on Moruroa, Tahiti-Polynesia, land of the Maohi. The British nuclear testing at Maralinga, Emu Fields, and Monte Bello in Australia. British and US testing on Kiritimati (Christmas) Island in Kiribati and Kalama (Johnston Atoll),[1] an outlying island claimed by Hawai'i, and, further afield, the Western Shoshone country of the Nevada desert (US). Few can comprehend the anguish of the "nuclear nomads" whose lands and life have been stolen. Fewer still can fathom the deep resilience of the Marshallese women who, with a strength that seems almost superhuman, find in their hearts the ability to forgive, as is reflected by Lijon Eknilang (1986):

I feel that maybe some day people will understand, and maybe they will change.

---

1. Kalama (Johnston Atoll) was heavily contaminated in 1962 when three atmospheric tests misfired, covering the atoll with plutonium. It has since been maintained as a Nuclear Testing Readiness Center, allowable under the Partial Test Ban Treaty. In 1971, on the return of Okinawa to Japan, some 72,000 chemical weapons, stored on Okinawa, were moved to Kalama after a hurriedly introduced law prevented them from being returned to the US. These weapons have leaked the chemical defoliant Agent Orange. A huge incinerating plant has been built on Kalama to destroy obsolete chemical weapons decommissioned in Europe. A leak from the incinerator, which places the entire Pacific in danger, has resulted in the South Pacific Forum demanding, in 1993, that the US close the plant.

WE HAVE ONLY ONE BELAU

– Belau –

Kayangel

Babledaob

Meyuns

Koror

Elabaob
(Rock Is.)

Peleliu

Ngeaur
(Angaur)

BELAU

Sonsorol

Pulo Anna

Merir

N

Tobi

We must protect our Constitution and our land. Belau is the only place on earth where we can express our Belauanness.

Gabriela Ngirmang. Belau. (Ngirmang, 1988)

The Belauans, a people mindful of their role as trustees for future generations, have taken care of their islands for thousands of years. A strong matrilineal culture survives. Gabriela Ngirmang, Mirair,[1] highest ranking woman of eastern Koror, capital of Belau, describes the position of women (1988):

> In Palau [Belau] women play an important role in issues of policy. Women traditionally own land. We control the clan money. We traditionally select our chiefs – women place and remove them. Having observed their upbringing closely we are able to decide which men have the talent to represent our interests. From birth, Palauan women are responsible for the men. When the men marry, the women arrange for the settlement, and when the men die the women bury them.

The Belauan story of colonisation is a familiar one. European traders, mainly British, brought western diseases which decimated the population. Spain claimed the islands in the seventeenth century, then sold them to Germany in 1898, who lost them to Japan in World War I, who in turn lost them to the US in World War II.

When the US set about trying to create "apparent self-government" in Belau, as in the rest of the Micronesian Trust Territory, they invited the Belauans to write a constitution. Bena Sakuma, Public Information Officer of the Olbiil Era Kelulau (Belauan legislature) in 1987, expressed the elation the Belauans felt at finally being able to throw off the colonial yoke:

> It was a feeling of unity, of pride, after about one hundred years of being a colony of different countries. Spain, Germany, Japan and now the Americans. When they told us, "This is your chance for self-determination". It was like a ray of hope. It was like a rainbow. This was our chance to be what we are, what we want to be (Collier, 1988).

The Belauans' euphoria was not to last very long. Since the Constitution was written, in 1979, they have been forced to vote repeatedly on the choice between protecting their culture and heritage or a Compact of Free Association which offers much needed funds but allows the US military and political control of Belauan lands and waters.

---

1. Traditionally, the people of Belau are politically divided into two balancing halves based on kinship lines. Each village is divided into two opposing and complementary sides. This ensures that the consensus process, upon which Belauans have relied for thousands of years, provides for all sections of the community. While, for example, as Mirair, Gabriela Ngirmang is the highest ranking woman of eastern Koror, her position is counterposed by the Bilung who is the highest ranking woman of western Koror. This division is repeated on the male side.

We're not asking or demanding something that is new to the world. What we are asking for is our rights and our land.

Bernie Keldermans. Belau. (Keldermans, 1987)

The people knew that the US wanted a third of Belau's land for a huge jungle warfare training ground, airfields, a nuclear weapons storage site and Koror's deep-water harbour to service the Trident submarines. They knew that the training area would swallow all the villages in five states of the republic on the largest island, Babeldaob. They knew that the US wanted to turn Belau into a military base, just as the Japanese had in 1935. The older people had vivid memories of the terrible consequences then, and having learned about Hiroshima, Nagasaki, Bikini and Enewetak, realised that here was a chance to protect their heritage from unimaginable destruction. So, they banned all nuclear and other toxic substances, and they said that no Belauan land should be used for the benefit of a foreign power. It was a move to protect their lands and heritage for all generations.

The inclusion of these clauses in Belau's constitution was a global first. Bernie Keldermans (1987) explains how it came about:

It was the people who made this constitution. Land is the main issue here. It is important for women because women control the clan and family land, not individual land because men and women can hold land personally. Clan and family land is passed down from mothers. Women have this talent that they can see beyond daily issues and themselves. We don't want to lose our land and with it our freedom, our rights.

The women said, "We want to hold onto our land". So, in Belau we don't pay land tax, that was the women's wish. There is no "eminent domain", so the government cannot take the land away from anyone, again women's wish. The nuclear [clause] is mainly from the women but many men were involved too. The Constitution was really formed by many people's voices. So when the US came to tell us to change it the people who wrote it said, "We cannot do that because this is not our work: it is the people's work". And so they did not change the Constitution.

Inspired by the Belauan custom of consensus, the nuclear clause is a tool to protect the land, and heritage for the generations to come. While it is this clause that has effectively blocked US military plans for over a decade, Bernie Keldermans (1986) stresses that it is the US that has emphasised the nuclear clause in an attempt to undermine the power of Belauans concerned for their land:

We think that the nuclear issue is important. We don't want any military here, not just American. We don't want Russian, Australian, Japanese, any military, here in Belau. But it's not nuclear that is the main thing. It is land. The US did not want us to emphasise the land issue. If that gets to the ears of every Belauan they will automatically say "No" to the compact. So they're using the nuclear issue as a diversion.

The care of the land is the essential ingredient in the Constitution, according to Cita Morei (1992):

Land is *the* issue. And tied to the land is the nuclear free issue in the Constitution, but it is there to protect the land, not to be contaminated or taken away by the military. There's not much land, it is all surrounded by water. If it is taken where do we go? You can walk across Koror in just half an hour – and that's it. And under the compact, if the US wants that it can take it. Where do we go? It is very simple, but the US has made it so complicated. We said in the Constitution, "This is how we want our life to be. This is how we define Belau". But then the US says, "No. That's not how you define Palau. This is how we define your life, so you better listen". That's the compact. It is very simple. Rather than complications like the compact, if you have a simple life, you should have a simple law. We fish, we go to the taro patch. What more do you want from life? Not complications like the US.

The Russians are falling apart. They are becoming a democracy. So why are we giving the land to the US? Even if the Russians are together, why are we giving the land to the US? If the land is taken our way of life will change in Belau.

We have been very good students of the US that we want our democracy and we want our freedom. What we're asking for is not different from anyone else. We want to be the head of a mouse rather than the tail of this big tiger. I don't know if you understand that ten times to vote to keep your country free from nuclear is democracy. To the US it is!

Bernie Keldermans. Belau. (Keldermans, 1987)

The pressure by the US has been without reprieve. Although the Constitution was originally voted for by 92 per cent of the Belauan population the US, through its ambassador Rosenblatt, immediately demanded that the nuclear provision be dropped. He directed the Trust Territory High Court to declare the Constitution null and void. A second constitutional plebiscite on 23 October 1979, rejected the new constitution by 70 per cent leaving a repeat vote on the original Constitution to be passed by 78 per cent. And thus in January 1981 the Republic of Belau was inaugurated as the world's first nuclear-free nation.

Meanwhile negotiations for a treaty with the US, the Compact of Free Association, begun in 1969, were continuing. The compact would grant the US control over Belau's military and foreign affairs in return for economic aid. The Pentagon would gain military use of the islands and the economic zone around Belau, designated under the

International Law of the Sea to be 200 miles, would be limited to twelve miles. This would not only divide Belau's archipelago but would make Belau's valuable sea-minerals directly available to the US. Under the compact, the US military demands the right to take any land within 60 days through eminent domain (the right of a government to take land in the national interest). The economic aid offered to the Belauans in exchange for all this is totally inadequate and will leave the small nation bankrupt within ten years.

The Belauans have been forced to vote repeatedly to protect their Constitution (eleven times by 1994). Millions of US taxpayer dollars have been spent on campaigning for the 11,000 voter population to accept the compact. Where that has failed both legal and underhand pressure has been brought to bear on the community. This has included the first devious assassination of a Pacific president, murder of and physical violence towards pro-Constitutional Belauans, and the building of an unnecessary power plant by British banks and companies. Built with the full knowledge of the US Department of the Interior, this power plant was a covert attempt to place Belau into immense debt, thereby increasing its dependency on the US. After a long court case the Belauans forced the US to accept responsibility for administering power under the trusteeship agreement.

Women have been in the forefront of the campaign to protect their Constitution, most particularly during the violence of August–September 1987. The government had forced a vote on the Constitution to amend the 75 per cent vote required to edit the nuclear provision, changing it to a mere majority. This was unconstitutional and the Ibedul, (paramount traditional guardian of Belau), on request of the *Machas* (women elders), led a lawsuit against the government. Threats of violence resulted in his unilaterally withdrawing the case. The *Machas* were furious. Calling on the powers that have rested with women throughout Belau's long history, they gathered women together from all over the archipelago. Led by Bilung (the highest ranking woman of western Koror) Gloria Gibbons, fifty *Machas* relodged the lawsuit in their own names. The threats became reality! Homes were firebombed; lives were threatened, especially those of the women plaintiffs and their children. The reign of terror, culminating in the assassination of Rubak (male elder) Bedor Bins, forced the women to withdraw their suit. Nothing like this had ever happened in Belau before. International outrage followed. Protests flooding in from all over the world demanded that the women should be given the protection needed to go ahead with their case. When, a year later, the women took the matter to court, they won.

This was a momentous event. It showed the power, determination and vision of the Belauan women. Despite terrifying odds, they stood fast to their beliefs. US terrorism did not deflect them. Although the women look back at this time with dread and pain, praying that there will never be a repeat, they are justifiably proud. To quote Bernie Keldermans (1987), the daughter of Rubak Bedor Bins:

> To your eyes we are very small: we don't exist! But as small as Belau is we have been fighting against the most powerful nation in the world and every time we have fought we have won.

Gabriela Ngirmang has always played a leading part in the struggle to protect the Constitution and has urged others to join her in filing lawsuit after lawsuit against the Belauan government. She explains why (Ngirmang, 1986):

It is a responsibility of any leader of any place to make sure that everyone in the community is taken care of. I do not want Belauans to accept the compact without knowledge, without a choice. There are many points in it that I don't like.

I am against the compact because I know the horrible things that happened during the war. I lived on Airai and I saw many Japanese ships on the ocean sinking, with so many people wounded and bloody. I saw many Japanese soldiers starved to death. I had two children. One was eighteen months old, the other I delivered during the war. And I just don't want to see those things happening in Belau again, or to our children.

Then there's also that the contract is for fifty years. If Belau decides that it wants to terminate the compact before fifty years and the Americans disagree then we can't terminate it. Both sides have to agree. I am concerned about our children. If they find that they really don't like the military then they can't do anything. So that means we'll be like prisoners to the US. I am very worried that once the military gets into Belau there may be no way to get them out.

But the main issue is the land. Land is a very touchy subject here because there is private land and clan land. The compact says that if the US wants any land the government must give it to them in sixty days. But it is not theirs to give. It belongs to the clans. The compact will create a lot of problems between people from the clans. There may be many lawsuits. I don't know how they will handle it. Whether they will file lawsuits against our government or against the military. Way back in the old days nobody would sell land. People would come, for example, and ask me to use a piece of land, but no one would sell land. It's only today, people are imitating the Japanese and Americans selling land for money.

Our lifestyle is very different from yours. You can move from house to house or city to city according to your job and where you want to live. Here we cannot move from one land to another. For example, this house is our ancestor's place. They are buried right here in this graveyard. This belongs to us. We cannot move and leave this place for someone else, we just can't. This land has been in my family going back seven mothers. Land has names here. Whoever is living around my house will inherit the title which goes with this land, the title that tells you who you are and your position in Koror. This is now telling everyone in Koror that I am *Mirair* [east Koror's highest ranking woman]. Whoever inherits this land inherits the title. Land is the most valuable thing we have. It is our identity. Without it we are lost.

The new generation has become less respectful to the elders. I blame the American administration that brought what they call "freedom". When you see cans and papers on the side of the road it's from the young people. Nobody used to pass this house and even throw their betelnut on the ground. It was highly respected. But now when they pass this place they shout and scream and throw beer cans. [In September 1987, in the violence against the women plaintiffs, Gabriela's house was firebombed.] Many men are not gentle and not humble, not merciful. So often it's the women who are struggling and not the men. Sometimes I feel it's all up to us. We all depend on prayer to ask God for help, because it's like going to the end of our tether. It seems like no woman ever started war in all of history.

Then there is the political education program. They don't teach the public everything that is in the compact. They never use the compact itself, they just tell people what they want to tell them, never refer to the compact document itself. They just tell people we were going to get more money, that they would put the money in an envelope and deliver it to us, and that you could even pack your baggage and go to the US to attend the school there without paying. This kind of talk fooled people. They didn't know any better, they just believed what they were told. Not many people know what is in the compact, so they just follow the others. I am not sure if there are even ten people in Belau who really understand what the compact is about. We try to educate people and hold group meetings but the preparation time is limited because they don't release the documents. So that it is very difficult.

I was very unhappy about the way things were, so I got up and told the UN Visiting Mission [election overseers] that nobody here knows what's going on. Our people will cast their votes for the compact, without knowing much about what it says. When the UN mission comes the president's office takes care of them. The only chance we get to voice our opinions is at the hearing, and that's only a matter of a few hours. And then they say that they really don't have the power to tell the US what to do – "The only thing we are here for is to see that the election is handled well", they say. But the election is not handled well because the political education is not being done well. They only come to witness the actual election, they don't see the preparation. When they are here they are taken to the Rock Islands for picnics and we don't know what they are told. The government handles them the way they want.

The US says they will use the military bases to defend Belau. I ask, "What for? What do they defend Belau for? Who wants to take Belau from the Belauans?". I don't believe the US military's interest in Belau is for the defence of the Belauans. I believe it is for the defence of the US.

Lorenza Pedro. Belau. (Connelly et al., 1987: p. 47)

The US is insisting that the Belauans need it and its military bases for protection, but experience has taught many Belauans that military bases result in death and destruction. With vivid memories of the battles between the US and Japan during World War Two, they fear that the US presence will threaten their nation once again. History has taught them that: "When soldiers come, war follows". Lorenza Pedro (1986) warns:

The US says they will use the military bases to defend us. This is the same excuse the Japanese used before World War Two but instead of defending Belau they fought their wars in Belau and, as a result, many Belauans lost their lives, our islands were devastated and we suffered from starvation and sickness. And so, we know that they do not defend us.

War has resulted in the loss of land, with a terrible impact on the people. Belauans, Roman Bedor (1986) asserts, are not too keen to repeat history:

We have seen the destruction of the land so many times. People had to build their homes from the ashes of World War Two. That's why we say, "Never mind about defence. If you have to destroy a society to defend it, then something is wrong with the whole concept of defence". They have used the Soviet threat to create fear that Belau as a small nation cannot survive without any defence: "the Soviets are moving into the Pacific!". As the years go on it will change. It is changing already. Who knows what will happen if the Soviet Union and the US decide to become allies again. What will happen to the Marshall Islands? Will they regain their healthy life? Will they regain the beautiful environment that they have lost? No way! And that's precisely what our concern is. They can change tomorrow, it's only a matter of negotiating. But our society has been destroyed, and there's no way you can create another island, no way it can be replaced. When we look at the Marshall Islanders we are afraid for ourselves. Look at the sacrifice that they have made "for the good of all mankind and to end all wars".

Belau, like many other Pacific islands, was the scene of fierce fighting between the US and Japan. The islands are littered with reminders from World War Two – war memorials, bombed Japanese wartime buildings and beaches carrying names like "Bloody Beach". For Micronesians "the war" is a terrible nightmare of only yesterday. There is a lingering anguish of the lives lost and nature destroyed. A plaque in Koror states: "Here in the Palau Islands Japan and the United States fought the most desperate battle of World War Two".

The attack of Peleliu Island began on 15 September 1944 when a US bombing raid destroyed 127 Japanese fighters and bombers on the airstrip. When, after three days of bombardment from air and sea, the US marines disembarked on the reef not a shot was fired. Relaxing slightly, they reached the shore and were wiped out. The Japanese had survived the bombing by hiding underground in an elaborate system of man-made tunnels. Their command post, under Colonel Nakagawa, was on Mount Umurbrogol, which the Americans called "Bloody Nose Ridge". After the three days of bombing, the Americans pushed the Japanese back into the tunnels and sealed up the entrances one by one. Hundreds of Japanese were buried alive. Others were blown up when the Marines poured aviation fuel into the caves. After two and a half months the battle was over. Thousands had died and Peleliu was devastated. Most of the Belauans had been evacuated to Babeldaob before the battle began, but many had also died. For those who survived, the simple acts of daily life were a hardship.

Ubad Rehetaoch and Maech Ngirakedrang,[2] her husband and a traditional seer, recalled their experiences of the war (Rehetaoch, 1986; Ngirakedrang, 1986).

Ubad Rehetaoch:

We were on Babeldaob during the war. We lived in the forest. We were very poor. Some of the people from Ngeaur (Angaur) and Peleliu moved into Babeldaob to get away from the

---

2. Maech Ngirakedrang has died since this interview was made. It has been included with permission of his wife Ubad Rehetaoch. Maech was a wise man and a seer. Belau and the world are a lesser place without Maech's counsel.

fighting so we had a big problem with food. The Japanese soldiers would stop us from getting coconut and taro and sometimes we couldn't even get seafood because of the bombing. We lived in huts of palm trees for the roof, and plain earth for the floor. Or we would stay in caves. The old people and young children stayed in the caves. Those of us who were strong collected food in the night time, we went to the farm, and the younger men would go fishing.

Maech Ngirakedrang:

If the Japanese soldiers saw us fishing they would beat us, kick us, take our fish away, and tell us it was dangerous. Also coconuts. When Belauans collected coconuts they would get kicked in the back, stepped on. I was beaten for taking a coconut.

Ubad Rehetaoch:

It was a very hard life for Belauans. Sometimes when the crops were ready to be used the Japanese would come and say, "We're going to bomb this place", and then they would move the people out and use the farms for their own food. They used Belauans to make farms for the Japanese soldiers. Sometimes the Americans would bomb a Belauan village in the forest, but whenever possible they bombed where they thought the Japanese were. Some Belauans were usually living with the Japanese so some Belauans died. But they didn't usually bomb a Belauan village. Still a lot of Belauans died for no reason.

Maech Ngirakedrang:

I was forced to train in the Japanese military for three months. We were trained to be Kirikomi, kamikaze frogmen. To carry big torpedoes and destroy ships – and die with them. They also used some Japanese but they were not good swimmers so they had to train Belauans. They used force. The Japanese didn't care, they just wanted to win the war. They would load a bamboo raft with explosives and make us swim with that raft to the ship. There was no way of returning before the bombs went off.

Ubad Rehetaoch:

The Japanese told the Islanders that the American soldiers were terrible people. That they would just come and get a woman, tie her legs to two horses and split her in half. We were very afraid. When Americans came we would hide and let them pass. We wouldn't look at them. Later we learnt that they were not like the Japanese told us. But when the Americans came they destroyed beautiful houses and roads. They used some of the Japanese refugees who were left on the islands after the war ended as labourers. After that they sent them back to Japan. Only one Japanese house escaped, belonging to a high government official. And some of the big buildings like the court house and the legislature. They are still the biggest buildings in Koror.

Maech Ngirakedrang:

When the Americans came they brought big changes for Belauan people. They brought more outside influence. During these first years it was very hard. The traditional chief would hold the title for the local people while the magistrate, or district administrator, held the government title. There was always a conflict between the two leaders. Belau was in a very bad time for leadership. When Belau's leadership still worked it was a good way of life, good laws. Now life is changed.

Resettling on Peleliu was not easy. When the Belauans returned home they could not believe their eyes. They could see right across the island. All the trees had been razed to the ground. Ubad Rehetaoch (1986) remembers:

> Peleliu and Ngeaur (Angaur) were like a desert. Trees are growing now because some of the people came to Babeldaob to get coconuts and plants to plant on the island. The chief of Peleliu asked for help.

The US had built a massive base from which to fight the retreating Japanese. Peleliu was covered with tarmac. The people have had a long court battle to get their lands back – land that the US military will tell you they fought hard for, to protect for Belauans. Only one of the original five hamlets has been resettled.

Ngeaur (Angaur) suffered a similar fate. It was bombed and covered with tarmac. But this was not the first violation. Ngeaur (Angaur) has been heavily mined for phosphate. Now the forest floor is bare spikey limestone – a lunar landscape. Balerio Pedro (1986) explains:

> They have taken our land and left us rocks to live on. They came and made us work for them, destroying our own island. The Americans paid low wages but for the Germans and the Japanese it was forced labour, and no government has ever paid us a cent for the phosphates they took. We were left with nothing. No land, no compensation – just destruction. Together the Germans, Japanese and Americans mined 3.3 million tons of phosphates. The Germans mined for seven years, the Japanese for thirty years, and the US for nine years. If we could get these rich nations to pay some of what they owe us, then we would be economically healthy and independent, like the Republic of Nauru.[3]

This raped island, historically and culturally significant to Belauan custom, is further threatened by the compact, Balerio Pedro (1986) continues:

> Ngeaur [Angaur] is separate from the rest of Belau. The reef that protects Peleliu, the Rock Islands and Babeldaob doesn't come here, it is the rough channel to the north that protected Ngeaur's independence in the old days. We were enslaved by Koror to "unite" us into the federation but we fought back and eventually regained our independence. So we were independent until the colonisers came, and so we are a very proud people. It's here that all Belauan spirits come before they leave the land. Ngeaur [Angaur] is a very enchanted

---

3. Balerio Pedro, representing the traditional chiefs of Ngeaur (Angaur), is attempting, under the United Nations' Trusteeship Agreement, to gain compensation against the US, Japan and Germany for the phosphate mining. Nauru, threatening to take Australia, Britain and Aotearoa to the International Court of Justice in 1989, has successfully gained compensation of A$107 million for the damage done to the small island nation.

place, very special. It was very rich and fertile, the best in Belau. It was rich in phosphates and now that is all gone, mixed into the fields in Germany, Japan and the US. Now the US say they want land for a new air base on Ngeaur [Angaur]. They want to extend the present airstrip over where we grow the taro now. It is our best land.

Women were significant actors in surviving the war. A story is told of how, although the Japanese had tried to evacuate all the Belauans to Babeldaob before the American attack, dozens had been stranded. They hid for weeks in the caves near the phosphate mines. With little food, they risked death from either side when they ventured out at night to forage for what they could. Eventually they decided their only hope was to leave. Ellen Pedro, a young nun, walked out first, waving a white flag. Somehow they got away to Babeldaob, where they found the rest of the community, also desperately short of food but away from the fighting. This brave woman leading her people to safety had followed the customary role of Belauan women in war. In the old days, when there was physical conflict between two sides, the women would sometimes walk to the front and end the fighting before too much blood was shed. The women of Belau are traditional peace makers.

Dilbelau Ues Petronina Pedro, Lorenza and Balerio's mother, is one of the few people to have witnessed almost one hundred years of colonisation. Bridget Roberts (1986) describes her:

> She was sitting on a pandanus mat in the cool shade of her living room, her sightless eyes looking back on more than ninety years. She had experienced four colonial rules and two world wars. I wondered at the changes she would have witnessed not only in the material world but in the spirit of the Angaur people. She would remember when Angaur was thriving, now it was dying as a result of a long history of colonisers and imposed cultures. This ancient woman bore the marks of custom, intricate blue tattoos adorned her arms. Dilbelau Ues (queen) of Angaur could help solve clan and family problems and pass on the old songs, chants and secret lore.

> *With the US it is like being tossed by the waves, back and forth, this way and that way. You are starting to become confused. There is nothing better than to lead your own life. To be with your own self. Governing self. It is better than anything.*
>
> *Gabriela Ngirmang. Belau. (Ngirmang, 1986)*

Alien social, political, and economic systems have been imposed on Belau, to the detriment of the traditional system and to the benefit of the colonisers. Gabriela Ngirmang (1986) describes the impact on custom, and its destruction of the ancient balance:

There is equality in the traditional system. Men respect the opinion of women, women respect men. There is an exchange of authority. Women do appoint the man but the men can turn around and say, "I want you to do this and this", and we consent to it. For example, if a man has to build a clan house he will tell women how much they must give, and we agree. That is a simple illustration. We appoint him, he does the work, and so we give him our support. It was a very good system that we live in, there was a balance in caring for each other.

Tradition still looks after the people, although men are in the highest position in the government. But there are few men who can buy their own land, or build their house on their own, and when they die we have money for their children. The majority, when they die, the Belauan custom takes over their responsibility to look after the children.

The government does not have respect for tradition. The traditional system was that the leadership was not paid, they took care of the people. The American system hurts the people. In the American system they made everybody equal, but equality is not really made to serve everybody. It is lacking in the care and concern for people, much less than the traditional way. When you are in the government you turn towards the US and then when you come into the tradition you put on another hat. It seems like a person who has got two feet, in two different places. It is difficult to be in two places – American and Belauan. But in most cases he has to comply with the US. He is tossed between the systems. If he has one eye to the US and one eye to Belau, then he is really cross-eyed. Belauans don't really know where they are, and for the government not to know which way to go reflects the people.

Cita Morei (1992) explains that the concept of "democracy" does not quite fit onto the Belauan template:

I think our Belauan democracy has a very different meaning than "democracy" in other places in the world. In the traditional system there is ranking. One of the things about "democracy" is that everybody is equal. It makes my vote similar to a chief's vote, and a chief's vote equal to a younger person's. Everybody is equal. That isn't so in Belauan tradition. We have "democracy" in our traditional system but it is very different from the US "democracy". Here we have the tradition and the electorate, two faces to a coin. We have to know both ways. We have to learn the US way, we have to speak their language, their politics, otherwise we drown in American "democracy". But we have to define what is Belauan "democracy", what is Belauan justice. The US are the "champion of democracy", but look what they are doing to the rest of the world. Interpreting democracy to their own advantage rather than to the advantage of the people who live in those places.

Belau is so small, we do not need to be so caught up in complicated processes of doing things the American way. The consensus way of decision is a good system for Belau, it is the best system for us, just to talk until we reach agreement. Problems get solved that way. But the American system is voting. It is the thing we have done most in this system. We have voted so many times. Eleven times in eleven years, to vote. We say, "What did Americans teach you?" – "Well, how to vote!"; "What is democracy?" – "Where we learn how to vote!".

Belau is a very stratified society. Everything is divided in two. Belau divides in two, Koror divides in two, even the smaller hamlets there is a chief for the northern part, and a chief for the southern part. It is the chief who oversees what is happening in his place. This is the nature of the Belauans. We have never listened to one chief, there have always been two, a check and balance. You have to have a consensus of everyone, you will never succeed, so you need different influences to get things moving. The smaller the group the better. Because we get things done in the smaller, rather than the bigger. Then we have a competition, who is better. Like with the men's *abai*, meeting house. Women compete in the taro patches. There is always a check who should talk to who or about what, among the older women. But among the young women, if you give your time then they listen to you. If you feed people then they listen to you. That's really Belauan. If you give your services, they will listen to you. It is sharing your wealth that you get respect. If you have lots of money but you don't share you will not get respect.

There are Belauans now who are totally American in their thinking, in their life. They work from morning to night, they do not go to the taro patch, or go fishing. And then you have people who go to the farm. There are two extremes. You have to have American skills to fit in Belau today, and at the same time you have to have Belauan skills to live with the custom.

Bernie Keldermans (1986) identifies a fundamental conflict between the communal basis of Belauan custom and the US concept of individualism:

No individual really owns the land because each plot is in the name of the family, clan or community. So when the US announces its desire for land for military bases, the whole community is directly and personally affected. There are no individual owners to be isolated and bought off. Still American individualism has crept in and land has been sold for hotels by people who have put the value of individual wealth above that of the common heritage. Those who support the compact and the American way of life are those who have sold their traditional values. To do that they have had to override or ignore the guidance of the women, whose main collective goal is to preserve the land for future generations.

Women ARE the government. It's really the women who make things move.
Bernie Keldermans. Belau. (Keldermans, 1987)

Belauan women are the caretakers and guardians of their people and culture, according to Bernie Keldermans (1986):

The constitution was mainly from the women. When US Ambassador Rosenblatt said we would have to delete the provisions on the land, on the two-hundred-mile economic zone, and on the nuclear issue, otherwise they would walk out with their foreign aid, the women said, "Yes, you can go with your money but we'll keep our constitution".

Whenever we have a plebiscite women will donate or buy paint, a board and so on, selling their taro, tapioca or whatever. We work all day and go to the villages after work. When we go everything has been arranged. The local women make sure they tell everyone and they are the people with the power in the community so when they say, "Come", then everyone will be there. We go through everything: the compact, the Constitution, why they are incompatible and why we think we should uphold our Constitution to defend our land, our rights. We never come out and say, "Don't vote for the compact". Everything has to be done by word of mouth, because most of the [older] women were educated under the Japanese, so they don't read or write English and they don't read Belauan in American script. The local women go back to the taro patch where they share work and talk, and they give the information out. Very few men stand up and talk and inform people what is going on, although they whisper here and there.

During the first and second plebiscites the government ignored us. They thought we were "just old women" and they didn't see what we did because it was done in the taro patches. That is where women carry out their daily conversations, teach each other or relay messages. But by the third plebiscite they were beginning to pressure us and tell people we were communists that really wanted to sell Belau. But the women are not afraid of the government because they feel that they are the government, so why should they be afraid?

Nowadays we have a problem. Most women are afraid to voice their opinions in public, especially young women. For older women it's not so bad because traditionally women have always spoken out. But most young women are really afraid. This is because of Americanisation. Before the westerners came, young women were always important in negotiations. If there was a fight people would negotiate, and part of that might be that a high-ranking woman would decide to go to another village to be the mistress of the high *Rubak* [male elder] of that village. She would make peace between the people and bring back money to her village. (It was good to have daughters.) It was always her decision but when the Spanish came they thought it was prostitution and banned it. All the foreigners imposed their own systems and now we have two completely different systems. Now men are in the government and they try to suppress the women. They are trying their best to keep us down.

A gender imbalance has been created by the carrot-dangling of an alien culture in which men have benefited from power over women. As many Belauan men, enticed by resulting privileges, adopt the norms of the American culture, women's status is being undermined, according to Isabella Sumang (1992):

What has happened to women under the American system? Look at the government, all of the high positions are men's positions. In the capitalist society men are always the head of everything. The men get more pay, and in the custom whoever puts in the most money has the most say. So men are able now to ignore what women say. He does not need her clan.

We live side by side with men. We cannot do without men. We need men. Men play a lot of roles. They keep the balance. They are the counterpart of the woman. They are equal. The work is kind of equal. The men kill the pig, get the wood, go fishing. It's equal jobs. The men have a role. There is a women's group, and there is a male's group, that balance each other. A sister and a brother who hold the same titles, like Ibedul and Bilung. For every clan there is a counterpart. She does the women's role in the community, the women's decision, and the men do the men's. It used to be very balanced. And there is a check of the balance there too. Even the Council of Chiefs they have a system – they have different roles, each clan has a role. That used to work. Before the Americans.

But for any society everything has to go through a change. The Japanese ignored our system. They did not force their government on us. We did not have any part of their government, we had our own. They left us alone, but there was just so many of them in

Koror (56,000) that you could not help but absorb it. They did not push it on you. Whereas the Americans, they forced their system on us.

The change is now that the men make the decision in the government, without the opinion of the women. He doesn't have to listen to the women because now he has his own money. That gives him power. Before he needed the women to pay his way. It is the capitalist system, that has been introduced very strongly by the Americans. It is man-orientated.

The hardest working females in Micronesia are Belauans. Then they can make the decision, because they have the power. It is not a dictatorship. Your son would be the clan chief while your husband wouldn't be. He will assume the clan title of the mother's family. There is the Council of Chiefs and when the son gets there he will make decisions. The council make decisions, but when it is unreasonable, women have the say. Women can withhold from the man, like if he wants to build a house he needs the women, he has to earn your support. It is like a balance.

Traditionally the woman goes to the man's clan, when he dies she goes back to her own clan. Or she earns something, she works to earn land from the family, she serves his womenfolk, then when he dies she inherits some land. It depends on the goodwill of the man's clan. But a woman also gets land from her mother. It is a workable system, not unreasonable. You find a good family, then they give easily, for not serving too much.

Women are strong because you are brought up that way. It is good to have the first born a daughter, because she can help you. It is sad if all your children are boys, then they cannot really help you.

You just assume your matrilineal power. It isn't something you think about. When you are growing up you see women taking the responsibility, so when they are gone, when it is your turn, you just do it. You know what your role is. You know what to do. When you are young you are told stories and taken to traditional custom, so you just grow up with it. I was asking my aunt, "Why is it matrilineal? Why is it that titles are coming from the women and not the men?". She said, "It is so easy. You are always sure that it is your baby, right, and you can never always be sure about the man. You can be sure that it is the blood of this family that runs in the child".

Isabella Sumang feels that women will inevitably come back into their power. She identifies the taro as having a significant role in that empowerment. It is, she claims, a way of keeping in touch with the land and therefore with what it is to be Belauan (Sumang, 1992):

With the US role of women coming up [improving], hand in hand with our own tradition, we will find very strong women, some of them young women. I think women are very strong, even in the cultures that are male-dominated. But we need to help other women who are depending on men to come out of it. If you are depending on men to provide the money then you are economically, socially and mentally dependent on that man. But yet, non-working women who stay home and work to raise her own food, to get taro to relatives, whatever, they are very independent. The women who work in the taro swamp. They have lots of gardens, taro, tapioca. So if she is just staying home and taking care of the children then she is dependent, but if she can work in the taro swamp she is strong.

It was not until I started working in the taro patch that I learnt the value of it. It helps you work out your mind, very clearly. All the time you are putting this soil back into the swamp you keep thinking. All the time in the world. You let your soul work on it by itself.

It is like you are not thinking of anything, but you think of everything. You work out all the problems in the taro swamp right there. You have the space, and the time, to do. So you don't have any problems no more. And at night you sleep well. It is very nice feeling. The taro I love, they respond to your touch. Even conservation you can learn from there, because you learn to preserve the water in the swamp, and you learn to recycle the leaves and grass. So there is a cycle, learning in a very practical useful way to respect the earth. If you treat it right, it will give back to you.

Cita Morei (1992) suggests that the taro patch has protected Belau in the past, and that it remains instrumental in empowering women against the taking of their lands today:

When the foreigners came they saw the men in the *abai*, meeting house, and they decided that the men were in charge. The women were left alone. They were left alone in the taro patches doing their own thing. So these foreigners they thought they had influenced Belauan politics but then they have not because they have not influenced the people who elect those men to talk and talk. That was a flaw in the outsiders' views. They left the women alone, to do what we did. Women went on and on and on, untouched by foreign administration, greed and all that penetrates the men's psyches.

The taro patch is a place to tell the women what is happening with the compact. When you tell them they will tell others. Taro-patch politics is very influential. It is sort of a sacred place in a way, you're thinking about the land. You are thinking, "This is what I value". You are not thinking of politics or of money. You are thinking about what it is to be Belauan. And that is played out in the taro patch. You get to think about what are *our* priorities, what are *our* needs, what are *our* weaknesses. If we want to keep coming to the taro patches then we have to look after Belau. We got to keep on going. Taro-patch politics. Men, they think about politics, they think about money. But women have been strong, because of the taro.

Palau [Belau] was independent before the Germans, Spanish, Japanese and Americans came to our lands. Now we live in a trusteeship for which we did not vote, more dependent than we were without it, and we have never had any other choice other than this deal which gives you [the US] perpetual military rights in land that is ours.

Gabriela Ngirmang. Belau. (Ngirmang, 1988)

As women have striven to protect the Constitution – and by extension the land and culture, the Belauan heritage – they have been confronted by a major propaganda machine set to alarm Belauans into a continued dependency. Gabriela Ngirmang (1986) describes the pressure behind the compact:

Some people pushing for the compact say, "Would you like to go backwards to where we were? To wearing grass skirts and eating coconuts?". They say this to people who are not thinking. These people are isolated, they don't understand and they are frightened. And that is why they are ready to be influenced by whoever has the most influencing story. All their lives they know the Americans, or some other coloniser. They have become dependent on the Americans. Most people are afraid to be independent because it's a very small country. First we will suffer for a little bit but after that, I am sure, there are other nations that will come to our assistance. Why we don't get other assistance is because the US is over us.

The situation in Belau is urgent. The rapid Americanisation of Belau is distorting the integrity of the nation and its future. Isabella Sumang (1992) expects that the hoped-for departure of the US will cause difficulties at first, but is adamant that it is essential to the long term well-being of the people:

The less interference from outside the sooner we get on our feet. The government is supported by US money. If they withdraw that, [the government] will fall apart and we will have to find another way. A way that is both traditional and part of what we have learnt from the US. People are so used to working two weeks and then get a pay cheque. They are afraid because they are dependent on the US economy. But if they would realise that the US is collapsing in on itself. The US economy is falling apart. How much can they give to us, for how long?

Women are actively encouraging education on the strength and potential of sustainable development. They claim that there are options to the dependency now binding the Belauans to the US. Gabriela Ngirmang (1992) warns that any development in Belau must care for the land:

With sustainable development we can cease living the other way, we can take care of our land. For instance, the sewer. Around Koror we cannot collect sea food because of the sewer pollution. This is another responsibility of the government. They created the system, they should see to it that the system works and benefits, not to pollute and poison. During the 1940s there were about forty thousand people in Koror – Belauans, Koreans, Okinawans, Japanese – and the toilets, they were above ground, and then people came to collect it and treated it as fertilizer. So we could collect sea food from the ocean, it was not polluted. Now there is not the forty thousand in Koror any more and it's polluted. The houses were next to each other, all connected. You could walk from one end to another without getting wet, it was crowded. The Japanese owned a few buses and trucks, and everybody walked. And the water-drains were better fixed than they are now – they were covered. And then there was the constant work to clean out the drain, so there was more work.

Before the war the Japanese planted here in a big way. We produced our own sugar, and tapioca was beginning to be sold. If we can do that again, among ourselves, instead of buying our food, then we are freer from the Americans. They started making their own soap, from coconuts. Maybe those kind of things could be started again. At least the Japanese tried to teach some things. But then there was the war and a change of administration brought a change of ideas. If they would have continued, it would have been good for Belau.

It is just like building a house. First we had our own house, with a thatched roof. And then the Japanese introduced tin and wood, so we are not really knowing how to do that house building. Then they sell us the cheapest material that you could buy so after a couple of years it is falling down. So then they introduced concrete. So then you built a house with concrete. But after a while they say that it wasn't a good way to build a house, you could have more space if you put in a two-storey house. So you do that. Where is the end of this thing? You build your own way of thinking, so that the situations and conditions suit the materials available, and you know how to do it, because you've lived with it. When you have to handle something new you have to re-educate. Start all over again. You are just starting all the time. There was German thinking, which really didn't affect us; then there was the Japanese way; and then, all of a sudden, there is a really big change. Education was entirely one-sided. So here we are.

Isabella Sumang (1992) insists that it is possible for Belau to become self-sufficient once again:

> When we started buying food, our people did not think what that would mean. Now we are dependent on imported foods. Big business is getting rich because we have forgotten that we can grow our own food. Many Belauans do not have the money to buy food. It is very expensive here. We could sell vegetables, rather than buy it from the US. There are gardens here now but they are all done in the bigger scale by Taiwanese and Filipinos. It takes money and knowledge of how to export these things. That has to be learnt.

Women have begun organising alternative economies. Based in a building on the main street of Koror, they are establishing a community centre with the intention of providing an outlet for women's produce. They have a triple hope of assisting individual women's economic independence, providing a networking hub that can educate the people and raising funds to assist in the continuous struggle to halt the US takeover of their lands and waters. Cita Morei (1992), instrumental in establishing the centre, describes the vision:

> We will have a market, we will have gift shop. Women will do the weaving to sell. Women will sell kukau (taro), bananas. There is a demand for taro on the island. And if the work they do in the taro patches makes money it will encourage more women to work on the taro. They used to can tuna. It is possible. If they did that, why can we not do it? We can make soap from coconut.

Belauan women, Bernie Keldermans (1986) explains, play an essential role in local development. Without their support and involvement true development is not only distorted, it is impossible:

> It was the colonialists that started to disrupt the traditional way and made men think they had the right. During Spanish and German times they utilised our way. And then the Japanese came and they completely ignored Belauan customs and imposed their own. And then the Americans. After World War Two they said we had to elect magistrates when we already had Rubaks who were appointed by the women to represent them. This caused all kinds of problems from the very beginning. We had to elect and only men were elected. The problem was that the magistrates were doing nothing while getting paid and the Rubaks did all the work. So the Rubaks became brainwashed saying, "Maybe we should run for election so we can be paid too", which did more harm than good.

The men say that they are strong but they don't make any decisions as far as the community goes. Nothing really happens until the women decide. Men might do the talking in meetings, but if men say something it's something that's already been decided, or doesn't need to be decided. So, then they revert back to the traditional way of doing things and women start making the decisions again.

In our custom we have sixteen villages each with ten clans. In each clan the women who belong to it through their mother's line will appoint a male member of the clan to represent them in the local meeting house. The men are our "public servants", even the Ibedul. They will work by consensus, and they will bring the issues back to the women and the women will decide. And they will reach agreement even if it takes one day or one year to agree. Now women have lost their respect within the community. They have power in their clan where they have blood community but not anywhere else. So now the clans are separate. The community has broken down. Clans only meet when they have something that needs to be done but the Americans came and took all their community responsibilities. So what do they need to meet for? Women have lost their responsibilities.

That is why there is little development here. The government doesn't ask the women what is a good idea. Women stand up and say, "We don't want our taro patch taken". And they have the right. Land belongs to women. So most projects don't succeed because the government doesn't follow the system that works.

Roman Bedor (1986) identifies the US, and all the members of the United Nations, as having a responsibility for assisting Belau towards true economic and political independence:

The [United Nations] Trusteeship Agreement states that these islands should achieve self-government or independence. This is the responsibility of all members of the United Nations. The trusteeship agreement was enacted without the knowledge of Micronesians, it was just a meeting between the US and the United Nations. Any member of the United Nations is a partner of the agreement that they accepted in 1947. They gave us to the US. They agreed that the US should be the administering authority. We are saying that the US and the United Nations should uphold the trusteeship agreement, which commits the US to give us true self-determination.

Experience has taught him not expect the US to keep to its international obligation but, he claims, Belau would benefit from the ending of US financial assistance which secures its political control over the nation (Bedor, 1986):

We have the analogy here, like other Pacific islands, that society is like a healthy human being that stands on two legs. The land is the right leg, the water the left leg. The two must complement and live with each other. If you destroy the ocean and the lands, as in many Pacific islands now, then you are crippling that society. And in order for us to survive we must beg. We have to depend on food stamps like the people in Guam. I think this is the reasoning of the US: in order to control us they must create dependency. Once dependency is created they can control our life. But it was not really effective because people still rely on the land for their living. Even now very few people on the islands are entirely dependent on a cash economy. Every family has access to land to grow their own food. Even people working in Koror. A lot of people in this village may be jobless, but they have their house, some of them have cars. There is no government welfare system but they are able to live because of our society and the land. They go fishing. They get what they need. If they need money, they sell their produce.

Losing US economic aid would be a good thing for us. An independent Belau would become a Third World country eligible for United Nations loans and aid. The natural resources are here. Belau was economically independent before the Americans came. It will take some time to develop an infrastructure, but I don't see that that will be a problem. In my view you must have political control of your destiny first in order to control the economy of your nation. Many Third World countries are politically independent but economically dependent, what's the big deal about that?

We are in a better shape than the people of the Marshall Islands because we still have our lands. Our fishing is some of the best in the world and the land is very fertile. We have calculated that if we had total control of our own agriculture, fisheries and industry we could raise at least twice what we currently receive from the US to fund our government. But once the land is destroyed for military reasons, or we are prevented from using it, then we are crippled.

We existed long before the US came to these islands. What makes them think we cannot continue to exist without them?

There's nothing wrong with Belau. It ought to be left the way it is. It fits the people here in Belau.

Liliana Isao. Belau. (Collier, 1988)

So what of the future of Belau? There is a growing desire for independence. This new status would enable Belau, free of outside domination for the first time in over a century, to determine its own path into the twenty-first century. The alternative is the distortion of Belauan custom, and the abuse of its land. Bernie Keldermans (1987) stresses the need for Belauans to be able to decide, without pressure, what their status should be:

The whole of Belau should seriously sit down and decide what we want, where we are going as a nation. Even though people are confused, even though they are afraid, they still have this gut feeling that they are Belauans. I think it would be good to use our system a hundred percent but I don't think that is possible now that we are dealing with the outside world. We must make it the Belauan compromising way. Co-operation, community co-operation, should stay. I would like to see ten Rubaks in each village, representing their clans, who would choose their leader for the time being. Women would make the decisions in the village. Rather than completely adopting a new thing. But it is only us Belauans who can do it, not outsiders.

The best thing for Belau now is to conduct some kind of political education on independence, compact, commonwealth, all kinds of relationships, come up with options, and really educate people on these options. If people are well aware of what choices there are and then they make a negative choice, then it's okay, because it's their choice. But if they don't know, and haven't looked at the possibilities, and just go for compact because of the money, because of false information, I really don't like that. Because one day we're going to wake up and find ourselves in a hole we cannot get out of. And in order to survive we'll have to sell our land. And pretty soon we'll be landless. It is impossible to be Belauan without land.

In exercising our inherent sovereignty, We, the people of Palau [Belau] proclaim and reaffirm our immemorial right to be supreme in these islands of Palau, our homeland. We renew our dedication to preserve and enhance our traditional heritage, our national identity and our respect for peace, freedom and justice for all mankind. In establishing this constitution of the sovereign Republic of Palau We venture into the future with full reliance on our own efforts and the divine guidance of Almighty God.

Preamble – Belau Constitution

Belauans have an inalienable right to sovereignty over their own lives and lands. Despite incredible odds they are determined to protect their culture. Fifteen years after creating a constitution that expresses the free wishes of the people, they are still being forced to vote, time and again, for that right. Roman Bedor (1986) identifies the role of the Constitution as representing the strength of the people and the problem that they face:

The Constitution is unique. A lot of people said it was selfish, but we saw that if it takes selfishness to protect us then maybe that's the only way, rather than resorting to nuclear armaments and such like. I don't think it's selfish to want to protect one's country. The whole idea of militarisation is to protect one's society – well, that's how they justify it. But we have a constitution that calls for the protection of our lands and the recognition of the culture and traditions. It's not just a question of nuclear substances – even guns are unconstitutional here – it dictates the course of our daily life. It takes everything into consideration – like how the land can be used. Only citizens can buy land and only Belauans can be citizens.

The Constitution is the supreme law of the land, while the compact is a treaty, an agreement between two nations. By the democratic principles of the US and of the rest of the world a treaty cannot supersede a Constitution. Any time a treaty contradicts a Constitution the treaty shall be invalidated. This is what we are telling the Americans now, which is unique because we learned it from them. They taught us in the first place that the Constitution is the supreme law of the land. We are practising the American democratic system now – the Americans are not. They are practising dictatorship.

Neither global shifts in military alliances, nor the end of the Republican era in US politics, has lessened the pressure on the Belauans to forfeit their lands, water and culture. The US in the mid-1990s remains committed to securing US military control of Belau. Secretary of State, Warren Christopher, made assurances in May 1993, that the US would limit its military use of the islands to periods of crisis or hostility, and that – should there be a nuclear accident – it would clean up after itself, are a long way from respecting their obligation, under their 1945 agreement with the United Nations, to "promote the development of the [Belauans] towards ... independence". Nor does it recognise the wishes of the Republic of Belau as inaugurated in the Constitution in 1981.

THE MOON AND WOMEN
Manami Suzuki (1987)

Belau's flag is very special. The blue represents the ocean, the yellow circle the moon and women. The moon is very important for Belauans, it controls the ocean tide and the growth of taro and fish, the most important things for Belauan culture. Look at the Japanese flag. It's called the Rising Sun – very masculine. But the Belauan flag is a symbol of femininity, of the female character.

Every country has both aspects, female and male, but when they try to set up their symbol, like a flag, they tend to use their male character. They are trying to show that, "We are strong", and "We are determined", and trying to show off their power. When Belau decided on the blue of the ocean and the yellow of the moon, it seems to me they were not looking at the masculinity of their country but saying to the world that Belau is a very female country. Not only in character, but historically, economically, culturally and politically too.

Belau has been invaded by modern culture, especially US, but still women are responsible for Belauan culture, history, politics and decision-making. Traditionally women are responsible for the generations, for the entire history of Belau. This is one of the reasons why women established the Constitution in order to protect their country. They discussed the Constitution while they cultivated the taro. The taro patch is traditionally, we say in Japanese, the "chattering field" for women where they discuss many things: what is happening in their families, in their clans, in their community. Of course, it was created by both sexes but the thing is that it was done not from the top but from the bottom. Everybody participated. The ideal practice of so-called democracy was alive here. Everybody was talking about the Constitution. All the articles of the Constitution were known by every-body. That's amazing. I don't know what the Japanese Constitution says.

In Belauan the word for "constitution" is "*kenpo*". It's a Japanese word, not indigenous. The Japanese taught their constitution while they occupied Belau. Until that period they had no word because they didn't need any *kenpo*. They listened to the elders. They learned from traditional customs and they learned from nature and their gods. They didn't need a constitution to rule people.

Today's women have been put in a very historic period in the entire history of Belau, because their generation had to decide whether they would join in modern society and the modern political system, or maintain their traditional ways of decision-making. It was their decision that Belau should make a constitution. They felt it was necessary for the survival of Belau, because otherwise Belau's resources, environment, nature and people themselves would be exploited and invaded by modern culture.

Belau is such a small nation, they don't really need a parliament or a constitution for themselves. Fifteen thousand people can rule themselves without such structures. They need it to protect themselves: it is because of the Constitution that the US cannot get Belau. They needed the Constitution because the world had become so masculine, so modernised. They needed to adopt a modern system to be recognised as a nation state. A constitution is a tool of masculine authority which seeks to exploit powerless people, so the Belauans needed their own to enable them to confront another government which is very masculine.

Modern culture is completely different from indigenous culture. European people tend to divide this world between communism and capitalism, a political division. But for me there is another world, the traditional, very feminine world. Even in western countries women were once respected, but then there was the witch-hunting. Men were afraid of women's power, women's mysterious power. We can give birth to a baby and this scares men because they cannot. For women a baby is actually a part of ourselves but men will never be sure that a baby is theirs.

And this respect for female values still operates in Belau. But modern masculine culture and technology have been invading Belau. In Belau the modern society and traditional society confront each other.

Many movements and groups talk about the nuclear free constitution and praise it without asking why it was needed in the first place. It's not enough to protect the Constitution of Belau if you want to protect Belau. They need to protect the traditional culture at the same time, otherwise Belau will become like Japan and other countries which already undermine their nation's female quality.

A Nation Divided

– Guam and the Northern Marianas –

GUAM & NORTHERN MARIANA IS.

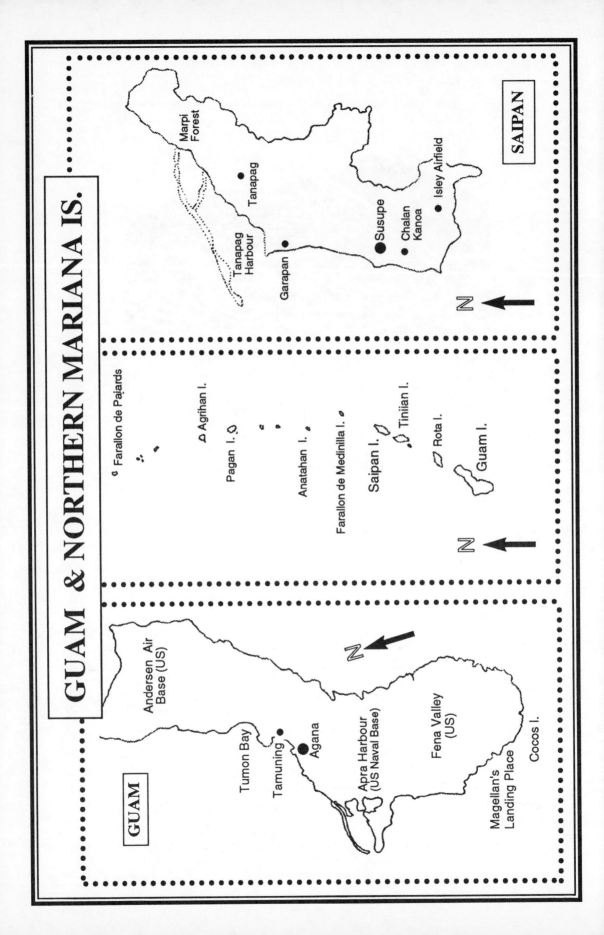

SAIPAN

Marpi Forest

Tanapag

Tanapag Harbour

Garapan

Susupe

Chalan Kanoa

Isley Airfield

N

Farallon de Pajards

Agrihan I.

Pagan I.

Anatahan I.

Farallon de Medinilla I.

Saipan I.

Tiniian I.

Rota I.

Guam I.

N

GUAM

Andersen Air Base (US)

N

Tumon Bay

Tamuning

Agana

Apra Harbour (US Naval Base)

Fena Valley (US)

Magellan's Landing Place

Cocos I.

While ours is a story of rape, is a story of conquest, is a story of destruction, is a story of genocide, is a story of division, is a story of alcoholism, is a story of suffering and degradation and loss of language, it is also and equally and most importantly a story of pride, a story of endurance, a story of continuity.

Laura Souder. Guam. (Souder, 1988)

The Chamorro were the first Pacific nation to be colonised by Europeans. Over the centuries that followed, they have been dominated by four different masters, each imposing their own cultures, each giving little and taking far too much. Finally the Chamorro, one people with a common matrilineal heritage, have been divided, north from south, and have become two separate political entities: Guam and the Commonwealth of the Northern Marianas.

The Spanish arrived with Ferdinand Magellan in 1521 who managed to sail right across the vast expanse of ocean without sighting land. He brought with him the arrogance of the coloniser, and before he left he began the wave of violence which would all but wipe out the Indigenous people. Forty years later, Guam was annexed by Spain and became a major port of call for the galleons plying their trade between Spain's American colonies and the Philippines. They established their colony at Agana, already a major Chamorro centre. Now the capital of Guam and three hundred years old, it is the oldest European city in the Pacific.

In 1668, the Spanish Jesuit missionaries arrived, bringing with them one of the worst campaigns of colonial genocide anywhere in the world. The Chamorro resistance against the Spanish presence with their Christian god was one of the longest in the Pacific. But the Spanish killing power was stronger and within twenty-three years they had decimated the Indigenous population. Those that escaped murder were killed by smallpox, influenza and other introduced diseases. Of between 80,000 and 100,000 Chamorro at the time of the Spanish arrival, by 1790 only 3,000 Chamorro remained (Oliver, 1985: p. 337). This story is one shared by other colonised peoples.

Chailang Palacios, a Chamorro from Saipan, the main island of the Northern Marianas, retells an old story:

The missionaries together with the soldiers began to Christianise our ancestors. They were very scared . . . they had never seen white people before. It was hard for us to embrace Christianity. The Spanish missionaries were blessing all the soldiers, while the soldiers were cutting my ancestors in half. Killing our men, raping our women (WWNFIP, 1987: p. 11).

The survivors, mainly women and children, were herded from their ancestral lands and crowded into containment camps on Guam, depopulating the northern islands completely, except for Rota where a few managed to escape the holocaust by hiding in caves. Many women were raped, others married their jailers; children were forced into Spanish schools and punished for using their language; all that was Chamorro was downgraded and banished. The devastation was so great that the Chamorro people, refusing to bring any children into this new world, "had begun to practise abortions and infanticide rather than raise the children [they] bore" (Wenkam and Baker, 1971: p. 18).

When, towards the end of the nineteenth century, the Chamorro were finally allowed to return to their northern homes, they found that Carolinians from Truk and Yap (now part of the Federated States of Micronesia) had settled Saipan in 1815, after their islands, also under Spanish rule, had been devastated by a typhoon. Co-existing with the Chamorro ever since, the Carolinians have played a significant role in the nation's development.

In 1898, another event shook the foundations of their community: the partitioning of the Marianas at the end of the Spanish-American War. Dividing the Chamorro nation, the US claimed Guam for its strategic value, leaving the northern islands to be bought by Germany. At the whim of the US military, a people was divided. Hope Cristobal (1986), from Guam, maintains that:

> Not only has the US separated Guam from Micronesia but they have separated the Chamorro people, the Northern Marianas Chamorro from the Chamorro of Guam. The Chamorro have been one people, one culture. We were one entity until the US came. We know though, as you drive around these military installations you see "Commander Naval Forces – Marianas". When you see titles like that it reminds you of how the military, for military reasons, look at the islands as one entity. Yet for political reasons we have been separated.

Since 1898, Guam has been under constant US control, except for thirty months of Japanese occupation (1941–44), while the Northern Marianas have changed hands from German to Japanese to American all within fifty years. No one bothered to consult the Chamorro people about this crude game of international netball. Chailang Palacios describes the shattering this has caused (WWNFIP, 1987: pp. 11–12):

> Another nation came. The Germans brought their own missionaries, who tried to teach us the Protestant religion. And this started making us fight amongst ourselves. That is always the way: when White nations come to conquer us, to colonise us, they divide us.
>
> And then there is this nation the Japanese. They came and were exactly the same. They wanted us to join their religion, Buddhism. They liked our islands so much they stayed. They took our land for sugar plantations, for pineapple plantations.
>
> After the [Second World] War the Americans came, like the early missionaries, in the name of God, saying, "We are here to Christianise you, to help you love one another, be in peace". We still have the Bible, while the missionaries and their White governments have all the land.
>
> [The Americans] are just another nation that has come to colonise our lands and our minds as the Spanish, Germans and Japanese did before. They destroy our religion and culture and give us a western White religion instead; they do all this in the name of the White god.
>
> My grandparents lived to be ninety-nine years old, so I spent a lot of time with them. I asked them, "Do you remember our old culture here?". They said that before the Spaniards arrived their religion is just nature. And when I asked, "What is nature?". They said, "Well, we work hard on the farm, both men and women. As a culture we live on the land and ocean. We respect the water, just sit down and contemplate the waves coming into the

shore, the sunset coming down". The Spanish said, "That's not good because nature is not God". They introduced the White god (McWomynus, 1985).

The Americans isolated Guam into a garrison island under strict naval control until 1962, and the Germans, in the northern islands only for fifteen years, established copra plantations, but it was the Japanese who were the greatest influence for the first half of this century.

Even before the northern islands were assigned to Japan, under the 1919 League of Nations agreement, Japanese settlers outnumbered the other non-Indigenous settlers and dominated the commerce of the islands. Very soon, Japan's economic tentacles reached right across Micronesia and far south into Dutch New Guinea (now part of Papua New Guinea) and Kanaky (New Caledonia). With over 40,000 settlers in the Northern Marianas alone, the Japanese developed a sophisticated infrastructure. Plantations of sugar cane, pineapples and coffee surrounded a city so developed that it was called "Little Tokyo". Increasing Japanese immigration was rapidly bringing further disinheritance and disease to the Micronesians.

In 1935, Japan withdrew from the League of Nations, which banned military bases, isolated the islands under their control, and built up its military might, thus preparing the way for the battles of the Second World War fought in the Pacific. The war displaced whole populations, and further decimated the Indigenous inhabitants of the region. Chailang Palacios tells a vivid story from the war days:

> We, the Micronesian people, were the victims of that war – World War II . . . the Japanese forced my ancestors up into the mountains. They made us dig a hole just in case the Americans and the Japanese fought. We would be safe in the hole. But it didn't happen like that. It was Sunday morning when the war came. Everyone was away from their holes, visiting grandparents, relatives, friends. All of a sudden – bombs from the sky and the ocean. The people were crushed fifty to a hundred in one hole because there was no way they could get back to their own place to hide. There was no water for those people. It was so hot, so dark, bombs all over. A lot of people died. Children died because their mothers' breasts dried up. No food. (WWNFIP, 1987: pp. 11–12)

On December 10, 1941, three days after the bombing of Pearl Harbour, Japan captured Guam from an unprepared American naval command. In March 1944, anticipating an American invasion, they then moved in 18,500 troops and herded the 21,000 local residents, Chamorro, Filipino and American, into concentration camps, where they remained to be "liberated" by the arrival of 55,000 US troops five months later. The fighting was bloody. Thousands died. Although it is recorded that 2,124 Americans and 17,000 Japanese were killed, there is no record of the numbers of local people who died. The Northern Marianas battle, the fight for Saipan, was among the most devastating battles of the entire war. The island was razed. The price of living on a strategic piece of real estate was heavy for the Chamorro and Carolinians.

By mid-1945, Guam had become an armed camp with 200,000 American troops.

While these numbers have since decreased, the full strategic value of Guam had been recognised and a new era begun. Situated in the western Pacific, where it is central to the Pacific and Indian Ocean regions, it remains one of the most militarised islands on earth.

In 1947, the United Nations granted the US control over the Northern Marianas. As elsewhere in Micronesia, the Americans set about securing permanent control by deliberately creating an economic dependency that has enabled them to trap the Islanders into a commonwealth status under US control.

The Chamorro, both in Guam and the Northern Marianas, remain determined to regain their inalienable sovereign rights to govern their own destiny, pitting their strength in a struggle against the Pentagon and associated colonial structures.

PLANTING THE SEEDS OF IDENTITY

– *Guam* –

We have a large airforce base in the north and in the south a big navy base. When we ask the Americans, "Why do we have all these bases, why do we have all these bombs in our island?", they say, "Oh, it's for your protection". Well, I say, "For an island that's only thirty-eight miles long, that's a lot of protection!".

Melissa Taitano. Guam. (Taitano, 1989)

Guam is an island where the old adages "behind every palm tree there is a military base" and "behind every military base there is a tourist hotel" ring true. Hotels mesh with military facilities, leaving little room for the people. Laura Souder (1990: p. 9) describes the situation on Guam:

On Guam, which is a piece of land 212 square miles total of land area, we have 11 military establishments; and those establishments are distributed throughout the island from the northern tip to the southern tip; they are typically located in beachfront areas, prime land areas.

One-third of Guam's land is controlled by the US Pentagon. Attempts to regain control of the land have long been on the agenda of the Organisation of People for Indigenous Rights, as Hope Cristobal (1986) explains:

After World War Two there was a lot of land-grabbing and as a result one-third of our island is in the hands of the military.

Much of the action that has to do with land rights is the result of the military takings. It all started back in the early 70s when people started questioning. You know, someone started a land claim, a legal suit, and then all of a sudden it popped open and everyone started looking at their lands. They started checking their roots, finding out that all that land was theirs at one time and that they were not compensated properly. Some were not even compensated at all, it was just taken from them. It seems a lot of people, especially throughout the Pacific have had a lot of land taken away from them for strategic reasons, for military reasons.

But that does not mean that the people necessarily want the military to leave. That thought is quite far down the road, if at all. Because in our lifetime, even in the lifetime of my mother, and even my grandmother, we've lived with the military around all the time. So there is this thinking, this mentality, that they've always been here. And we really can't see whatever negative impact the military has. One of the issues that has brought about the negative impact of the military is the land issue. That's close to the heart of the Chamorro. From there they can see, and they can feel, the negative impact of the military. Otherwise, probably half of the working people are employed by the military. So really, at this stage of the game, I don't think we're going to ask the military to leave.

There's a lot of concern outside of Guam about the military being here, about the role of Guam in the global nuclear strategy of the US. A lot of people would like to see Guam demilitarised. But really, before anyone decides that, I think the Chamorro people should be asked whether that's what they want. I think really deep down inside that is what they want and that's what they would like to see, but many people today are not willing to give up their comforts of life. But I think that to be independent is not to have this military on our lands. There is a lot we can do with our lands. Much of the land they have is fertile land, farming land. Fena Valley [a nuclear weapons storage site], with the only lake on this island, is being held by them. We can't touch it. I've never been to it. I can only see it from fifteen miles away. The only deep harbour, where the naval ship repair facility is, is held by the military. All the flat land to the north: Andersen Airfield. So, much of the area that we could use for farming, for export, is being held by the military. It wasn't an accident that they got all this. I'm sure it was well thought out.

They made their wars here and now they're getting rich, the Japanese and the Americans.
Chailang Palacios. Northern Marianas. (WWNFIP, 1987: p. 14)

Tourism has also taken precious land. Tumon Bay, with the island's best beaches, has become a ghetto of Japanese tourism. A "red-light" area, run for Japanese, American and Australian businessmen, it offers Filipina sex-workers, desperately moving to Guam following the closing of the US Subic Naval Base and Clarke Airforce Base in the Philippines. The tourist industry is claimed to be Guam's ticket to prosperity but, according to Hope Cristobal (1986), there is little benefit in all this for the Chamorro:

The tourist industry is supposed to be the industry to raise everybody's standard of living but what's happening is that the tour packages are being bought in Japan, by the Japanese. They ride in their Japanese aeroplanes. As soon as they get off the Japan airlines they go to Japanese hotels and they're driven around in Japanese tour buses with Japanese tour guides explaining the Chamorro culture. Not only that, the jobs are taken by military wives who are Japanese, or Oriental. They speak Japanese. The government of Guam right now has a program. It's trying to encourage a lot of investors by giving ten-year tax rebates. So now a lot of these companies come here, set up shop for ten years and make their millions, and then take off and we never see them again. They can actually come in and have a business without having seen or heard of us. People who come here never really came because they were interested in us. I think that's the bottom line. The military came for the strategic real estate and the tourists came because of the sun and the sand.

When the tourist industry opened up, a lot of Japanese started coming up here. One of the first things they did was to organise Japanese tour groups and comb through the jungles and collect all the bones of the Japanese people, Japanese soldiers. They looked in all the caves, we have many man-made caves the Japanese had used for refuge during the war. The tour groups collect the bones and have worship service and cremate them. They have a lot of respect for the Japanese bones but they don't care about Chamorro bones. They're doing a lot of building in Tumon Bay. The area was actually a flourishing Chamorro community long before contact with Europeans and there are a lot of burial sites and a lot of artefacts all over the place. Almost everywhere you dig you find bones. Chamorro bones. These are our ancestors.

When we realised this was happening, we approached the construction company but they said they couldn't possibly stop construction. So we hurriedly asked the bishop, who's now the archbishop, to say mass. A sort of reconciliation. It was our only consolation at the time because the bulldozers were moving in as fast as we were gathering people together. We had our Christian services with over 200 of our elders. The church in Tumon was packed with our elders. And then we invited them over to the park to see the way our ancestors had been buried, layer by layer. The next day the machines came in and turned everything up. Destroyed everything.

So there's these Japanese people who we've always thought revered the dead, or regarded remains as sacred, looking at Chamorro bones as not sacred and just running them over with bulldozers.

This desecration of the Chamorro ancestors continues as the tourist industry develops unabated. While Japanese corporations exploit their own people's respect for the dead, they wantonly neglect and destroy the sites sacred to the Indigenous people.

Through a deliberate immigration policy, controlled by the US, the Chamarro have become a minority in their own island. While in 1940 they were 90 per cent of the total population, that figure had dropped to 48 per cent by 1991. The Chamorro have increasingly been pushed into the southern region of the island. It is here, in the furthest reaches of the island, that the Chamorro have managed to retain and strengthen their language and traditions. But now Japanese developers are rushing to build huge tourism complexes in this stronghold of Chamorro culture.

The influx of US, Japanese, and now Filipino, Korean, Chinese and Micronesian, immigrants has impacted upon the Chamorro sense of identity. Hope Cristobal's (1986) story of her finding her Chamorro identity, and her refusal to accept the lies, and deceptions of the colonisers, is an experience common to many Indigenous people:

My OPIR [Organisation for the Protection of Indigenous Rights] participation, and all my activities prior to that, were re-education for myself. I went through a school system that taught me to be American, where I struggled really hard to speak good English, to dress American and just be American. If you were anything else you were an outcast. I tried really hard to prove I was a good American, but I was constantly reminded of how different I was from everyone else. And I thought, "Heck with them! I'm American. I'm one of you. Why do you keep telling me I'm different?".

Then it dawned, you know. I realised then that I was different and that I had to accept that. I'd look in the mirror every day and say, "Yeah, I really am different, I'm me". It was a big re-education on my part having to re-learn that I am Chamorro. I was punished when I went through that school system for being Chamorro. I was physically punished. Every time I spoke the language I was given a stick across my finger nails. So I went to a school system that punished me for being me. It was a real contradiction going home, because at home we spoke Chamorro with our grandparents. You know, I got challenged as to who I was when I got back home, inundated with questions of, "You're not here. You're not you". And I kept saying, "Yes, I'm here. I'm Chamorro. I'm me!". But they kept on telling you who you are, and the school system tells you the same, only different.

And so the language was the first thing I started working on. In 1974, the *Pacific Daily News* refused to print an advertisement in Chamorro. It was just a simple advertisement inviting people to something and they refused it. So we gathered over four hundred people and had a big procession around their office. We had all our elders chanting Chamorro songs and we had a big mass resistance. We took our newspapers and had a burning session right there. Everybody was down there. When it comes to the language they are not going to stop us.

The language was slowly getting eroded away. People tried to tell us it didn't exist, that it is a creole, but it does. We still have a culture that is unique. And we're still here. But we have a lot of work. We're trying to get people to realise that we still need it, that we still use it. We need it to pass on our beliefs. For example, it is difficult to go out into the boonies [country-side] and point out the herbs we use, the medicinal herbs, without using our language.

We have made significant gains in terms of the language. The Chamorro Language Commission is doing well. The government has passed a law that mandates that the Chamorro language and culture be taught in schools. We have signs printed in Chamorro. And when you arrive at the airport you are welcomed in Chamorro. This is all important, but we still have a long way to go.

So my participation started with myself, realising how I had been lied to. Then I got involved in the language issue and continued on to the Constitution and now Chamorro self-determination.

Hope Cristobal (1986), explaining the establishment of the Organisation of People for Indigenous Rights (OPIR), stresses the importance of upholding the inalienable rights of the Chamorro people to self-determination:

OPIR was first organised in 1981, as a response to a plebiscite on political status that was not limited to the Chamorro, that allowed everyone to vote on a political status that should have been the Chamorro's decision.

People ask why it should be the Chamorro who make the decision about political status? Why shouldn't everyone on Guam make that decision? But why should everyone? Why should people in Wisconsin come now and make this decision for us? Why should Filipinos, who have decided in 1946 to become independent, come over here and decide again, when they came here because of the invitation of the military? Many of the first Filipinos that came out here were construction workers who later stayed and made Guam their home. They came not because they were interested in us. They come because they want to help themselves, and because of the structures that are set up by our colonial masters.

They come and they can go home and they have a place they can go to feel good about themselves. We have no place to go to feel good about being Chamorro except here. So why should other people come and decide our fate for us? It's immaterial how they're going to vote. We just don't want them to participate. They say, "We Guamanians who love this island should be allowed to exercise our right of self-determination". But "Guamanian" is not Chamorro. It is not a matter of love. It is a matter of justice.

It's been a long struggle to get people to recognise that the Chamorro even exist. You know, the question used to be: "There are no Chamorros, you're half this and half that!". But we see ourselves as a whole being, a whole person. We never see ourselves as half of anything. But the next question came about as to, "Who are Indigenous? What is Indigenous? What does Indigenous mean?". "Indigenous" was a very new word, but now you hear little kids talking about "Indigenous people".

Recently the question is: "Yes, we understand there are Chamorro, but don't you think it's a little bit too late to exercise your right?". That right exists in the Organic Act [1950]. It reserves the right of the ultimate political decision to the Chamorro only. And it also defines the Chamorro as "those people who were given US citizenship in 1950, August 1st, and their descendants". In fact, it goes back even further than that, to the United Nations Charter. As a matter of fact, the Organic Act impedes that right of self-determination. It really looks like we were made citizens to legalise the land-taking. In 1950 we were renamed "Guamanians". We were the newest kid on the block. It is as if you wake up the next day and are completely different because you are a US citizen! They renamed us because they wanted us to forget that we are Chamorro. But we are remembering. People are now rejecting the name, the word, "Guamanian".

In 1987, a local plebiscite on the future political status of Guam was passed, which fully recognised the Chamorro people's right to determine the future of their island. It intended to change Guam's relationship with the US from that of unincorporated territory to commonwealth status thereby granting a greater degree of self-government. As created by the people of Guam the Act called for, amongst other things, full internal self-government, control over Guam's 200 miles Exclusive Economic Zone (EEZ) (as defined by international law) and recognition that the 1950 Organic Act guaranteed to the Chamorro the inalienable right to self-determination.

Ten years in the making, the Act was placed before the US Congress in 1990 for consideration. The US, insisting on the right to equal representation, responded by demanding that the reference to self-determination for the Chamorro be deleted from the commonwealth draft. Although the US had, in 1988, recognised the Chamorro rights as declared under the Organic Act they had within a year unilaterally removed any reference to Chamorro self-determination from the United Nations resolution on Guam.

Further, the US rejected Guam's claim to full internal self-government. The 1950 Organic Act granted the US the power to revoke Guam's limited self-rule, and to influence its external relationships, at any time, without the consent or even prior knowledge of the people of Guam. As if that wasn't enough, the US has been reluctant to relinquish control over Guam's EEZ, because it is rich in mineral deposits and strategic materials. Guam's EEZ has been under the control of the US since 1983, when US President Reagan claimed it through an Executive Order.

The pressure for self-determination growing throughout Guam's diverse community is reflected in the statement of Guam's Government Committee on Self-determination:

> The People of Guam will no longer tolerate being treated as less than other people throughout the world. We will no longer tolerate living, as we have, bereft of natural rights enjoyed thousands of years before there was a Spanish Empire, for thousands of years before America was a dream in Colombus' eye. We must have our sovereignty restored (Pacific Concerns Resource Centre [PCRC], February 1991: p. 7).

The Chamorro welcome the Commonwealth Act (as drafted by Guam) as a step towards decolonisation on the proviso that the right to self-determination remains solely the domain of the Indigenous people as described under the Organic Act [1950]:

> ... it must be made emphatically clear that [the Commonwealth Act] is a document which was created based on the status choice of US citizens and not one based on Chamorro self-determination ... While the Organization of People for Indigenous Rights maintain that only the Chamorro people have the right to change Guam's status from a non self-governing territory to one considered as having a full measure of self-government, based on

the principle of self-determination, we are not opposed to an interim federal-territorial act as outlined in the present Commonwealth Act. We are not opposed; because the Act, as written, acknowledges the Chamorro right to self-determination … However, it must be clearly stated that the current Act is not an act of self-determination, but it is a significant prelude to the eventual exercise of self-determination … We would like you to know, however, that our organization is prepared to defeat the Act, if in the final analysis, it does not recognise the Chamorro people's right of self-determination (OPIR, nd).

Past actions have proven that the Chamorro have the power to enforce that claim. In 1977, the US invited people living on Guam to create a constitution, but insisted that the US retain sovereign power over the island. The Chamorro organised against it and it was rejected. They have made a clear statement that they are "prepared to defeat the [Commonwealth] Act if in the final analysis it does not recognise the Chamorro right to self-determination" (OPIR, nd).

Years pass as the US, the United Nations and the Government of Guam discuss and negotiate over the future status of the nation. The US, insisting on maintaining control over Guam as a vital strategic outpost off the coast of the Asian-Arabian-European continent, threatens to withdraw funding and facilities from Guam if it does not get its way.

You rarely hear about our quest for self-determination, or about our struggles, our colonisation, our suffering, our very existence as indigenous people, or about our hopes and dreams. We come to you with music and song and may have caught you by surprise. Because many of our Pacific brothers and sisters have readily admitted, it is a well kept secret that Guam is the homeland of Chamorros. We invite you to listen to our music, enjoy our dancing, but understand too that, while we are a fun-loving people, we are also a people of struggle.

Laura Souder. Guam. (Souder, 1989: p. 4)

The Chamorro people's determination to reclaim their birthright, their sovereignty, is growing at a rapid pace. In 1991, a historic event happened: a group of activists calling themselves the "United Chamoru Chelus for Independence" declared the "Chamoru Nation" into existence.

Following upon a heritage laid down by the OPIR, and other land and self-determination initiatives, the Chamoru Chelus (translating as sisters and brothers) shook the comfortable pretence of the US that the Chamorro were content with their political status. With a massive influx of migrants into the island and the recent economic recession in the US, there has been a growing sense of urgency among

Chamorro that they must move now to protect their lands and heritage. Angel Santos (1992), one of the main initiators of the Chamoru Nation, describes the process:

On 21 July 1991, the Chamoru Chelus proclaimed the existence of a people. Our right to exist as a nation of people. Just like the nation of Korea for the Koreans, a nation of the Philippines for Filipinos, Japan for the Japanese. We felt that we had the inalienable right to proclaim to the world that we are a People. We did not quite grasp what we did. Three days later we met again, and realised that what we had done was history. For four hundred years of colonisation not one Chamoru had stood up to proclaim the existence of a peoplehood, the Chamoru Nation. We had done that. Then we had to ask ourselves: "Great, now that we have proclaimed the Chamoru Nation, where do we go from here? How do we define the Chamoru Nation? What constitutes the Chamoru Nation?".

There were only six members in the United Chamoru Chelus. It was simply a public awareness that we were promoting, so we didn't have a membership. Obviously those few could not carry the responsibility of the Chamoru Nation, so we invited other organisations to join us. The Organisation of People for Indigenous Rights (OPIR), Protehi I Tano'ta (Protect Our Land), Achaot Guahan (Chamoru Artists' Association) and the Guam National Party. We agreed to work together under the same banner. Not as one organisation. An attempt to form one organisation would be an insult to our mission – we are an entity higher than any organisation. We have a god-given right to exist as a people. Now we have a thirty-three member council that reflects the different villages. Comprised of everyone from administrators to farmers, it reflects the entire community. We came together and swore in the council members with the Bible and the Guam flag. It was a formal ceremony.

We found that we had to define the word "sovereignty" – the right for us to control our destiny – before we could plan a course of action of how to perpetuate a nation. We came onto the concept that no nation can survive without protecting the six elements: the tano, land; the hanom, water; the *aire*, air; *hinnenghe*, spirituality; *linguahe*, language; and *kottura*, culture. That it is our responsibility to protect these six elements in order to survive as a peoplehood. We established working committees accordingly. They are responsible for identifying what it is that threatens our nation, our sovereignty, our right to exist.

We were considered radical at the beginning. Our people are not accustomed to standing up against the government, to speaking out. You have to understand four hundred years of colonial domination of our people. They have been intimidated to the point that what you tell them, they'll do. So people are not used to protest; civil disobedience; non-conformity; challenging the system. The seeds of loyalty have been planted in the minds of our people. Especially through World War Two, when my grandparents enlisted in the US military. Then came Vietnam and many of our young men were drafted into the military against their will. So the need to go to war to defend the US in the "national interest" is in the hearts of our people. Never mind the social injustices against us. Our history has been rewritten. We were brainwashed into thinking we were liberated but when you look back at the facts after the war, and at what happened before the war, then you realise the lies.

Guam was invaded by the Japanese on 6 December 1941, but in October – two months before – the US evacuated their active-duty personnel and dependants to Hawai'i and left only non-essential personnel here. The Japanese were only two islands away, on Saipan. The US knew of the impending war but they did not warn our people. Instead they left quietly and allowed the enemy to come in and take our island. Then they came back and made it look as if they had liberated us.

So it has been embedded in our minds that we have been liberated, and that that is equal to all the injustices. Our people have been numbed to the past. And now it is the loyalty that is paramount. That's the biggest obstacle. But we have begun to tear it down block by block – just like the Berlin Wall.

In the early 1900s, the US naval government regulated our cultural practices. They even went so far as to do away with the matrilineal system – replacing it with a patrilineal system. The US government required all parents to give their children the father's name, and anyone who refused to comply would be fined. So, three thousand years of living under a matrilineal system was done away with in one day, at the whisk of a pen. Our culture was almost destroyed.

We have been taught that we are not Chamoru. That there are no Chamorus any more – they're all dead – and that we are Americans. In 1922, naval Governor Dorn imposed the Californian school system, he wanted to make Guam a loyal possession of the US. I can see how they set out to do that. At the age of five or six, when we entered school, we were immediately taught to memorise the Pledge of Allegiance to the US; we were taught to identify the four seasons (which we don't have in Guam); we were taught American history. The US methodically set out to destroy our culture, our language, our identity.

Chamoru are a lost people – we almost have no identity. Right now the Chamoru are living in two cultures, two different worlds. Many of them are imitating cultures of other people. Today they are into materialism, capitalism. They have lost sight of the basics – to respect each other, to survive. (What other threat is there?) They think that if they own three houses and two Mercedes, then they fulfil the ultimate dream. But they are not content with their lives. They are missing the most important thing – identity. What we are trying to do is to plant the seed of identity in the lives of our people – from there it can grow. We can have a sense of direction, a sense of belonging – belonging to a peoplehood. Everything will fall into place after that.

After we have rallied the support of our people, we hope to go to the United Nations. The US signed an agreement in 1946 with the UN that they will respect the rights of the Indigenous people. They promised to develop Guam's social, political and economic structure until such time that the people were able to self-determine their status. It is an agreement protected even under the US Constitution. So the road, the legal process, has already been paved for us. But each year the US reports to the UN that the Chamoru are content. They are stalling until there is a greater percentage of outsiders than Chamoru.

We're hoping to draft up a constitution that would protect the indigenous rights of Chamorus while, at the same time, safeguarding the civil rights of the non-Chamoru. We have to find a happy medium. We cannot kick out the foreigners. So, there is still a lot work to do, things to iron out. Still, I thought it was going to be more difficult than this. I'm not saying that there's no valleys and troubled times – we have a lot of work ahead of us. We know what we have got to do, and we're doing it step by step. We will free our people from the bondage of colonial slavery. It is now or never. It is almost too late. We have to save what's left.

TOURISM IS NOT GOOD FOR CHILDREN

– the Northern Marianas –

If you are rich and you are flying over the Pacific, you'll hear on your radios all about "Paradise in the Pacific". Beautiful islands, calm, clear water. Beautiful women – very cheap. You can get anything you want. Lies. Lies after lies. You don't hear anything about the war, or about nuclear testing, or about people who are dying slowly. No! You will just see beautiful pictures. Paradise in the Pacific!

Chailang Palacios. Northern Marianas. (Palacios, 1985)

The Chamorro of the Northern Mariana Islands are being assailed by a deluge of tourists streaming to their small islands in search of the eternal paradise on earth. And in that process the local cultures (Chamorro and Carolinian) are being distorted and the environment irredeemably polluted.

In 1991 the islands were inundated with 424,458 tourists, and while this was an increase of 400 per cent in ten years the numbers continue to rise (Marianas Visitors Bureau, 1991). Seventy-two per cent of those visitors were Japanese, 17 per cent American, and the remainder predominantly from Korea (4.9%), Australia and Taiwan (9% each) and Hong Kong (8%). The vast majority (412,004 in 1991) arrive and stay on Saipan, the main island of the Northern Marianas. This means that, on any given day, there is a ratio of almost twenty visitors to the islands for every resident (22,500), a population that includes American expatriates, Filipino labourers, Carolinians and Chamorro.

There are as many foreign labourers and their dependants as local citizens. Coming from the Philippines, Korea and Taiwan, they are drawn by the promise of work. Because they are not unionised, they will work for less money and do not demand their rights. The men are in demand as construction workers by the tourist developers and the women work as hotel staff or as domestics.

This rapid influx of tourists and foreign labourers places a massive burden on the nation's limited resources. Huge hotels are being built at such a rate that a local joke has named the construction crane as the national bird.

Chailang Palacios (1992), whose ancestral land is being lost to the tourist industry, complains:

They are turning Saipan into a concrete jungle. It is really bad. Soon there will be no room for the people. Where do we go then? There is only one home for us. It is here, Saipan. And what about Tinian? And Rota? We are losing our land, our spirit, to the tourist.

Members of the Northern Marianas Women's Association have been outspoken against what they claim is the resultant "misuse of resources". They have consistently warned that a lack of proper planning jeopardises Saipan's future. Maria Pangelinan argues (Tighe, 1985):

We do not have the infrastructure to allow for the wholesale conversion of Saipan into a tourist colony ... economic development is not one and the same as tourism. It is, instead, the planned development of a sound economic base for present and future citizens.

Tourism will place an additional burden on our water, sewer, and electrical systems, on our schools, social services, health facilities, courts and government agencies . . . Our Association favours economic development and recognizes the importance of the tourist industry. But we favour planning, rather than the haphazard approach that provides no protection to the citizens.

Can [we] really support, or afford, the growth in the tourist industry that will come when present hotel-building is finished? Where will the water and power come from? What about sewage disposal? Will they all be provided to the hotel by being taken away from the people in the nearby villages? They do not employ local people; they import and exploit alien labour; pay almost no taxes; use subsidized power; pay incredibly low rentals; and use Saipan's limited water. Let's first assess our infrastructure, especially water and power, to ensure that Saipan is capable of providing the foundation of facilities necessary to support the economic and social development we seek.

But inappropriate tourism affects more than infrastructure. Chailang Palacios (1992) complains that the unchecked tourism on Saipan is rapidly eroding both land and culture:

It is not really helping the economy – most of the money goes back to Japan. The tourists bring money but psychologically, socially, it is destroying the people. Half of the Chamorro, they lease their land for fifty-five years to the Japanese, so now they are landless. The land is bulldozed for hotel. There is no land to get back. They don't think about that. Once you lease your land you start fighting with your own family, because in our culture, when you have money you give it to all your family. That is our island culture, what you have you share. So if you lease land you share that money equally. In my generation you never even think of selling land, it goes from one generation to another. Until these Japanese start coming here and flashing their Japanese dollars. So money changed people here.

The Japanese came because they realise that this is a pearl, a gem, a paradise. They are here because they love it, it is not like Japan. But now they are making Saipan into Tokyo. They come here and they build ugly hotels that don't fit into the environment. So these Chamorro they build themselves big house, new cars, but they forget that they are Chamorro, they forget their family. Before we had strong family, now even in the small village the kids they lose the family. They are much closer to their own peer group. They think that's their family. That is because of our overnight changing of value – now it is fast cars going to overnight disco. Even parents are confused on disciplining their kids, because money is so abundant and the kids demand it.

Everything now is to be American. They want to be White. They think they are ugly because they are not White. So it is destroying not only our value, but the way that you are made up. The image they see in the television, they want to be like that. Just like in New York. Poor kids growing up, they don't know their identity. Our young people no longer speak Chamorro. They say, "Hey, I'm not Chamorro!". This is hard. When I was growing up I knew myself as a Chamorro but when we became a commonwealth of the US I notice the young ones they are ashamed to be their own selves. I know politically we are American, but when it comes to our values and culture, when it comes to Chamorro, I am very strong. But our young people are all confused. That is why we are having these problems of the Western world – depression, suicide, drugs. In my generation we don't have that because we don't have that conflict. We don't have money, we were poor, but we had ourselves. Now the youngsters they have money but they don't know their identity. They are confused. They have so much money but they are losing the happiness of our community style.

They think if you eat our own fruits it is too low. You have to go to the store and cash your money and buy very expensive Japanese fruit, and half of them are rotten. They will sell their coconut and bananas to the Japanese, and get money and buy coke and doughnuts to give to the children. That is why a lot of us are becoming obese. All the best food, we sell it to the tourist and then go to the store and buy chips, coke. We are even selling our young trees to the hotels to beautify the hotels. Then they have the money to buy food from the Americans, Japanese, Chinese, Koreans. So a lot of our people are getting sick because all they eat is processed food. Even the fish, people sell them to the hotel. Yes, we still fish but in the long run too many people going to the ocean will damage that, and we will get sick from eating seafood.

The tourists will not be here forever. Once the ocean is polluted, bye-bye. Saipan is so beautiful. All the people come here and say it is so nice. It's just the fast foreign investors, they want to get rich quickly. They don't care. They will go back to wherever they are from and we will be left with the pollution. They are so polite to begin, but once they get their feet on the land, they do not even greet us. There will be a lot of stresses because of tourism. There will be no land, no homes. People who lease their land, they come back from San Francisco – no land, no house – they are on welfare. Now they hate the Japanese, they hate the Americans. Many become mad. Overnight you become a millionaire, but then you come back here and the rich American, the rich Japanese, the rich Chamorro treats the poor Chamorro like they are shit. Who will end up helping these people? It will be us.

Margarita Sarapao (1992), a Carolinian elder who works as a cultural educator, is equally concerned about the impact of tourism, again from a perspective of culture:

I don't blame the people. Time is changing. This is the time, now, for many people in Saipan they sell their land. Because they need money and long time they have suffered. But now they need the money they sell their land. I know it is good to pass on to next generation but the people this time they not smart, not like those old people, they don't think about the future, about young generation. They go to school and they have a different life.

Not like Japanese time at our age. We suffer, we just be patient. But these children, these American time children, now they learn many things. So they need money for anything, like cars, everything. So I don't blame them. Because time change everything. You are the one selling your land, they don't force you, but you need the money. So they sell the land, and they divide it into how many brothers and sisters. So now they have a good house. It's up to them. For the island it is not so good. But what can we do? We can't stop somebody from what they want because they been hunger, or they been suffer and they like to change their life or their children life. They pay their school so they can have a good knowledge, be smart, so when their parents die they the one looking for their life.

So, sometimes I don't blame too much. I only need to maintain our culture, because if we maintain our culture it help. It help some problem, like heroin, marijuana, alcohol, you cannot stop. If we keep with culture it help prevent some of these problems. So many problems. Culture tell them what to do, and they obey. Nowadays you tell these children to obey you, they cannot.

But if we listen to culture, culture help us. It is a rule, like chief in community. That help mother. Maybe her son do something bad, or suicide, culture can bring peace. I believe that if we follow our custom it is safe. But how can we follow? They like to follow what they see in the TV. That's good for the TV, but for our children it gives trouble. These children they watch TV and then they disobey their parents. It is the time. Our culture will stop the problems because when you talk to them they obey.

We cannot just follow American way, but we have to follow our culture too. I don't think Japanese throw their culture in and just follow American because they lose in the war. They carry their culture to take care of their people. But people here they don't take good care of their culture. They use their culture for decoration, but not real. They just say, "I am Carolinian", but you can see that they don't care about their culture any more. They think only what they can earn from their job.

It is not really bad to adopt American way, but we have to think that we are native, we are Carolinian. We have to respect our own dignity. Yes, it is good to dress like American, I have house like American, but I am still Carolinian. We have our own language but in my village now they speak Chamorro. No more Carolinian. In Japanese time the Chamorro people in Tanapag they speak Carolinian, at that time Chamorro were a minority in Tanapag. Now in American time Carolinian speak Chamorro. Maybe there is another war and they change again and speak what? Carolinian? The Chamorro now they speak English, they don't want to be Chamorro. Carolinian don't want to be Carolinian so they speak Chamorro.

They come here to make money, and anybody wants to can come. Who are these people who let these people come? They are responsible. They get big money for this beautiful island, Saipan. But even though we talk, we cannot do something. We wasting our time saying we don't like Filipino, we don't like Korean. We cannot stop them. I know it really bothers my culture, but I have to work hard on my culture. Americans don't care about my culture, even Carolinian don't care about their own culture. So how can we maintain that culture? How? Who can do it? I don't think American, Japanese, Korean, Filipino can help me. They don't care. They care only they come here making their business. They lease the land, fifty-five years. They collect all the money. They make hotels. They make good money. And then they leave.

In my heart I am still holding onto my culture. There is one thing can help. If there is a cultural centre that can help keep our culture alive. So many tourist. We cannot stop. But tourists, they going to spend a lot of money, and that money can pay for students to have knowledge. I am in the cultural centre, I will wear Carolinian clothes, not American. I will speak Carolinian. Those children, they will sing Carolinian. They learn, once they grown, they can teach their own children. So it pass to them. And money, why not use our culture to get money for our children? How many tourists? Too many. Where they go? We don't have anything native, from this island. That be good for this island. Tourists will see what is Saipan, not some Japanese hotel. Why not use that talent? I am teaching traditional dance, how to make pandanus weaving, how to make Carolinian dance. There are other women too. Once we die, no more. If we have a cultural centre we can let young people learn culture. So to me that is how culture can be coming back. We start little by little, then it grow.

In keeping with Margarita Sarapao's desire for a cultural centre, Chailang Palacios (1992) suggests that there is a more humane way of maintaining the tourist industry:

Saipan is too small for any industry except tourism, but there is a good way to do it. What do you call it? Bed and breakfast. Even the Japanese tourists they want that. It is only these rich developers that want the big hotels. The tourist come here and they don't see Chamorro, only Filipino. So tourism here is not even encouraging local people to share with other people. It's all Korean, Chinese, anything but Chamorro. Japanese tourists, they would like to share the beautiful dream to let nature introduce itself. A lot of the richness we have here. The local food. The weaving. And all of the building will be in Chamorro style. There is a group of concerned people here – Japanese, American, Korean, Filipinos, Chamorro – who want to improve our environment for the future generations. It just takes a little time. There is a demand too, to open your home to tourists and it is a way to learn about the people.

It is women who change things. If women gathered together my dream is that this suffering will end.

Chailang Palacios. Northern Marianas. (Palacios, 1985)

The Northern Marianas, like other Micronesian nations, is traditionally matrilineal. Chailang Palacios (1985) claims:

This is a matrilineal custom. The power is with the women. It is the women who decide for the people. The chiefs are the old people, very powerful because they have experienced so much. And do you know who is behind these chiefs? Women.

Heritage, power and guidance has traditionally been passed down through the generations on mother's side. Margarita Sarapao's (1992) story of her genealogy, while Carolinian, is also representative of Chamorro:

My ancestors they come from Truk, from a small island we call Piserach. That's in English, in Carolinian we call it Piherarh. That is the real name of that island. My people they come from that chain of small islands in Eastern Truk District.

This story they call it Inefeeri, the name of the lady they pull up from the fishing trap under the water. This is very important, it is the beginning of Carolinian people. This man he pull up his fishing trap and there's this lady inside. He just about to throw it back but this lady tell him, "Don't throw me back, you have to take me to this island". So he take her to this island they call Unanu, that is island near Piherarh. This story long time ago. These people they kill strangers. This woman, she half human and half ghost, she knew these people always kill the stranger people.

So this guy he went to chief and told him that she should have meeting, so she can talk to them. So she the one who create the *ainang*, the clan. She the one divided all the people and gave them name. She explain what it is *ainang* mean. *Ainang* mean it will bring all the peace among the people, and all humans on Earth. She create the *ainang* so that the *ainang* can help stranger. That Carolinian custom. She told them how to build *utt*, boathouse or manhouse beside beach, so anyone who came could be put there and give them food and everything. So that's the time they began to make the *utt*. That lady come so that she can make peace among the people, they killing people long time ago. This is very important story because this lady is the one bringing all the peace, *gunammwey*, all the good things, to these people.

When she finish her time on this island she told them to put her on a boat so she can float on the ocean. So she float to this island called Uman. This island have a mountain. It is the second island she come to. This big mountain the long time people of Tanapag, they call this island Talabwog. But in English we call it Tanapag. So they adopt the name when they come to Saipan.

So this woman she make clan. Woman is the one has pure clan. It is woman, not a man. So this woman her clan is Uun. What means *Uun*? Uun means *Uu*, fishing trap. Because she is half human and half ghost her clan is not going to spread. There are only a few on the island. My father is real *Uun*. But my mother is Wite, that is her *ainang*. So myself, I am pure Wite, because we carry the clan of our mother. And we take on half from our father. So I am part of this lady too, I am part Uun. When I come to my father's *ainang* they make me high, because they respect someone's clan. So they make me high. But my mother's clan they give me the land. So I am strong in this land, but I am not so strong in my father land. I'm not strong with my mother's clan.

Before colonisation began to distort the traditional culture, matrilineal cultures were egalitarian societies where women and men worked together in balance, each having different responsibilities and rights. Women's power was and continues to be tied to the land, as Margarita Sarapao (1992) describes:

Man cannot hold the land – always the woman. Women make decisions for the land. She the boss in the house. Other things the man know what to do. Man go fishing, bring some food. Woman is the one who does everything. Before we have chiefs. Men. Even the woman if the father is dying and she doesn't have a brother. So most chief is man. Women they have big say in who that chief be, the clan appoint the chief. Women have say in the clan, in the village.

Chief is the boss. My father-mother-father, the one who came from Truk to Tinian. He is chief. They call him *Rufag*. So this chief made rules for the people, because if you do something wrong they have to tie you in the *utt*, manhouse. Until you pay fee. Then they untie you. Like you bring some food. Or maybe these people they make loom for their *lava-lava*, out of banana tree and hibiscus fibre. They make boat. Many things. So you make trouble they tie you. Man and woman. But what the woman going to do? Maybe she go with her brother, that's a big sin. But I don't think she can go into a man's room and try to rape him. They tie men, maybe for woman problem [rape]. The payment go to the chief. There are not many rules, not like American. It is really simple.

Chailang Palacios (1992) recounts the changes imposed by the Spanish:

Chamorro is matrilineal, but the Spanish came and conquered the Marianas, and the Spanish mentality is that in everything men is the boss. So when the Spanish came here they completely switched our culture. They said that everybody should have the land. It is typical of the Spanish mentality that because us women would be marrying a man that we should have less land, because once we are married we get the land from our husband. In my parents' generation they gave three lands to my brother and to us sisters only one land. My mother and father they both have their land, but my mother, because of the Spanish influence, she gave her land only to her sons, not to us daughters, because of the Spanish mentality that men have to support the family. My father gave to the daughters and son, but not my mother. While my brother has several lands, I only have one. It has not been a problem, I don't have kids. But sometimes the daughter will do everything that the parents need but they don't get the land, while the son has all the land and takes off. But my sister she change that. She realise that her own daughter should have equal land, that it is not healthy when you give more land to the boys. She says, "Look at us, in the end all of us sisters come back to Saipan to be with the family while the brothers are gone".

Despite the obstacles women have, according to Chailang Palacios (1985), remained strong forces within their communities:

Women's power is very, very subtle here. The woman is the one in charge of the house, the decision-making and all that things. Even when the Japanese came here and wanted to make all the Chamorro Buddhists. A group of women gathered together and they said, "These Japanese are not going to come and boss us around". The Japanese general, the military, he is very mean, so the Chamorro men are very scared of that, but these Chamorro women, twenty-three of them they went to the office of this general. They didn't even make appointment, they just went there, and they said, "We demand to talk to the General!". So the general man came out. And they said, "You send all the Spanish priests back to Spain because you want us to be Buddhists. No way! We're Catholic! So, okay, maybe you don't like the Spanish but within a year, if you don't send us a Catholic Japanese priest we will never listen to you!".

So, yes, it is us women, even now. But with this Western mentality we always have to make our men number one, serve the men. It's still going on. When it comes to work it is us women who take the hard work. We cook and serve our husbands, but that big decision it is the women. So after three hundred years of the Spanish conquered us, it seems like the men. If you see all the leaders it is the men. But it is the women who make the decisions. Very subtle. The men will say this and that, but then the women at the back will be really criticising. But we are under the US, it is all the men who make the decisions out there, but when you go back into the house it is the women. Women are the force behind the men.

Women, responsible for the land and children, have consistently played an instrumental role in the fight to protect their culture. Chailang Palacios tells a story of how, when a casino was planned for Saipan, the women mustered their forces and prevented it:

In 1975, they tried to bring a casino and prostitution to the island for the military but women organised themselves, we realised what destruction it could bring. Five women working against this, and we won. We now have a group of twenty-one women. Remember that Saipan is small: 17,000 on 176 square miles. As a group we are very strong (Francke, 1985: p. 30).

Women campaigned against nuclear waste-dumping when, in 1979, Japan announced it would dump 50,000 barrels of low level nuclear waste annually (a total of 1.8 million by the year 2000) into the Marianas Trench, the world's deepest ocean only 600 miles north of the Mariana islands.[1] They strove to protect their ocean because, as Maria Pangelinian said:

---

1. Japan is building a series of nuclear power plants that use plutonium instead of uranium. Japan plans to import the plutonium from France and Britain in 30 shipments over 18 years. The first shipment of 1.7 tonnes in 1992 received condemnation from 15 African, South American and Pacific nations along

continued next page

The ocean is our life. It's our food. If they contaminated the ocean we have no food to eat. We would live a nightmare, waking up wondering whether the food we ate would poison us and kill us – not only us but our children and future generations (WWNFIP, 1987: p. 27).

They challenged the producers of nuclear waste to take care of their own waste. Jacoba Seman insisted:

We believe that we should not be – our beautiful Pacific Ocean should not be – a dumping site for any garbage of the industry of the superpowers who profit from that industry, the nuclear power technology (WWNFIP, 1987: p. 26).

We do not benefit from nuclear power. It is not justice for us to be burdened with your waste. Where is the guarantee that we won't be dying of cancers, leukaemia, and having deformed babies (Seman, 1985).

Scientists may come up with beautiful statements to "prove" sea dumping is "harmless" – but it is also a moral issue. This garbage belongs to the nuclear powers – let them dispose of it in their own lands, not in our backyard (Dibblin, 1985). If you don't have a place to store it then stop making it (WWNFIP, 1987: p. 26).

In 1993 the campaign to which they had contributed was successful. Under the London Dumping Convention, forty-five countries agreed to a world-wide ban on nuclear and industrial waste dumping at sea.

If the United States truly and honestly wants to defend [us] they should protect us from nuclear [war]. They should protect us from war. I don't believe fighting will make peace. I don't believe nuclear will make peace. Our neighbouring island suffered from nuclear tests … I question why the US use these tiniest islands in the Pacific to defend this great big country.

Lorenza Pedro. Belau. (WWNFIP, 1987: p. 24)

The US has its own interests in the islands. Close to the Asian subcontinent, the Northern Marianas is a vital strategic location for the Pentagon and it is here, in Saipan, that the US has built the final link in its Pacific Barrier (PACBAR) system.

1. *cont. from previous page*
   its route – plutonium is much more toxic and easier to convert to nuclear weapons than uranium. More than 49 tonnes could be stockpiled by the year 2000, and eventually a total of 500 tonnes. Reprocessing, the separation of plutonium from spent nuclear fuel, increases the volume of high level nuclear waste by 189 times. This, together with the waste Japan plans to import from Europe, will create a disposal problem that may eventually result in a renewed push by Japan to dump nuclear waste into the Pacific.

Giff Johnson reports that the PACBAR system is designed to "pick up Soviet satellites in the first few minutes of their initial orbit over the Pacific and identify their flight paths. This information is immediately communicated to the North American Air Defense Command Center (NORAD) which in turn generates targeting data so the US can shoot down the Soviet satellites on subsequent orbits ... First orbit tracking by the Pacific Barrier network, for destruction on the satellite's second circuit, gives the US an important edge in ASAT [Anti-Satellite] warfare" (Johnson, G., 1984: pp. 61–64). This facility places Saipan into the network of other bases in the region designed for the essential role of surveillance and communication which support its first-strike capability. A weapons system is only as effective as its command, control and co-ordination.

The PACBAR Radar, built in the Marpi Forest, was pushed onto the local people. The US Air Force, concerned that they be seen to be acting in the best interests of the inhabitants of the island, and aware of growing protest on Saipan, held an unpublicised "public" meeting hoping, no doubt, to escape local objections, as Chailang Palacios (1986) recalls:

The US Airforce came here to have a public hearing. But nobody knows about this meeting. Only the government people. No publicity. Luckily my husband told me. He said, "Hey, did you see the *Focus*?". That's our local newspaper. And I said, "What?". He said, "Go and read it because it has something to do with Star Wars". When I read it I was panicking. They wanted to put it in the Marpi Forest. Just next door, five minutes drive from here. It's a beautiful place up there. A very high place and you can see the ocean and all the beautiful view of nature.

So I started calling some of the women. That was Friday and the hearing was Tuesday. We had only three days, but a few of us were there, including my older sister Maria. She's sixty-five years of age. All the rest were American, air force. They were all in uniform, everybody with their badges and stars and everything they have. One Chamorro man, an airforce man, was with them.

So in the beginning they were all speaking English and we have people there like my sister. This scientific word of "ionise" and whatever they have for the radar, the "laser beam", she couldn't understand. So she stood up and said, "Hey, wait a minute. We are here. It's our place. I'm just next door to this place where you're going to build the radar station. You have to talk Chamorro!".

My sister Maria, she's very strong. It really shook the governor, because she is a strong Republican. She told the governor, "We don't want the radar. We experienced the war, and we don't want another war". This place is a natural forest, we have birds there that you only find on Saipan and Rota. We have coconut crabs which from time to time people will go there and catch, and deer. And they've already bulldozed some of the forest to have a road. Already they have gone there and bulldozed it. It is lucky that we were there.

The military are all lies. They're just lies. Saying, "Oh, no, this is just for us to track our satellites". But an American came and said, "Just tell us, is this for you to see the Russian missile?". And the air force said, "Well, if we start answering some of these questions we're going to reveal the secrets of the Pentagon".

Since then we have been working hard, the women and some men. We drafted this petition and we went to the stores and asked people to sign.

The petition against the radar collected over a thousand signatures. The Northern Marianas Women's Association proudly announced, "That's equivalent of over thirteen million signatures in the United States!". They stressed that out of every one hundred people approached about ninety-eight had signed, "showing that well over 95 per cent of our people do not want the radar station". The question everyone seemed to be asking was: "Why should we voluntarily commit suicide to protect people in the Continental USA?".

The military responded by insisting that the people knew about their military obligations when, on 17 July 1975, they had voted, by a 78.8 per cent margin, for the Marianas Commonwealth Covenant. Under this agreement the US claimed two-thirds of Tinian Island, including the San Jose Harbour which they would lease back for civilian use "compatible with intended military use"; a large section of Saipan's Tanapag Harbour; Isley Airfield, Saipan, for joint use; and the entire island and waters of Farallon de Medinilla for target practice. In addition the US would have eminent domain in the "national interest", which means it can take any land at any time. This agreement lasts for fifty years with an option for a further fifty years.

By 1991, the US military was using Saipan's harbour for the four-ship Maritime Prepositioning Squadron deployed in the Guam-Tinian area. Two similar squadrons were already in operation in Europe and the Indian Ocean. Each squadron carries sufficient supplies – food and weapons – to support a 16,500 man Marine Amphibious Brigade for thirty days of combat. This enables troops to be airlifted directly to their fighting area while the ships bring their equipment. With the ships, of course, military personnel have come. Jacoba Seman (1987) reports them as "waltzing around the islands":

> I, for one, do not feel any protection or security seeing military war supply ships anchored right over our reefs visible from my kitchen window, backyard, and anywhere along the beach road (our main highway), which everyone uses daily.

Many people claim that the people had no real choice over their political future. Some said "the US bought us overnight"; others, that it was inevitable after 400 years of colonialism, particularly the recent years of American control. The US, needing to ensure their military objectives, rigged the Commonwealth Covenant plebiscite. Despite protests from both the Marianas people and members of the US Congress, the US Department for the Interior worded the ballot paper making it impossible for anyone wanting commonwealth status to reject any section of the covenant agreement. There was no consideration of any other possibilities of political status. Public discussion was made difficult by retarding the release of the educational booklets on the covenant until only three weeks before the plebiscite. Not satisfied with that they rushed through the plebiscite despite attempts by many prominent Islanders to call for a delay. After the covenant had been passed in the islands it was adopted by the US House of Representatives through voice vote after what the *New York Times* described as "perfunctory moments of debate with fewer than twenty-five members on the floor". On 15 March 1976, when US President Ford signed the covenant into law, yet another island nation was acquired for the US military.

Chailang Palacios describes the impact of the US policy:

We never had political power, we never wanted it. We organised ourselves in our own way. The Americans destroyed this self sufficiency. We are just ants to this big, big monster. A powerless thing to be played with. They cannot allow us to be independent (Francke, 1985: p. 31).

They indoctrinate us and tell us that we cannot survive without them. The reason is that we are in their strategic area, they can keep a check on Russia and China from here. They buy us with their food stamps and social security which we didn't need but are now dependent on. They have contaminated our support systems, breaking up the family by putting our elders in old people's homes (Francke, 1985: p. 30). We are really a very simple people trying to survive. Working with nature. With the family all together. Taking care of our families and our lands. Helping the poor. Helping the old people. They are our books. They are our encyclopedia. In our culture we have no written books. It is the old people who tell us our story, our tradition, from one generation to the next. They will be the ones teaching us to make rope, to weave baskets. So they are very important in our lives.

I have an extended family and also a clan outside the family. If I had a kid – which unfortunately I don't thanks to the nuclear madness – and they wanted to get married within the clan, it would not be allowed because we are considered a family. It is that strong. Now the US is trying to destroy our clans because all of us have a lot of land. How come when the island is so small and there are so many people? Because of the clans! We build our own house. We are not greedy. We take what we need, that is all. Then the rest of the land is empty to feed all the clan. So one family will plant something there and the next there and we will exchange. And whatever is extra we will try to sell. Everything is give and take and everyone is taken care of. When we go fishing we don't want to take all the fish. We say, "Leave it, there will be another family to come and fish". You know what? The coming of the refrigerators brought change. Very subtle. It is how the Americans wanted it – "Everyone is an individual. Just take care of your family. You and your family and that's it. Don't go out extra to take care of your neighbours". The icebox is making us say, "Now I will go and fish for the whole week and put everything in the freezer and I will not share it" (Palacios, 1985).

Before we had our lands that gave us fish and clams, but now the people don't want to work the land because they can get food stamps to buy processed American food. We eat "Spam" which the rich Americans don't even give to their dogs. They buy us out the easy way. We have become lazy, unwilling to work the land, just waiting for food stamps. We used to have a simple life, working hard upon the land but enjoying a community, family life. We were healthy without polluted minds and bodies. But the Americans have created an environment that gives us high blood pressure, diabetes, heart attacks (Francke, 1985: p. 30).

The Americans are trying to divide us. Telling us that it is an oppression for all the clan to own all of the land. They couldn't understand, but that's our way. And they're dividing us. Those that have so much money are now giving a little bit to the clan to get half of the land. Who's behind that? The US! But we are waking up, beginning to understand (Palacios, 1985).

Because of recent events we have come to realise that if you starve a person, he'll eat anything he is given. We have been getting only crumbs. Our land is precious and scarce, we cannot condone the use of it by a foreign government. We are Chamorros and proud of it and want to stay that way. We steadfastly oppose the military takeover of any of our Beautiful Island for purposes of destruction, and instead offer a life-giving alternative – the growing on our super-rich soil of food for our Struggling Nation.

Tinian Students at the University of Guam, 1973
(Micronesian Support Committee, 1982a: p. 38)

Surrounded by an emerald sea teeming with hundreds of flying fish, their bright blue bellies glinting in the sun as they dart along the surface of the ocean, the small island of Tinian holds a story that should be told and retold.

Scarred by the massive battle fought between the US and the Japanese, Tinian is covered with what, in 1945, was the world's largest airfield. It was this small, isolated island that witnessed the start of the Nuclear Age when, on 6 August 1945, the *Enola Gay* took off from Tinian to devastate Hiroshima. As if in some macabre nightmare, the loading pits where the bombs were stored have been planted with frangipani and coconut palms, and are now a prime Japanese tourist site. Amid markers commemorating the Japanese dead, stands a plaque which promises lasting peace. But the coconut palms, one over each pit, have never borne anything but dry misshapen husks! Is the soil there contaminated? And if so, why? The old people tell stories that speak of "things" down there under the ground. There was no way that the Tinian people could have comprehended what the Americans were doing on their island. Few knew then that Tinian, island of the ancient latte stones, harboured the nuclear nightmare that would haunt humanity.

Today, the island is still thoroughly criss-crossed with long, straight roads stretching from one end of the island to the other, the skeleton of the four wartime airfields now softening at the edges as the tropical creepers and scrub reclaim the land. One of the runways has been rebuilt, the dock has been updated and, under the former airbase at North Field, under what is now cattle grazing land, cables for up to 800 telephones have been laid. This island, once the most fertile in Micronesia, has not been returned to farmland because the US military has other plans. Tinian is slated for the development of a joint service Air Force, Navy, Marine Airfield/Logistic Facility. In 1974, the US military announced that it required the entire island: the northern two-thirds for the base and the southern one-third to be returned for civilian use, and Tinian's protected, deep water harbour for an ammunitions wharf. The people of Tinian would have to be relocated from their village at San Jose to the swampy southern part of Tinian bordered by rocky hills. Tinian could expect approximately 5,000 to 6,000 troops, and their dependants, with another 7,000 arriving periodically for war training manoeuvres. Additionally some 8,000 to 12,000 civilians would be required for construction and base operation activities (Micronesian Support Committee, 1982b).

The nine hundred Tinian Islanders immediately protested. Tinian's mayor sent a petition to the United Nations demanding a stop to the US "land grab". A 1974 US Air Force Socio-Economic Impact Study considers that the projected population density of such a build-up will severely limit agricultural activities, and thus result in a deterioration of the Islanders' standard of living (Micronesian Support Committee, 1982a: p. 37). The study was not released to the public until after the vote on the Commonwealth Agreement. Despite local protest, the Pentagon continued with its intentions, although it has agreed not to relocate the village and to only take two-thirds of the island. While the US has not yet taken up its option the threat hangs over Tinian. The people are campaigning for the US to release more of their island back into local control. Unless the military can be stopped, Tinian is destined to become another Ebeye. Even before it has been developed it is being visited every six months by 300–500 US Marines from US bases in Japan and Okinawa for a series of amphibious assaults and manoeuvres called "Operation Quick Jab"! The island is scarred by the target practice and exploding shells of those who prepare for war in someone else's land.

Chailang Palacios (1992) complains:

> The army is training on Tinian. They bring over a thousand soldiers to the island for exercise. I saw them. I said, "What is this? I thought the Cold War is over!". This American soldier, he said, "No, we make ourselves ready for the Persian Gulf. So we are always ready in training". Here they were running around, camouflage. Bombing the tank. Sick! It scares me. I see them with guns. Who they going to shoot? Amongst themselves? Who pays? All the kids, the Iraqi kids, Iran kids. They are so hungry because of all this war. And the American are so proud of it. It's terrible!

The impact of the Pentagon's presence is already being felt. The people of Tinian, particularly the youth, are leaving their island and, seeking the promises of the Western world, are moving to live in Saipan or Guam. There seems no future for them on Tinian if the military comes in force. Already the island bears the scars of the American society: bars and brothels for the US servicemen.

But still the people of Tinian strive to maintain their culture. They seem to draw their strength from the Taga Stones. These huge stone pillars, ancient monuments left from the time of the ancestors, from the world before the Spaniards came with their sweeping devastation, pulse with a formidable strength. The stones hold the power of the ageless land and the promise that the Chamorro will survive.

The people of the Marianas – Guam and the Northern Marianas – continue to withstand pressure to submit to the colonial power. Whether in Tinian or Guam the Chamorro (and the Carolinian) are opposing the take-over of their land. The resistance begun over 400 years ago during the "War of Extermination" continues today in many forms. It is this persistence that enabled Melissa Taitano (1989) from Guam to exclaim:

> I'd like to say that I'm proud of my people because we have survived. We still have some of our language, and if that's just some, it's enough. We still have our customs. We have times when we can get together and say, "Yes, we're Chomorro. We weren't a country that gave up to the big power. We didn't change our ways totally. We still survive!". Now, our people in this generation, my friends, have grown to become proud of their country. We've grown to realise that this is part of our history and to accept it and say, "Hey, we're still alive and we are going to fight for our culture and it's not going to die, not any more! We've suffered enough! We've all suffered enough!".

ALOHA 'AINA – LOVE THE LAND

– Hawai'i –

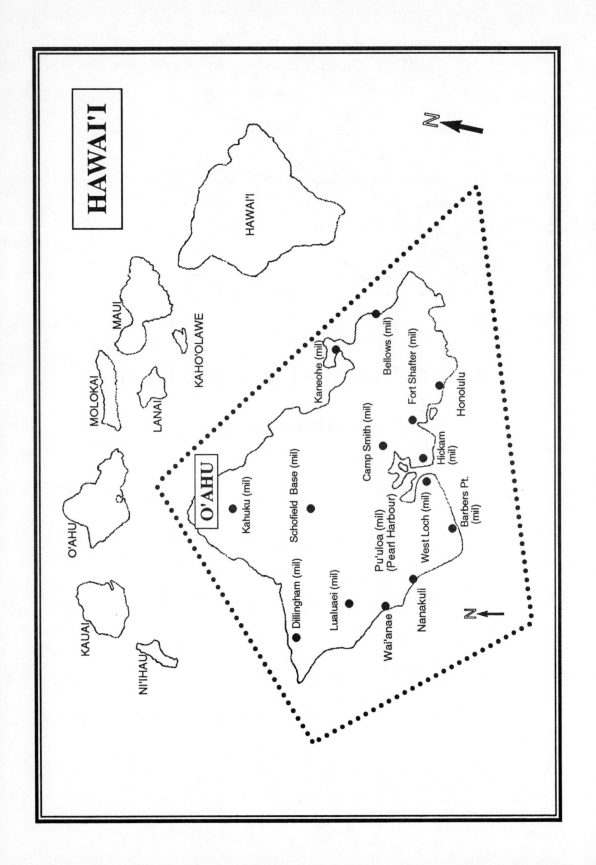

As Hawai'ians we trace our ancestry to the land and the deities who are the life forces of nature – the moon, the stars, rain, native plants and animals and ocean life. We believe we must aloha 'aina, *love the land.*

Ku'umea'aloha Gomez. Hawai'i. (Gomez, 1986)

Sitting in a turquoise ocean – an ocean that goes on and on and on – emerald mountains rise majestically above silver crested waves. The scent of frangipani, the sweet song of birds, tall glistening trees, moistened by massive waterfalls. This is Hawai'i. Hawai'i is also Honolulu: a mass of city buildings stretching across the coastal plain, tourist hotels full of Haole (European/foreigners) pushing out, onto the dry side of the island, the Kanaka Maoli, the Indigenous people of this land. Hawai'i is military bases, the US Pentagon, the "Belly of the Monster". Hawai'i is a stolen land.

At its root, Aloha 'Aina *is the belief that the land is the religion and the culture. Native Hawai'ians descend from a tradition and genealogy of nature deities:* Wakea, Papa, Ho'ohokukalani, Hina, Kane, Kanaloa, Lono *and* Pele; *the sky, the earth, the stars, the moon, water, the sea, natural phenomena as rain and steam; and from native plants and animals. The Native Hawai'ians today, inheritors of these genes and* mana, *are the* kino lau, *or alternative body forms of all our deities.*

Noa Emmett Aluli. Hawai'i. (Aluli, 1987: p. 6)

The Wai'anae Coast, the dry coastal plain on O'ahu Island, is home to the majority of the Kanaka Maoli, Indigenous Hawai'ians. It is a place of serenity and beauty where the people of the land live overshadowed by military facilities, golf-courses and tourist meccas. It is a place of immense strength.

Puanani Burgess (1986a) stresses the role of Wai'anae in social change:

Wai'anae is a rebellious place. People in ancient times used this as a place of retreat. These were people who survived battles. There are two kinds of folks: those who will never fight a battle again, are so injured that they have lost heart, and those who are rebels. So this is a very rebellious place. It is living out its heritage.

That strength is reflected in the land, as Eloise Buker's description of Wai'anae makes apparent:

Wai'anae is a rural community located on the western tip of Oahu. The drive from Honolulu to Wai'anae provides a transition from the urban hustle of the city to the quiet country life. Crowded residential developments give way to open fields. Mountains burdened with homes, reaching up their slopes, give way to mountains rich with vegetation – green and brown grasses and tropical forests . . . rocks whose bold form shapes the mountains . . . a sweeping view of the ocean. At that moment one feels the presence of the Wai'anae coast and leaves the city behind . . . The sharp mountains with their valleys flow into the ocean; ocean waves stretch towards the mountains . . . In the midst of this, the people of Wai'anae make their homes, cultivate the land, and rear their families. The mountains and ocean together cradle these homes and offer food and pleasure. But the land needs care and offers its own challenges (Wai'anae Women's Association, 1982: pp. viii–ix).

Wai'anae is a place of change, a place of contrasts, and a place of survival. Sister Anna McAnany (1986), a Maryknoll nun who has lived in Nanakuli (a neighbourhood of Wai'anae) since 1970, describes some of the issues that arise for Wai'anae residents:

The Wai'anae coast is where most Hawai'ians live. The whole situation in the islands has been a struggle for land. The Hawai'ian people, of course, had all the land in the beginning. It was gradually taken away from them, step by step. The military began to claim it in the Second World War promising to give it back, saying that they were defending our islands, but they have not given it back. The Hawai'ian people have gradually been displaced from Waikiki [Honolulu's tourist centre], and other areas, and in order to try to satisfy them land was given to them, by the government, out here on the leeward coast – Nanakuli and Wai'anae. It is not good land. It's not easy to live here. There is a lot of tension, a lot of frustration, that leads to physical illness. A high percentage of cancers – the highest on the island, a high percentage of ulcers, high blood pressure, diabetes and other diseases. People want their land back. There is a feeling that is strong here, about land.

Women in Wai'anae have joined together to assist each other in their move for a better life. One such initiative has been the production of a book, *A Time for Sharing: Women's Stories from the Wai'anae Coast*. It contains stories of strength and determination, as well as stories of betrayal. This is how one woman remembers the way her family's farming land was stolen (Wai'anae Women's Association, 1982: pp. 48–49):

In the early 1920s, my mother and her *'ohana* moved to the Kalia area of O'ahu, where Ala Moana [a major shopping centre] is today. They planted taro, bananas, coconuts, and vegetables. They raised ducks, chickens and other animals and harvested fish from their pond.

Food came from their gardens, and life was pretty good, our *Kupunas* [elders] say. In those times, our 'ohana worked together, always sharing what they had. My parents' stories taught me respect for malama – taking care of the *'aina* [land] ...

One day, some foreigners came to their house. They said that a big tidal wave was coming. Everybody should move up to the hills ... , they said. Many families left their homes. When they came back, their *taro lo'i* [field] and fishponds and food gardens were filled with coral rocks and salt water.

But it wasn't from a "tidal wave". It was from Dillingham's dredge. The dredge had chewed up the fishing reefs along the shore. They dumped the coral in our taro fields and ponds. The salt water killed everything. Many families were forced to leave.

Today at exactly the place where my mother's family lived, stands the Ala Moana Shopping Centre.

... In 1929, when my mother's family moved to Nanakuli, it was barren. The land was dry. It was covered in *kiawe* and coral rocks. There was no water.

... The years went by. Like my mother and father, many Hawai'ian families who had gotten kicked out of their homes settled down once again. From a barren area, Nanakuli slowly changed. Through the people's *aloha* [love] and *mana* [strength] it became the beautiful Hawai'ian community it is today with gardens and fruit trees.

Ho'oipo De Cambra (1986) expresses pain felt by the legacy of such violence perpetrated against her people:

We *Po'e Hawai'i* [Indigenous Hawai'ians] come from a gathering society. We were at one point very much meeting our own needs and would like to continue to do that for ourselves. My son is nineteen. He's a gatherer. He hunts, he fishes. But there is no part of society that supports him, except his family and a few friends, and the community that we are building – or, should I say, re-building. "Progress" is the destruction of this self-supporting lifestyle. And we raise our children in the context of this "progress", and we live in two worlds. We live in a world of our culture that orders us to be Indigenous, to live out those values of our history. Yet, at the same time, we are conditioned to assimilate by a dominant group – your Western culture. You make us crazy. That's really difficult.

The women living at Wai'anae hold the spirit of their people. The poet, Puanani Burgess (1986a), angry at the plight of her people, speaks of the strength of the women and their spiritual connections with the *'aina*:

In the language of the *Po'e Hawai'i* [Kanaka Maoli] the ideals presented by the words "justice", "righteousness" and "hope" are inseparably entwined in one sacred word, that word is *Pono*.

As part of our search for *Pono*, what Indigenous people do is challenge. We challenge long-held and loved myths. We challenge powerful, organised structures in our society. We challenge long-held beliefs of our grandmothers and our grandfathers, who have believed somehow in a new god. And it is with pain that we challenge this, but we must.

As part of the process of change, we have to reclaim our cultural concepts. We have had to promote them, and find new meaning for them: for example, the concept of *aloha 'aina*, which can be translated to mean love of the land, but it is so much deeper than that. When you consider how the *Po'e Hawai'i* considers herself or himself in relation to the land, and everything else, I think you will see clearly that *aloha 'aina* means to love everything.

Along the genealogical line of the Po'e Hawai'i are the snail, the *limu* [seaweed], the earth. So my relationship is a relationship to all living things. We are sister and brother, we are mother and father, we are daughter and son. And therefore the way that we work for, and protect, and preserve are much, much different from the modern western conservation attitudes towards the environment. It is not just a mental-emotional [thing]. Hawai'ians believe the connection is real. It is not one of, "I am the steward of the earth and therefore all these resources are mine to command and I conserve them because I want to produce more for my use".

You know, the first time I was up in the *lo'i* [taro fields] I understood what that meant. Really understood. I was there, pulling the weeds, just pulling the weeds, and suddenly I no longer existed. I don't know how long that feeling was but I no longer had a body. I had an essence. The land and I were one. That's the first time I had felt that and I thought, "This,

this, is what happens, this is how my ancestors lived!". I knew it. It was in me all the time, but I had to find the place and time, the opening, for it to come back. And it did. That gave me a lot more understanding of what those connections are. And that is why I work in the *lo'i*.

In Hawai'ian society a lot of work that was separate for various reasons has come to be blended. I was telling a meeting recently that I had just come from the *lo'i*, the taro patch. My fingers and toes were stained black. One of the *kupuna* [elders] who teaches ethnobotany at the university said, "That's really interesting because in other parts of the world, Micronesia especially, the taro cultivation is done by women. In Hawai'i taro cultivation is men's work, totally men's work, to such a degree that sometimes when men went off to battle for long periods of time the women would not go into the *lo'i*. So they starved. Even if they did go into the *lo'i* they didn't know what to do".

I respect that there are things that are men's business, because there are things that are women's, and I want them to respect that also. But now here I am in the *lo'i*, and I'm determined to stay there because I want to know. It's part of the spiritual existence that I want to have. That is a tradition of Hawai'ian women – to challenge even the *kapu* [the sacred]. As far back as I can remember women have challenged and changed *kapu*. That's our position, and that should be our position.

Because they don't understand that they are relevant a lot of women are willing to give up their Hawai'ian culture. They don't see their relevance to their community, their family, their children. They think that they are just baby-making machines, or sexual machines, or house-cleaning machines. I was fortunate, I grew up in a family where women were really the most relevant and men were in the background. I come from a family of women who were in total control. I lived with my grandmother who was a very powerful woman in spiritual terms, in healing terms. She was a giant. Literally. She was six feet tall, she weighed four hundred pounds. She healed by massage and medicine, and she ruled with an iron fist. Then my mother also ruled in my family in her own way.

So when I was growing up it wasn't a matter of feeling oppressed as a woman, but feeling oppressed as a Hawai'ian. While my mother taught me I can do whatever I set my mind to, the world told me that, as a Hawai'ian, you're below below.

I'll tell you the story of one woman's needs. About ten years ago I was sitting with a lot of women, most of them fifty and older. They were all local, mostly Hawai'ian. We got talking about welfare, and how Hawai'ian women are all on welfare and are looked down on. And how people always presume that Hawai'ian women have more and more children because they want to have more welfare. And how the social workers are always asking who you're living with, and all these personal, harassing kinds of questions.

One woman, closest to the oldest, was really quiet. She said, "I think I know why women have lots of babies – at least I think I know now. When I have babies they really love me. I can teach them how to pick *limu* [seaweed]. I can teach them how to do this and to do that. I can teach them to sing to birds. They love me and respect who I am and what I am. But then my babies go to school. And then they find out I cannot read, I cannot write, I cannot do maths, that I cannot help them in all the ways that society tells them makes a valuable person. So I make another baby, and another. And they betray me every time, every time". That's what western education has done – it has taught the children to betray their parents.

But I believe in history. The history of my family has been that the women have made the breakthroughs and brought the men with them, and brought the children along.

The women of Wai'anae are strong in their determination to reclaim their lands, and the control over their lives and the futures of their children.

Oh, honest Americans, as Christians hear me for my downtrodden people! Their form of government is as dear to them as yours is to you. Quite as warmly as you love your country, so they love theirs. Do not covet the little vineyards of Naboth's so far from your shores, lest the punishment of Ahab fall upon you, if not in your day, in that of your children, for "be not deceived, God is not mocked." The people to whom your fathers told of the living God, and taught to call "Father", and whom the sons now seek to despoil and destroy, are crying aloud to Him in their time of trouble; and He will keep His promise, and will listen to the voices of His Hawaiian children lamenting for their homes.
Queen Lili'uokalani. Hawai'i. (Burgess (aka Laenui), 1982: p. 23)

The story of how the Kanaka Maoli came to the Wai'anae Coast is a microcosm of a much larger process.

Hawai'i, as a nation, was stolen. In 1893, in a pact between US economic and military interests, a small handful of US businessmen overthrew the Hawai'ian monarch, Queen Lili'uokalani, and stole a people's nation.

But to begin at the beginning: the story of how the Kanaka Maoli became a minority in their own lands is contained within the Hawai'ian flag: it bears the trade mark of British colonialism – the Union Jack. When Britain's Captain James Cook arrived in Hawai'i in 1778 he brought with him the cultural arrogance, guns, alcohol and disease that began the destruction of the strong, thriving, and vital Hawai'ian community. Opening the way for British imperialism he was followed by British fur-traders, whalers and sandalwood-getters, bringing with them more guns, more alcohol, more disease – and rape. Next came the missionaries, condemning the customs and beliefs of the people, attempting to abolish a religion they could not understand. It was their sons who were to become the businessmen who stole a nation.

The British opened the islands to exploitation by the US. From an estimated 800,000 the Kanaka Maoli had been so decimated that, a hundred years after the British arrival, when the nation was seized, they had become a minority in their own lands. Reduced to 40,000 – an 80 per cent decrease – they were outnumbered by 20,000 Haole (Europeans) and 30,000 indentured Asian labourers. In 1993, a century after the taking of Hawai'i, the Kanaka Maoli numbered 200,000 but, because of immigration into their islands, that was only 20 per cent of the total population.

It is important to realise that Hawai'i had been recognised in the international community as a sovereign nation as early as 1779. It had treaties and other agreements with numerous nations, including Denmark, France, the German Empire, Italy, Japan, Netherlands, Russia, Samoa, Sweden, Norway, Tahiti, and the US. Even Britain recognised Hawai'i's independence when, in 1843, unknown to Westminster, a group of British merchants took possession of the islands for five months, until they were reprimanded by the British Sovereign and the Islands returned to the Hawai'ian monarchy.

British and US business interests vied for control of the fertile islands and in 1842 the US unilaterally declared Hawai'i to be within its sphere of influence. The US colonialists then set about changing the laws of the Hawai'ian nation, thereby establishing their access to the land.

They forced two big changes that undermined the basis of Hawai'ian society. The first was the Great Mahele of 1848, which took the land away from the *maka'aina* (commoners) and gave it to private ownership of the chiefs, a move totally incomprehensible to a people to whom ownership of the earth was impossible. The *maka'aina* got one per cent of the land and 70 per cent of Hawai'ians were made landless. This freed land for sugar plantations. The colonialists became the new landlords, the sugar barons. Importing indentured labourers from Japan and China, they quickly made the Kanaka Maoli a minority in their own islands. They engineered themselves into positions of power and soon controlled the government, the land and the labour.

But they still weren't satisfied. They wanted duty-free access to the US sugar market. In exchange, the US military wanted Pearl Harbour. So, in 1887, threatening death to King Kalakaua and his family and supporters, they enforced a new constitution, later known as the "Bayonet Constitution", which disempowered the monarchy. This done, they granted the US exclusive rights to Pearl Harbour as a naval refuelling base.

When Queen Lili'uokalani ascended to the throne in 1891, she received a petition from two-thirds of the voters of Hawai'i, not only the Indigenous Hawai'ians, imploring her to return control of the land and their lives back into their hands. By January 14, 1893, she had drafted a new constitution and was about to enforce it when she was taken prisoner and her monarchy overthrown.

The sugar barons had enlisted the assistance of US minister Stevens, Commander of US Forces in Hawai'i, a strong advocate for annexation. And on January 16, under Stevens' orders, 162 armed marines, backed by the USS Boston, supported the establishment of a "Provisional Government" consisting of the colonialist families.

Queen Lili'uokalani, under threat of bloodshed, surrendered in protest – not to the barons, but temporarily to the US government – and demanded an impartial investigation. She sent messages imploring the British queen, whom she considered her friend, to intervene. Her request was never answered.

The sugar barons, assisted by US President Harrison, attempted to push a treaty through the US Senate, that would place Hawai'i forever under American control, and guarantee permanent access to US markets. Before the Senate could vote on it, however, President Cleveland took office. He withdrew the treaty and conducted an investigation concluding to the Joint Houses of Congress that:

By an act of war, committed with the participation of a diplomatic representative of the US and without authority of Congress, the government of a feeble but friendly and confiding people has been overthrown. [Queen Lili'uokalani] knew that she could not withstand the power of the US but believed that she might safely trust to its justice. [S]he surrendered not to the provisional government, but to the US. She surrendered not absolutely and permanently, but temporarily and conditionally until such time as the facts could be considered by the US [and it could] undo the action of its representative and reinstate her in the authority she claimed as the constitutional sovereign of the Hawaiian Islands (Burgess (aka Laenui), 1982: p. 22).

Cleveland refused to forward the treaty of annexation to the Senate for as long as he remained in office, but his attempts to restore authority to Queen Lili'uokalani proved futile. The self-proclaimed "Provisional Government", whose members had earlier used their American citizenship to justify the landing of US marines in peaceful Honolulu, conveniently claimed that they were not American citizens and that Cleveland had no jurisdiction over them. On 4 July 1894, the "Provisional Government" simply declared the islands the "Republic of Hawai'i" and waited for the next US president, William McKinley, to accept the annexation which was hurriedly pushed through as a joint resolution rather than the legally required constitutional act in July 1898. The Kanaka Maoli had become US citizens overnight. Hawai'i was annexed under the shadow of the Spanish-American war – US Congress having been convinced that Americans needed a forward base off their western shore. Later, in 1959, under the shadow of the Korean War, Hawai'i was "granted Statehood".

The Nation of Hawai'i is being held hostage by the US for strategic interests, but the Kanaka Maoli, recovering from the onslaught of foreign oppression, are demanding their sovereignty. Poka Laenui (aka Hayden Burgess) declares:

The facts are clear. The US conspired with a handful of business men living in Hawai'i to steal a Nation and a People of their independence and the right to self determination ... The passage of time will not make a theft, especially a theft of a Nation's freedom ... legitimate. Indeed, the passage of time simply enlarges the theft (Laenui [aka Burgess], 1982: p. 23).

Land/religion is the foundation of native Hawai'ian culture: our beliefs and the practices of our customs and traditions. Without the land, we native Hawai'ians are nothing. Without land our language, culture and people cannot survive.

Noa Emmett Aluli. Hawai'i. (Aluli, 1987: p. 6)

When Hawai'i was formally annexed, the US Congress placed 1.5 million acres of Hawai'ian land into the hands of the Kanaka Maoli. In 1921, the Hawai'ian Homes Commission Act limited the land available to the Indigenous people to 200,000 acres. The US military seized a large percentage of the remainder.

Sixty per cent of that land designated in 1921 has been rented cheaply to non-Kanaka Moali, most particularly local and foreign businessmen. Tourist interests have claimed a large portion, as have local and federal government bodies. Only 17.5 acres remain in the hands of those Indigenous people deemed by the government to be of at least 50 per cent Kanaka Maoli descent. But only a third (5,800 families) of those on the Department's waiting list have been awarded land, and most of them are barred from living on it because the state has not provided infrastructure. The Department of Hawai'ian Homelands, claiming to be underfunded, has consistently sat on what money it has received, or has used it for the development of non-Kanaka Maoli corporations utilising Indigenous lands.

With 21,000 people still waiting for access to land, the Kanaka Maoli have responded by setting up camp on land deemed to be Hawai'ian trust lands under US law. They are returning to live with their lands, in a bid to escape urbanisation, and its associated hardships of homelessness, housing shortages, and poverty, and to connect with their *akua*, gods. Inevitably, they are perceived, by many of the settler community, as public nuisances, and are arrested. But it is the military, the tourist and corporate interests that, even by US law, claim land illegally.

Because these interests have taken over much of the limited *'aina*, there is an acute shortage of housing in Hawai'i, particularly on O'ahu Island. The cost of housing, far greater in Hawai'i than in the US, puts the dream of owning a home out of the reach of approximately 90 per cent of Hawai'i's people. Renters are no better off. Hence, more than 40 per cent of families suffer from heavy overcrowding and sub-standard housing.

The recent move back to the land echoes efforts of the early 1980s when many Kanaka Maoli had been forced to live on the beaches because of poverty. It was there, crammed together, that they had created a strong community voice for the right of the Indigenous peoples to their land and to affordable housing.

Defying orders to "move on", many were arrested as the government responded with violence. The Kanaka Maoli, resisting being pushed into sub-standard housing, sought creative alternatives to homelessness. They wanted homes that were low-cost and self-sufficient. On the windward side of the O'ahu they wanted a village orientated towards the Hawai'ian culture housing community programs such as co-operative child care, adult skill-sharing and community health care. While in Wai'anae, people wanted self-help housing and set about doing just that. These initiatives challenged the popular notion that the Kanaka Maoli were "lazy, irresponsible, good-for-nothing welfare people".

The women of Wai'anae, with their menfolk, established the Maili Land Project. Insisting on change, they had, within one year, forced the government to build an estate of small, affordable flats. Sharkal Aweau (1986) of the Coalition for the Homeless, and

Earnestine Marfil (1986), from the Maili Land Project, with Ho'oipo De Cambra (1986), tell the story of the Wai'anae initiative:

Sharkal Aweau:

We were living on the beach and we didn't have our self-esteem. We thought everyone was better than us. And then we said, "We have to make a change". So we started to pull together. We got the land and negotiated with the city to build houses. And we felt better about ourselves because we knew we could do anything if we really wanted to.

Ho'oipo De Cambra:

When the windward side did their resistance, the government went in forcefully and removed people to the point of injury. I believe this points out that they will not tolerate us making it a political native Hawai'ian land struggle. They will use force, brutally if they have to, to suppress that kind of statement – that Hawai'ians are landless, that the state is not being responsible. They have mismanaged our lands. Today we are at the bottom.

Sharkal Aweau:

But we're coming up. That's what they are afraid of.

Earnestine Marfil:

To be political is just to fight for your rights. Your right to be Hawai'ian, your right as a person, your right as a homeless person. We haven't done anything to make them afraid of us. We're just making changes because we refuse to lay down.

Sharkal Aweau:

All the women on the beaches went through a lot. The women work really hard, and always pull our struggle together. When it comes – not to a fight – to a negotiation, the women will be out there, the men will be behind to support. Although when we go home we've gotta put up a fight with our husbands, when it's time for a struggle they'll be behind us giving us support. When it's time for talking and stuff the women are together. That makes things so caring – that people can be together, willing to give up all they have.

But we didn't want to see our kids go through the same struggle we had to go through. We wanted to see them have a good life. We seek for their education, their health and their finances. That's what counts – the kids, the future.

Women can go on and on, and never give up. Men get so tempered fast. The leaders had a hard time. We didn't just have to cope with the city and the police, we had our husbands complaining as well. But to the outside it always looked like we were always together.

It damaged my marriage, because I was always gone, gone, gone, never home, home, home. I told him, "You gotta understand this is my commitment – gotta, not try to!". Then afterwards he was so proud of me.

When we go we can feel it, the island has a lot of mana *[power]. As soon as you step on it you can feel it. It's a hurt vibe, it is wounded, sad. The shape of Kaho'olawe is the shape of a foetus.* Kohe Malalmalama o Kanaloa, *the original name, means The Shining Vagina of Kanaloa. It is like a birthing spot, like a womb. The whole of Polynesia is connected by it.*
Luana Busby. Hawai'i. (Hawke and Rafkin, 1984)

In 1941, the US Pentagon began using Kaho'olawe Island, one of the eight main islands of Hawai'i, as a bombing and shelling target. Then, in 1971, they began inviting their allies to join them in what has become the Pacific's largest comprehensive naval exercise. Code-named "RIMPAC" (meaning Rim of the Pacific), and held biannually, it once culminated in the targetting of Kaho'olawe. Australia, Japan, Aotearoa (New Zealand), Canada, Britain and South Korea have all participated in the exercise, although only Canada has accepted the US invitation to shell the island. The Kanaka Maoli responded by organising to protect Kaho'olawe and reclaim their culture. Kaho'olawe became a symbol of a people's culture, an inspiration for land rights and sovereignty struggles across Hawai'i and the Pacific.

The movement has been successful. In 1990, after more than a decade of protest, US President Bush ceased the bombing and the rights of the Kanaka Maoli, as *kahu* (stewards), to fulfil their obligation to honour and nurture their *'aina*, were officially restored. In 1993, a 1953 agreement was finally honoured. It committed the US Navy to restore the island to a suitable condition for human habitation. The Protect Kaho'olawe 'Ohana was granted US$125,000 to reafforest the eroded land with native trees. It is based on the Hawai'ian concept of *ahu'pua'a* (the traditional division of an island whereby each clan cared for land running from the mountain summits to the ocean) and it will take two years. While this is less than the US$300 million originally considered necessary to clean up the island over a period of ten years, it is a significant step in returning the sacred island to the Indigenous people.

But it has been a hard struggle. The Kanaka Maoli have defied the military, found their way to Kaho'olawe on surf boards and, hiding in the bush, risked their lives to stop the shelling. These days have not been forgotten, nor the two young men who were lost at sea in their passage back to Maui during a storm and did not return.

For many years the Kanaka Maoli and their supporters have been going to Kaho'olawe, to make their *ho'okupu* (offerings) to the island's *'aumakua* (gods and goddesses) and *akua* (ancestral spirits), and to *malama* (take care of) the *'aina*. Every full moon, people gather on Maui, under the banner of the Protect Kaho'olawe 'Ohana. With boxes of food, bottles of water, and polythene-wrapped bedding, they travel seven miles by boat across to the small island, their common purpose to honour the ancient and inalienable rights of the Indigenous Hawai'ians, to reclaim and renew their heritage. As the authorised *Na Kahu O Ka 'Aina* (stewards) of the island, they have a court order which grants them monthly access for religious, cultural, educational and scientific purposes. In these visits, they seek to tend the wounds inflicted by forty-five years of shelling and the over-grazing by the large goat population, a legacy of European settlement. Their established camp consists of traditional *halau* – thatched wooden longhouses – and a vegetable and herb garden.

Kaho'olawe, recording nearly a thousand years of Hawai'ian settlement, is a recognised treasure of the US. It was placed on the US National Register of Historic Places in 1981, but the bombing continued. The hills are covered with the foundations of stone shrines, workshops and houses – "archaeological sites" for some, but places of worship and living cultural symbols for the Kanaka Maoli. Abandoned shell cases adorn sacred sites such as Pu'umo'iwi, an ancient adze quarry which once serviced the entire archipelago, and which is still in use today. Pu'u Moa'ula, the highest point on the island, is the site of one of the ancient schools of wisdom of the Pacific. It is a place dedicated to the study of sea currents, fish movements, astronomy and navigation. Although relatively low in altitude, especially compared with the Haleakala volcano across the channel on Maui, it commands a view of most of the Hawai'ian islands and a large area of ocean. It overlooks Kealaikahiki, "Pathway to Tahiti", from where the Hawai'ian ancestors set out in canoes to visit their neighbours in Polynesia.

Spiritual connection with the land is a central part of activities while on the island. Hula ceremonies, not the commercial hula of tourist packages but the true ceremony of traditional dances and chants are now being reclaimed on the island. Bridget Roberts (1986) wrote about her experience when, hosted by the 'Ohana, we visited the island to protest British and Australian involvement in the 1986 exercise:

> We were involved in the preparation, weeding the rock platform and carrying small flat stones from the beach to pave it while the *hula* [sacred dance] group made skirts, *leis* and bracelets from long green *ti* leaves specially brought to the island. The ceremony began at noon, when our shadows would be shortest, almost within the body, and therefore our energy centred allowing the *mana* [power] to flow most strongly.
>
> After the *hula* mound had been purified with salt water and decorated with sacred stones and plants, the dancing and singing began. Pu'a, the teacher, who had received the *hula* through her parents and grandparents, beating a gourd on the ground, led the singing, as the dancers, five women and two men, responded, weaving their patterns in perfect unison. This *hula* was in honour of Lono, god of peace and fertility. One of the creation stories for Kaho'olawe is that Hina, the moon goddess, and Wakea, the sky god, got together and made a child – the island is shaped like that unborn child. *Papa*, Mother Earth, was so jealous that she banished the child. The people here say that Kaho'olawe is being abused by the US military because of that curse. The *hula* ceremony was to ask *Lono* to bring rain to cleanse the curse and to green the island after decades of abuse.
>
> As I watched I felt tears welling up from deep inside. It was not just that the dancers were bright, strong, supple and eloquent. It wasn't only my awareness of the long heritage of the ceremony, nor the contrast between this and the Honolulu freeways, skyscrapers and nuclear arsenals. Nor was it my sense of shame for the harm done to the Kanaka Maoli. The

tears just flowed freely for life itself, unblocked by the dance, cleansing and strengthening. Many of us cried. That evening, the rain prayed for in the *hula* came in abundance. It fell warm and fresh.

Kaho'olawe has lent its *mana* to the people of Hawai'i. According to Alohawaina Makanani (1986), it is like a beacon pointing the way towards self-determination:

> Kaho'olawe is a baby, an island that is born, where there is a lot of energy. It is a place like no other in Hawai'i, where there is a dream happening, for children, for Hawai'ians. Kaho'olawe has given us a chance to look through all the distractions, to look at the *'aina*. And, believe it or not, the military have really helped us. They have helped us to learn who we are, what we are, and what we are doing. Kaho'olawe has given us the opportunity to show them, the government and the military, what it means to be Hawai'ian. The *'aina* has opened a lot of doors for the Hawai'ians and the general public to share, and to find a common ground on how we can help one another. Hawai'i is changing very fast. The longer we stay in a city life like this, the more we're beginning to change our attitudes. For our children, we have to look for alternative ways to share and to hand on the *mana'o* that our ancestors left us.

When you see how strong we feel and how much we hurt for the land, for the culture, then you will know for sure that the bombing of Kaho'olawe is a racist act.
                                                            Noa Emmett Aluli. Hawai'i. (Aluli, 1986)

There are 110 US military facilities on Hawai'ian land – most of them on O'ahu (Albertini *et al.*, 1980). Every time a plane lands at Honolulu airport, it heads straight for the nuclear weapons bunkers at West Loch, before turning sharply for the domestic runway. The risk of an aircraft crashing into this nuclear minefield places the entire western Pacific in grave danger, many times daily. Military planes, including large nuclear weapons transporters, also use the same airspace. And this is only one of many danger areas. The island of O'ahu is literally covered with military bases and installations, occupying a full quarter of the land (Albertini *et al.*, 1980). Large areas of Hawai'i, including its surrounding ocean, are under military control.

Since 1887, when the Pentagon gained control of Pearl Harbour, Hawai'i has been treated as a vital forward-defence base for the US. It has become even more significant since the key strategic shift to the Pacific in US defence policy in the early 1980s. Pacific Command Headquarters on O'ahu, headed by CINCPAC, the Commander in Chief of the Pacific, controls US forces for over half of the earth's surface, from the western coast of the Americas to eastern Africa, and from the Arctic to the Antarctic.

For this purpose, the military has built airfields and harbours, bunkers for nuclear, chemical and conventional weaponry, powerful communications, surveillance and tracking stations, maintenance depots and waste dumps, houses, hospitals and schools, land, sea and air training areas, golf courses and holiday homes. They often occupy the best land: residential land close to town centres or the best hills, valleys and beaches. They have it rent-free or for a token fee from the state and private landowners. Some of it is land designated for Hawai'ian homesteads. The military limits access to, and therefore the survival of, cultural and religious sites, as has occurred on Kaho'olawe. They claim that by keeping people away from wild country they are assisting in conservation, but this is heavily offset by the environmental damage done by, for example, nuclear waste from submarine reactors in Pearl Harbour (which was once a very rich fishing area) and electro-magnetic radiation from the high frequency stations in the residential areas of Wai'anae.

Military forces stationed in Hawai'i, their dependants, direct employees and some 94,000 ex-service personnel amount to over 25 per cent of the population. Their votes, along with the military's influence among the big businessmen who control the Hawai'ian State and its media, ensure that Pacific Command's land and resource hunger continues to be satisfied. The economy depends on military bases and tourism, a fate experienced by, or looming for, many other Pacific island nations.

Kanaka Maoli, realising that regaining their sovereignty means challenging military and corporate occupation, have instigated many land struggles. Kaho'olawe, as Makanani said, is a beacon showing the way.

We Hawai'ians are sovereign! We are a distinct people! We share a common culture! We inhabit a definable land that our ancestors first occupied for over fifteen centuries.
Pro-Hawai'ian Sovereignty Working Group. (1990: p. 1)

On 8 October 1989, Ka Pakaukau, a coalition of sixty Kanaka Maoli was formed, representing fifteen pro-sovereignty groups. Its mandate was to reassert the inalienable sovereignty of the Indigenous peoples over their lands, ocean resources, and lives. Denouncing the present governing structure as illegally imposed by the US, they are working towards the construction of a viable indigenous alternative.

The groups differ in their perceptions of the pathway to sovereignty – some calling for immediate and absolute independence, others for a nation-within-a-nation status similar to that of the Native American Nations (as an interim step), others wanting local self-government within the US federal structure. But they are bound by one goal, to restore to the Kanaka Maoli the lands and rights stolen from them one hundred years ago.

This desire for justice is rising so strongly within the Hawai'ian people (Kanaka Maoli and others) that they have become a formidable force, as was recognised, in 1993, by the Clinton Administration's official apology for the US government's over-throwing of the Hawai'ian monarchy in 1893. The Kanaka Maoli will not be content until their inalienable and divine right to govern their own nation is fully restored.

HAWAI'I PONO'Ī

Puanani Burgess (1994)

On Friday, August 7, 1987
Forty-three kanakas from Wai'anae,
In a deluxe, super-duper, air-conditioned, tinted-glass
tourist-kind bus,
Headed to Honolulu on an excursion to the Palace,
'Iolani Palace.

Racing through Wai'anae, Ma'ili, Nanakuli —
Past Kahe Point, past the 'Ewa Plain —
In the back of the bus, the teenagers – 35 of them
Rappin' and snappin', and shouting to friends and strangers
alike: Eh, howzit, check it out, goin' to town . . .

(Along the way, people stop and stare, wondering
What are those blahs and titas doing in that bus?)

Cousin Bozo, our driver, (yes, that's his real name)
Spins the steering wheel, turning the hulk-of-a-bus,
Squeezing and angling it through the gates made just
Wide enough for horses and carriages and buggies.

Docent Doris greets us:
"Aloha mai. Aloha mai. Aloha mai.
"Only twenty per group, please.
"Young people, please, deposit your gum and candy in the
trash.
"No radios. No cameras.
"Quiet. Please.

"Now, will you all follow me up these steps.
"Hele mai 'oukou, e 'awiwi."

Like a pile of fish, we rushed after her.

At the top of the steps,
We put on soft, mauve colored cloth coverings over our
shoes and slippers,
to protect the precious koa wood floors
from the imprint of our modern step.

Through the polished koa wood doors, with elegantly etched
        glass windows,

Docent Doris ushers us into another Time.
Over the carefully polished floors we glide, through the
        darkened hallways: spinning, sniffing, turning,
        fingers reaching to touch something sacred, something
        forbidden – quickly.

Then into the formal dining room, silent now.
Table set: the finest French crystal gleaming; spoons,
        knives, forks, laid with precision next to gold-rimmed
        plates with the emblem of the King.
Silent now.

La'amea 'U.

Portraits of friends of Hawai'i line the dining room walls:
        a Napoleon, a British Admiral . . . But no portrait of
        any American President. (Did you know that?)

Then, into the ballroom,
Where the King, Kalakaua, and his Queen, Kapi'olani, and their
        guests
        waltzed, sang and laughed and yawned into the dawn.
        (No one daring to leave before His Majesty)
The Royal Hawai'ian Band plays
        the Hawai'ian National Anthem and all chattering
        and negotiating stops. As the King and his shy Queen
        descend the center stairway.

And up that same stairway, we ascend – the twenty of us.
Encouraged, at last, to touch . . .
        Running our hands over the koa railing,
        . . . we embrace our history.

To the right is the Queen's sunny room . . . a faint
        rustle of petticoats.

To the left, we enter the King's study:

        Books everywhere. Photographs everywhere.
        The smell of leather, and tobacco, ink and parchment –
        The smell of a man at work.

        Electric light bulbs (in the Palace of a savage,
        can you imagine?)

        Docent Doris tells us to be proud, that electricity lit

the Palace before the White House.
There, a telephone on the wall.

Iwalani longs to open those books on his desk,
Tony tries to read and translate his documents,
                written in Hawai'ian, just lying on his desk.

La'amea 'U.

Slowly, we leave the King.
And walk into the final room to be viewed on the
            second floor.
The room is almost empty; the room is almost dark.
It is a small room. It is a confining room.
            It is the prison room of Queen Lili'uokalani.

Docent Doris tells us:

"This is the room Queen Lili'uokalani was imprisoned in
for nine months, after she was convicted of treason.
She had only one haole lady-in-waiting.
She was not allowed to leave this room during that
time;
She was not allowed to have any visitors or
communications with anyone else;
She was not allowed to have any knowledge of what was
happening to her Hawai'i or to her people."

Lili'uokalani. 'U.

I move away from the group.
First, I walk to one dark corner, then another,
            then another. Pacing. Pacing. Searching.
            Trying to find a point of reference, an anchor,
            a hole, a door, a hand, a window, my breath . . .
I was in that room. Her room. In which she lived and
            died and composed songs for her people. It was
            the room in which she composed prayers to a
            deaf people:

            "Oh honest Americans, hear me for my downtrodden
            people . . . "

She stood with me at her window;

Looking out on the world, that she would never rule again;
Looking out on the world that she would only remember
            in the scent of flowers;
Looking out on a world that once despised her,

And in my left ear, she whispered:
'E, Pua. Remember:

This is not America.
And we are not Americans.

Hawai'i Pono'I.

Amene.

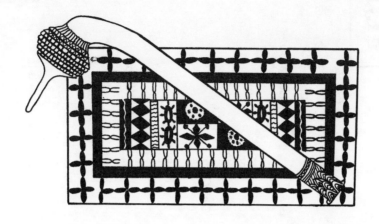

ONE VOICE SAYING MANY THINGS

– Fiji –

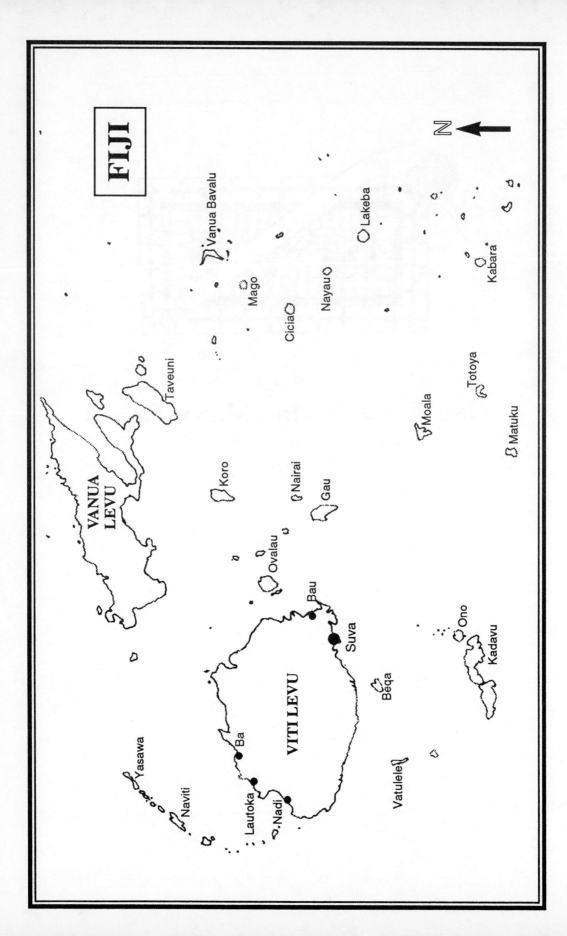

It is said that the Pacific region "enjoys a good human relations record". Shatter this myth. The general feeling is that the violation of human rights in this part of the world may not be of the nature of those violated in other parts of the Third World. But they still undermine the dignity and threaten the physical survival of peoples.

Sau Chee Low. (Sau, 1985)

Fiji lies in the realm of British imperialism. The British legacy overlays every aspect of Fijian cultural, social and political life, on the foundations of a spirit that is distinctly Fijian. A patchwork of crowded townships, thatched villages, canefields ploughed by bullocks, rice paddies washed by wide rivers, women carrying babies and produce to the markets, men carrying pigs – this is Viti Levu, the main island of Fiji. Fiji is beautiful, but the exploitation evident in the Micronesian and Hawai'ian islands can be found here also. Local townships and villages contrast vividly with grand tourist resorts.

The story of Fiji's early contact with the European world follows the same pattern as elsewhere in the region. The usual collection of explorers, blundering onto the islands as early as 1643, were closely followed by the inevitable stream of loggers, fishers, traders, beachcombers, gun-runners, planters and missionaries. Once again, economic, political and cultural exploitation was the basis of European contact with the indigenous world.

Perhaps the best example of the attitude of the invading exploiters is expressed by the story of the sandalwood fellers, who began operating in the islands in the early nineteenth century. Within a mere fourteen years, 1800–14, they had cut out all the accessible sandalwood trees, seemingly with little concern about the effect of their practices on the welfare of the local people. They were there to take and they took whatever they wanted, including women.

Then came the ships searching for trepang (sea slugs), and settlers to establish plantations on the rich soil. They brought with them changes that would distort the Fijian culture forever. The missionaries quickly followed, bringing their crosses and Bibles, and, in the name of their god, set about "benevolently" destroying local belief structures and undermining the Indigenous identity.

Concerned at visits by American and French warships to Suva harbour, the British, pressured by their colony of New South Wales, claimed control over the islands to safeguard what they considered their "economic interests". Settlers from the British colonial outposts flooded Fiji.

The Deed of Cession, which recognised the authority of the British sovereign, was signed on 10 October 1874, but only by chiefs of eastern Fiji. The people of western and central Viti Levu rebelled. They were an egalitarian people and did not want to be dominated, either by the British or the eastern chiefs. Although the western resistance continued throughout the 1870s and 80s, and in some ways into the present day, the British had successfully imposed colonialism on the western *mataqali* (clans) by 1876.

Determined to maintain lasting control, the foreign administrators then set about restructuring the Fijian social system. The process was begun by Fiji's first governor,

Sir Arthur Gordon, who arrived in 1875, only months after a measles epidemic had raged through Fiji killing a third of the Indigenous population. Placing themselves at the top of the political pyramid, the British administrators strengthened the rule of the chiefly elite. Utilising the age-old custom of obedience and loyalty to the *mataqali* (clan) authority, they secured their own domination. They favoured the eastern system, based on the Polynesian hierarchy brought by the earlier Tongan arrival, over the west's relatively egalitarian structure, and inevitably, they favoured the eastern chiefs over the western.

Gordon was also responsible for the arrival of the Indian Fijian people. Fearful of a "native uprising", he ended the ten-year-old use of Fijian and blackbirded (kidnapped) Islander labour in the colonial cotton and sugar fields, and replaced the "kanaka" system with the indentured labour scheme. Over 62,000 Indians were brought to the *narak* (hell) of the Australian monopolised sugar industry. Between 1879 and 1916, two thousand Indian peasants arrived every year to work in crowded and filthy conditions for very low wages. They suffered corporal punishment, fines, imprisonment and ill health. Many died. Although many had been kidnapped or tricked into leaving India, most agreed to stay after their initial five year term, and, when the system was finally abandoned, 40,000 remained to become small-hold farmers and retailers. Mixing with the newly arrived Indian-born free immigrants, they became Fiji's middle business class. By 1936 the Indian population had increased to 85,000, three quarters of them Fijian-born. When Fiji gained independence in 1970, over one hundred years after the forced migration of Indians had begun, there were as many Indian Fijians as Melanesian Fijians living in the islands.

Meanwhile the Melanesian Fijians had been restricted to their villages. Although often presented as a benevolent act designed to protect the Fijians from the European settlers, it was another method of keeping control. If the British could contain the Indigenous population in semi-subsistence village groups, separating them from the growing Indian community, there would be little opportunity to organise against the colonial oppression. It was the old divide-and-rule doctrine. Melanesian Fijians were isolated in the villages, Indian Fijians in the cane fields.

But, as members of both groups drifted into the towns and cities, those barriers began to collapse. And then, on 14 May 1987, the nation erupted in violence.

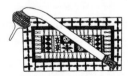

Please spread the message: we are in danger and fighting for the whole Pacific, our home.
Judith Denaro. Fiji. (Denaro, 1987)

It was on 14 May that Dr Timoci Bavadra's Labour government, the elected representatives of the Fijian people, was ousted from parliament by a military coup. Ten masked men led by Lieutenant-Colonel Sitiveni Rabuka had taken Dr. Timoci Bavadra's coalition government hostage. Bavadra's government during its few days in power had shown itself to be the voice of all peoples of Fiji, particularly the poor and women.

Judith Denaro (1987) wrote:

On Thursday, May 14th, just after 10am, Lt. Col. Sitiveni Rabuka was present in Parliament. About ten soldiers of the Royal Fiji Military Forces, in battle dress and gas masks and carrying rifles, entered the House.

Rabuka walked up to the Speaker and said, "This is a military takeover. Stay down and remain calm". With lightning efficiency, the Prime Minister, Dr. Timoci Bavadra, his eleven Cabinet ministers and sixteen Labour-National Federation Party Coalition members of Parliament were arrested at gunpoint. Within minutes they were whisked away in army transports to Queen Elizabeth Barracks. Almost immediately there was a news blackout and the Fiji public were left in an agony of suspense, watching the balaclava-masked commandos with rifles patrolling around Government House.

The next thing we were told in an official communique from Rabuka was: "I am in complete control . . . I took this step to prevent further bloodshed". This message was repeated over and over while we asked ourselves where on earth the previous bloodshed had been.

Thus began the political, economic and social turmoil of a nation. In a wave of violence, political treachery and international confusion, Rabuka played dictator to the Fijian people. Not satisfied with the results of the first coup, he instigated a second on September 25 that same year, abrogating the Constitution and declaring Fiji a Republic on October 7. However, while Rabuka was seen to be the main player in the crisis unfolding in the islands, he has not been the only beneficiary. That role has also been reserved for the leaders of the Alliance Party who, in power since independence, did not savour the idea of losing their political and, economic control. There is circumstantial evidence that the CIA were also involved, concerned, it seems, by the coalition's consideration of an anti-nuclear policy in keeping with those of Vanuatu, the Solomons, Belau and Aotearoa/New Zealand (Robertson, 1988: pp. 91–93). Perhaps the Pentagon feared that its arch-enemy, the anti-nuclear virus, was catching on in its sphere of national interest!

The violence that erupted in the streets, where Melanesian Fijian fought Indian Fijian, was unparalleled in Fijian history. Coming at a time when Fijians of all cultural backgrounds were uniting in a shared vision of a prosperous future, it set the small nation spiralling into chaos. Fiji's political status was in tatters, but it is the social impact that irredeemably wounded the people.

Five years after that disruptive day in 1987, the first general elections since the coup, were held in May 1992. It is indicative of the lasting tensions in Fiji that some of the candidates for that election included the "repatriation" of Indian Fijians in their platform. The election follows upon the implementation of a constitution, enacted in 1990, which disadvantages Fijians of all backgrounds.

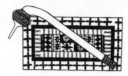

Let's not be mistaken, there is a lot of resentment against the people who have done this thing to Fiji.

Vijay Naidu. Fiji. (Naidu, 1987)

Vijay Naidu, of the Fiji Anti-Nuclear Group, had warned about the possibility of trouble several months before the coup. While recognising that there was some tension between Melanesian and Indian Fijians, he believed that the problems were being worked through but was concerned that a group of men was trying to cause havoc. "They're dangerous!" he insisted. That group, which came to be known as the Taukei Movement (indigenous movement), acting under the order of Sitiveni Rabuka, instigated widespread violence throughout Fiji.

Vijay Naidu (1987) explained the process that led up to the coup:

The claim is that race is at the root of all this. In the last five elections, race has been an issue, but in April 1987, when the Labour Party was elected, there was no real race issue. The Alliance Party tried to use the land rights issue, but clean and open government, allegations of corruption and the use of government finances were bigger issues. The Alliance lost power for the first time in seventeen years.

In all honesty, no one can say that the Labour-National Federation Party Coalition government resulted in an Indian domination of government. It did result in Indians in majority in the lower house of parliament, but not in government itself. The administration was dominated by ethnic Fijians, as was the justice system, the governor general and the military. The Great Council of Chiefs continued to dominate the Upper House. The Cabinet was fifty-fifty Indian and Fijian, and all the major institutions close to ethnic Fijians, such as land, etc, were given to Fijian ministers. So it was not Indian dominance per se that made the coup happen. It was perceived that the Labour Party was a challenge to the hegemony of the chiefs and their associates who led the Alliance Party.

The trouble was orchestrated by a small number of Alliance Party people together with the military. The Taukei [indigenous] movement is just a term for extreme elements of the Fijian Association, one of three organisations within the Alliance, which renamed itself the "Taukei movement". They overtly used the military to return themselves to power, using the racism issue. All this controversy about Indians taking Fijian land is for the international media: the Indians never confronted the Fijians over land, never threatened their land. They couldn't anyway. It has always been protected under the Constitution in safeguards that would require the ethnic Fijians to give away their land themselves. It is pure nonsense that Fijian land is threatened by the Indians. Fijian land is safeguarded in the Constitution.

The history of the coup goes back a long way. It is a mistake to see the Indigenous Fijians as a monolithic block. There are many tribal differences of dialects and customary practices. For example, the eastern tribes are more influenced by Samoa and Tonga. The east of Fiji has been divided from the west since 1874, when the eastern chiefs joined the British. The eastern chiefly hierarchy was the first to convert to Christianity and co-operate with the British, while the western chiefs fought a war until 1876. Many western and interior people were then exiled or executed. So easterners have looked down on the western peoples, calling them "devil tribes". The productive region of Fiji is in the west – the sugar-cane industry, tourism, petroleum refinery, a major portion of the pine forest industry and Fiji's only goldmine – but the government posts have largely been filled by people from the eastern part of Fiji.

When, in the mid-60s, the United Nations was putting pressure on the British to declare independence, the Alliance Party was opposed to it. But the British and the chiefly elite got worried about the consequences of the United Nations coming in and getting one person one vote, which is what the National Federation Party wanted. So, to prevent that more democratic solution they decided to give independence fairly quickly, on the basis of the interests of the colonially established elite. On the withdrawal of the colonial administration, on 10 October 1970, the mantle of power went naturally to Ratu Mara and Ganilau and other easterners.

It's quite true that ethnicity is important in Fiji and it was important in justifying the coup, but it was used in the interests of the dominant class in Fiji, who have never given Fiji a sense of commonality. From the beginning of the colonisation process, the state acted to define people by ethnicity. So the Indians are still called "Indians" after three to five generations in Fiji. And the General Electors (Europeans, Chinese) even call themselves "GEs" – that's how much the state defines us! This was what the Labour coalition was trying to change. The Alliance Party was based on ethnic Fijians, and the National Federation Party (NFP) on Indian cane farmers, but the coalition represented all Fiji's people. It was truly multicultural.

The Taukei movement opposed equality and liberty as foreign concepts. It is as if the National Front had taken over Britain. It's that kind of extremist position taken by a few people, and said to be the position of everyone in Fiji. If that is the opinion of everyone why not have a referendum on the 1970 Constitution, or on the idea of a republic? The regime is racist, inegalitarian, anti-liberal and works very closely with the military. It is difficult for us who believe in peaceful, non-violent resistance to change things, because it is almost like the apartheid regime in South Africa. We are not dealing with rational thinking people.

Racial issues are often used to divide people, and although there was tension in Fiji, as Judith Denaro (1987) reports, Melanesian and Indian Fijians had shared the nation peacefully:

Yes, there is hostility between the Indians and the Fijians. Yes, the Fijians are jealous of the Indians in high-powered commercial, vocational and civil service jobs. Yes, the Indians are afraid of Fijians who hold the land tenure and could ruin them any day by confiscation. [But] when you go down to the lowest levels you will find [that] between the Indians and Fijians [there is] no racial strife. The strife becomes greater the higher one rises in the hierarchy. On the day Fijian youths ran riot through Suva, Fijian market women hid Indian women under their stalls and behind their vegetables to protect them from their own people;

an Indian whose shack was burned down suddenly found all his Fijian workmates collecting timber and taking days off to rebuild his house. These are the real people of Fiji, the common working people, who got on fine until the politicians stirred them up, for reasons they do not even understand.

After the coups human rights abuses were rife throughout Fiji. Under the military dictatorship of the imposed regime, all sectors of the community risked imprisonment, and in some cases torture. Daily life was directed by the military. No one was safe as the racial tension became exacerbated and the co-existence of the two major ethnic groups was upset. A Melanesian Fijian woman (1987) was able to give me a woman's perspective on the coup, some of it positive. It is indicative of the present Fijian situation that, fearful of repercussions, she has asked not to be named.

Fiji had always been so peaceful, but suddenly people lived in fear. Enmity arose between Fijian and Indian. Indians, Chinese, Europeans, whatever – everyone lived in peace. But the coup put Fijians against Indians, Indians against Fijians. Suddenly the outlook was, "You are all Indians. We are all Fijians". Hatred came between us. But it was the people in power who hated each other, or were against each other, and that hatred filtered down to the people in the community. It was very hard for us to accept at first, because we were on friendly terms with Indians, especially our neighbours. But soon many followed the powerful, as they always do. It was very hard to cope with. We were hating them for nothing, including those who had been good friends. Hating them for nothing! It was all so sudden.

It really touched our lives in a very personal way, as Fijian people. You know, "This is our country – what are we going to do? What will our children be after this thing has happened?". The women were looking ahead, they were concerned about the future, about what the future holds for their children. They were the ones who really felt this. They are the mothers. They have feelings of looking ahead while the men, the chiefs and politicians, were only concerned about what was happening there and then with the Government. But it wasn't just a case of sitting around worrying, "What will become of our children", women were actually doing things, active as they hadn't been before.

Another positive outcome of the coup is that the Fijian people have begun to realise that they have to work, instead of being so dependent on the Indian people. "The Indians run the businesses. The Indians will surely have the top jobs. The Indians will surely do best at school. The Indians are this, they are that". Before, the Fijians just sat back and let the Indians run everything, but now they were saying, "What will happen if all the Indians go? Who will run the shop?". This was what went on in our minds. They were determined to do their best, they encouraged their children, "Make use of time, make use of money, make use of land". And so the coup pushed the Fijians, challenged them, and that has been a good thing that came from something so terrible.

It has also led to a greater understanding of each other. When the truth of the coup, why it had happened, became known, people began to talk to each other again, Indians and Fijians. It brought us closer together.

Don't get me wrong, Fiji suffers badly from the coup, but there have been some good things come from the middle of the disaster.

The coup has brought women, of all cultures, together, sharing a common determination for justice for their people, their nation.

Vanessa Griffen. Fiji. (Griffen, 1988a)

Vanessa Griffen (1988a) explained the impact of the coup on women:

One of the obvious ways women were affected by the coup was the increased violence generally, which led to more violence against women. After the first coup, in the brief period when there was actual racial violence, many rapes of women took place, which the women in the Women's Crisis Centre heard about, but which were not reported to the police. So, overall, there was increased male violence, and women were the first targets of that.

Many of the incidents have gone unreported, particularly when the courts and police were replaced by the military. A group in Fiji, compiling human rights violations for Amnesty International, listed cases of women being raped by soldiers, sometimes in front of their children or husbands. Unchecked military powers, and the breakdown of judicial and police controls, resulted in women being more vulnerable to sexual abuse and violence.

Now, women are bearing the full brunt of the economic situation, because many of them have been made unemployed. The Women's Crisis Centre reports that many women are coming in, because it's the only place they can think of to go for economic and social help. They can't meet the costs of school fees, food, etc., because their husbands, or they themselves, have been laid off. The economic situation is being carried by the women – they are the ones stretching the finances.

Unemployment increased following the coups. Many women domestic workers lost their jobs, or had to accept less money, as their employers themselves suffered pay cuts, or losses in business. These burdens passed on to the women – the most lowly paid employees.

The Women's Crisis Centre is acting as a support for women who are victims of the coup. They are trying to work out economic projects to help women – it is not what they were set up to do, but they felt they had to do something for all the women who were coming to them in desperation. There is no social security in Fiji, and there were women who were supposed to be getting maintenance payments from their ex-husbands, but the courts weren't functioning to enforce that, and many men had lost their jobs.

A lot of Fijian women have become politically involved, for example through the unions, the Young Women's Christian Association and the University of the South Pacific. So, for some women it's a matter of participating in progressive organisations. There has been a cross-fertilisation of work and action.

These women are now being told that this is not the way Fijian women act. Except for a few women in the elite, this new Fiji is not going to be a place where women can speak, it will be reactionary for women. The return to tradition means losses for Fijian women, in terms of political rights, decision-making power and personal freedoms. The church-going mother and supporter will be the ideal image of Fijian women promoted. Militarisation is a step backwards in women's status in Fiji, a glorification of men and the obliteration of women by even more men holding power and being the key political actors.

The opposition is women and church people, teachers and university people. When Bavadra and the MPs were arrested after the first coup, it was women who offered support. As time progressed and the army hold tightened, women organised peaceful protests around government buildings, organised women to make *leis* to put over the statues of respected Fijian leaders – and got arrested and held for questioning. Even my mother had pamphlets that she distributed anonymously around the church. Women are doing things they would never have done before. Women continue to protest. It was women who protested outside the cinema screening Rabuka's film on the night of the premiere. It was very courageous, when most of the people going in were supporters of Rabuka.

Women's and community groups have come up with a very principled defence of Fiji society. They are fighting for a demilitarised Fiji, a less violent Fiji, a more just Fiji. Promoting an alternative way of doing things, and presenting the idea of justice and political relations, based on sorting out economic and social relationships, women have taken the leadership roles, and are doing the consciousness-raising. They have done this quite naturally.

I think most of us see that a return to democracy needs a lot of work. We have to really start at basics, educating people to see Fiji the way it is, removing some of our racist and other stereotypes. Working for real participation and democracy. I think many of the male politicians are shortsighted and think only of a return to power. Some of the official men don't seem to have the humility to work at consciousness-raising. They think in terms of getting back into parliament, when such structures no longer properly exist.

The coup has been an opportunity to activate women, to talk about the status of women. In the flux that the coup has caused, we are having to examine our whole society, our racism and extremism. We have a chance to think about a whole new society we want to work for.

But, I think this is a struggle which will grow stronger rather than weaker, and which the military has underestimated. Because Fiji was quite a good society in the past, people are outraged by what is going on now, and those with memory don't like it, don't want children to grow up in this society. Because now it isn't a solid society. On the one hand the army has got stronger in terms of repressions, but other elements are rising – women, community groups, lawyers, and others who have been supporting people protesting peacefully. The army can rely on its balance of power for the moment, but it cannot rely on this for too long.

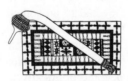

Tradition and culture are very much alive in Fiji custom. It is a must for every Fijian person to know their culture.

Rusula Buretini. Fiji. (Buretini, 1989)

Fijian women have always been strong, Rusula Buretini asserts, but colonialism has placed them second to men. But now, women, particularly those in the towns, where they have more opportunity for schooling, and therefore contact with women's issues, are beginning to get back their power. They are working together for the advancement of all women (Buretini, 1989):

> It's true, men are more dominant than the women, especially in the villages, but women have grown up with it, it's part of their lives that men should be superior. The women believe that they are there to listen, they do not take part in the decision making. That is the men's role. It is their belief that it should be that way, they have grown up with it. It is not that the men keep saying, "You listen to me, I am the man". It is just in their hearts that this is the way life is.
>
> In the towns it is different. It is the thing that comes up most in family arguments. Women there are more educated, and they show their power. They are both working, and she is out all the time. She's working. She's part of the Catholic Women's League. She's a member of the National Council of Women. And so no one is home to look after the kids. That brings on a lot of arguments: there are more divorces in the towns than in the villages. And where men are working and the women are at home it's different again. Oh, yes, that is where the male dominance really shows up. The man is working, he has got the money, he's earning, he's out all the time, and the woman is at home looking after the children. There's a lot of work needed to change that.
>
> And it's happening. Together women are making changes, in the towns and the villages. The educated townswomen are going back out into the villages to help the women there, women who live a pattern of just getting up in the mornings, making breakfast and just staying at home and doing the housework. You see, young women just leave school at the age of sixteen or seventeen and they think, "This is where my life ends". It's a set pattern. They don't realise how much they have to offer and that they are needed.
>
> The townswomen work with the village women to make them aware of what talents they have, and get them to share them with their community. To know that they are capable of a lot more than washing clothes, cooking the dinner, and going to look for fish. They set up women's clubs, have meetings in the village and the women have a voice. They are speaking from what they feel should be done in the villages, rather than the men making decisions for them. Men don't feel what women feel, so how can they help?
>
> It's no longer a matter of, "We in the towns are educated, who cares about the women in the villages". We are in this together. And so educated town women have gone back out to the villages to bring up the voices of the women. We are being heard together as one voice saying many things.

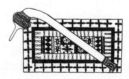

I've learnt a lot from older women about what women can do for the country. You don't have to be a strong man to be a politician or do something. You can have a woman who really believes she has the strength and power and believes what she has learned and gained, she can do something with it.

Rusula Buretini. Fiji. (Buretini, 1989)

The Women's Crisis Centre is at the forefront of moves to improve the social environment for women. Created to care particularly for the needs of both Melanesian and Indian Fijian women, it has provided services in the absence of adequate provisions by the government. During and since the coup its importance has increased, as Shamima Ali (1986), instrumental in establishing the centre, explains:

> In 1983, a group of women got together because there was a spate of nasty rapes. Women had been accepting rape as something they couldn't do anything about, but they started saying, "Something's got to happen, it's getting worse". They formed a collective and in August 1984 opened the doors.
>
> We help women who have suffered rape, and also victims of incest and child or marital abuse. They have mainly been referred to us by other people like doctors and the police. The police have been good at times. There was one case of a girl who wouldn't and couldn't talk about her rape so the police brought us in to help her while she was making a statement.
>
> Rape is a problem here. Although I don't think there is more rape here than elsewhere, it is very under-reported. In Fijian culture if I am raped by six Fijian guys everything is taken out of my control. The parents take over. The men's relatives come round and say, "We are really sorry this has happened". They bring the whale's tooth as an offering and say, "It will never happen again", and so on. The woman's parents negotiate and agree not to report the case to the police. It has to be a very strong woman, with a lot of support, who will go out and report a case. And in court, one of the main arguments for the defence can rest on her past sexual life, which is dragged through the courts while the guy sits and smirks. She has to prove herself. Just recently a fourteen-year-old girl was raped by a policeman when she was working as a housemaid for him. She was illiterate and couldn't tell the time, and on that basis the guy won the case!
>
> If an Indian girl gets pregnant, even by rape, they will try to get her to abort, whatever the risk to her. If it is known that she has been pregnant the chances of her marrying are nil, unless it's to a widower who needs someone to look after ten children. For the Fijian woman it's a bit different. She might get beaten up by her father or brother, but they will always accept her and the child into the family, and she can still get married.
>
> In both the Fijian and the Indian cultures, the women play a very submissive role, and a lot are not educated, or if they are educated, once they are married the husband won't think of letting them work outside the home. In rural areas they might have left school at nine or ten because maybe there was only enough money in the family to send one child to high school, and preference was given to the brother. A daughter over twenty who is not married is a shame on the family. If you go to a village you will see many women with a front tooth missing because their husband has punched them. And women are ashamed and blaming themselves. Suicide is on the increase, especially for Indian women. Living in an extended family you've got your mother-in-law and sisters-in-law to cook for. Oppressing your daughter-in-law is like a custom and there's a lot of hardship ending in women hanging, burning or drowning themselves.
>
> In Suva, a lot more women are educated, but it is rare to find a woman who is independent. She is still the one who will cook three meals a day, and take care of the children. If you go to the government and ask why women are not in the top jobs, they say they can't afford to have them getting pregnant, having periods, taking time off for sick children. All the old excuses. Women's promotion is delayed, they are threatened by male colleagues. We need women in the government and the media.

At the centre, we believe that women need to talk about their problems, instead of internalising them. They have no one at home to talk to. Their mother, mother-in-law or sisters will just say, "You have to put up with your husband, because you are nothing without him, and you should be thankful you've got him to look after you". When a woman comes here we'll listen, not immediately try to solve her problems. Maybe she'll come in one day look around, go away, and come back two days later, beginning to trust us.

We try to be as up to date as possible on women's rights to social services and things like that. We have a woman lawyer who offers her services for free or for what the woman can afford. If a woman wants to go ahead with a rape or a divorce case we let her know what is in store for her, and let her make the decision. A lot of people think we teach women how to leave their husbands, so when we go out to give talks we make it clear we are not doing that. It's hard to get people to see that women can make their own decisions and take control of their own lives.

It's very hard to leave a husband because parents don't want you back, unless they are rich enough to look after you and they can stand the shame. Social welfare gives about $10 [Fijian] a week for four children, and maintenance is hard to get.

There is the Women's Rights Movement. That's a movement that came out of this organisation because we said we had to do something about the law. For example, there is no such thing as a non-molestation order for a wife who has been bashed up. We called a meeting of all women in Fiji who were concerned about the law and women's rights. We tried not to attract too many expatriates, although there are a lot who are very aware and concerned, because if there are too many white faces other women will dismiss us as a western thing. Over seventy women turned up – we were bowled over – all races, all walks of life. The five of us who had called the meeting each talked about an issue – rape, violence against women, how the laws stood, how we wanted them changed, and so on. The other women all wanted something done. Of course one or two said, "It's traditional to be beaten up by your husband – he has to take out his frustrations, and if you don't cook his food you should expect something like that to happen".

When we challenge traditional attitudes to women, some people say, "Oh, but our identity – we mustn't lose our identity". So we have to tell them that some things like wife-beating are not Fijian, they happen all over the world. And also that some traditional things have been accepted, others rejected, depending on whether they develop or improve our society.

Given the chance, women in this country can become very strong. A lot of changes of attitude have to take place, but I think the Women's Crisis Centre, and the Women's Rights Movement (I'm biased!) do a lot for women here. It might take twenty, thirty or fifty years, but it's a beginning.

The women who have lived through the frightening atrocities of 1987 will not rest easy until their dreams of a Fiji where all people are free and equal are manifested. Their strength and vision is an inspiration.

Since the Dawn of Time

– Australia and the Torres Strait Islands –

AUSTRALIA and TORRES STRAIT ISLANDS

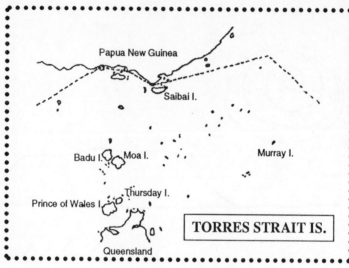

Papua New Guinea

Saibai I.

Badu I. Moa I.

Murray I.

Thursday I.

Prince of Wales I.

TORRES STRAIT IS.

Queensland

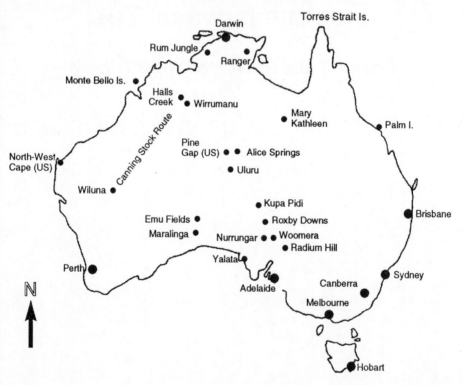

Torres Strait Is.

Darwin

Rum Jungle

Ranger

Monte Bello Is.

Halls Creek

Wirrumanu

Mary Kathleen

Palm I.

North-West Cape (US)

Pine Gap (US)

Alice Springs

Uluru

Canning Stock Route

Wiluna

Kupa Pidi

Emu Fields

Roxby Downs

Brisbane

Maralinga

Nurrungar

Woomera

Radium Hill

Yalata

Perth

Adelaide

Canberra

Sydney

Melbourne

N

Hobart

ALL human life is sacred, and all people throughout the world have the right to life. Aboriginal people living in Australia are no different. We too are human beings. We too love life, our freedom.

Helen Corbett. Yamagee. (Corbett, 1987a)

In 1788, proud, egalitarian peoples, living in harmony with a vast, sometimes difficult environment "since the dawn of time", confronted invaders who, spiritually alienated from the Earth, considered themselves a superior race with a mission: to "civilise" the "heathen savages" and claim the world's resources as their own.

Before colonisation, there were over 700 distinct peoples indigenous to this continent and its islands – each with their own language, culture, history, social experience, and lands. Called "Aborigines" (meaning the original people) and Torres Strait Islanders by Europeans, they know themselves by their traditional names – Koori (NSW and Victoria), Murri (Queensland), Nunga (the Adelaide area of South Australia), Meriam (just one people of the Torres Strait). These names break down again: the Wadi Wadi, the Yuin, and the Bundjalung people, all call themselves "Koori". They are names which bind them to the land which is their country.

Europeans now concede that the Aboriginal peoples have been living in this continent for over 80,000 years, and have been busy tracing the pattern of their arrival from southern Asia; but the Aboriginal peoples claim that they have always been here. They are adamant that, as Bundjalung, Pauline Gordon (1990) asserts:

We were here the first sunrise. That's our Law and our culture. You might have come from a monkey, and come out of the ocean, and evolved from fish and walked on the land – but we certainly didn't. Our Creator Spirit put us here. He was here the first sunrise. I don't know where you come from.

European settlement of the continent began only 200 years ago and yet, when the British arrived, they declared the land *terra nullius* – empty land. In contradiction, they then set about an elaborate campaign of genocide against a people they insisted did not exist. The violence is typified by the attitude of William Cox, remembered as a hero in school-book history, and quoted in Bruce Elder's *Blood on the Wattle: Massacres and Mal-treatment of Australian Aborigines since 1788*:

The best thing that can be done is shoot all the blacks and manure the ground with their carcasses. That is all the good they are fit for! It is also recommended that all the women and children be shot. That is the most certain way of getting rid of this pestilent race (Elder, 1988: p. 50).

Massacres, supported and condoned through silence by the European settlers, were carried out by European men. Whole communities were hunted down and butchered. Those Aboriginal people who survived often witnessed the brutal killing of their clans.

Aboriginal women and girls suffered the double burden of being repeatedly raped and assaulted before they were slain. Others were captured, abused, and then dumped by the European settlers. Janine Roberts records in her book *From Massacres to Mining: The Colonisation of Aboriginal Australia* (1978: p. 29):

> In 1900, a station owned by the Queensland National Bank had "eight or nine gins[1] fenced in with rabbit-proof netting next to the house". One man "sent a gin away with the mailman to Burketown to be sent south to some of his friends as a slave. Parties of men use to go out to capture "gins". These women were traded between stations. A government report in 1900 stated that women were "handed around from station to station" until discarded to rot away with venereal disease.

Although syphilis was the largest single cause of death amongst Aboriginal people, it was just one of the many illnesses, imported from disease-ridden Europe, that raged through the bush.

Truganini, portrayed incorrectly as the "last Tasmanian", had a life typical of many. Bruce Elder records that:

> By the time she was seventeen she had been raped, had seen her mother stabbed, her uncle shot, her step-mother kidnapped and taken to China, her three sisters sold and enslaved to sealers on Kangaroo Island and her betrothed murdered (Elder, 1988: p. 31).

These were not one-off incidents. They happened everywhere! Throughout the continent, Aboriginal people were slaughtered by bullet, disease, and starvation.

Aboriginal resistance has continued from the arrival of the first fleet until the present day, taking many forms. Until the early decades of the twentieth century, this resistance often consisted of armed warfare. Despite the Europeans' economic and military advantage over a society unaccustomed to war, the Aboriginal peoples' determination to protect their lands and people was strong. Janine Roberts reports:

> The Aborigines resisted the invasion . . . As the whites attempted to take their lands, the inhabitants banded together to fight guerrilla campaigns . . . Despite having only spears to fight guns, this warfare lasted some 160 years from the first battles at Sydney to the last massacres in the Northern Territory around 1930 (Roberts, J., 1978: p. 21).

Threatening the viability of the pioneer industries, resistance made settlement difficult and the settlers retaliated by even more slaughter. Whole tribes would be exterminated if any Aboriginal people tried to resist, and often when they did not. It is impossible to estimate the numbers of Aboriginal people killed during those early years, but it was tens of thousands.

Henry Reynolds, writing *White Man Came Took Everything* (1988: p. 5), observes that "the frontier settlements bristled with guns", and quotes a pioneer of 1869 commenting that his community "had its foundations cemented in blood". This echoes

---

1. "Gin" is an extremely racist term, so it is included here with hesitation, but it reflects the racist attitudes of many settlers.

Bruce Elder's quotation of a letter to the editor printed in the *Launceston Examiner*, on 26 September, 1831:

> We are at war with them. They look upon us as enemies – as invaders, as oppressors and persecutors – they resist our invasion. They have never been subdued therefore they are not rebellious subjects but an injured nation defending, in their own way, their rightful possessions which have been torn from them by force (Elder, 1988: p. 195).

The very presence in Australia of the European community was, until 1992, based on the pretence that Aboriginal people did not exist. Although Captain James Cook's orders were "with the consent of the Natives to take possession of convenient situations" the lie of *terra nullius* was politically expedient. It "excused" the British government from having to recognise a prior nation, and therefore from having to deal with the issues of treaties and land rights. And, it allowed them to turn a blind eye to the atrocities of their own people. It enabled them to satisfy their national greed, stealing a huge and wonderful land from its people, and, building their empire, extending their tentacles out across the Pacific.

Brought up on history-book lies, most European Australians have only recently begun to learn the extent of the violence, but the majority still do not fully comprehend the impact. For Aboriginal peoples the story is different. As the recipients of the violence and the continuing racism, individually and collectively, they have always known the pain of the invasion. As Erica Kyle (1989), a Bwgcolman of Palm Island, asserts:

> In the history book we read that Captain Cook discovered Australia in 1770. Aboriginal people say that Aboriginals discovered Cook! Through the sad history it's important for us to know that there is the other side of it.

We come from 40,000 to 50,000 years of history and that's what gives us pride inside. That God has given us a race that goes way, way back, with so many wonderful stories. We talk about the Dreamtime stories, but they're not just stories – it's the Law of that land and the connections between us and the trees, the birds, the animals and the songs and dances. All intertwined.

Erica Kyle. Bwgcolman. (Kyle, 1989)

Rachael Cummins (1989), also of Palm Island, tells the story of the invasion from an Aboriginal perspective:

> I think one of the biggest things for us is we've been confused. I mean, it happened when White men first stepped foot on this land. The Black people thought he was a spirit of the

ancestors but they soon found out that that wasn't true. When they found the Whites killing kangaroos they thought, "This is my country. I let him stay here, and now he's killing my kangaroos. So okay, I'll go and kill a sheep". And then he and his community were killed in retaliation for the sheep. He thought, "Well, what's happening! He's using my water and killing my kangaroos, and yet when I want a feed, I'm being killed for it".

And then after wiping us out failed, they turned to "protecting" and assimilating us.

In the earlier days the government decided to "protect" the Aboriginal people. So they put Aboriginal people in small pockets of land that no one wanted. People weren't allowed to move freely. If you came into the town it was because you were on a special order. You came to town to work, usually on a cattle property or in the shearing sheds. The owner of this place was responsible for you, and once you left his employment you had to go straight back to the reservation. If you got off-side with the manager he would just move you out. Doesn't matter if you had family and children. For punishment he would move you to another reserve, and you wouldn't see your family again.

The women on Palm Island were sent to work on the sheep stations and cattle properties. It didn't matter if you had children, they were put into the nursery section. In some cases mothers didn't come back for three or four years, and they'd find their little babies grown up. In a lot of cases those children were adopted out. That's one of the things used to break up our culture, one of the things that's broken our spirit. The dormitories were only pulled down in 1969.

There were some people who escaped round up, and over a period of time the government said, "Oh well, we'll leave them there". These people formed little fringe camps around the towns. They lived in the rubbish tips, and were moved on all the time. And some poor confused people even said, "Okay, I'll do everything right. I'll be a good Black and live in the White community". And they'd go and apply for jobs, or they'd live next door to the White people, and they'd find out quick smart that they don't measure up. That they're "only Black fellas" anyway!

Before 1969, on Palm Island, there was a Black area and a White area. And you couldn't go into the White area unless you were a "Boy" or a "Mary", to clean out their homes, or do their gardening. And we'd get a police escort, be dropped off at their house and picked up at five o'clock, and walked back to the dormitory. My mother was a cleaner in the manager's office in the early 60s, and she got friendly with the White staff. I thought they were really lovely people, and they had kids my age. They invited me up to play with the kids, so I went up to their place, but someone reported me. That same Saturday afternoon the police came around, and told Mum she was wanted at the manager's office. Mum went up and she had to spend the night in jail, as punishment for letting me play with the White kids.

And now they're saying, "Listen, let's all live together and be friends". So, of course, there's confusion!

Peace and justice go hand in hand. You can't have one without the other, you can't have peace without justice and in Australia today Aboriginal people have no peace and they have no justice.

Helen Corbett. Yamagee. (Corbett, 1987b)

The violence against Aboriginal people continues in European attitudes and government policies. Helen Corbett (1987b), a Yamagee woman from Ingrada country in Western Australia, stresses that the violence still isn't over:

There's a war going on against Aboriginal people. They're no longer poisoning our water holes or poisoning our food or giving us blankets covered with smallpox to wipe out our nation. But it's another form of genocide being practised against our people. Aboriginal lives are not considered valuable, they are not seen as the same value as White people's lives in Australia.

Joan Wingfield (1988b), of the Kokatha People, South Australia, speaking at Greenham Common Women's Peace Camp in Britain, explained the Aboriginal situation:

Our unemployment rate is six times higher than the national average, and we earn only half the average income of non-Aboriginal people. Our life expectancy at birth is twenty to thirty years less that for non-Aboriginals. The infant mortality rate is three times higher than the national average. On top of that, our young girls are being given a contraceptive called Depo-Provera which is banned because it causes infertility. This is to girls aged ten, eleven, twelve! Girls who haven't even thought of having a family! Also Aboriginal women are being given caesarean sections, just because doctors make more money from that. They are increasingly waking up to find their tubes were cut and tied, thereby preventing them from having any more children. So, the genocide that started in 1788 is still going on, only in more subtle ways.

The imprisonment of Aboriginal people is higher than for non-Aboriginal people, and is certainly higher than for South African Blacks [per percentage of population]. For years and years we asked the government to have a royal commission to find out why so many Aboriginal people are dying in police custody: what's the causes of death? If the same proportion of White people died in jails it would be seen as the massacre that it is, thousands would have been killed. We were consistently refused, until the bicentennial year, when the government wanted to be seen, by the international world, to be doing the right thing. An attempt to placate us, so that we wouldn't protest too much. They never gave enough money. Even for the cases of deaths in prisons. And we're also interested in the deaths that occur outside the cells, like those people who've been shot in the back in the streets, in their homes. When you think that they spent $26 million on finding out what happened to one White baby near Uluru [formerly Ayers Rock], then you know that Aboriginals are not equals in Australia today.

We're living in a very racist society. We have White people saying to us, "Well, how come you don't live like us?". They're forgetting a few thing. Firstly, that we don't have the economic means to do it, that's if we really wanted to. And secondly, that we've only been citizens of Australia since 1967. Before that time we couldn't vote, we couldn't work, we couldn't own land. We couldn't send our kids to school, and we couldn't go to cinemas, or swimming pools, or hotels. Or do other things that White Australians could do, unless we had a little piece of paper, a licence, from the government saying that we were a "White person". So, then we're expected to learn everything about White society in twenty years, how to speak the language and how to live like them! I doubt whether White people could go out into the bush and learn to live like Aboriginal people in twenty years, and learn our language, and learn our culture. I don't think that they could do that at all.

The events of January 1788 [arrival of the "First Fleet"] was the beginning of a new life for my ancestors. It marked the beginning of the end of the old way.

Erica Kyle. Bwgcolman. (Kyle, 1989)

If you find the mid-way point on the Western Australian–Northern Territory border, and then step into the setting sun, you find yourself in the most isolated region in Australia. This desert country of rolling, red sand dunes and vast plains of spinifex, graced by huge, red rock mesas, is the home of the Kukatja people. Amongst the last Aboriginal people to have contact with Kartiya [Europeans], the Kukatja did not begin coming into European settlements until the late 1960s, early 70s. Indeed, the Kukatja, insisting that the desert is "alive", say that there are still people living a traditional lifestyle, who keep away from Europeans. The last people who came in from the bush, as recently as 1984, stayed for a week and went back into the desert.

Nestled on the edge of a spectacular mesa, is Wirrumanu, an Aboriginal settlement, also known as "Balgo". A former Catholic mission, it is home to approximately 200–300 Kukatja, Ngardi, Jaru, Walmajarri, Wankajunga and Warlpiri people, and thirty Kartiya [Europeans]. It is a meeting place of cultures.

The elders of this community, remembering the life before the arrival of the Kartiya, have themselves experienced the massacres, the children being stolen, the attempts to destroy their culture. Today they live among the deprivation caused by that violence, in situations akin to any to be found in the Third World. But, a proud people, they maintain their culture.

Tjama Napanangka, a senior Law woman for the Ngardi-Kukatja people, remembering the old way, guides her community, with wisdom and courage, into the future. Her story moves through the coming of the Kartiya into her country to the present problems that have arisen as a result of their arrival (Napanangka, 1994):

First time Kartiya [Europeans] bin come in bush, in desert, my mother still young. She have me inside. They bin have ceremony – all the mothers, having ceremony for son. One old man, my grandpa, he bin come back from hunting. He bin see Kartiya with women, and big mob stockman [Aboriginal]. He bin get real angry. He worry for them women. Stockmen they bin say to my grandpa, "Hey, old man, don't throw boomerang. This Kartiya is no good, he too cheeky". My grandpa he bin say to Kartiya, "What you after? This my wife. Leave 'em!". "No!", that Kartiya bin say. Then my grandpa throw boomerang at that Kartiya. Kartiya bin get 'em rifle, and bin kill my grandpa. From there that Kartiya keep going, look around for more people. Go find another people, another place. Find another ceremony. That Kartiya bin take three young girls, take 'em home for self. And from there keep travelling to another soakwater, to another place. People there they bin have big ceremony. They bin get up, look. "Hallo, who come?" Some women they bin run to hill, keep watching, "What's that? Might be devil there". My mothers they bin run to hill. That Kartiya he bin take people away, take 'em away for good.

Alright. Another people they bin come out of ceremony, they bin follow that Kartiya. They bin tell everyone, "This Kartiya bin shoot one old man. We bin angry for that Kartiya. We gonna have fight". Big mob bin come, sons for my grandpa. They bin follow that Kartiya. My father bin really worried, my mother too. They bin in bush, they bin say to that Kartiya, "We gotta catch you now. You know why? You bin kill my father. We gotta kill you now". Everyone they bin fight that Kartiya. Fight really hard. Finish, that Kartiya.

Long time, another Kartiya come. Old people living in country, they bin have plenty bush tucker. That Kartiya come. Oh, that big mob people they bin run! Go in, the tree. And that Kartiya bin chase 'em, bring 'em back. Those people they ask him, "This country for Aboriginal people. Why you fella bin come here?". That Kartiya never understand, they bin talk language. "What for you come here?"

That Kartiya bin build house, Aboriginal people they bin watch. No clothes, no anything, nothing. He bring 'em bullock, bin shoot him, tell 'em, "You fella can eat". He teach 'em flour and sugar. People they bin work for that Kartiya. After that he give 'em tobacco. Ration. They learning little bit English. Young boys, they bin doing work, riding horses – stockmans. Still no clothes – women, old peoples. Stockman they bin wearing trousers and hat. They bin working for Kartiya. They bin bringing lotta sheep. Making well, mud house. They Aboriginal people from Halls Creek way. But people from this country [Kukatja], they bin run to cave, hide, some people. We don't like Kartiya. We bin live in country, eating goanna, kangaroo. 'Till I bin grown up little bit I never come close to Kartiya.

First time I bin see Kartiya, me and my sister we bin making mud. Waterhole. Me, little girl. We bin sitting down. I bin getting mud all over. My father and mother they bin sleep. Kartiya bin come up, horses. I bin run, wake 'em up. "Something there! *Lipi* [white]!" My mother she bin look – my mother bin run, *tiiwa* [long way], into spinifex. Kartiya bin round up all the people. Horses right round. We bin really shaking. "Okay, you fella run, to hill. Come on, get going! Run! Run really fast!" We bin run. My daddy bin carry me. That Kartiya bin throw 'em big stone. "Run!" We run to hill – long way. We bin get tired. Running. Running. Running. Running. One Kartiya and five stockman, but them stockmans they never stop that Kartiya – they too frightened. "Quick, run!", they bin say. We bin sit down on top of hill, watching Kartiya. That hill really high and high. We bin sitting down watching. We bin wait for my mother, she still running, she come around long way.

Another time, me, Marti and Bidi, we bin sit down and play. Mothers and fathers all bin go hunting. They bin look in bush, kangaroo. Kartiya bin come up. We go in under tree, all the sisters. We bin shaking and crying. That Kartiya bin wait, long time. He bin talking to us, but we never understand. We bin lay down and sleep. My father and Marti father bin come back from hunting, really hungry, "Hey, where all the kid? Where the kid gone?". And that Kartiya bin run and grab 'em. He bin ask, "You fella bin kill anything?". But my father and uncle they never understand. "Right!" They bin take my father, and Marti father, put chain on, round neck. That Kartiya bin tell 'em, "You bin kill 'em bullock". But never. He liar. For nothing wrong they bin put 'em chain on. They never kill anything. We bin sit down really hungry. We bin cry for two daddies. They pull 'em on chain, drag 'em. They bin take 'em and keep 'em for two days, and let 'em out. Everyone bin look, bin ask 'em, "What trouble? You fella bin kill 'em anything? Bullock?". "No, nothing. We bin sit down hungry. All the little kids bin cry, hungry one. We never kill anything." They Aboriginal people told Kartiya, "He not do anything wrong. He not kill 'em anything. You gotta let him out". They let 'em out. We keep going bush. We don't like that Kartiya. We keep going back to country. We bin living there for good.

We go bush sit down long way from Kartiya, long way. But still that Kartiya bin come, look around for people. I don't know what for. That Kartiya bin sit down long time ago. All bin making house now: Lake Stretch and Lake Gregory [once stations, now the communities of Billiluna and Mulan] and Balgo. We bin watching Kartiya build house. People bin talk, "Where from this Kartiya bin come? You fella seen him before, in this place?" "No! All bin come from nowhere. This country for Aboriginal people". "Why for they come to desert?". Still bushman bin come out [of desert] and that Kartiya still put chain on 'em. Look around and find 'em. Ask 'em, "You fella bin kill 'em bullock?". But we never say nothing. Can't understand. Every time that Kartiya bin come bush he bring trouble.

We bin sit down Billiluna, I bin little bit grown up now. Government bin taking all the kid. Kartiya kid, half-caste, away to school. They bin cut 'em out [term derived from mustering] from mothers. We run all the kids, my sister, and that Ivy and sister, whole lot. We bin go bush, sit down, hide. All the mother bin say, "You gotta go long way and sit down somewhere: the government gonna take you mob away to school". We run away. We bin come back before sundown. We bin come back to mother.

I bin big girl now. Mother and father bin take me to Tjaliwarn [Old Balgo]. We bin come out of bush and find 'em Kartiya. Catholic they bin come. Sheep, and chicken, nanny goat, donkey, everything. We bin sit down there. Make 'em windbreak, put 'em fire. No blanket, no clothes. Little cock-rag. No shame. One Kartiya woman she bin make dress. Not really dress – blanket.

Sometime we bin leave mother and father behind, we just follow Kartiya for tucker. We hungry for tucker. Some Aboriginal people, they bin work, making soup-soup. They bin sing out, "Come on, all you kid! You want soup-soup?". We bin run and get. They tell us, "You fella gotta go back mother". "No!" We never hear. Keep walking. One Aboriginal man got wagon and took us back to Old Balgo. We bin go back. Mother and father, they bin look, "Where you fella bin go?". "We bin follow that Kartiya for tucker." And every time they bin take 'em sheep, take 'em to another place, still we bin follow 'em. I don't know what for. "Hey, you fella gotta go back to Mother." We never listen. Nothing.

Then that father [priest], he come kill all the dog, so we go back bush. "Okay, we'll leave this place. Go back Yaka Yaka way. Find 'em soak water. Sit down four days, get all bush tucker – *karnti* [yam]." Then two fella bin come. From bush. Aboriginal. For ceremony. Tjakamarra and Tjapanangka [skin names]. They bin talk, "We gotta have ceremony". We go to another place, another soakwater. We keep travelling. We bin find 'em big smoke. We going long way. "We gotta go for ceremony, everybody", my mother bin say.

Two women they bin sit down dancing all night 'til sunrise. It really hard, that ceremony for share-'em out culture. People come from everywhere. All bin dance for three days. That two girls never sleep. They bin dance all night. Dancing all the way. Husband making big fire for wife. Fire in the middle. They bin dancing to fire and go back. All night. For three days. They share that culture. It is learning one. After, we bin come back to Balgo and bin have ceremony. My mother bin learning, now she bin teaching others from Balgo mob. Share 'em out. After that, all bin take 'em to Billiluna and share 'em out again, learning and teaching. When all bin learn 'em in Billiluna all bin take 'em to Stuart Creek, right up to

Gordon Downs. All the way. Share 'em out one culture.

After that we all bin sit down Billiluna. I bin growing up there. I bin get married, my husband, promise [marriage arranged at birth]. I'm big enough now. Sometime I leave [husband] behind. I run away. I frightened of man. I go back to mother. He come, get me. We go mustering, for Kartiya. Old people bin get 'em bullock, make 'em big fire. Cook 'em and eat 'em. And from there everyone say, "We go bush. Leave Kartiya". We sit down bush, for might be one year. Come back to [Old] Balgo. Catholic people. I bin learn Kartiya. I know now. Everything. We bin stopping there until I bin grow up proper. Just walking around a little bit. We bin learn work. After work we get ration. But no money. Just ration. We sleep in windbreak. Only two houses – toilet and kitchen. Sometime I get away. Take off. Hard work, I don't like. Sit down maybe three days. They come get me, "You want to work?". "Yeah." Too hard that work. One time Kartiya he belt me and other girls for not working. Beat me too hard. I just walk away. Sit down in camp. Next morning they bin come, "You want to come for work?". "No", I bin tell him. "I can't go back. You can do yourself." No one go work there. Really rotten job we bin doing. Hard work. From morning to dinner time. Washing, ironing, cooking, all the time. Get up before sunrise. I go to Balgo. Kartiya there he say, "You want to go Canning Stock Route?". "Yeah, alright. I'll be there."

I go three times on Canning Stock Route. Bidi and me, we doing cooking. Make 'em bread. Meat. And tea. Get dinner. Bring in horses. I bin riding camel. Three womans. Five hundred bullocks. Two Kartiya. Lots of stockmans. We bin go up front, cookie. Get up sunrise, making fire, making tea, cut 'em bread, cut 'em meat. Call up people for tucker. After, I go back and sleep. Sometime we dry camp, no water, and morning we ride up to well, fill 'em up water, straight away. Fill 'em up water in trough, for bullock and horses. My camel bin work hard. Fill 'em up water. Up and down, up and down, up and down. Riding camel. Get 'em wood. Cooking. On holiday, two days, we do washing. All the way. Every days, every morning, every night. Hard work. Right up to Wiluna.

From Canning Stock Route, I bin work Christmas Creek, for three years. Then I bin thinking, "I want to go back home". I bin walk to Billiluna, work there two years. Then [New] Balgo. When I get there Father bin say, "You want to work in Balgo?". I bin work in church. I bin living there for good. Four years. Then we have meeting for Mulan. We bin talk, "We gotta get that Mulan community. Aboriginal land". Big meeting. "Alright, you fellas can get that station." Lotta people go live in Mulan. Growing up little by little, that Mulan. Building houses.

But that father he don't like any culture. All the girls and boys, keep 'em in dormitory. Aboriginal children bin live in dormitory until they bin married. Keep 'em away from mother. Sometime they take 'em camping out in bush, might be two or three womans. Not teach 'em singing. He [priest] don't like. Only hunting. That's all. Not culture. Until they bin grown up, big enough. They married. They have wedding in church. Everyone be married in church. Then they can start ceremony for mens. No ceremony in dormitory. All here in camp, after dormitory. Then the people say, "Finish! No more dormitory!".

Balgo is little bit good place, now. Sometime boys they make trouble. They get 'em petrol and smell, or drunk. Only boys. Girls, nothing. Girls all right. I don't know why. Girls, they good. Mother and father don't look after properly, that why boys they make trouble. Mother and father gone for grog – Halls Creek, leave 'em behind, that's why they get mad. Before, in old time, boys bin make trouble, father he give 'em good hiding. Boys make trouble because they don't listen to Law. Ceremony can teach boys be good. Kartiya way make it hard for boys to grow up properly. Then boys get in big trouble, go to prison, maybe two years, or three sometimes. Them boys they gotta listen to Law, then they be good. Law teach 'em be quiet.

Sometime, when mother and father give 'em to married [arranged marriages], then he alright, no trouble. Sometime he worried, "What time I gonna married? I'm not little boy!". That why he start making trouble. Sometime, if little boy start making trouble, he get taken for culture, might be three weeks, and he listen. He say, "Oh, I bin culture. I can't make trouble". Some time they never listen. We tell 'em, "You fella got big Law, you gotta sit down, listen. You don't listen. You don't like culture. Big Law. You gotta learn listen, stop quiet. If you don't listen how you gonna learn strong culture?". If they don't listen they make trouble, then for sure they go to prison, maybe then they learn to listen.

Women's culture, *yawulyu*, really strong. I bin learn culture from my granny, from mother, in Old Balgo, when I bin young. I bin watch womens. All bin doing painting. Doing dancing. Teach 'em all young girls. Some young girl, they frighten. It's really hard, this culture, for the women. Sometimes they grab 'em, with the little boys, they start doing painting, dancing, with mother and aunty. Father they separate. I know culture now. I big enough. "Hey, you woman now. You want to come to culture, learning, dancing?", all bin say old people. "Oh, yeah!" Right. Old people bin take me bush for teaching. Do 'em painting. And do 'em dancing. After finish in culture, we can go hunting for goanna. We bin kill 'em goanna, present for old ladies. When I bin young, we bin come to [New] Balgo, old womens bin do dancing, bin share 'em *Tjipari*, and *Mina Mina*, and *Nakarra Nakarra* – every culture. We bin dancing and learning. We bin have big ceremony. Singing. All the mothers, for the son. Only the women. And old people they come and get tucker for the mens. And soon as they ready mens come. The people they talking, "All the mothers, they ready?". "Yes." The mother they paint up, they ready. That woman side. We sit down all night. All the man, old people, they come. We put 'em smoke – all the mothers. We bin have ceremony all the time. Separate from mens.

Women bin grow up with *yawulyu*, women's culture. They say, "This culture, for women's side, it's from *Tjukurrpa*, Dreaming. That's why we got to hold on this culture. We can't leave 'em. We gotta keep 'em for kid. Still teach 'em. What about grand-daughter?". That's why we hold 'em. And man, old people, they learn from woman side. They learn. They understand. Woman take it really hard and hard. Strong, really strong, more than man. If anyone gets sicks and from fighting they get 'em red ochre. Whatever, they put 'em red ochre. Old days, no medicine, only ochre. And this time, doctor do 'em in hospital, put 'em medicine, 'till long time they sick. But when they bin have this culture, before hospital, they bin fix quick. They get up and walk, is right. That's why we keep this culture really strong. We hold 'em really strong. Land and culture. Whatever bird, animal, he's culture too. Turkey, he's culture, goanna, anything. Whatever. Bush tucker is culture too. Strong culture.

But now women bin say, "We not really strong. Nothing. We not strong. Only men". Only woman is strong, not man. Only woman. We work really hard. That why we set up this Manungka Manungka [Women's Association]. To hold onto that culture, to hold onto the land. We all bin talk, all the womens, "What we gonna do? We gotta help Aboriginal women for the culture". So, we make *Manungka Manungka*. *Manungka Manungka* is *yawulyu*. Dreamtime. That *Manungka Manungka* woman [who kept this story] she bin pass away, and they bin lose this culture. That why we put this name, *Manungka Manungka*, to hold onto that culture.

In every one of us there is a severe and serious responsibility to protect these places [sacred sites] in which we are prepared to lay down our lives. In fact a lot of people have in the past, and will continue to do so in the future.

Barbara Flick. Gamalroi. (WWNFIP, 1987: p. 30)

British nuclear involvement in Australia took up where the initial Britain colonial invasion left off: on Aboriginal land! Uranium mining began in Australia in 1944 to serve British desires for their military program The British have destroyed sacred dreaming sites and desecrated land – at Rum Jungle in the Northern Territory, now a massive area of radioactive death, Mary Kathleen, Queensland, itself also deserted, and Radium Hill in South Australia on Kokatha land. This uranium was taken to Windscale (Sellafield) nuclear processing plant and the Aldermaston armament industry in England, turned into nuclear bombs and returned to be tested upon Aboriginal lands and people. That uranium mining continues today, at Roxby Downs, again on Kokatha land, shows that British oppression of the Aboriginal peoples is far from over.

The British military abuse of Aboriginal lands reflects that of the US, which maintains some of its most important command, control and co-ordination facilities in Australia. Facilities like Pine Gap and Nurrungar, essential to the US nuclear capability, are operated by the Pentagon without the consent of the Australian people. Aboriginal people, Helen Corbett (1987b) observes, are directly affected by the war games of the nuclear powers, from uranium mining to military bases:

It's Aboriginal people who are at the front line, who are suffering, because the mining is right there in the Aboriginal communities. It's not happening in the cities; it's happening on the doorsteps of Aboriginal people. And the same goes for installations in Australia which the Americans have got. Pine Gap is close to Alice Springs which is a very big Aboriginal community. With Nurrungar in South Australia, Pine Gap monitors the Indian Ocean and the Pacific for the US military. Those installations are sitting ducks, they're nuclear targets. Once again Aboriginal people are at the forefront because those installations are right there in our communities. White people aren't there – not the ones who make the decisions – they're down in the cities. It's our people who are victims again.

Joan Wingfield travelled to Britain in 1988 to tell the story of her people, the Kokatha, to the British company British Petroleum (BP) which is mining uranium at Roxby Downs. The Kokatha have experienced almost every aspect of the nuclear industry, from uranium mining at Radium Hill and Roxby Downs, through nuclear testing at Maralinga and Emu Fields, to military bases at Woomera Rocket Range (British) and Nurrungar (US), notable for its role in the US Star Wars program. It is a story that reflects, again and again, the continuing disregard by the dominating race for the first peoples of this land (Wingfield, 1988c):

My people were forcibly removed from our land in the 1950s because of the bomb testing at Maralinga and the rocket tests at Woomera. We were put in trucks and buses and scattered thousands of miles throughout the south of Australia. I should say that not all my people managed to escape Maralinga. A few of them died because of the actual bomb tests. Some who were in the area when the bombs were tested suffered blindness, my relatives can talk of that. Some of them suffered skin diseases, cancers and thyroid problems, unknown diseases, and they are still suffering today from illnesses largely attributed to the bomb tests.

So, having been removed from those areas, we came back in 1980 and said to the government, "We'd like to protect our religious places at Roxby Downs". Well, the government turned around to us and said, "You haven't been living in the area for so long, so you can't claim that you have an interest there. You haven't been practising your traditional ways, and because you haven't been there you've shown that you're not interested in the land". But they are the ones who moved us forcibly from the land. We had a very hard time to get our perspective included in the environmental impact statement. And even when we were successful, we had to have a White professor verify that what we said in our report was true. That it was Kokatha country and that there were sacred and religious places in that area. That was a big insult. We knew whose land it was, and we're not going to lie about that land, because if we're claiming other Aboriginal people's lands then we'd be doing the wrong thing by our traditional law. It's just another way they try to prevent us from having our rights.

The mining operation denies us our human rights. In the United Nations Convention [of Human Rights] it says that everyone's right is to practise their religion, no matter what it is. The mining operation prevents us access to our religious places, as well as destroying those places. Even before we got to the impact statement, forty to fifty of our sites in that area were destroyed, and they're still being destroyed today. There's no guarantee that further destruction will not happen.

They dug up a stone arrangement outside Roxby, and placed the stones outside the primary school. So when I went to the annual general meeting of British Petroleum I asked the chairman if he would dig up Stonehenge. Of course, he said that he wouldn't. That just goes to show his disregard for Aboriginal people, and our culture and traditions. His attitude was just typical of the way the mining companies in Australia treat Aboriginal people. He said that everybody's got sacred sites and some of these are going to have to be destroyed for the sake of "progress". He said, "For instance, we're looking at mining Pooh Corner!". Well, that's a kid's story! It was a big insult. He was equating that fictional story with our sacred stories and places.

That's just typical of multinationals. And they tell the government what to do. They make TV and newspaper ads that play on the basic racist feelings of White people and causes a lot of hysteria. They put on ads, like Black hands building a wall across Australia, saying that if land rights legislation went ahead it would mean that White people would have access to lands denied them by Black people. Never mind that access to our lands has been denied us for two hundred years. And that's not what we would have done anyway. Because we believe in sharing with everybody. We want to live side-by-side with White Australia. But the multinationals were successful, and national legislation still hasn't happened.

Why is Roxby important to us? I can't talk about the secret, sacred stuff because our tradition is still alive, but I can explain basically what Dreaming stories are. They are stories about ancient beings or animals that travelled across Australia a long time ago. And depending on what they did it made the different land forms, like why the hills and mountains are there and why the mineral deposits are there. Where the food sources are, and things like that. They are like mental maps. Our stories, our Dreaming stories were passed on from generation to generation. If you'd never been in an area before but had been told the Dreaming stories you could locate the waterholes and find food, or know where the mineral deposits are that you should avoid. It's a map in your head and helps you survive. Also Dreaming stories aren't just stories, they dictate to us how we should relate to each other, how we should relate to the plants and animals.

There's a saying we have, that we come from the land, we belong to the land, and we return to the land, and it's got to be left the same way it was when we came into the world. That we should only take what we need and no more, and certainly we weren't allowed to dig up the minerals from the earth. That was taboo. We say that the land is our mother, that the plants and animals are our sisters and brothers, so we're concerned about the harm that's being done to our mother and the damage being done to the plants and animals through mining operations, and through neglect by White people today.

At Roxby they're mining gold, copper, lead, silver and uranium. Well, the Dreaming at Roxby is sleepy lizard. In our language we call it *Gulda* [sleepy lizard]. The main shaft of the mine goes straight through the stomach of the sleepy lizard. When you open up the stomach of the sleepy lizard, in real life, you find the same colours that are found thousands of feet underground. You find the yellow of the gold, the silver and the copper colours inside the stomach of the real sleepy lizard. I think it's amazing how my people knew that those minerals of that colour were down there. How could we know? But somehow we did, and we knew that they were very dangerous. We were always told that if we ever went anywhere near the area, or if we dug it up, or harmed it in any way, we would get very sick, we would have a lot of vomiting and that we'd eventually die from it. I don't think it's any coincidence that our Kokatha people's stories and other Aboriginal peoples' sacred areas and stories give the same warning. This should be recognised by governments and mining companies. But they don't want to listen.

We Aboriginal people are trying to stop the mining of uranium, because if we can stop that then you won't have any uranium to fuel your nuclear power stations, and if you can stop the power stations then there's nothing to mine uranium for except nuclear weapons. We've all got to work towards stopping these things. Aboriginal people know that you don't need those things, because we've lived for thousands and thousands of years without nuclear power, without atomic bombs, and things like that. We're really worried about what's happening to the earth. We've all got to start working together for the earth and everything that's on it.

That's why Aboriginal people are strong. We've realised that we have a political right. We have started to enforce that right. It's our land, it's always been our land.

We were told by our elders not to disturb the place. Not to dig, not to touch anything because these things are very dangerous . . . The creation spirits they destroyed this evil thing and put it below and said no one was allowed to touch it. But when the White men came they wanted to put their hands on it for the sake of money and it is going to destroy nearly everything on earth.

Barbara Flick quoting a Yeerlirrie Elder.[2] (WWNFIP, 1987: p. 30)

---

2. The title "Yeerlirrie Elder" has been used because I have not been able to discover whether the speaker is still living. This has been done in respect of Aboriginal Law, which does not name a person after they are dead.

When Britain decided to get into the nuclear arms race, they chose to test their nuclear devices in Australia, as far from Britain as it is possible to get. Maralinga, Emu Fields (both in South Australia) and Monte Bello (in Western Australia) resounded with nuclear detonations. Many Australians, Aboriginal people and others, were contaminated by those blasts. Whole cities (e.g. Adelaide and Melbourne) were covered in massive fallout clouds that registered hundreds of times above the so-called "safe level". Vast expanses of Australia have been contaminated; particles of plutonium have been left blowing in the wind. Australians continue to pay the price for Britain's "nuclear deterrent".

In 1988, Helen Corbett (1987b) visited Britain in an attempt to alert the British people to their responsibility for the legacy of their testing program:

> That we're expendable: that's the mentality that was operating in the 50s when the British and Australian governments collaborated to do the bomb testing at Maralinga, Emu and Monte Bello. Monte Bello is very close to my home town in north west Australia. It's a small island just across from the mainland. During those tests the scientists got their weather conditions wrong – the wind moved the fallout cloud over the coastline where the people lived. When the scientists did their investigations to find out what effects the tests would have on people, and on animal and flora life, they decided Aboriginal people were not living in the area. The British scientists came up with the number of ducks, hens, pigs, cattle, sheep in the area, because they had statistics on them, but they didn't have any figures on the Aboriginal people, although they were the largest percentage of the population. Aboriginal people weren't considered human. We weren't counted in the government census until 1967. We've only been considered citizens since 1967. And that was only a result of Aboriginal people pushing for recognition.
>
> At Maralinga, which is in South Australia, it was the same. A large population there is Aboriginal. The government appointed one patrol officer to search for Aboriginal people, to remove them from the bomb blasting area. One! That man had to search for four years, in an area five times the size of Britain! It wasn't until four years later, that they appointed another patrol officer. Anyone who knows anything about the bush, knows that, when the rain comes, everything gets flooded in. Most of the time those patrol officers spent isolated and not able to move. They said that they had reduced the level of the bomb testing to what they called "Level A", because Aboriginal people, at that time, were living in a semi-traditional lifestyle. But the testing was twelve times higher than the bombs they dropped on Hiroshima. Those people who were from the test sites faced other problems. They were relocated. Different tribal groups were mixed together, and put into areas that belonged to other people. That caused a lot of social problems. A lot of the people of Maralinga were forced into Yalata Mission, and there were huge problems there.
>
> Recently, the Australian government did an inquiry into the Maralinga bomb testing, and found that there's something like twenty kilograms of plutonium still lying on the ground. That's ten times more plutonium than originally estimated. It was supposed to be buried by the British, but it wasn't, it's just blowing loosely across the land. That land is the land the Australian government gave back to the Pitjantjatjara people. It's their land, and they want to go home. But it will cost something like three million dollars to clean up, and the British and Australian governments are wrangling over who should clean it up.

Joan Wingfield (1988b) insists that it is the responsibility of both governments to clean up the land:

Maralinga?! It needs to be cleaned up by the Government. British, Australian? I don't care whose Government! They were both party to it, so both of them should clean it up. The British were in there forcing the things they wanted on Australian society. It's about time they just left us alone, and cleaned up their mess and got out of Australia. British society has been responsible for the destruction of a lot of people's culture. That's what they're doing at Maralinga. It's alright to come in and bomb us, but then they don't want to pay compensation to our ex-servicemen or civilians, to the Aboriginal people, or to fix up the country.

They can never really know how many Aboriginal people were killed by Maralinga because they didn't do a census. They wouldn't know. They couldn't know. We weren't even considered. Aboriginal people were expendable in their eyes. And that's the thinking – all Indigenous people are expendable, and our culture is expendable. That's why they can dig up uranium, mine our land – they don't have any respect for it. That's why they go and test bombs on Aboriginal people, on Tahitian people. That's why they go into Belau, into the Marshall Islands, dig up North American Indians' land. The same in South America and Africa. Because they think they are better than us. But they're not. Because we don't think like them. We don't think that we're better than anyone else. That's the first area of fault: when you think you're better than somebody else.

In 1993, the British Government finally agreed to pay half the cost required to clear the land of plutonium. The Australian Government would be responsible for the rest of the cost, plus compensation to the Maralinga people. This agreement was a direct result of the persistent demands the Maralinga Tjarutja elders presented to the British people and Government in many exhausting trips to Britain. A reversal of British rejection of its obligations – the British had understated the amount of plutonium left in the soil after its earlier clean-up attempt. The Thatcher Government had refused to provide vital documentation to the Australian government during its 1985 Royal Commission into British Nuclear Tests in Australia, and had, in 1991, ignored the request of the Australian Prime Minister Bob Hawke for a lump sum of A\$94 million. The clean-up, which will take six years, will attempt to clean up only a small part of the affected desert. The major proportion, 500 square kilometres, which is too contaminated, will be fenced off for a quarter of a million years. This is the decision of the Maralinga Tjarutja: their feeling for their land is too strong to allow it be to further desecrated by the removal of its top soil.

Aboriginal lives have already been damaged by the testing. Joan Clifton (1989), Elaine Yasseril (1989) and Gwen Rathman (1989) recall their experience of the Maralinga tests.

Gwen Rathman:

What happened at Maralinga? They chased everyone away. But not all the people went. They were the ones who got hurt. The White fellas wanted the land. They said there shouldn't be anybody living there, that it was waste land. But the people who lived there, they knew where to get food, where to get water. They was fat and healthy. But the Whites reckon there was nothing there. They wanted to use it for their atomic bombs.

Elaine Yasseril:

We was at Mable Creek [near Kupa Pidi/Coober Pedy] that time, when the bomb went off. We was busy working inside. People told us to look for the big cloud, but we didn't see it. Maybe the mens saw it, but we was busy working in the house – ironing, washing. But later, when the wind was blowing, maybe a week or something, that dust it come real black. It was real bad. When we used to go out to the bore [water hole] we used to see dead cattles everywhere, sheep, whatever. We reckoned it was the tests that was killing them. People got sick too. I remember I suffered eye trouble then. I still don't know what it was – it must have been the tests. I couldn't see the fire, couldn't go out in the sunlight. My eyes they was just burning. They said it was sandy-blight and gave us drops from the store. They only made it worse.

Gwen Rathman:

Some of the old Black men they used to say that the White men who was there had masks on but the Black men just stood there with nothing.

Elaine Yasseril:

You go around Mable Creek today, you see the trees. They're not the same as they used to be, you know. Real dry looking, not much leaf on it. Even after the big rains the trees didn't come on good.

Gwen Rathman:

One bloke got blinded from the tests. People died. Not only the Black ones, the White ones too.

Joan Clifton:

Same as at Woomera – the rocket range. No way in the world did they contact anybody, any Aboriginal people, when they built that rocket range there.

Gwen Rathman:

They was told to go. Even those ones working on the cattle stations. They never got any help. They didn't say, "I'll get you a job in Adelaide where it's safe". They didn't tell 'em. They never told them anything. They just said, "GO!". Yet the station owners they were still up there. Like the bombs only hit Black fellas!

Elaine Yasseril:

Like they was saying, they been hunted all out there. Spread around about. They didn't make one place where we could all be together. Kokatha people together. All families. Some ended up in Whyalla, Iron Knob, Port Lincoln, as far as Ceduna. All over the place. They pulled the community apart.

Joan Clifton:

Families were split up and kids were taken away by Welfare.

Elaine Yasseril:

> They took my childrens away. Fostered them out here and there. That was really bad. And when you want to go see them you got to have a pass to go to Adelaide. They was really mean about that. We'd go down for a day or a night, or something, and you'd only see half the kids because they was everywhere. Scattered. I still don't know where one of them is. She came back looking for me, but we was away. I don't know if she's still living, you know. It's hard.

Aboriginal children suffered in a unique and horrific way under White colonisation. They were stolen from their families and separated from their people in a deliberate policy of assimilation. The idea was to destroy their identity as Aboriginal people and to bring them up "White". It was an attempt to "breed out" the Aboriginal race. Between 1883 and 1969, in NSW alone, over 5,500 children were stolen from their parents.

Aboriginal children were isolated in institutions, missions, or White middle-class families, with little or (usually) no contact with their parents, and fed propaganda about the inferiority and vileness of their own people. Living under the control of harsh wardens, in conditions that often equated those of concentration camps, they were reared to service White society. Girls were trained as domestics, boys as station (farm)-hands, both as a source of cheap labour.

When they reached eighteen, they were "allowed" to go home. But many had been taken so abruptly when very young that they often had no knowledge of who their parents were, or where they came from. The only home they had ever known was the institution. Others had been successfully indoctrinated to think of Aboriginal people as dirty and dangerous. Those who did go back often found that their families had moved on or were dead. Others who were successful, found that they couldn't stay on the reserves, because there weren't any jobs, especially for the women. Many Aboriginal people are still searching.

Joan Wingfield (1988a) discussed her feelings at being separated from her mother and brought up in a European family:

> What did it feel like to be taken away? What did it feel like to be brought up "White"? It felt horrible! Really strange. You're a kid with black skin. You're not like the other kids, so you feel different. And then you notice that the other kids have relatives – grandparents, aunties, cousins – but you don't. Lots of things are different, so you always feel different. I felt terrible – until I went back and found my own family, and found that they loved me just as much as the White people loved their children, and that I had this wonderful culture, and that I was part of it. And that's when I started to really work hard for protecting what's left, because I realised that there's so many bad things in White society, that Aboriginal society seems so much fairer. It will never let anyone suffer. No matter who you are, they'll always try to help you, because that's the way of the bush. We have strict rules that make sure that people don't destroy society, like is happening with Whites. White laws are designed to protect the rich and their money. That's one thing about Aboriginal society, we didn't have material wealth. Everything was shared by everyone. And that's what should happen in White society, because there's no reason on earth why we should have people who are starving, or why people are homeless, because we can all look after each other.

[The 'Bi-centenary' is] a celebration of an invasion in which thousands of Aboriginal women were murdered and, of course, raped. A celebration of a thing as sad and distressing as what happened in the concentration camps. Black women particularly should not celebrate. They have lost more than anyone.

Faith Bandler. (Hutton, 1988)

Aboriginal women have carried the double burden of colonisation: racism and sexism. They are raped and abused. They have had their children taken from them. They have had to keep their families together, to provide for and protect their children. This is a common story for all women, particularly women in the exploited world, but it has a unique Aboriginal context. Joan Wingfield and Helen Corbett speak about the experience of Aboriginal women.

Joan Wingfield (1988a):

Colonisation of this land has been quite drastic for women. Their traditional roles are being altered; their power taken away from them by Aboriginal men using the power of the colonialist to their advantage and disrespecting Aboriginal women's rights. Our sacred sites are being destroyed; our kids are taken away from us in the past and even today in more subtle ways; we are losing Aboriginal women's culture – like traditional births, having them out bush – which in turn affects the traditional structure.

And then there's all sorts of problems, like being raped. By White men. Being gang raped. Being raped by police. There's a woman who has nine different kids to policemen. Rape wasn't something that happened in our society before. We're being beaten up. Those people who transgressed the Law, who raped and beat us, would be punished under our traditional Law, but that doesn't happen under White law. Our powers have been taken away.

Also, the money is given to the heads of the families, which in White law is the men. But in traditional Law, it's the women who are responsible for the children. They should be paid the social security payments, or the wages, because they're the ones who have to look after the children. But, instead, it's paid to the men, who go out and spend it, and consequently the women get very little money, and have to make do. It's the men who've got all the money, and the power that money brings. There are very few women who are wealthy, even in White society. And in Aboriginal society, the ones who've got the top jobs are the men. And yet there's many more qualified women who don't get the jobs. The men won't let them anywhere near them.

But, in the past few years, Aboriginal women are suddenly being more forthright, more political, and fighting for our culture and our rights to be respected. More so than for Aboriginal men, because we've lost more than them. We have! I mean, every time mining companies come out to talk about sacred sites, they never send women out to find out if there's women's sites there. Women never get consulted in this process. So, consequently, it's always men who have had their sacred sites protected, and not women.

Maybe women in the bush might have a say, maybe, but what about the urban Aboriginal woman – they're going to be the last of all. If you're Black that's hard enough. But if you're Black and you're a woman, you're way below the Black men. You're suffering twice as much as Black men. They suffer, but then they put us down, just like the rest of society does. Under traditional Law they couldn't do it! The White system is responsible for the way we are being treated today.

Women keep the culture. We've got a lot of educated women who have been keeping our culture strong, working hard for years and years. If they hadn't done that I don't think our society would be as strong as it is today.

Because the children are always in the company of women, that's where they learn their survival skills. Where they learn their language. Because women are always talking to them. That's where they learn the traditional way of life. And we've been doing that since the beginning of time.

I might add that men wouldn't be able to perform their initiation ceremonies without women. When the boys "go through the rules" it's the women who make the food, and keep the men going, through these lengthy ceremonies. So, we have an important role to play there too. As well as our own ceremonies, of course.

I hate saying it, because it seems like I'm disregarding everyone else's culture, but I think ours is such a rich culture. I'm very proud of it, very proud of being Aboriginal. There are so many wonderful things in our culture. Even after two hundred years of being massacred, and being taken away from our parents, and told not to speak the language, not to speak to other Aboriginal people, our culture has still survived.

They say Aboriginal women were inferior to men, having no say, belonging to the men. But that's not true. They say one man had lots of wives – that's a very limited view. Firstly, you've got to realise that it did make sense for a man to live with a number of women, especially after a war. It's one way to keep the population from dying out. But the women weren't there primarily for the man, for sexual gratification. They were there to help the other women. Bringing up the children, providing food, supporting each other. They are not owned. They wouldn't be there unless they really wanted to be. They could leave any time they wanted to. And they often did, to live in the women's camp, or whatever. And they can go with any person they like, which is quite different from White society, because once you're married to somebody you've got to stay with them for the rest of your life. But in Aboriginal society we are free. We still live in extended families, because that's the only way we can survive. That's the only way we've known. Helping each other to look after the kids. Grandparents, aunties, people like that, will always look after your children if you're not able to do it. And they're always around. For instance, my son would be called "son" by my sisters, and their kids are my "sons" and "daughters". Our extended families give us a lot of support – which is different from Whites.

In the old days there were single women's camps, where you'd go if you had an argument with your husband, or if you just wanted to be with women. If you had just given birth you'd stay in this camp until you were ready to go back. But the single women's camp is no longer there. There's no place where a women can get away from men today. There's no way to escape being raped or beaten. It all goes back to the fact that our traditional society is being destroyed, and the things we are suffering from today come down to that.

Another thing that they say about Aboriginal women is that the men always take the lead, and that the women are always subservient and walk behind. That's stupid! It's done because the women have to carry the children, walk with the children who can't walk as fast as the men. It's purely practical. And anyway, in some places the men walk behind the women, because just after menstruation women can smell the crocodile. So they walk in front.

Sure, men do have power over women, and they can be violent with that. There's domestic violence, for example. But the men are just learning to copy the White men's way. And it's the system. I mean, how can people live in big cities, so close to each other, with all this noise, and no peace and quiet? It's crazy. And then they're made to feel that they're second-class citizens, and aren't being given the chance to do anything about it. That's why women get raped and beaten up.

White women talk about feminism as if it doesn't exist in Aboriginal culture. Of course it does. We're all women. We all care about our children, and the future of our children's children. We Aboriginal women work together with the White women. But we work in a different way. We have our traditional Law. But basically it's the same, because we're all women. We all care about the same things, like what's been done to the land, and being dissatisfied with the way men have been running the show.

When I get together with other Aboriginal and Indigenous women it feels really close. We call ourselves "sisters". Because their society is much the same, they can understand a lot better than most Whites. It's just so much easier getting on with them, because you don't have to explain anything: they understand and accept. We're not all the same, we have differences but they can accept the differences without trying to change us to being the same as them, which is done by White society. Many Whites don't accept differences – they think they're better and that we should change to be like them. That's not right. No society has the right to impose their structures on another society. There is no need for it. We can all live side-by-side.

Helen Corbett (1987b):

Women have challenged what's been happening over the past two hundred years. A lot of women are running Aboriginal organisations, community organisations, that we, not the government, set up. Since the late 70s there's been a national movement built up, so now you can easily pick up a phone and ring anyone in the country. And it's Aboriginal women who are doing that networking and running our community organisations.

If you track back in history, the roles that Aboriginal women play are completely different than the roles women play in western society. The relationships between the sexes are different. You've got a hunting and gathering society, the women had their business and the men had their business, and you've got a White culture coming over and imposing White values on to that sort of society. "Men have to be the breadwinners." "Men have to look after the family" – play that nuclear family role that is completely different to the extended family system. A lot of Aboriginal communities were matriarchal. You've still got those. I still have very little to do with my father's side. But, you've got this White image of men's and women's roles placed on to our society. And that causes a lot of problems.

They say Australia is a lucky country, but lucky for who? It's certainly not Aboriginal people. It's Aboriginal women who are having their kids die at such a huge rate – we have one of the highest rates of infant mortality in the world. The laws are so discriminatory against Aboriginal people that it's us that are in the jails. There's a very high percentage of Aboriginal women, compared to White women, in prison. So people have to rely on the extended family network. Black women can get jobs more easily than our men, we get all the dirty jobs and get paid less. That's part of the "protection" era, when Aboriginal women were taken away as kids, and raised in homes where they learned how to work as domestics for White women. This policy came about mainly during the Second World War. Men went away to fight in the army, White women took over the managerial jobs, the migrant women who usually had the domestic jobs moved into the factories, the munitions factories, and there was the gap for Aboriginal women.

So Aboriginal women were able to get more jobs and dare that bit of independence from men, and you start getting a strong women's movement. Whereas men were largely kept out of that. They've got no role to play, or in the Black community there is a role for them, but like in White society, it's very limited. Most of the men are in a cycle of despair. If we look at four Aboriginal men when they're forty: one has died; one is in a circular path of alcohol, homelessness and prison; one is institutionalised in jail; and one has been successful and married into the non-Aboriginal community, and because of pressure doesn't relate back to the Aboriginal community.

There's been attempts in the late 70s, by the government, to employ Aboriginal men in key positions in policy-making areas. All that thinking about Black women being castrators of Black men and matriarchs! Your stories of contact are the same as those experienced by other Indigenous peoples throughout this continent, and the ocean region. But, here, the older people are the ones who have been through all the community organisations. That's where all the action is taking place, not with the policy makers. There are some men who know not to mess with Aboriginal women. They know it's the Aboriginal women who are the activists, and there's respect for that. No way would they go and bulldoze through to put their own views across. But another element there is chauvinism, Black chauvinism, amongst Aboriginal men towards Black women.

Look, one of the things we rarely talk about is the division between sexes, because we've got to unite. We know sexism is there. We know that Aboriginal women get raped by Black men. We know things like incest happen. We know all that. But racism is so sharp, that it's at the forefront. That's one of the reasons why you don't get many Black women coming into the women's movement in Australia. Aboriginal women realise they've got the same issues as White women, but we've got to unite against racism as one people.

Aboriginal people are building self-determination within our own communities. We are surviving the killing times.

Helen Corbett. Yamagee. (Corbett, 1987b)

One example of women organising, against great odds, to better the social and political environment for their people, is found on Palm Island, an Aboriginal island community out from Townsville in Northern Queensland. Erica Kyle (1989) outlines the history and difficulties of that initiative against a poverty and a racism that White Australia attempts to relegate to the so-called Third World:

Palm Island was set up in 1917 because the government wanted to use the lands of many different tribes for sugar cane and cattle. Because our people were powerless, they just moved wherever they were made to move. It was either you moved or got shot, or jailed. It was the "out of sight – out of mind" policy: put Aboriginal people far away.

My tribe is no longer a tribe in anything but name and kinship. We were a coastal people, but we were moved when they were bringing the cattle up from down south. So that the cattle had land we were moved to the Townsville area, to the Hull River Mission near Innisfail. But it wasn't just one tribe – it was happening everywhere. Lots of people coming to Hull River. They brought in people from the west. I remember my mother telling us stories of the old people at sundown, sitting on the beaches crying because the sunset reminded them of the west. If you think of how those people were forced to eat sea food! Their diet was kangaroo. They were forced to change their diets. Many of those people died of a broken heart. There were forty different tribes. It's like sending Italian, German, Japanese and so on together and saying, "You live here now and you get on". They hoped we would all die off or kill one another. There were fights between the different tribes, but we managed, we came together and survived through that. Then in the early 1900s a big hurricane came and flattened everywhere. I don't know why they didn't rebuild there, but that was when we were moved to Palm Island.

I'm proud that my grandparents and others went to Palm Island and proud that I was born on this beautiful island. We now call ourselves Bwgcolman – that means people of Palm Island. But we lost the different languages, the dances, the culture. We struggled to keep them and we're reviving them again. And then, there's the people's spirituality. The big tree [on Palm] is a very special place, we used to see a special spirit there. It is an important part of the life of the community. We lived with the spirit world, the Dreaming. Today all that is gone. There's an emptiness, a void, in our lives.

But Palm is a community that's struggling for its independence. It's time to take hold of our situation, our dreams, a time of healing. And Aboriginal women are in the front of that change. We have always been the strength of our society. All around Australia we have always played a very strong role.

My mother was seven years old, and my father was nine, when they were brought here. So they grew up here. But, because my mother's skin was lighter, she was put into a dormitory. They separated them from what they called "full bloods". That was the government policy, separating and breaking up the family. So my mother didn't know her mother that well. They married on Palm, and raised a family of thirteen. It was a time when there was very strict control. Our men woke up in the morning, the bell rang for them to come to work. A bell rang for them to go home and have lunch, to go to work again, to go to bed, even. Worst of all, our people liked to go fishing at night and while they were out there, along the reefs, the bell would go, which meant that they had to go back and go to bed. I remember one of our women saying to me, "Look, this night we went out and we were catching fish, and so when the bell rang everyone knew that they had to be off the streets. We said, 'Oh, blow it! We're not going to listen to them!'. And so we finished our fishing and when we came in there were police lined up with torches". That's the kind of control.

I remember my mother saying that the child endowment, an allowance for mothers with children, used to come to our community, but went to the administration and our mothers had to line up to get eggs, milk, rations. Well, my mother weighed it up and said, "We've got our own fowls, we've got our own vegetables, we got plenty of fish, and we have fresh milk from the cows. I'd like that money to go into my hand so that I can go and buy some clothes". She asked the women at that time to go with her to put the case forward, but when the time came she was the only one there. The changes came, but the administration made it very hard for my mother. I think that's where I got my strength, from her – to stand up even though it's difficult. And it was very difficult for her, so difficult that she had to leave Palm, had to get away from that control.

There's problems. We have very little employment, young and old. We would like to have more positions, better positions for our people. For example, the White hospital does not take into account our identity, does not consult with us. Women want to move out of domestics into other areas. It's happening. More and more women are in the workforce today. But all the positions of power are mainly held by non-Aboriginal males.

The conditions on Palm are not good. Our people have got nothing. *Nothing!* It's a cycle. You leave school, get pregnant, and have one baby after another. The men are off looking for another woman. They don't see any responsibility to care for their children. So grandmothers are left caring for the kids. It's really hard to bring women together, because they're held back by jealous husbands. The problem comes because the men have been stripped of their role in Aboriginal society. They feel: "You've taken everything from me, you're not going to take my woman!". I work with the women to tell them that, "You are an individual. You have a right to do what you want to do". I'm seeing changes now. Women are saying: "I want to do this. I want to do that". Some have made a bigger stance and moved right away from the community, have vowed never to come back, because it's been such a terrible experience.

In 1986, we set up the Palm Island Women's Centre, to stand up for the rights of our women. It was a time when there was a lot of fear towards the men. The men ruled. They ruled the council. They had all the jobs. They ruled with an iron fist in the homes. So we set up the centre to say: "You ain't going to hurt our women any more!". The message was out. A very quiet message, but the violence dropped in a matter of three months. Dropped drastically. We were warned that the men would retaliate. But what could we do? We had to stop the suffering. The men got the message that the women weren't going to take it any more.

You've got to understand why the men treat our women like that. It's the effect of colonisation. The spirit of the men was broken in 1957 through their stand for better conditions. There was a group of seven men who said, "We want better conditions. We want better wages". It was the first big strike in Australia in a place like Palm Island. They were determined that there was going to be no work until they got what they asked for. The government got the police to come in in their fast boats overnight, and, in the early hours of the morning, they went and took these men and sent them away to different communities all over Queensland. Their families were sent with them, they were never allowed to return to Palm. They broke up the leadership completely. Six out of the seven turned to be bad alcoholics, the seventh a fanatic about religion and change. It broke the strength of our men. It is very difficult, even today, to get our men active and involved because of that fear. And then alcohol came in. All the men could do with their anger was take it out on those closest to them. There were so many examples of it happening. You take your anger back to the home. And with all that alcohol it was just one big explosion.

In 1967, the Australian government had a referendum, and asked Australian people if they would agree to the federal government looking after Aboriginal people. The Australian people said, "Yes!". But it's never happened. We still have to work with the state government. Anyway, what followed was that they were going to "give Aboriginal people on Palm their rights". It wasn't their right to make their own decisions about their community – it was the right to drink alcohol! Forty women got together at the time and said, "We don't want that here. It's going to do so much harm to our people!". They put the canteen up anyway, and restricted the drinking hours from five to seven o'clock. And so people sat around all day – no work, no say in their lives – and at five they went to the canteen where they'd drink, drink, drink, drink. Trying to drown out the bad feeling. And at seven, when they went back into the community, violence erupted. All that caused very, very severe suffering. I used to live next to the canteen and so I thought, "What can I do?". I got together with six other women and we decided that we would get some control over our land. Things had got to the stage where something had to be done.

It was from that little group of women that we began to get strong. Things began to happen. We started off giving ourselves a little newsletter so that we could pass information around. It was called, *We the People*, so that people would feel a part of it. But even the fear of taking a piece of paper and reading it – coming through all that history. They'd fold it away. But I knew that they read it, because the feeling was starting to get around. Strong. People started to see changes. Small, but they were there.

The women emerged out of it all. We have continued to survive and demand our right, and justice. It is always women who will come together, because they have been through so much. There was a time when our women were pushed to the limit, they took their lives through kerosene, petrol. Those who didn't do that are still very strong, still very concerned. The strength of women is talking one to one. We've got to encourage each other, because we carry a lot of pressure.

We want to see that we have a better quality of life, keep the homes together, get our kids through an education system that is not the system we have chosen. And we must try to help those in prison, in the parks. We want better education. better health and legal services. We want to see something done about the police. We want better goods for us to buy – and cheaper. Everything is so expensive. We are poor people and we are tired of being poor, not even having enough beds in the family. People don't know where to turn. They're really bogged down, trying to get through one day at a time.

It is women who must be everywhere. It is women who are everywhere.

Melanesians do not leave their own land and family responsibilities easily.
Evatt Memorial Foundation. (1989: p. 10)

South Sea Islanders are another people who, while not indigenous to Australia, have suffered from Australian imperialism. Descendants of the Islanders beyond Australia's shores, they were taken as "indentured" labourers to the sugarcane fields of Queensland and northern New South Wales, between 1863 and 1904.

Over 60,000 women and men were taken from the Solomons, Vanuatu and Fiji, some even from as far away as the Marshall Islands, Kiribati and Tuvalu (Maude, 1985). Many were "blackbirded" (kidnapped). A few came by choice. All were "Kanakas", forced to live and work in slave-like conditions for the benefit of European Australia. Australia's sugar industry was built on the blood and sweat of these people. A submission by the Evatt Memorial Foundation to the Australian Commonwealth Government "on behalf of the South Sea Islanders" states that:

Now known as the "blackbirding" era those years produced incalculable distress to the island communities, souring relations between Europeans and Indigenous people for decades, and condemning thousands of victims to disease, slave-like working conditions and race discrimination (Evatt Memorial Foundation, 1989: p. 5).

Women were in high demand and were often sold for twice to three times the price of men as they could be used to propagate more labourers. Although the Islanders resisted, (in the Solomon Islands it was war between Islanders and the Europeans), their spears and clubs were little protection from the European guns. Few "recruiters" worried about how many Islanders they killed, many were also involved in the head-hunting trade – if they killed someone they could still make a profit. Stories abound of whole communities murdered.

In 1901, the year of Australian federation, one of the first acts of the new Commonwealth government was to formulate the "White Australia Policy", which, until it was revoked in 1967, insisted that white skin be a prerequisite for citizenship. The union demand of "Jobs for Whites" brought an end to the trade in human lives, and by December 1906 most of the Islanders had been "repatriated". But it was not a case of returning individuals to their home islands. Many had been born in Australia. Those who did come from the islands were often dumped anywhere, and if they arrived in hostile country, they risked being killed. Those who did return home, carried diseases with them that further depleted their already depressed communities. The 1,500 to 2,000 Islanders who, either through exemption or hiding, stayed in Australia were marginalised along with the Aboriginal people. Forced to live as fringe dwellers, they survived through a subsistence lifestyle. Their children are today's South Sea Islanders busily reclaiming their culture and history.

The price paid by the South Sea Islanders has been immense. Their cultures have been distorted – they have lost their lands, and with that much of their heritage. As a social and political force, as a separate people, they are often ignored. They are subject to discrimination, having their unique history erased by being expected to assimilate into a "multicultural" Australia. There is little understanding among the general Australian population of the difficulties which challenge the lives of the Islanders. According to the Evatt Memorial Foundation:

... the Islanders do not have the benefits of their own strong culture with its deep roots in their own soil. They have been completely disenfranchised from the Melanesians' most important birthright, their land. This crucial issue is not generally understood. Land, as it is to Australian Aborigines, forms a vital link for Islanders with their ancestors as well as providing their own survival. Without their land, a vital cultural support, Islanders suffer much greater marginalisation than immigrant groups from countries with different cultural traditions. Islanders and their descendants, should not be classified along with various ethnic migrant groups which have come to Australia during its history. These cultural supports do not disappear in a few decades ... Islanders should not now be expected to assimilate, as they have in the past ... all minority groups are given specific rights to maintain their culture by International Human Rights Instruments through the United Nations Organisation ... The Islanders are ... caught in no man's land, through no fault of their own. They are discriminated against due to their colour ... and they are denied the benefits given to

> Aborigines – welfare, land rights, education assistance etc. Culturally they are strangers, yet born in this land with a parentage further back than many white Australians (Evatt Memorial Foundation, 1989: pp. 7–8).

Another people indigenous to Australia, who have a parallel and yet also distinct experience of colonisation, are the Torres Strait Islanders. Their seventy islands stretch like stepping stones between Papua New Guinea and the Australian continent. Traditionally, the Islanders have had cultural contacts with the northern Aboriginal tribes, although they are more culturally aligned with Papua New Guinea – not only materially but also with strong language bonds.

The first European to visit their islands was the Spanish navigator, Torres, who, in 1606, gave his name to the region. During the eighteenth and nineteenth centuries, the Strait was used by ships sailing between Europe and India. It was increasing exploited for its rich resources of trochus, pearlshell and fish. Jeremy Beckett, in his book *Torres Strait Islanders. Custom and Colonialism* (1987: p. 33), records that women were abducted to "serve the sexual needs of their foreign crews".

The London Missionary Society (LMS) arrived in 1871, and proceeded to ban dancing and destroy sacred places. Islanders were forced to clothe themselves, and headhunting and infanticide (a practice largely caused by economic factors imposed by colonisation) was ceased (Dept of Aboriginal Affairs, 1988). Forty years later the LMS left the "heathens" to the Anglican Church, which began to take on Islander-style church services and encouraged the indigenous language. Christianity has become a major element of Torres Strait Islander culture.

In August 1879, the British annexed the islands, administering them through their Queensland colony. Upon federation of the colonies in 1901, the islands were ceded to the Commonwealth of Australia. In keeping with their policy of "protection" of the Indigenous inhabitants, the Australian government then isolated the islands and began to exploit the Islanders as a cheap labour source for the pearling industry. The process of dependence was continued as the self-sufficiency of the Islanders was broken down. In 1967, with the abolition of the White Australia Policy, the restrictions were finally lifted and thousands of Islanders, mostly males, left their homelands in search of employment in Queensland. This left a high predominance of women and children in the home-islands, especially on Saibai Island where women outnumber men by 80 per cent. By 1988, two-thirds of the Torres Strait Islander population lived on the Australian mainland, under conditions akin to those experienced by the Aboriginal people.

The Islanders are moving for self-determination. They insist that by the year 2001 the Australian government should grant them self-rule that would recognise their right to form their own parliament, have greater control over the delivery of services, and the power to determine policies which affect their natural resources. This would be a step towards eventual independence. The Australian government, reluctant to lose control over the strait because it straddles Australia's sea route to the Middle East and provides a defence buffer zone to the continent's northern shores, has warned that independence would result in the withdrawal of services, including welfare upon which the Islanders are presently dependent.

It's time for a new change. Where is our culture within [the White man's] lifestyle? It is now time to look at a better system. We know that we must live together, White people and Black people. We want justice. We want to have our land.

Erica Kyle. Bwgcolman. (Kyle, 1989)

The three hundred Meriam people of the Murray Island in the Torres Strait instigated changes that promise to restore their ancestral lands to the Indigenous peoples of this continent.

Wanting to administer their own island, they took a land claim to the High Court of Australia. On 3 June 1992, they won the "Mabo" case and changed the course of Australian history. Their traditional ownership of their island had been recognised, and with it the native title of all Indigenous peoples governed by Australia.

This was a major moment in Australia's history, because it was the first time that prior native ownership of land was recognised. It was the first time in over two hundred years that the European immigrants officially recognised that the Aboriginal and Torres Strait Islander peoples were the original inhabitants, and therefore owners of the land.

The finding of the highest court in Australia shook the foundations upon which the continent had been settled. Abolishing, once and for all, the myth of *terra nullius*, it undermined the power of the squatocracy that has dominated this country for 200 years. Under a regime of death threats, misinformation, racism and intolerance, mining and pastoralist companies, and other vested corporate interests, lobbied Commonwealth and state governments against "Mabo". Some state governments lobbied the Commonwealth government. Meanwhile, Prime Minister Paul Keating was making statements that recognised the crimes of dispossession and murder committed against the Indigenous peoples, and the institutional and individual racisms that continue today. He was the first Australian prime minister to do so.

For a moment, it seemed as if the government would side with the corporate elite. The High Court had ruled that the Queensland government, as administrator of Murray Island, could only extinguish the Meriam people's claim to their land provided it did not contradict any existing laws of the Commonwealth, in particular the Racial Discrimination Act, 1975. Demands were made that the Commonwealth government nullify its commitment to the International Convention on the Elimination of All Forms of Racial Discrimination, which it had ratified in 1975. Indigenous people met around the continent, determining what compromise if any they would be willing to make, and what to do if the government failed in its obligation.

Then, on 2 September 1993, over a year later, and twenty-five years after the Indigenous peoples were first recognised as citizens of Australia, the Commonwealth government made its landmark decision. The Racial Discrimination Convention would be honoured. Indigenous people still had no veto over mining companies on their lands but the companies could only mine under negotiation with the traditional owners, and mining leases validated after 1975 would not extinguish native title. A national land acquisition and management fund would be established, and those peoples who could not access their lands would be compensated. A comprehensive social justice package would be established with the aim of overcoming the continuing social and economic disadvantage that Indigenous Australians have faced as a result of European arrival and the stealing of their lands.

Time will determine to what extent these obligations and promises are fulfilled. European Australia has the opportunity to regain its dignity by the active recognition of the abuses that have continued for over two hundred years. The recognition of the rights of Indigenous Australians is inevitable. Australia, as a nation, has the chance to walk proudly into the twentieth century – will it take up the challenge?

IN THE BEGINNING WAS THE DARKNESS

Kiri Potaka-Dewes (1989)

We come from a long way back. We in Aotearoa can trace our beginnings right back to the Dawn of Time. We have in our songs, in our chants, in our prayers, the references to the beginnings of our people. We trace ourselves back to the heavens of the gods.

In the Beginning was *Te Kore*, the Darkness. In our rituals and songs we recite an incantation that refers to the Beginning of our people. It talks about *Te Kore*. The Darkness turning, the Darkness changing, the Darkness moving. And the Darkness thrusting forth into *Te Ao*, World of Light. And it is telling us to Seize the Light, seize that moment, grasp the Breath of Life. If you ever come to my people's country you will hear this incantation over and over again.

Our women claim to be the first of the mortal race, of the mortal world. The world began with the women, the world ends with the women and in the long run everything that matters is because of the women. We are the beginning and we are the end of life.

So we have a very special place in Aotearoa. The women have a very special place. We call it *Mana Wahine*. The dignity of women.

Our mythology begins with *Rangi*, the Sky Father, and *Papatuanuku*, the Earth Mother, held together in a clasp which was unending. And the children born of the two struggled in the darkness, and so they gathered together and plotted and separated the two. The Sky Father was sent asunder and the Earth Mother was left out here. And so the world was created.

Then the children of *Rangi* and *Papatuanuku* decided to create people, ordinary people, and they created them through the formation of a woman's body. They copulated with the woman's body and the first issue was a woman. And so we say in our mythology that the beginning of our race was a woman.

When this woman was an adult, she discovered that her lover was her father, and because of that she fled to the underworld and has become for us the Goddess of Death. Everyone who dies goes back to her. So, she both began it and she ends it. And we know that when our time is over we go back to her.

One of our favourite stories of the creation of our country is of Maui fishing up a turtle that carried Aotearoa on its back. Now Maui was very skillful, but he couldn't do it unless he had access to his grandmother's jaw bone. It was her jaw bone with its magic, with its strength, with its power, that enabled him to pull up Aotearoa. That's one of the myths we have about the beginning of our islands.

Today we have to reclaim all those stories. So many of them. All about women. They're beautiful stories. But I can remember in my childhood at school only learning about this guy who did it. I never learnt that he couldn't do it unless he went to his grandmother.

And so we have to rediscover the stories, we have to rewrite them, retell them. And they are beautiful stories. We need to reclaim that. We are doing that very actively. Against all kinds of pressure. And that's a difficult struggle and it's one of the struggles that we have in common with you.

The women still hold an important place in our community. The big issues of today are in fact led by women, ordinary women, women who have had children and are grandmothers now. And they have worked, and done the washing, and everything. They haven't had the sort of education I have had, and others like me. They are the ones who lead the land marches, the ones who tell us where it's at, how to get rid of all the other bits, the superficial bits, where the *take* [mandate] must be, that is, where the issue really is. It's they who teach us not to be distracted by other things: that in the long run our land is where we're at, that if we lose that then we've lost everything.

So, Papatuanuku, the Earth Mother, is a very real woman for us. Very real. When I was born the afterbirth was taken and buried in the soil where we were all born. All my sisters and brothers, all my mothers and grandmothers, my fathers and grandfathers. The afterbirth was buried into the Earth Mother. That's where we belong. I know where I come from. Wherever I am in the world I can say, "There is my placenta – there! That's where I belong. I am a part of the earth". It's not just a dream. It's real. For us it's real. So when we talk about the land, it's not just a political issue, it's not just an economic issue. It's an issue of our survival as a people. As a people distinct from any other people in the whole world.

A Partnership Denied

– Aotearoa/New Zealand –

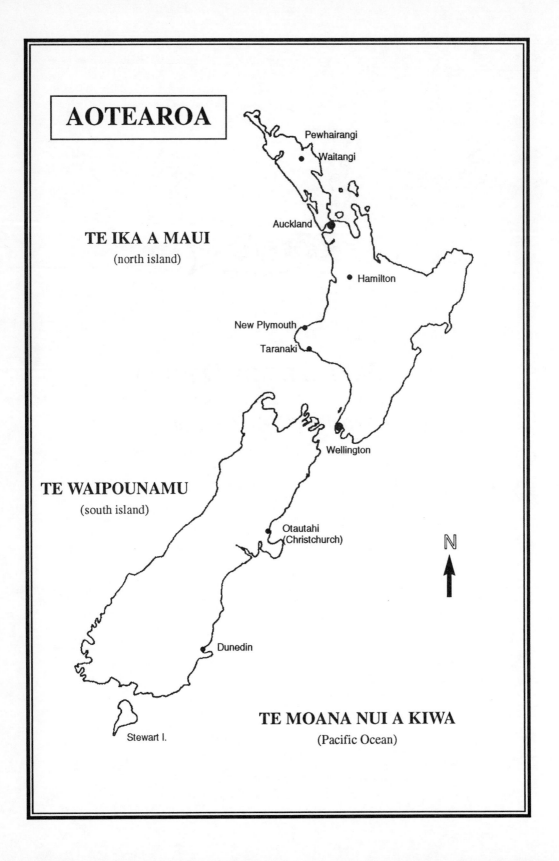

AOTEAROA

Pewhairangi

Waitangi

TE IKA A MAUI
(north island)

Auckland

Hamilton

New Plymouth

Taranaki

Wellington

TE WAIPOUNAMU
(south island)

Otautahi
(Christchurch)

N

Dunedin

TE MOANA NUI A KIWA
(Pacific Ocean)

Stewart I.

It is difficult for most people to understand the Maori situation if you don't live in Aotearoa because on the surface it looks as though everything is wonderful. But we have had the guns. We have had the bullets. We have had the British military. We've had the confiscation of land. We've had the introduction of diseases and sickness that caused the almost death of our people. And what we have now is sheer survival. The survival of the race.

Nganeko Minhinnick. Ngati Te Ata. (Minhinnick, 1989)

Aotearoa, the Maori name for New Zealand, was first colonised, and later annexed, by the British, predominantly to keep it out of French hands, as the empire builders vied to gain control over the region.

Titewhai Harawira describes her country before the Europeans came:

Aotearoa is the name that my people gave to our country and means the land of the long white cloud. For thousands of years First Nation people have lived in harmony with the earth, the sea, the trees, the animals and lived in harmony with one another. We are of the land, from the land, and our countries belong to us. For thousands of years we have worked as Maori people to nurture the land, to develop the land, and to trade with the rest of the First Nation people throughout the Pacific. In trading we learnt the languages of our neighbours, we learnt their cultures and their lifestyles (WWNFIP, 1987: p. 34).

Then the Europeans came. The first to arrive was Abel Tasman who, never setting foot on the land, named it after his home province of Zeeland in the Netherlands. Over a hundred years later, in 1769, Captain James Cook made his appearance. His introduction of European culture to the Maori was far from pleasant. Landing in Pewhairangi (the Bay of Islands) he killed ten Maori, (two for refusing to answer questions!), before departing to carry news of his rich discovery home to Britain. This contact was soon overshadowed by the arrival of French Captain De Surville, who burnt the nearest village and kidnapped their chief Kinui for "stealing" a boat. He was followed by more French who raped the local *wahine*, women. The Maori retaliated by killing their captain. The French responded by massacring two villages. Such was the beginning of Maori-European contact.

Only twenty years after Cook, in 1792, settlers began arriving to exploit the land rich in timber, flax, seals and whales. By 1815, sealers from the colony of New South Wales, Britain and the United States had almost wiped out the local seal population: one United States ship carried off 60,000 furs to markets in the north. The trade quickly changed to whales and the devastation repeated. During the 1820s there were 130 whaling stations churning out whale oil; the industry had to be abandoned within ten years. The settlements which grew up around the mills rapidly distorted the life of the Maori.

In 1839, the call "Ships, Colonies and Commerce" echoed through London's chambers of commerce. The New Zealand Land Company, enticed by the rich, fertile islands larger than Britain, laid claim to twenty million acres within three months. It was difficult for the Maori to understand that these strangers were intending to do the impossible: to alienate Maori land, communally passed on by the *tupuna* (ancestors) and held in trust for the future generations. The company, wanting protection for their land grabbing, lobbied the British government to annex the islands. Although initially reluctant to claim the colony, Westminster succumbed when the church, wanting title for the large parcels of land it had itself acquired, added its voice to the demands. The deciding factor was the interest being shown in the islands by France and the United States. On 29 January 1940, seven days after the first load of settlers descended on the *whenua* (land), Captain Hobson arrived to annex the archipelago within the political boundaries of the Colony of New South Wales. In a matter of days, on 6 February, Hobson initiated the Treaty of Waitangi: a document designed to ease the movement of British settlers into the Maori lands.

Conflict over land was inherent in the British government's attitude to Aotearoa. Occupied with the loss of America, fighting the French and colonising Australia, the British paid little attention to their new dominion. In keeping with the Treaty, Hobson immediately proclaimed that only land issued under the British queen's authority would be recognised, and that it would be amply paid for, but there were no funds forthcoming from London. His hope was that the demise of the Maori nation, already suffering horrendously from introduced diseases, would make land available. Meanwhile, however, the New Zealand Land Company kept sending shiploads of colonists with the false dream of an endless supply of free land. These events caused panic among the immigrants who rebelled against the arrogance of the British overlords. The uprising was suppressed but antagonism towards the Maori increased. And so began the battles, known as the "Maori Land Wars", by which Pakeha (Europeans) set about seizing Maori land.

By 1845, the British military presence had been increased to enable the enforcement of land "sales". Land was taken either by direct confiscation through a series of legal acts, or it was seized. The 1863 Suppression of Rebellion Act proclaimed all resisters as "rebels" to be punished by "death or penal servitude", while granting immunity to the military committing atrocities in the name of the government. The New Zealand Settlement Act allowed the confiscation of any land belonging to any tribe or group of Maori which the "Governor was satisfied had engaged in rebellion" (WWNFIP, March 1990: p. 15). Millions of acres were stolen from around Taranaki, Waikato and the Bay of Plenty. In 1862, the Native Land Act abolished the Crown's right to pre-emption in land purchase. Three years later, they abolished the right of collective ownership of land, so basic to Maoridom. By 1901, one-third of *te Ika a Maui*, the North Island, had been stolen. Today the Maori nation controls only three per cent of the total land area with 50 per cent owned by the Crown and 47 per cent privately in non-Maori hands.

The Maori people are the Indigenous people of Aotearoa ... We are the children of the Great Ocean of Kiwa (Pacific) and we trace our ancestry back to the lands of Hawaii and Tahiti Nui.

Hilda Halkyard-Harawira. Te Rarawa, Te Aupouri, Ngati Whaatua. (Halkyard-Harawira, 1986a)

Considering the events of the 150 years since the arrival of the Pakeha, it is appropriate that Waitangi translates as "Water of Weeping". The ethos of Waitangi is caught in the 1990 speech of the Maori Anglican bishop, the Right Reverend Whakahuihui Vercoe, guest at the Waitangi celebrations. His sentiments stirred the nation:

> Some of us have come here to celebrate, some to commemorate, some to commiserate, but some to remember what happened on this sacred ground. We come to this sacred ground because our *tupuna* [ancestors] left us this ground. A hundred and fifty years ago a compact was signed, a covenant was made between two people ... a treaty was signed to give birth to a nation – a unique and unusual circumstance ... But since the signing of that treaty ... I want to remind our partners that you have marginalised us. You have not honoured the Treaty ... the partner that has been marginalised is me – the language of this land is yours, the custom is yours, the media by which we tell this world who we are, are yours ... I don't want to debate the Treaty. I don't want to renegotiate the Treaty, I want the Treaty to stand firmly as the unity, the means by which we are made one nation ... The Treaty is what we are celebrating. It is what we are trying to establish so that my *tino rangatiratanga* is the same as your *tino rangatiratanga* (absolute sovereignty). And so I have come to Waitangi to cry for the promises that you made and for the expectations of our *tupuna* ... As I look at the tranquil waters of Pewhairangi [Bay of Islands] as I remember the words that were spoken on this land, as I remember the history of my people ... as I remember the songs of our land, as I remember the history of our land, I weep ... (Vercoe, 1990).

There were many versions of the Treaty of Waitangi/*te Tiriti O Waitangi*, two of which have a prominent role – one Maori, the other English. Although 512 chiefs signed the Maori version, only 30 signed the English version which, created after the Maori document, contains many discrepancies, some extreme (Halkyard-Harawira, 1990a: p. 5), and yet it was the English version that the Pakeha seized upon to justify their annexation of the Maori lands.[1]

In the First Article, while the English stated that the Maori "cede ... absolutely and without reservation all the rights and powers of sovereignty" the Maori distinctly gave the British limited administrative powers: "*te Kawanatanga*" or governorship. "*Tino Rangatiratanga*", translating in Maori as "absolute sovereignty", is not used. The Second Article "guarantees ... the full, exclusive and undisturbed possession of the lands and estates, forests, fisheries and other properties ... so long as it is their wish and desire to maintain the same in their possession but the chiefs ... yield the exclusive

---

1. According to Pania McArdell (1992) women played a significant role in the Treaty. Five women were among the Maori chiefs who signed the Treaty on behalf of all the Tangata Whenua, men and women, while Captain Hobson represented the British sovereign, Queen Victoria.

rights of pre-emption over such lands as the proprietors ... may be disposed to alienate, at such prices as may be agreed ..." The Maori version stresses this strongly. It uses such terms as "*te tino Rangatiratanga*", promising full chieftainship of their land, their villages and all their possessions, their "*taonga*" – everything held precious. It expresses the concept of full sovereignty. The Third Article "... extends to natives ... protection and imparts to them all the rights and privileges of British subjects", but it does not make them British citizens. And a Fourth Article, not present in the English version, guarantees religious freedom, customary law and, specifically, Maori custom (Halkyard-Harawira, 1990a: pp. 4–5).

Clearly, the Maori did not cede their sovereignty. The Treaty merely allowed the Pakeha to remain in the islands, governing themselves, but subject to Maori *tino rangatiratanga*, sovereignty (Jackson, 1990: p. 12). It exchanged settlement rights with the promise that Indigenous rights, the rights of the *Tangata Whenua* (the People of the Land), would be respected. If it had been honoured by the British in the spirit in which it was signed by the Maori, then Aotearoa would have witnessed a true partnership.

The Maori chiefs who signed the Treaty wanted an agreement that would protect them from the lawlessness of the settlers, protect their trade (the Maori had extensive trade networks both within the country and overseas) and guarantee their control over their land and resources. Some actively sought the Pakeha presence, believing that it would bring new riches and opportunities to their people. And indeed it could have, had the British settlers recognised the Maori as anything but "mere savages". This contrasted acutely with the Maori willingness to share the land and to exist alongside Pakeha culture. They did not require that the newcomers lived as they did, but simply that their culture and values be respected.

A Maori perspective towards the Treaty is expressed by Titewhai Harawira (1985):

The Treaty guaranteed us our land, our language, our forestries and our fisheries. It in fact recognised our sovereignty . . . Three years after that treaty was signed the British began their large land wars and confiscations . . . The whole of the South Island was taken in one big confiscation. Other areas were confiscated. Our people were killed, our women raped. In areas around New Plymouth and Taranaki where our people were made to believe by the missionaries that Christians don't fight on Sundays my people were massacred. The four tribes in that area were having a service on Sunday morning and they were going to continue talking about the land confiscations. The British arrived on horseback, with their guns, and slaughtered them. Killed all the children, raped and killed the women.

Today there are over three million people in Aotearoa, and the Maori people are only 12 per cent of that population. Seventy-five per cent of Maoris are under twenty-five years old. Sixty five per cent of Maoris are women. But we are a strong nation. We have a strength that has been built on our awareness of our past. Our past is our present, and our present is our future. The whole White teaching says, "Look at today. Look at tomorrow. Don't look back". But for us, Maoris, we look back. And we look back in anger, because we know what the British have done to our people. And that gives us strength. We know our history today, and we have the real determination to build a new way of life.

*My people are loving. That's why we let the Whites in. We wanted to share because we do
not own the land. Then the Waitangi Treaty came into being. Now we walk across a land
that has been stolen, ripped from under our feet. Our anger is strong. Passionately angry,
furious. But we learn to sing our pain, to handle it. I've learnt to haka, to sing, my anger
instead of perhaps getting a revolver and shooting the whole lot of you. Sometimes that is
how I feel.*

Hinewirangi Kohu. Ngati Kahungungu, Ngati Ranginui. (Kohu, 1987)

Culture and identity remain essential elements of Maori community. Hinewirangi
Kohu (1987), a Maori poet, echoes the passion of *wahine Maori*, Maori woman:

One of the most beautiful things is knowing that you are brown, knowing that you are the
same colour as *Papatuanuku*, the Earth Mother.

As a *wahine*, a woman, I've grown in Maoridom because I keep the *waiata*, the songs,
and the medicine. I am trained in that by my old *tupuna*, my elders, my grandmothers. I was
taken to special places from the time I was born, because I am also the first born of Kohu,
the sky clan. My grandmother's name was Sky-Woman or Hinewirangi. There I learnt
about putting my hand in the earth. Early in the morning, when everyone was sleeping, they
picked me up and they put my hands beneath the earth. I didn't know what for, but it didn't
matter. Then one day my hands began to turn upwards, and I thought, "I'm not doing that.
Who's turning them under there?". When I felt that, my grandmother was right behind me.
She gently led me out of the place, and I went for a long walk into a very green and gentle
place by a river. There I had another teacher. She had vibrant, long red hair. I don't
remember her skin colour, except I remember the lights shining around her hair. I remember
my grandmother saying, "I'm bringing you here my child because there's going to be a day
when you need to run, to come to a place like this and be safe". Many, many times, as I
struggle as a Maori woman, I have been there, to the beauty of learning about the things of
the sky, my clan.

Instrumental in founding the Learning House of Women, in her hometown, Hamilton,
Hinewirangi Kohu (1986) told this story in Hawai'i:

I bring greetings to the *whenua* [land], *aina*, that allows us to be here. And I bring the love
of the *wahine Maori* from Aotearoa to you all. And I pay homage to the spirits that linger
on or around this *'aina*.

I come with the *take* [mandate] of women. I belong to the Maori women's group in
Hamilton part of the national women's group, *Te Kakano* – the Seed, which concentrates
totally on Maori women.

We believe that, while we are fighting for the *whenua* [land] – the *'aina*, if our women
are not safe, then how can we embrace the *'aina*, which is female? How can we embrace the
whenua, which is female? We in Aotearoa call her *Papatuanuku*, Hawai'ians call her *Papa*.

But if our women are raped, battered in domestic violence, and all these things, how can we say, "*aloha 'aina*" [love the land], because we are just battering her? We believe that the women of Aotearoa are the ones who are going to work really hard to win us our independence. So I come with that *take* [mandate].

We have a Learning House of Women where women come and learn about traditions. They learn to see that they have been oppressed and denied so many things, and that our lands have been stolen from us. Women learn to see politically. Then, when women go to *hui* [gatherings], they will know all of that, rather than becoming political cripples. We, as political women working with women, have decided that we don't want to see our women crippled by something they are afraid of, by something that they don't know much about. So we have this really big job of helping them learn what they already know.

The *whanau* [family], we believe, consists of our *wahine* [women], our *tane* [men], our *tamariki* [children], our *tupuna* [elders]. They are all important. We work with the whole family, but we give priority to women and children. That is because they are the most disadvantaged. Maori women in Aotearoa are doubly disadvantaged – we are women and Maori.

We work from a Maori perspective. Totally. Looking at traditional things that belong to Maori people, and looking at using these as models of healing. As Indigenous people of our country, we have these skills of healing. We lived as a *whanau*, what you would call an extended family, but it wasn't only that – we had our gods and goddesses. So, we work as a collective of women, because that's how we operate in our *whanau* – we work together.

We're sort of like the middle people. We work in with the Waitangi Action Committee (WAC) and the Pacific People's Anti-Nuclear Action Committee (PPANAC). They are really important to us, because they are the ones upfront. We are the middle link, so that women are a little more prepared than they would be if they went straight to the top.

It's not a rosy picture. It is very hard for Indigenous peoples to keep up the struggle, to maintain the traditions that are deep inside of them. We have to confront and prove ourselves daily.

And, now that we are a force, the government wants us to write down the way of the Learning House of Women, so that they can control it, control us.

And the reason women's way has never been written down is because the early recorders were all men, who are not allowed in the Women's Houses. So it never became something that was talked about in common language, but it's still something that is very *tapu*, and very sacred, and it still holds the rituals.

We had a certain law, and a certain order in our lives, because we had sacred things, called the *tapu*. We had a place where women could be and birth. And when women reached their moon there was a place for them to go and be loved, for that is a sacred time in their life. The White man teaches us to chuck it down the trash can, and so our woman dies, mixed in muck and yuck. When, once a month, we, as women, are in our moon, the Maori considers that really sacred. So we had a place for that to be.

We believe that the truth never disappears, *nei*, the truth is always there. It's just that you get lost to the truth. We get lost. And so we have to bring ourselves back and find ourselves. So that the truth can come back. So that we can sing again.

And no one has the truth. No one is better than the other. We are all equal. We all recognise that some of us were born to be memorisers, some were born to keep the secrets of the song and the *waiata*, not one of us was born to be hopeless like the White system tries to tell us. And so we try to instil in our women that there is not one of us that was born that does not have some beautiful little thing about us. That is totally ours. That we can learn about. That we can share.

Once we know that the women are really strong within themselves, then we begin the political campaign of saying, "Now, what do you think of the Treaty of Waitangi?". And we start that process very gently. We know that Waitangi Action Committee can't do that, because they have to be right up front all the time. And so, my role in the political movement, is working in the Learning House of Women, so that by the time women get up to doing that work our Black Women's movement needs us to do, that our *hui wahine* [women's movement] need us to do, we have gone through a very basic grounding. And therefore, there's not one of our women burdened with fear and scared because they might say the wrong thing, scared because they don't know anything politically.

So that's mainly our *take* [mandate]. Our job is working with grassroots women and bringing truth to light, so that we can go together and claim what is ours.

The basic tool of resistance is culture. Embodied in culture are all the things that keep the life force of a people together – language, histories, songs, traditions, land, families, and the passing on of knowledge. Culture retention and revival is essential. Culture is our main weapon of resistance.

Hilda Halkyard-Harawira. Te Rarawa, Te Aupouri, Ngati Whaatua. (Hanly, 1986: p. 34)

Language, the root of culture, is one of the greatest *taonga* [treasures] that distinguishes one people from another. If a language is made extinct, then the foundations of a nation crumble.

The Maori people were faced with such a threat. The Native Schools Amendment Act (1871) demanding that all education be in English had a devastating effect on the Maori cultural identity. While, in 1923, eighty per cent of Maori children could speak their own tongue, by 1975 that figure had dropped to less than five per cent. And so in the late 1970s the *wahine Maori* [Maori women] swung into action. Establishing kohanga reo, [language nests], they placed Maori heritage back into the hands of the *tamariki*, Maori children.

Titewhai Harawira stresses the importance of the *kohanga reo* (WWNFIP, 1987: p. 36):

My parents were strapped for speaking Maori! A law was introduced banning it in the schools. You have almost a generation of Maoris, my age, who don't speak Maori because our parents said it was no use learning the language if you were going to be strapped for speaking it. So the language almost died, and the people and culture with it.

Now we are setting up our own schools. We are teaching our history to our children. As told by us, not the history as told by the oppressor. And it's a good history, a positive one. Today Maori women have gone out and we are teaching all our pre-school children to speak Maori. Because when you learn the history, when you learn the language, you revive the people.

Hinewirangi Kohu (1987) recalls the pain inflicted upon her because of the Pakeha schooling system:

> They took from us our beautiful history. We are an oral people, and we learned wonderful lessons. We learned that everyone was born with a special, special gift. Everyone. Some were born to be keepers of the *whakapapa*, the genealogy; some were born to be keepers of the *waiata*, the song; some were born to be keepers of the medicine, *waiora*. I'm born *waiora*. Some were born to take care of others, the *kai awhina*. No one was born good for nothing. In this time of colonisation we have "good for nothings". The people in jail are eighty per cent Maori. Maori people fill the mental institutions, seeing all those supposedly learned people. We have a lot of rape, incest and domestic violence, alcohol and drug abuse. Those are symptoms of the real problem, which is that we have an identity crisis because of colonisation.
>
> I want to say something to the non-Indigenous. "I am a colonialist. Today you'll take all those clothes off and you'll get into the clothes of Indigenous people. You won't live in your houses. You'll give away your cars. And I think we had better put you out in the sun 'cos you're too white. You mustn't speak your language at all. No English whatsoever. You will speak my language. You will no longer live in your nuclear families, you will all come and live in a *whanau*, where there are untold numbers of us, beautiful, wonderful communities."
>
> Some of you will think that's trendy and fabulous, but most of you wouldn't like it. To be forced. Well, that's what happened to the Maori people. We got whipped for speaking our language because it wasn't a matter of choice. The British were very wise. They said, "Let's marry them. Breed them out. That way we'll make sure that the language will disappear".
>
> I grew up hating being Maori. I was ashamed of it basically because I was told that White is right. I got strapped in school one day for talking to my cousin. The teacher was asking me something, and I didn't know the language, and I only wanted to know so that I could be obedient. And she slammed my nose in the corner and beat me with a stick and said, "You dirty little savage, you'll learn one day". So I became ashamed. I decided I was never going to speak again, and I didn't speak for a whole year, until I could speak English absolutely perfectly. They stuck me in a class for dyslectic children, thought I was disabled.
>
> I went to university as "a clever little Maori" who has been made an example of. But I was alienated from my own people. I could no longer go home and eat with my fingers and taste the food, because I had been taught to eat with a knife and fork. I used to hate it. I went through the system beautifully, got the degrees I wanted, and I fight for my people now. I work with the women who have been beaten, with the men who have been jailed.
>
> We have an identity problem and we are doing something about it. We have *kohanga reo*, language nests, where we are putting our babies to school. Where our babies can learn Maori ways and traditions. We are making demands for this kind of school, and if they are not met we'll meet them outside the government system. They can't lock up every Maori. The solution is for us to take up our sovereignty and do what we want to do. It's a matter of equal power.

The movement to establish *kohanga reo*, was so successful, and in such demand, that the government, unable to ignore the issue any longer, integrated it into the school system. At the same time declaring *te Reo Maori*, the Maori language, to be an official language. However, this has, to a large extent, placed control of *te kohanga reo* into the hands of the government, undermining the Maori intentions. Maori organisations are now working to reclaim the initiative by establishing language nests outside the government's domain.

Children lose their fluency in Maori four years after leaving the *kohanga reo* and moving to primary school level, where instruction is in the Pakeha tongue, so the Maori have established *kura kaupapa Maori*. These are primary schools that focus on Maori *kaupapa* (philosophy) and *taonga* (culture and heritage), mixed with the best elements of Pakeha education. Thus Maori children are being raised strong in their own culture, but with the skills to enable them to utilise the Pakeha system to the benefit of their own people. Maori are now moving to create *Whare Waranga*, houses of higher learning, to cater for adults. Their goal is to learn from the *tupuna*, elders, about things Maori, in an effort to retain their history and language.

Maori people are moving to recreate their communities, and to provide for themselves those structures they consider essential to the retention of their culture, as Hilda Halkyard-Harawira declares:

> ... Maori communities have withdrawn from Pakeha societies ... We have withdrawn into our communities and are trying to rebuild ourselves. [Maori communities] are preparing to run themselves. We are creating things with and without Pakeha authorities. It is good if they give us help, and we don't care if they don't give us help. We are going ahead (Halkyard-Harawira and Boanas, 1992: pp. 322–3).

Before the signing of the Treaty of Waitangi we, the Maori people, had and we still have, our own mana, *our dignity, our authority, our own sovereignty. The New Zealand government governs illegitimately.*

Nganeko Minhinnick. Ngati Te Ata. (Minhinnick, 1989)

The steep mountain ranges of Te Waipounamu, the South Island, the spine of Aotearoa, are the *whenua* of the Ngati Tahu.

The entire island was annexed by the British only four months after Hobson's arrival in the islands – again in an effort to beat the French government to fertile lands. The British administration, becoming aware of French attempts to establish a colony on shores it claimed as its own, had sped from Pewhairangi (the Bay of Plenty) to the South Island, arriving only two days before a French ship carrying colonialists. The French, admitting defeat, sailed off to colonise the Marquesas (Tahiti-Polynesia), but left a small community behind to intermarry with the British. French Bay exists today as a reminder of the French endeavour to share in the profits of Maori land.

Initially the Maori were keen to experiment with Pakeha ideas. They controlled the shipping trade, carried out their own whaling and fishing, and ran cattle and sheep on their land. They might well have prospered, but they were pushed off the land into reserves. Forbidden to hunt, and not having money to buy food, they suffered malnutrition and starvation. By 1868 the community had been severely decimated by disease. Only 2,400 Maori survived, making up only 1.7 per cent of the population of Te Waipounamu. This made the colonisation of the South Island far easier than the north, and many settlers were grateful for it.

It is here, in Otautahi (Christchurch), that Lenis Davidson, of the Ngati Maru people, and Mona Lisa Johnson, born of the Ngati Porou and Ngati Kahungunu (Rongomai-Wahine), work for justice for their people. They spoke of the strength of women in Maoridom and the effects of colonisation, stressing the role of women. They were particularly clear on the concept of partnership between the two distinct cultures (Johnson, M. L., 1990; Davidson, 1990).

Mona Lisa Johnson:

The Pakeha doesn't know what "biculturalism" means. They tend to abuse that word. For me, as a Maori, it means giving back the power to the Indigenous people of that land. It's really simple. Everything. I mean, you look at the Treaty (1840), look at the Declaration of Independence (1835). For years since the colonisers came to our land we were doing okay, we had a strong base. They sent the dregs of their society to our land. We've had enough. What's happened with my generation is that it's not going to continue – my children ain't going to pick up the scraps. They made 1990 [150 years after the signing of the Treaty of Waitangi] a big celebration, but its not a celebration! Maoris are still struggling for education, we're still struggling to have *korero kaupapa Maori* [the rights of Maori to live by the Maori philosophy] recognised.

I'm on my way out. Soon, thirty years down the line, my kids are going to pick up the *hikoi* [march/struggle] – they're going to have to walk. And so I train my boys now – politically. I've got to get them on board, because they might see it on their way out. Change has got to happen. If it doesn't, it will get out of hand. They've got to start listening to our needs. We're not sitting back any more. They tell us to "fit into the box", and if we don't they say, "No wonder you're down the bottom of the heap!". Maoris keep getting blamed: "Why aren't you people up here where we are?". How the hell can we get "up there" when we have a different way of doing things? So what we're saying is, "Recognise our way. We have values within our culture that you can also learn from". Partnership. True partnership. It's not going to happen until they give the political power back to the Indigenous people. I really don't think it's ever going to happen under the White system.

Lenis Davidson:

Partnership? I suspect that, in 1840, when the Treaty was signed, there was a lot of for and against it. Like any other community, you will always get leaders of the tribe who would have trusted the senior people of the Pakeha society. But, those who are actually on a lower level got to see the greed of the lower level of the Pakeha, they would have seen that there would probably never be a partnership. In Maoridom, you were born to your position and could advance yourself in the tribe by your ability, but in Pakehadom, if you're shrewd and cunning, you can cut someone else's throat and acquire his wealth. If not literally, then certainly in other ways. The *mana* of our leaders was so great that the people followed these leaders. And then they had affiliations because of kinship, blood and so forth. That system probably helped the Pakehas gain the momentum to take control.

Mona Lisa Johnson:

If the Treaty had been honoured we wouldn't be where we are today. One thing is true: Maoris did not sell off their *rangatiratanga*, our sovereignty. We opened the way for the colonial settlers to remain in our country, but we still maintained our *rangatiratanga*, we merely allowed them to come and settle in our land. Once they set up their system, they brought in the military forces to support their government. Legislation and violations of the Treaty were put into place. In 1909, Maori women could no longer breast-feed their children. That was a law passed in 1909. There's many land acts that were passed. These violations were imposed on our people, with no political say, and as time went on we actually lost it. For the sake of our children we've got to go on the *hikoi*, we've got to go on with the struggle.

Lenis Davidson:

Even though we live in this Pakeha alien world, we are Maori, now. It's got nothing to do with a cupful of Irish in one, a cupful of English in another, all the blood that came into us as tribes. It's to do with our own identity. If we see ourselves as Maori, we are Maori. I don't blame people for choosing not to be Maori. The thing is, you've got to take it on, mentally and physically. Those people who choose not to, lose something forever – themselves. They've got children that might not feel the same as the years go by. There's a chance that if we keep the *kohanga* going, the language will always be available for the people to learn later, that the children will come back. It's when they actually stop *kohanga*, stop the little step to start on the journey, that's when we'll really be in trouble. Your language is your identity – as a nation, as a people. It is your cultural anchor. Unless you have your language you can lose so much. It's all very well learning about your tribal identity in Pakeha, but if you have it in Maori, then that immediately clicks you into place – mentally, physically. Your psyche is actually tuned into the *tupuna*: the people who were, the people that are, that you are. You are the representative, you are the face of the people that have been before.

Mona Lisa Johnson:

I think what's happening now, is that Maori women are becoming politicised. It's really exciting to see. We aren't alone any more. We have good networks in place. We learn different ways of empowering ourselves. The young women are coming up, getting aboard the *hikoi* [struggle]. We always thought we weren't good enough. Now we're saying, "Yes, we are good enough. It's our life!".

Lenis Davidson:

It was different for women before colonisation. Although it varied from tribe to tribe, there were quite a few Maori women who were leaders in their own communities. When children were born into certain positions the elders of the tribe watched them develop, and if they thought the child showed the grace, or had the ability, then that child was groomed to do a certain job, regardless of whether it was male or female.

Mona Lisa Johnson:

Maori women always held positions of power. There were roles that women had, and roles that men had, but in decision making process Maori women always had an input. Like the Treaty. Maori women signed the Treaty. Maori chieftains in their own right. Maori women were part of the decision making at that time. The way sexual abuse was dealt with was very interesting. The men who abused women in any way were given justice by the Maori community. It was an eye for an eye. They were put to death. They were hung for a period of time, and then they were buried standing up – they didn't lay them down – in front of the *marae* [tribal gathering place] so that when people walked onto the *marae* they walked over them. Men who abused their power were dealt with severely – and it was death.

Lenis Davidson:

The beliefs of Maoris in those days was much more spiritual. When you attacked a living person you were actually attacking their *wairua*, the essence that is around you, that is you, that goes on forever – the Pakeha call it a soul. The *wairua* connects all people. People were individuals as far as personality were concerned, but they were part of each other. In the past you recited your *whakapapa* [genealogy]. The thing is you had a name, not a surname, surnames came with the British. So you had your name, and you belonged to a *hapu*, which was the clan or village in which you lived. You are so-and-so's daughter, or your *tupuna* [ancestor] was so-and-so. You might recite three names before your name, so everybody always knew who you were, exactly where you fitted into a *whanau* [family]. You had an identity with your *tupuna* [elders/ancestors] and your immediate *whanau* [family].

Mona Lisa Johnson:

Women hold a lot of power now. Where my mother's from, women spoke on the *paepae* (the bench where the Tangata Whenua speakers sit during the *powhiri*, [welcome]) on the *marae*. There are other places where women don't speak. Thing is, women don't have to speak. Their body language can cut men off. Like at one *hui*, a man on the *paepae* was abusing – what the women done was get up and walk across the forecourt, straight across him, and he had to sit down, he couldn't speak. So even though they might not be able to say anything, women have power with actions and body language. It's becoming more frequent for women to talk on the *paepae*, which I think is positive, but once again we have different roles. Some of the things that I wouldn't dare do, my husband would do, and he wouldn't cut across my boundaries either. This is getting personal, but there are certain times that my husband and I don't sleep together, during menstruation and a week after, usually two weeks of every month. The same with my mother. I mean, you're *tapu* [sacred]: a man doesn't come across your boundaries. My husband accepts that.

I'm teaching my boys, my sons, their position as protector of *te whare tangata* [people of the home], their role with women. We walk on the *hikoi* [struggle] together – men don't walk ahead, women behind – we walk together. That's how I'm teaching my boys. Some of our men are on such a power trip that what we're doing is getting our men back into line with us. Our own men, our Maori men. They've been so colonised that they think, "We're better than the women". What we got to do is educate our men, bring them back onto the *hikoi* that we walk together.

Lenis Davidson:

The men can come on the trip of being in power because they're male. One of the problems of men is that they always assume women are going to make their decisions from an emotional point of view no matter how sound something is. So it's very hard for women to get across a genuine point of view. We've almost got to draw pictures. It's as if you have to go to the bowels of hell to get information before they'll accept it. They're very sceptical of women.

It was the Pakeha men who influenced our men. The first Pakehas were whalers and sealers, pretty unscrupulous individuals. They realised the only way they were going to get their hands on land was to marry Maori women, because, in lots of tribes, the land went down through the women, because men went away to war and got killed. So, often, the land was attached to women. Your *whakapapa* [genealogy] came down through women. The Pakehas wanted to fence the land, they wanted exclusive rights to that land. Maoris found that very alien, very threatening. Land belongs to the *whanau* [family], it wasn't necessary to fence it, it was just a thing that was known.

It was different for Pakeha women. Pakeha women didn't have any status, for them, in Victorian times, it was necessary to be married to a Pakeha man to have your soul saved. So, you see, it was quite different for Pakeha women. A lot of spinster women who came expecting to marry Pakeha men, ended up married to Maoris, because the Pakeha men wouldn't have them, being judgemental of women over a certain age. You were an "old bat" by the time you were twenty-five, and then they'd work you to death producing a child every year – you'd be dead in ten years.

What colonisation did to Maori women was make them the bottom of the pile. The Pakeha, especially the missionaries, brought a certain value system with them. Sin. It was important to have sin. I mean, if you don't have sin how can you save somebody's soul? It was very important to lay guilt on people. The idea was that you needed to have your soul saved, and that they were the only ones who could do it. Often a tribe would send their children to the missionary's schools, and they would come back to the tribe and do the dirty work, by talking to them and saying, "You shouldn't do this. You shouldn't do that". They were quietly cutting across the *kaupapa* [philosophy] of tribes, their beliefs, and undermining their law. They brought in new values, the Pakeha concept. Some people accepted that, because they were hungry for the new things the Pakeha brought. Others didn't. And women literally became the "wearers of sin". The person who was sinful was never the male. Their perceived idea of sin was that women were to blame. They were the ones who committed adultery – not the men, who were supposedly beguiled by the woman's charms. The double standards of Victorian men came into Maori society. I'm not painting Maori men as angels, because I'm quite sure some of them were right little rat bags, but the point was that the Pakeha came in with their version of what was right and what was wrong. And Maori men just automatically thought, "Oh, I can benefit from this!". They were quite happy to take on certain aspects of the Pakeha teaching. It was always the woman who was to blame.

Mona Lisa Johnson:

Women were considered the weaker sex, especially with the churches: "They're not quite up to our level yet, we'll just keep them at bay, keep dominating them".

Lenis Davidson:

The position of Maori women – under Maori men, under White society – that makes me angry. I think there's a great deal of suppressed anger. A great deal.

Mona Lisa Johnson:

I want for us to have the right to determine what we want. I think we should have the power back – control of our own destiny, of our own land. The whole sexism, the whole racism, has got to end. Women in general have always been down the bottom of the heap, but mainly Black women. So yeah, we need our independence – our own right to determine what is right for us as Tangata Whenua here. That's what I want. I want control. And keeping our *kaupapa* [philosophy] intact, retaining our heritage – all that is ours.

Lenis Davidson:

I want a genuine share, if not all, of the resources available in Aotearoa to return to the Tangata Whenua, to do things by our criteria. For instance, Maoris have always been conservationists, aware of the need for the land to recuperate itself, same with the sea. You didn't fish in one area because it was the easiest place to get to. Pakehas have only just begun to understand that, but they've never attributed it to the Maori – they can't cope with that, because it would give credence to Maori values.

But the Pakeha doesn't understand partnership! They're hooked into what they call "democracy", and because we're only 12 per cent we would never get 50 per cent of anything out of this system. So we have to go for 100 per cent. Pakehas can't adjust their concepts. It's impossible for them, because they can't accept the idea that there's anything worthwhile in Maoridom. Oh, yes there are Pakeha that are beginning to get on board, but they're very few.

Mona Lisa Johnson:

Time is running out. We've got to get on board the *hikoi* [march/struggle]. Looking at Maori people and Indigenous women globally, we're all on the same *hikoi*. We're all on the same *hikoi* in our own lands: fighting rightfully for what is ours as women, as Indigenous women. We want a place too. We got a place under the sun. So, we've got to take it back. It is ours.

I am Maori and I'm Indigenous to Aotearoa. I am Maori and I'm one with Mother Earth. I am at one with Mother Earth, and Mother Earth with me. And so the pains and the hurts suffered by our people, through the transgressions of others over our lands, has caused many of us to fight for the retention of those lands, in order that we might survive.
Nganeko Minhinnick. Ngati Te Ata. (Minhinnick, 1989)

In 1877, under the climate of hostility that followed the taking of the Maori lands, Chief Justice Prendergast, labelling the Maori people "savages", unilaterally revoked the Treaty of Waitangi. The Privy Council of the time protested, but the local courts, controlled by Pakeha greedy for land, ignored their ruling.

It was this legacy that the Waitangi Tribunal, established in 1975 to consider Maori claims under the Treaty, inherited. The tribunal has the power to investigate claims going back to 1840, but, without the power to enforce its findings, it is obstructed from returning justice to the Maori people. Moves to reassert Maori right to their *taonga* (treasures, natural resources) are progressively being undermined.

In 1988, the High Court, determining that, under the Treaty of Waitangi, the fishing grounds around Aotearoa belonged to the Indigenous people, recognising the rights of the Maori to their fishing resources. At the same time, the government instigated "Individual Transferable Quotas", granting corporate interests permission to fish the same waters. When the High Court then found that the government had not gained the permission of the Maori people to fish the waters guaranteed them under the Treaty, the government set about an elaborate plan to rob the Maori of their rights in perpetuity. They offered to pay NZ$150 million to some Maori people to buy a part share in the country's biggest fishing and processing company. The deal hinged on the reciprocal agreement by the Maori people involved to extinguish all Maori commercial fishing rights and to discontinue all claims before the Waitangi Tribunal.

Although twenty-five *iwi* (tribes) and *hapu* (clans) opposed the contract, the deal went ahead. Court cases followed as the Maori community, shocked by the transaction, responded. The Waitangi Tribunal originally denounced the deal as contrary to the Treaty and declared that the rights could not be extinguished. But it then recommended that the deal should proceed.

And so, the Maori people were then declared to have given up their traditional fishing resources worth NZ$1500 million annually, and their right to compensation for over 150 years of exploitation of these resources by Pakeha companies – for a mere NZ$150 million.

The settlement between the Maori negotiators and the government threatens other rights under the Treaty. In 1993, moves were taken to eliminate Maori rights to land in the same fashion. The government aims to settle all Maori claims to land by the year 2000.

Nganeko Minhinnick (1989) of the Ngati Te Ata, long involved at the cutting edge of the struggle for Maori territorial rights, as her people move against the desecration of their lands and burial sites by the mining company New Zealand Steel, speaks of the difficulty of obtaining justice under the Pakeha system:

> Our tribe has sought through all the due processes of law to find the solution, but nobody wants to know. We have been going to courts for the lands, for the waterways, for the total environment – something like a hundred cases before tribunals and high courts in the country, for about ten consecutive years. And it is almost to no avail. Because each time we reach a decision in the courts which is in our favour – that acknowledges our existence, that

acknowledges that we have something that is unique to that country, and therefore to the world, that we have something to give to save the environment, that we have a real contribution to make, that we can no longer sit and take what is imposed upon us – justice is still denied us.

It is hard to see what is happening because it is cultural genocide. We have imposed upon us all kinds of legislation that on the surface looks good, it sounds good, because it talks about empowering Maori people, at long last – after 150 years of control. But, in fact, it still keeps us in a state of dependency.

And so, my tribe will not accept any of the carrot-dangling. What that means is a total deprogramming of our people in order to regain our culture. It won't be an easy task, but I know that we will succeed. We have made a commitment to working towards self-determination on a daily basis.

It is in this spirit that Moana Kohu (1990) voices a challenge to the Pakeha peoples:

I challenge the [Pakeha] to recognise the Tangata Whenua, to recognise the Treaty, to recognise our sovereignty. They cannot be at home in this land until then. I suppose it will take them another 150 years to get it right. I hope it doesn't. I am of the learning generation, learning to pick up the struggle. I talk to my generation, and the feeling is that, "Hey, after 150 years of White failure, we're getting sick and tired of being pushed around by these people!". A lot of us are getting impatient, and the sooner we get this struggle over, the less of our people will get hurt. Slowly, very slowly, our people are coming up. We have had enough. It is time for the Pakeha to honour the Treaty.

The Maori have offered the Pakeha a challenge – true partnership, an alliance that was agreed over 150 years ago, that benefits both parties. Increasingly Maori are coming back into their *mana* (power). They are a force to be recognised. The Pakeha have one choice only, whether to be tossed gently in the shoreline breakers, or to be tumbled by a tidal wave. The choice and the responsibility is theirs. The Maori are going for justice.

VISIONS : MORUROA

midnight: beach walking, star gazing
singing
sweet madrigals
of gentle revolution
and confronting
fearful futures

midnight: Moruroa
visions of her bleeding womb
torn apart and left to drown
in a millennium of poison

midnight: oars and fingertips
dipped in blue-white
phosporescence –
sisters delight
in wet stars sparking

midnight: Moruroa
gendarmes and warships
drip violence
from their eyes
the sons of Caligula
blind to their own blindness
they come
to witness their excrement
but this time
she will fight

o gentle womyn,
keep on singing
sirens of the night
crystals of light
sailing in violet seas
it is time
for your gentle revolution
have no fear
sing your pleas
the world will hear
Moruroa.

Lynx. Aotearoa. 1985

BEHIND A CURTAIN OF FLOWERS

– *Tahiti-Polynesia* –

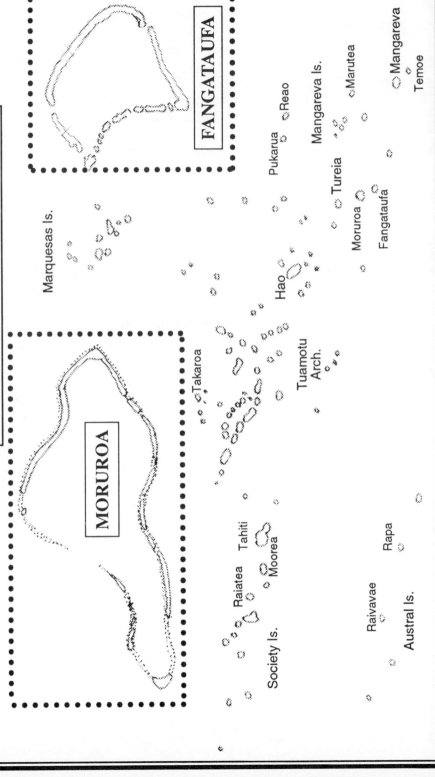

We protest in the name of all those who have no voice, who have been abandoned by this new society without mercy, a society where money decides our future, where the existence of a small minority living in luxury constitutes an insult to the majority living in poverty and degradation.

Tahitian Women's Statement. (Robie, 1980)

The pattern in Tahiti-Polynesia, Te Ao Maohi (Land of the Maohi), is typical of the colonisation, and disruption of spiritual beliefs and lifestyles, imposed right across the Pacific. It is a story of land stolen, religious sites and objects destroyed, and the brutal massacres of those who demanded the right to their ancestral beliefs. It is the story of the dispossession of a people, but it is also the story of their resistance. The Maohi people, still struggling to throw off European imperialism, have never been subdued, resistance has continued side-by-side with the oppressions.

The Maohi have been exploited by France, England, Spain, the Netherlands, Chile, Peru and Russia. The devastation of the Peruvian slave raids has been clearly expressed in H. E. Maude's book *Slavers in Paradise*:

The slavers descended on a region totally unprepared for, and on a people who had never conceived of, the possibility of such a visitation. There was nothing of a like nature or scale in Polynesian history to make it conceivable that anyone, let alone persons professing to be radically and culturally superior, could be capable of kidnapping thousands of men, women and children by violence and treachery, tearing them at a moment's notice from their parents and children for compulsory transportation to an unknown fate at an unknown destination (Maude, 1985: p. ix).

With the arrogance that attended these voyagers, the 130 islands of Tahiti-Polynesia, scattered over an area the size of Europe, were named and renamed, and progressively collected into five archipelagos, (bearing such differing titles as the Society, Tuamotu, Gambier, Austral and Marquesas islands), along lines that bore no semblance to the Maohi world. Tahiti itself has variously been known as Amat, King George III, Nouvelle Cythere, and Otahiti (Carter, 1984: p. 540).

Now, under the French, these islands scattered over 4.5 million square kilometres of ocean, an area as large as Europe, with diverse cultures, languages and histories, have been drawn together to be administered by an alien culture from the other side of the world.

Although Tahiti is a French colony today, the English got there first. John Carter (1984: pp. 140–143) presents a potted history of Tahiti. In 1797, the London Missionary Society (LMS) sent eighteen missionaries to Tahiti, but they received such resistance that by 1799 most had departed for the British colony of New South Wales. It was not until 1815 that they succeeded in converting Tahitian Chief Pomaré II and solicited his help in spreading Christianity throughout the archipelago. The LMS became increasingly influential and when, in 1836, two French priests arrived to form a Catholic mission they were driven away. Outraged by the attack on its citizens, the French government responded by sending Captain Du Petit-Thouars, who threatened to bombard the island unless "reparations" were made and there was agreement to a gun salute to the French flag. He was followed a year later by another French commander (Captain La Place) who again threatened to bombard Papeete (Tahiti's main settlement) unless Tahiti's sovereign, Queen Pomaré IV, allowed the Catholic religion into Tahiti and her other domains. The queen agreed. Meanwhile she had written to Britain's Queen Victoria asking that the islands be made a British protectorate, but the British were too pre-occupied colonising other Pacific peoples. The French, wanting the islands to service their whalers, gunboats and merchant ships, took this opportunity to seize control over Tahiti Island in 1842 by forcing Queen Pomaré IV and principal chiefs to sign a protectorate treaty. The French then established a provisional government which the British, returning to the island only months later, refused to acknowledge. England meanwhile had accepted the protectorate, but the news did not reach Tahiti until after the French had ratified the treaty earlier signed by Queen Pomaré IV. The British consul, George Pritchard, insisted that Queen Pomaré had been forced into the treaty, and she refused to strike her personal flag. The French responded by forcibly annexing Tahiti. In November 1843, 500 French soldiers marched to Queen Pomaré's palace, hauled down the Tahitian flag, and raised the French tricolor in its place, proclaiming that, "In the name of King Louis Philippe I, our august master, we plant the French flag over this land … As for you, the people of the country, we have come to protect you and bring you civilisation and peace". The Maohi people resisted. The British consul was arrested, charged with inciting resistance, and deported, and Queen Pomaré IV fled to the nearby island of Raiatea (where the Islanders fought to retain their independence until the bloody French massacre of 1897).

When news of the annexation reached Europe, both Britain and France were so outraged at the other's behaviour that war was only averted when the French king, Louis-Philippe agreed to pay indemnity to the British consul. Meanwhile, back in Tahiti, the French were busy crushing the Maohi resistance, and, in 1847, Queen Pomaré IV finally accepted the French protectorate and returned to Tahiti. In the same year France and Britain agreed that France should gain control over Tahiti and Moorea, the domains of Queen Pomaré IV, but that the leeward islands of the Society group (including Raiatea) would remain independent. Gradually the French gained control over the neighbouring islands and archipelagos and in August 1957 the entire territory was constituted as "French Polynesia".

Today the Maohi are still fighting for their inalienable sovereign rights! Their resistance has continued unabated: from the refusal of Queen Pomaré IV to accept the missionaries (and the inevitable destruction of Islander culture) to today's efforts to stop nuclear testing and claim full-scale independence.

You come with your civilisation and you got them to go to your schools. You promised them good work, good salaries. And now they have to leave their families to live in Tahiti which is more like a punishment than a reward. Tahiti is like a double-edged sword – no house, no family, exploited as a worker, as a prostitute. That's what the French have brought to Polynesia!

William Tcheng. Tahiti-Polynesia. (Tcheng, 1987)

Tahiti was an island of scattered homesteads and fertile gardens until, in a bid for greater control and the desire to take the most fertile land for plantations, the colonial government herded the people into settlements on the coast. The main city of "French-Polynesia", Papeete, for example, is built on a marsh. When, in the 1960s, the military, the tourist industry and the French settlers arrived claiming the beautiful beaches and coastal plain for themselves, the Maohi were pushed back into the hills. Today, heavily overcrowded and deprived of land for self-sufficiency, the Islanders are dependent on the imported French society. Papeete is a city of contrasts: rich and poor, White and Black, locals and tourists. Its obvious militarisation is reminiscent of the Marshalls and Guam. Bridget Roberts (1987) wrote:

As in Micronesia, the nuclear issue is just one of the coloniser's tentacles: we could see the urbanisation, the destruction of the culture and the language, the theft of the land, the power of foreign capital, the exploitation of the environment, the influences of the churches.

The Mayor of Faa'a, Oscar Temaru (1987), leader of the Tavini Huraatira (Polynesian Liberation Front), the nation's most prominent pro-independence, anti-nuclear political party, is adamant that the French presence has impacted heavily upon his people:

In 1962 it was decided by a French man, General de Gaulle, that our islands would be used to make French bombs. He didn't ask our opinion. Nobody did.

When the French came they changed everything. There were only two thousand people in Faa'a, we knew everyone. It was sort of a big family. It was a beautiful life. We made copra, went fishing, and we planted. When the French army came here, people came from the outer islands looking for work. Then they would ask members of their family to come and join them. Later, when everything was built, there was no more work, everyone was laid off, but they stayed. They never went back home. Now they are living in the urban zone in a very precarious situation. We are twenty-five thousand people – just in Faa'a!

That's why the independence of this country is our very urgent wish. French people are flooding into Papeete. They come and take jobs. All the best jobs are for the French. All the administration, business and education is in French, so it's easier for them. They can even vote after being here six months. They take up housing and land, they have all the land on the flat and own the beaches. They make money while our children starve, our children have nowhere to play. Our people are dying of diseases because the living conditions are so bad. There's public housing, I call it "incarceration", "social imprisonment". That is not the way we Maohi live. We have to have land, a place to plant, to raise up some animals, go fishing.

The French tell us they are here to protect us. But we have no enemy! We are living in the Pacific! And that's what we want: to live peacefully in the Pacific. The French are doing their nuclear tests here to protect themselves, not us! You know, there were two wars 1914 and 1939. Our ancestors went with the French army to France to protect the French. They didn't come here to protect us, we went to France to protect them! People say, "But don't you know the Russians are taking over the Pacific?". We don't have any problems with the Russians or the Libyans, we have problems with the French! They are our enemy. We have to protect ourselves from them!

We have started to inform our people about our sovereignty, about our own culture, about our education and economic problems. And it is very hard. But the idea of independence is growing fast. And the French government knows it. They say that the people don't want independence, but we are convinced that they do. Why do the French refuse to organise a referendum on the issue if they are so sure?

When the French army started to come here, people were not aware of nuclear radiation. We welcomed the military with *leis* of flowers. The French do not have the right to trick our people like that. It is criminal. We don't want our children to be a nuclear target if there is a nuclear war. No, do it in Paris! I was born here in Faa'a and my umbilical cord is buried in our soil. I am tied to this land. I belong to this land. The connection is very deep. I love my country, and I am not alone in that.

For the Tahitian people . . . the radiation is making us ill and creating cancers in our bodies . . . The French . . . derive huge profits from our suffering and exploitation. They have also managed, with absolute disregard for all Pacific peoples, to arrogantly and callously damage the environmental safety of our large ocean region.
Myron Mataoa. Tahiti-Polynesia. (Connelly et al., 1987: p. 40)

France has held Tahiti-Polynesia hostage to its dream of being a *puissance mondiale moyenne,* (a middle-sized global power), with an independent nuclear deterrent. A dream that, for the Maohi, has been a nightmare.

Today, France rings the world with a chain of military bases and communication facilities, and is second only to the US in the number of military installations outside its own land (McLellan, 1989: p. 7). Increasingly, nuclear powered and armed ships visit Tahiti, and many troops and legionnaires are stationed there. Tahiti-Polynesia has been a vital link that enables France to have the capacity for unilateral military actions anywhere on the globe. Consequently, the political grip over the islands has been held tight. Military flexibility, however, is not the only reason why France has maintained its imperialistic control. Tahiti-Polynesia has had a more sinister role: the testing of French nuclear devices. Moruroa and Fangataufa atolls hold the laboratories which have enabled the French to become the world's third-ranking military power.

When the Algerians gained their independence in 1962, forcing the French colonialists to look elsewhere for a site for their nuclear detonations, Polynesia was decided upon. Despite promises that France would never test nuclear bombs in Tahiti, in 1963

President de Gaulle announced that, "In order to thank French Polynesia for its faithful attachments to France I have decided to set up the *Centre d'Expérimentation du Pacifique* (CEP) there". Immediately an outcry of anger resounded through the islands. Political, church, and civic leaders led local protests calling for independence. France responded with the empty promise that bombs would only be exploded when winds were blowing from the north, across the empty ocean between Polynesia and Antarctica. In July 1966, atmospheric testing began, first on Moruroa, then Fangataufa atolls. This was three years *after* the US, Soviet Union and Britain had agreed to limit their tests to underground detonations.

The first test was on Moruroa. It was catastrophic! An eyewitness reported that the blast had sucked up water from the lagoon and the islands had been covered with contaminated dead sea life. Two months later, President de Gaulle arrived to witness the second test, which was postponed because the winds were blowing towards inhabited islands. Although the wind had not changed direction, de Gaulle, impatient to get back to Paris, demanded that the test proceed. Monitoring stations in the Cook Islands, Niue, Samoa, Tonga, Fiji and Tuvalu immediately registered heavy radioactive fallout. So much for the promises that the islands would not be affected by nuclear fallout. Between 1966 and 1974 a total of forty-four atmospheric tests were detonated on Moruroa and Fangataufa. Fallout spread throughout the southern hemisphere. Increased concentrations of iodine 31 (which affects the thyroid gland), strontium 90 (the bones), and caesium 137 (intra-cellular) have been recorded as far away as Australia and South America. Measurements in Tahiti-Polynesia and its neighbours are far more alarming.[1]

I ask, why are they doing this to us? I think it is because we are all Black people. I believe that racism is at the base of the whole nuclear issue. You wouldn't be testing in the Pacific if it was populated by Whites.

Chailang Palacios. Northern Marianas. (Palacios, 1985)

France has responded to international calls for information on the impact of the testing with false or misleading statements. With health statistics and environmental information suppressed, or "laundered", since the testing began, scientists have difficulty linking

1. In 1974, the last year of French atmospheric tests (a total of 44 since 1963), the French Commissariat à l'Energie Atomique (CEA) measured nuclear contamination in the atmosphere over the Gambier Islands. They found that compared to Christchurch, Aotearoa, with a total beta reading of 1.9 mBq/m3, the Gambiers indicated 1460 mBq/m3. Similarly, the average iodine 131 concentration in milk was 161 pCi/L, compared to 1 pCi/L in Australia and Aotearoa. (WWNFIP, 8/1989: p. 13)

the increasing physical and psychological problems to the French nuclear program. The people, however, do not have the same difficulty making the connection. Stories abound of radiation related illnesses and birth defects, and those concerned blame the bomb. Toimata's story, which first appeared in Greenpeace International's *Testimonies: Witnesses of French Nuclear Testing in the South Pacific*, is a prime example of this (Greenpeace International and Toimata, 1990: p. 63):

> Our first and eldest child was born in 1975. She always seems to be sick with a chronic cough and stomach pains but she goes to school and is doing all right there. My second baby was born prematurely at seven and a half months and died the day he was born.
>
> My third baby was born at home at full term but died there two weeks later. She had a skin problem. Her skin would come off immediately if it was touched. The doctors said that the baby was fine but obviously she was not. No one knows the cause of her condition.
>
> Eugene, my fourth baby was born at full time but died when he was two months old. He had diarrhoea and we took him to Mamao, the hospital in Tahiti. The diarrhoea continued for some time. When it stopped, it was replaced by another condition. The baby became rigid, like wood. Every part of his body was racked by continuous muscular contractions and he had a high temperature. It was impossible to open his fists. The doctors would not talk about his condition. He was at Mamao for two weeks and then he died.
>
> The doctors did not tell us anything and refused to fill out his death certificate. Without a death certificate the baby could not be buried so I pleaded with the doctors. They told me to get my general practitioner to fill in the form. The nurses at the hospital told me to tell people, if anyone should ask me, that my baby had died en route and not in the hospital. In the end I had to give in and ask my general practitioner to fill out the death certificate so that my child could be buried. I have no idea why all this happened and there was nothing we could do about it. On top of that, we are angry that we were not allowed to stay with him in hospital when he was so sick. Because of that we weren't there when he died.
>
> Our fifth child is alive and well. The sixth was born at full term in a clinic. Everything went well during the pregnancy and at her birth but the doctors said she was premature and she was transferred to Mamao and put into an incubator. She died the next day. She weighed over three kilos at birth and I am sure that I carried her for a full nine months.
>
> The seventh is alive and very well. My eighth was still-born prematurely at six and a half months. My ninth baby, a girl, was born at full term but she died when she was eight months old. She was a very fat baby and they said she had a blood infection.
>
> The tenth child was born mid-1985. She has had an airway infection and a heart condition since birth. We were told that she had a hole in the heart and she was sent to France to have an operation to correct this. The surgeon said that she would need only one operation but she has to go back to France for a checkup soon. She seems to be doing well.
>
> I feel physically well myself. I have two sisters. Neither of them have had any problems with their children's health except for having had two premature stillbirths, one as a result of a bad fall. I think that my children have died because my husband worked at Moruroa.

This is just one of countless anecdotal reports of the *"bébé martyre d'atomique"*, of the children born with genetic abnormalities, and the miscarriages of genetically damaged foetuses. There are reports of Maohi suffering from cancers being secretly transported to hospitals in France and Aotearoa (WWNFIP, August 1989: p. 13). Fifty Maohi brain cancer patients were secretly sent to Paris. Women are suffering a high level of breast and other gynaecological cancers.

According to long-time Tahitian activist Marie-Therese Danielsson (1987), there have been no studies done to determine the extent of the impact on the health of Islanders:

> We don't know how many people have cancer. You only know when you hear that someone has died of cancer or leukaemia. They send a lot of people to France, more and more, but they are not all on the list. They arrive in Paris, but no one knows what treatment they are getting. It's a big problem. There is an association of parents of handicapped children because we have many handicapped children, since the atmospheric tests. But when the authorities looked for the children they didn't find any. Why? Because the Tahitians don't like to show their handicapped children to people. Then the French said that there wasn't any. These are children born to people on those islands during the atmospheric tests, or to people who have worked at Moruroa.
>
> We are only just beginning to see the effects of the atmospheric testing, only the tip of the iceberg. When will we begin to suffer from the underground tests? Ten years, twenty? The government says everything is safe for a thousand years, even if that were true, which it isn't, what legacy do we leave the future generations?

They are killing our spirits: that's the most dangerous part. That they have made us think that we are worthless.

Chailang Palacios. Northern Marianas. (Dibblin, 1985a)

A major effect of the testing that scientists have been able to monitor is the increase of *ciguatera* (marine food poisoning), which results in vomiting, diarrhoea, physical weakness, miscarriages, premature births and neurological disease in the newly born, and can sometimes be fatal. *Ciguatera*, which is particularly common in the larger fish that form the basis of the Maohi diet, flourishes when reef ecology is disturbed, whether by natural causes (storms, earthquakes, heavy rains) or human activities (construction, dredging, and explosions). Tahiti-Polynesia suffers from a *ciguatera* rating six times the average of the Pacific as a whole.

In Hao Atoll, where building of a military facility to support the testing in nearby Moruroa, had resulted in the dredging of the lagoon, the first case of *ciguatera* was in 1966. By mid-1968, 43 per cent of the population of 650 had been affected (WWNFIP, August 1989: p. 14). On Mangareva Atoll, the closest inhabited island to Moruroa, almost all of the 528 locals have suffered the associated neurological symptoms with a mortality rate of one in six annually (WWNFIP, August 1989: p. 14). Widespread throughout the region, *ciguatera* has a massive social and nutritional impact in a community where fish is the main food. Islanders are dependent on imported fish, mostly canned, from Japan which has the fishing monopoly for Tahiti's ocean.

It is interesting to note that Moruroa means "place of the great secret", and that the atoll bore that name long before the French testing began. Were the ancient Maohi seers into the future? Marie-Therese Danielsson discussed the effect of the testing program on Moruroa, Fangataufa, and their neighbouring islands:

> Moruroa is safer, it is the biggest atoll in the region. Fangataufa is a small island and they had to build a pass there but Moruroa was chosen because it had a pass deep enough for ocean vessels to get through to the lagoon. A big island with a broad pass is very rare. With the size of Moruroa it is possible to put a village on the east side and have a pass on the west side, leaving the north and south for the tests. It's a town. It has a church, a hospital, even cinemas and its own television and radio station, sports facilities and a shopping centre. Three thousand men and twelve women live there. A lot of the men are Maohi. They've made too many tests at Moruroa. They've made them wherever they could because they need space for living. They've made them on the coral reef, around the inside edge of the lagoon, and in the middle of the lagoon, where the layer is thin and without protection. It's not possible to do so much testing there now and so they are trying to go back to Fangataufa which is already contaminated. The first underground test was made there, and the atmospheric tests, but something went wrong and Fangautaufa is very much irradiated. It is too radioactive to work there. But now that there are problems on Moruroa, they are trying to get back to Fangataufa (Danielsson, 1987).

There are many other inhabited islands in the area. There is Mangareva. Today the population is little more than five hundred. Catholic missionaries disembarked in Mangareva in 1834, and within ten years converted the population to their faith and the European way of life. The casualty rate was high, because during this period the population diminished from 5,000 to 500, as a result of the many introduced diseases and the changed living conditions. In and around the only village, Rikitea, there are several ruins, dating from two distinct periods. On one hand, there is a convent school, where the girls were locked up during the strict rule of the early Catholic missionaries. On the other hand, there is at the opposite end of the village an atomic shelter, where the whole population was locked up on several occasions, during that period that nuclear test were made in the atmosphere at Moruroa. In the meantime, the army technicians "decontaminated" their houses by spraying them with water from the lagoon, which cannot be considered an efficient method. During the same period, contaminated French warships also anchored in the lagoon to be rinsed and cleaned.

Before testing began at Moruroa in 1966, the lagoon teemed with fish. Only two years later, all fish in the lagoon were poisonous, and many people sick from having eaten them, displaying all symptoms of *ciguatera*. Ever since, the people have had to live on canned food or, if they want fish, to travel by small boats to Temoe Atoll, 25 miles to the south. Much direct radioactive fallout must also have occurred at Mangareva, and it is strange indeed that no cancer statistics are available. A high cancer incidence today is even more likely. I have seen two freshly dug graves in the cemetery, containing, I was told, cancer victims.

The people of Mangareva have complained on many occasions in the past to the French authorities about these health hazards, but nothing has been done to improve the situation. When I asked them during my recent visit they all seemed very resigned and hopeless saying: "Who cares about what we say, we are such a small people". So why do we not give their voices more strength by joining in and protesting more loudly, by the thousands?

Almost more isolated than Mangareva is the island of Rapa, 700 miles south of Tahiti, as there is no airstrip. The island is the emerging portion of an ancient crater, communicating with the sea. The 480 inhabitants live in two villages on each side of the entrance to the bay thus formed. The Rapa islanders are fortunate not to have any ciguatera problem and can thus eat the many species of fish. French navy ships call at the island every three months or so. The aim is to give the sailors what commonly is called "rest and recreation". Each time, the whole population is invited on board, "discos" are organised for the youth, drinks are offered and the women are tempted to prostitute themselves (Danielsson, 1985).

There is Tureia. It's less than a hundred kilometres away from Moruroa. In 1968 there was an election and only one person in Tureia voted. That was really strange and people started questioning. We found out that all the people of Tureia had been taken away. They stayed away from their home for two or three months, quite a long time. Only one man had refused to go and he was the one that had voted. They were taken away from the tests. When they were allowed to return they were told, "Don't eat fish from the lagoon, locally grown food, or drink local water". How else could they live?

And there's Marutea. That's a very good island for pearl shells. Once after a test on Moruroa had resulted in a rock slide it caused a tidal wave there. This French farmer complained about the destruction caused by the wave, he was told "close your mouth". These islands are contaminated.

There are other inhabited islands close to Moruroa, like Reao and Pukarua. But the whole of Tahiti-Polynesia has suffered from the French, although not necessarily directly related to the tests. One example is the story of Takaroa Island. The French decided to build an airstrip. At an astounding low price, they compulsorily purchased ancestral lands and, in May 1986, at forty-eight hours notice, they moved in their bulldozers and demolished everything. There was no right of appeal for the people whose lives were destroyed by this arrogance, nor any assistance to help them start again.

And there's Hao. That's one of the biggest islands. There's about a thousand Tahitians [Maohi] living there. A lot of people there are against the French military because they have left all their dirt there. Hao is so dirty. And they suffer a lot from cyclones too. It's a very hard life. There used to be a lot of military activity during the atmospheric tests but now less personnel are needed. Now it's a military airport. Civilians can land there, but there isn't a regular airline. It can be used by the US, NASA, as an emergency airstrip for the space shuttle (Danielsson, 1987).

The environmental impact on Moruroa itself demands urgent global attention. It is one of the most heavily contaminated islands in the Pacific, along with Bikini, Enetwetak, Rongelap (all US testing sites) and Kalama/Johnston Atoll and Kiritimati (Christmas) Island in Kiribati (where the Britain and the US have both tested).

Massive accidents have occurred at Moruroa. On 22 March 1981, a hurricane swept a pile of radioactive waste (previously dumped on the western section of the atoll) into the ocean. This included plutonium from a July 1979 accident that killed two technicians. There is enough waste on Moruroa to fill 200,000 concrete containers, each holding 200 litres. An internal report of the Atomic Energy Commission engineers and technicians on Moruroa, leaked in 1981, indicates that the atoll is sinking 2 cm after each test (a total of 1.5 metres from 1975–81); that there was a 30 cm wide 800 metre long crack in the atoll; and that radiation leakage into the ocean had been occurring for years. Coral atolls, being fragile and permeable, are recognised as the worst geographical testing situation. Incredibly high temperatures and pressures vaporise and melt the basalt and fracture the surrounding rock. The French government insists that radio-activity would be retained in the test chambers, bored 800–1500 metres deep and sealed with concrete plugs, for a thousand to ten thousand years.

All we want is a better future for our children – a future that is good for everyone.
Hilda Halkyard-Harawira. Aotearoa. (Magnall, 1987)

The women of Tahiti-Polynesia have a long history of strength, wisdom and endurance. The proud independence of Maohi women was remarked on by the first Europeans to contact the Islanders. When Samuel Wallis arrived in Tahiti in 1767 it was a woman, High Chieftainess Purea, who governed the people, and in 1843 it was Queen Pomaré IV, again a woman, who was ousted from the throne. The women were free, they did not "belong" to any man. Their world was a long way from the disempowerment experienced by European women of that day.

Since time immemorial it has been acceptable for a Maohi woman to choose to be a "Firebird", that is, a free woman (Lewis, 1977: p. 156). Operating from a high status, women determined when, and indeed whether, they would engage sexually with a man. This freedom of choice came as a shock to the European men who were enculturated into believing that women did not experience sexual pleasure and were only there for male gratification. Played with by the women, they began to pull the nails out of their ships to pay for the women's attentions. This autonomy of Maohi women has been exploited by tourist companies, creating the image of Tahiti as the archetypal South Sea Island: women – ever-smiling and always available. It is a myth that misrepresents Maohi women, a myth created by a male-dominated culture that simply could not comprehend a society where women were free. Certainly the autonomy of the Maohi women has been far above that allowed to European women.

But the arrival of the colonialists shattered women's power. Making it very clear that the limitation of women's power is a product of the French colonial culture, Marie-Therese Danielsson (1987), describes some of the difficulties that women face under the alien regime:

> It's difficult to get women organised because they are dependent on the men. In Tahiti many women who work and are well off are not interested in politics, they just think of money and what they can get for themselves. They just want to have a good time, run a car, go to dances, have babies and then educate them. That is the French way, they have become

French. And at the same time they are Tahitian women, *vahine*. It makes problems in their lives. And then you have the poor women. They have to work very hard. They have a lot of children. They are beaten by their husband. They have to make money because there is no money because he has spent it drinking. They have many problems, these poor women. How can they do anything? It's a terrible situation.

For the women who are not in Tahiti, that are still on the outer islands, it is different. I know a lot of women from the Tuamotu Islands. They are very strong. They have their own land. If a woman marries a man, he has his lands and she has her lands. The man might work on his wife's land but, many times, she would pay him for the work, although the money would be used for the family. She has the money and is more independent. In the old day, twenty years ago, the couples didn't marry. They waited until they had been living together ten, fifteen, twenty years and they had many children. Sometimes they were grandparents before they married. Because there were no social services, no insurance for medical assistance, they didn't need to marry. The woman was free. She felt free to leave her husband. And the man, if he wanted to have his wife, was more careful, because he knew that she could go away when she wanted to. She could go with another man if she wanted. There could be fighting, but finally she could do what she wanted to do.

Now that is not the case. She has become more "civilised", and has more problems. In the Tuamotu Islands it was the last place where they were so free. They were Catholics, but led a less religious life, much less, because very often there was no priest for most of the time. So they had no feeling that they had to be religiously married. And the old missionaries there were very wise and encouraged them to wait and see if they would stay together before marrying, because then, in the Catholic church, if you married it was for ever. So they preferred to wait because they knew there would be changes. The Protestants did group marriages. Twice a year they go to the villages, and say, "All those who have been living together should get married. Now!". With the new religions, Mormons and Jehovah's Witness, it's worse. You have to be baptised into their religions before you can be married. All this has changed the culture so much because the woman now belongs to the man. So the situation of the woman is not good.

One example of how colonisation has undermined women's power is in the area of sexuality. Maohi women have traditionally taken pride in their sexual behaviours, there was status in sexuality. Now, the French have created a trade in women's bodies: under French rule, they have become "prostitutes". According to Marie-Therese Danielsson (1987), women are paying a heavy price for the French presence:

Women come from the outer islands to work in the tourist industry. A lot come to be prostitutes. This is new. Before, it was not really prostitution. Before, women just went to the men they chose. They liked to have fun and went to bars. A girl would think, "Here's a man with a little money so I can have fun with him". And so that was all. And if he had a lot of money she would say, "I need a new dress", or "My mother is very ill, I need money for her". There was no tariff, no charge. The women were responsible for themselves, and if she didn't like one man she would throw him out. And often, after the women went out the whole night with the men, they would just disappear at the last moment. It was very amusing. Some were considered prostitutes because they had been to hospital with venereal diseases and had to go to the police from time to time. They were looked down on.

After the military came it was different. A lot of women, and a lot of men too, came to be prostitutes. Now it is a problem with a price, pimps and studios. It's very different. You have parents taking their young daughters to the Korean ships, very young girls because Korean men like young girls. You have a lot of prostitution with the fishing ships. No one speaks about it. But if you go to the quay at night you can see them. And rape. Rapes are terrible here, you can't imagine.

Women in any society are strong – women survive – and Maohi women have a strength inherited from their traditional culture. Maea Tematua, recognising the hardships, stresses that women are beginning to come back into their power. They have been actively involved in the move towards an end to nuclear testing and independence for the nation (Tematua, 1991):

> Right now I am telling you what I think, but many other women of course have their own opinions on life, on Polynesian society, as they are at present. These are mine. There are many women who are against independence, but there are also many who are for independence. There are many who are against nuclear testing. There are some, however, who support it [nuclear testing]. Try to understand them and the situation in which they live.
>
> There are many problems that women face with regard to day-to-day life. Everything is linked by a vicious system. That is, economically we depend on the outside world, whereas we could be self-sufficient. In Tahiti, despite appearances, there is poverty – what we call the "needy". Life is too expensive. There is too great a gap between the well-off and the majority of the people. This is why there is poverty.
>
> So, in Tahiti women do a great deal to help in their family life. They are craftswomen; they do a lot to help buy everything their families need. They also help in their children's education. There are women who speak French, who can help their children, but there are also Tahitian women who do not speak French very well, or who speak a mixture of French and Tahitian. These women are not able to give their children an appropriate education, they can't help the children – and it is the children who suffer the consequences of this. There is a growing rate of failure at school, but at the moment the government is in the process of drawing up an education charter, based on an education adapted to local children. Because, don't forget, we have our native language, but a French curriculum is at present applied in the schools. That is why there is a problem with education. So, when the parents can help their children, the children in those families make it, but in the purely Polynesian, purely Tahitian families, the children have difficulty in pursuing and reaching educational goals.
>
> Family planning is also a problem. There are too many children in each family. There needs to be some education concerning family-planning, and at the moment our government is setting up family-planning structures which are adapted to society as it is now, adapted to life as it is now in Tahiti. Also, we have had a health system for some years but this still needs to be promoted. That is, the Polynesians need to be educated and informed, within the context of their day-to-day life. So there are many problems.
>
> Women are very involved politically. Polynesian women are being included and they have a lot to say. At the moment we have two women in government: one is a minister, and the other is a territorial adviser. What I would like for Polynesia is many more women in power speaking at a governmental level. This is what I most wish for my country. Because women have also come a long way. They try to obtain jobs which are important in Polynesian society today. They are no longer the Tahitians of a century ago. They have moved forward with time, with education and with society in general. We must become aware of what Polynesian women have to say. That is why I call on Polynesian women to

move into the political arena, because I know that Polynesian women are very frank – if they have something to say, they say it up front.

Money from the bomb does not interest us. It is better to be poor and in good health than rich and sick.

Ida Bordes-Teariki. Tahiti-Polynesia. (Robie, 1980)

In 1992, after twenty-five years, the French government announced a temporary halt to its nuclear testing program, provided the other declared nuclear powers also refrained. Coming more than a year after Russia's unilateral halt to testing, the offer was rejected by the US and Britain, and responded to by China with the detonation of one of its largest devices. Since then the US, Russia, Britain and France have agreed to a temporary suspension.

The French government seems to have been forced into that position because of growing public demand, particularly in France where the opposition to the testing program has increased threefold over the past five years. Rallying behind the Maohi people, 60 per cent of French citizens now favour a permanent end to the testing, in contrast to only 30 per cent who want it to continue. This growing pressure is evident in the election results of March 1992 where the ecology parties received 14 per cent of the votes compared to the Socialist Party's 18 per cent, forcing the socialist government to negotiate with them on several major issues, including the nuclear testing program. The moves towards unification of the European Community in 1992 also provided its own impetus: nuclear testing in Tahiti-Polynesia became a European issue as much as it was French. In addition, the bilateral cutbacks by the US and Russia, coupled with the modernisation of the French arsenal, had resulted in France having a comparable nuclear force. Thus the alleged reason for the testing program, to maintain a *force de frappe* was removed. However, the respective governments facing mounting pressure by their own militaries, it is questionable just how long this respite will last. One thing is certain, the damage has already been done. Tahiti-Polynesia is highly contaminated, and its people, living in poverty, face increasing health problems.

Despite the moratorium on testing, France remains reluctant to relinquish control over its colony. With the Pacific recognised as the hub of the world's new economic and political order, France is determined to expand its position in the region. France claims eight million square kilometres of the Pacific Ocean. This includes not only Tahiti-Polynesia, but Kanaky (New Caledonia), Wallis and Futuna and the little-known Matthews and Hunter Islands, mere rocks between Kanaky and Vanuatu, populated only by Foreign Legionnaires stationed there to "fly the flag". By merit of these colonies, France exploits the world's second largest Exclusive Economic Zone, some 4.6 million square kilometres.

Nevertheless, the departure of the French is inevitable, and the Maohi are mobilising with a renewed strength to move towards independence. There has been a large scar left upon the Maohi lands and people, and it will take time to recover, but the determination evident among the Maohi underpins achievable goals. Their memories of life before the French flooded into their islands provides the template for their efforts.

In 1963, when the French announced their plans to shift their nuclear testing program to their Polynesian colony, large numbers of French technicians and troops began arriving in the islands. And thousands of Islanders flocked in from the outer islands for employment in the construction industry, and were later made redundant as the infrastructure was established. When the French government reneged on its promise of free passage to return home, the majority remained. The population rose dramatically. On Tahiti alone it rose from 600 in the early 1960s to 114,000 in the late 1980s – 70 per cent of the nation's population crowded onto one small island (WWNFIP, August 1989: p. 14). Islander life was transformed. With precious land taken up with military bases and personnel accommodation, the Maohi people were left with devastating social effects.

A massive tourist industry was encouraged, and the Maohi people were dumped into poverty. Today many live in *bi donvilles* (slums) on the steep mountain slopes, often with no water or sewerage, while the French settlers and hotels claim the luxury of the green plains and splendid shoreline. The wealth disparity between the Indigenous and the substantial French and Chinese communities increases daily. The Maohi suffer from domestic violence, alcoholism, drug abuse and juvenile delinquency. Since the urban environment necessitates the importation of 90 per cent of its food supplies and other needs, the nation is economically dependent on the testing program (PCRC, June 1992: p. 6). Tens of thousands of Maohi live directly or indirectly off the CEP. This economic dependency makes the struggle for political independence more difficult.

The French have intentionally undermined the economic integrity of the islands, asserts Marie-Therese Danielsson (1987):

> The French have had a big influence on Tahiti. Just before the tests we had reached a point where we could balance our budget because we produced enough for the people's consumption. Cattle. We never imported meat from Australia or New Zealand before the tests, never. We had better cattle. We ate more fish. We had coffee and vanilla. We had just developed a new breed of coconut just right for here. We could have managed very well, but it's all gone now, because people prefer to work for money, cash, quick money.
>
> Before, we were self-sufficient and did not need "employment", now there is a lot of unemployment. The outer Islanders were drawn to Papeete, to the big city. People came from the Austral Islands where there was plenty of food and abandoned their plantations. They settled in Papeete where the population just keeps growing, people just keep coming. The women of Raivavae are coming here because of the life here, and the men of Raivavae cannot find enough women to marry. Also the Marquesan women. They come to work in

the restaurants and bars and become prostitutes. All these problems are very mixed.

There's a lot of rebuilding that needs to happen. The bomb has destroyed the economy. The French encouraged the people to come to Tahiti. I think partly because the military thought there would be fewer people to be contaminated if they moved the people. And the Catholic Church also. The bishop told us that he was happy about it because now all the people from the Tuamotus who were really difficult to reach would be in one place. You had one missionary for five to ten islands, and he could only get to the smaller islands for a week once a year, and to the larger islands for one month, and it was dangerous to travel between the islands. People in the Tuamotus and the Marquesas, who are mostly Catholic, came and the church built houses for them on their lands, they own a lot of land, keeping them in one place. So the church helped the military to keep control of the people. All these things have done a lot to transform this society and make the problems we have today.

The French presence has created a false society: the present economic and social structures, based upon the nuclear testing program, are not sustainable or just. Many Maohi people are committed to stepping beyond what Maea Tematua (1991) calls the "curtain of flowers":

I believe that independence is a legitimate demand for us, for Polynesians, to become responsible for the destiny of our country and for future generations. And I am firmly opposed to any weapons which kill: nuclear weapons are among these. There are too many injustices in Tahiti, too many differences between the Tahitian people and the wealthy minority. I hope with all my heart that there will be progress towards independence, and towards the denuclearisation of the Pacific. Then we will be able to say that Tahiti is really a beautiful island, but, at the moment, there is a curtain of flowers here – separating reality from all that is artificial, all that is plastic, all that is false. There is this curtain of flowers that you have to look behind.

That is why I would like the CEP and the CEA to withdraw from the territory, to go and carry on their experiments elsewhere and not in Polynesia, not in our paradise. To support independence, I am thinking above all of the departure of the CEP, because if there is an increased amount of money coming into the territory, it is solely because of French nuclear testing. Tahiti has come very far in thirty years, but this development has been for a minority of the population. I do not know whether you have already seen how we live, the very high cost of living in Tahiti.

But independence has to be prepared for, that is certain. When the French leave Tahiti the people will automatically become responsible for our country. They will turn to agriculture and fishing, which are the raw materials of our country. For example, after the cyclone that we had in 1983, the people who had suffered damage began to cultivate the land so as to sell their products all around the island. But as soon as the territory received the obligatory aid from the state and elsewhere those people once again became *des assistés* [dependent on state welfare]. I think that as soon as we are able to eat our fill, using our own resources, we will be able to stretch further, to see further – and why not? – to independence. This is my most fervent wish – I have never hidden it, and never will.

The independence parties have begun to consider possible solutions to the problems that arise from the French presence and its anticipated departure. Oscar Temaru (1987) believes it is possible to recreate a self-sustaining nation:

The economic situation is the responsibility of the United Nations. Resolutions have been made at the UN that requests all the UN members who have colonies to help those colonies attain independence but that law has never been respected. We want them to respect that and get the French out of our country. And they have to look at the economy. The French destroyed our self-sufficient lifestyle and implanted an economic structure where the Maohi are at the bottom and the French and Chinese at the top. You go anywhere, all the stores belong to the Chinese or French.

We know we are going to have problems for the first few years but we are very hopeful. We are only 150,000 people, we have a hundred and thirty islands and the biggest ocean. This country is bigger than Europe. We can see what we can do with our ocean. We can build fisheries here. Our ocean is used by the Japanese and Koreans, we can sell our fish ourselves. We can educate our people in animal husbandry. We can farm. And we have tourism. At the moment all the money goes to foreign investors but we can do it in a way that is good for our people. Bring in just enough foreign currency so we can develop our country.

William Tcheng (1987), living on Raiatea, argues for a style of tourism that benefits the people directly and aims towards a self-sufficient economy:

I want to see small people given a chance. Lots of our youth are unemployed, I want to see them going into tourism, real people-orientated tourism. Ten people to run twenty bungalows, let them out cheaply, feed the people fish and food from the land. Do it in the right spirit, the right awareness. It would be good for the Polynesians too, strengthen their identity, make them know they've got something to be proud of. It's easy, we can do it.

The economic survival of an independent nation depends upon land, assert the Pomaré Brothers (1987), direct descendants of the royal line of Queen Pomaré IV:

We must address land issues now. If not, what will it be like after independence? Will the Maohi people have the land they need or will they be oppressed as they are now? The people of Tahiti have nothing any more, a few bare patches of land. Our people live on the slopes surrounded by dust and mud. Nothing grows there. The French have all the rich, fertile land. We have become tenants to the colonialists. The French signed a treaty with our forefathers that they have never respected. They agreed that all land would be under a Tahitian tribunal. This has not happened. The French have bought it all – and the Chinese, Americans and Japanese. Just like in Hawai'i. Soon we will have no land left. And so the Maohi have begun to occupy the lands given to us by our ancestors. There is no other choice.

The movement to take back the land is increasing throughout the Pacific, but in this instance that land has been contaminated by nuclear testing.

It is urgent for us Tahitians to struggle and gain independence in our own country. The sooner we rid our country of France the sooner the Pacific can become calm again. While France remains in the Pacific the bombs will continue to explode. But when you tell France to go home and bomb, they will say, "I am at home". If you give us a hand at getting rid of France it is definite that soon we can make the Pacific independent and non-nuclear.

Charlie Ching. Tahiti-Polynesia. (Ching, 1988)

Tahiti-Polynesia, home of the Maohi, has witnessed over 150 nuclear detonations. The French government has indicated that it has little regard for the lives of the Maohi people, or for their future generations. They have refused to allow any true study of the impact on the environment or health, and have persistently denied the evidence that does exist. With an arrogance that has been displayed throughout the colonial era they continue to maintain their military forces in the region. Tourism flourishes at the expense of the Indigenous people, forced into slum areas on the sides of steep mountains without adequate infrastructure. Prostitution and rape scar the women. Babies are miscarried or born deformed.

There is an anger mounting in the land. The people have suffered enough. They are finding a voice – a strong, defiant, rebellious voice – that speaks from their hearts. Increasingly they are demanding the freedom to determine their own lives. Demanding their independence, they are uniting with other Indigenous peoples to create a future Pacific that honours life.

French Polynesia, which is said in the tourist brochures to have the closest islands to paradise, is nurturing the fire of death, the fire of the disaster of humanity.

Louis Uregei. Kanaky. (Uregei, 1987)

A SCAR ON THE MEMORY OF THE PEOPLE

Please fight to stop them with this nuclear madness. But tell them to dismantle it all, not to send it to the Pacific.

Chailang Palacios. Northern Marianas. (WWNFIP, 1987: p. 14)

The "end of the Cold War" and the "relaxing of tensions" between the US and Russia has not benefited the Pacific peoples.

The "era of nuclear demilitarisation" heralded in Europe has not been mirrored in the Pacific arena. The region has witnessed only a change of emphasis: not a withdrawal of nuclear weapons but a restructuring of the nuclear weapons systems in the region (McLellan, 1990: p. 8). The US Pentagon has decommissioned some nuclear weapons and has limited the number of troops stationed in foreign countries. But this has been coupled with an increase in rights of access to regional facilities, the involvement of allied and "friendly" nations in US strategic plans, and the "modernisation" of US weapon systems and its command, control and communication facilities. On its part, Russia has reduced the deployment of nuclear vessels from extended patrols in the north Pacific but continues its nuclear activities along its Pacific coastline.

The "nuclear demilitarisation" moves made by the US should be considered with a good deal of suspicion. Many of the nuclear warheads once deployed by the Pentagon are now in stockpiles awaiting redeployment. Nic McLellan (1994) of the Pacific Campaign to Disarm the Seas writes:

> The Pentagon has been forced to decommission nuclear weapons for a combination of reasons: the obsolescence of many delivery systems; the increasing cost of nuclear deployments; and the significant political costs of nuclear visits – most clearly seen with the anti-nuclear policies of Aotearoa and the Philippines, and through bans and protests in countries around the region: Australia, Japan, Vanuatu, Belau and more.

In addition, as the world's biggest debtor nation, the US must put on a pretence of channelling finances into the needs of its own people who have increasingly demanded that their government deal with local issues, such as poverty and health. In the absence of the great Russian "enemy", the people of the US are less prepared to allow their sons and daughters to be stationed away from home for extended periods. The world's people are ready for an end to the nuclear "deterrent", and yet, although the world's social climate has changed, the "arms race" continues.

The US considers it necessary to maintain its hold on the Pacific because the region, heralded as the "Ocean of the Future", has become the economic hub of the twenty-first century. During the late 1970s and 1980s, as the Pacific Rim countries of Asia – Japan, China, Taiwan and Korea – increasingly exerted economic clout on the world's markets, the Pacific region overtook Europe as the US's major sphere of economic interest. In 1980, when Japan became the US's paramount trading partner, US trade with the region already had begun to outweigh its trade with the European Community. The region, rich in natural resources and cheap labour, straddles the sea-path of the US to resources in the Middle East and Africa.

When, on 3 February 1988, US Naval Secretary, James Webb urged the Pentagon to shift its focus into the Pacific, he was simply voicing a policy change that was already well under way (Jones, 1990). During World War Two the US Navy and Marines were the predominant force in the Pacific arena; the US Navy were involved in the administration of Micronesia in the 1940s after the war; and the US Pacific Command which covers the Indian and Pacific Oceans has long been established. But now the US is moving to integrate its economic involvement in the region with its strategic and military interests. As the twenty-first century dawns the Pacific region has become the global hub of US military activities. It is the Pentagon's intention to "safeguard" US interests in the region, and it has never hesitated to maintain control over its most prized possession.

The US nuclear presence in the Pacific was increased when, in 1987, the Intermediate-range Nuclear Force (INF) Treaty removed Ground-Launched Cruise Missiles (GLCMs) from European soil. The US Navy had planned the deployment of Sea-Launched Cruise Missiles on a range of ships and submarines since 1984, thereby escalating the US first-strike capacity. As US missiles were removed from Europe in the late 1980s, sea-based forces increased their sway. The number of US Sea-Launched Cruise Missiles almost doubled the missiles abolished under the INF Treaty and, by early 1990, almost one third of the world's nuclear weapons were at sea – an estimated 16,000 nuclear weapons, belonging to the US, Russia, Britain, France and China. The Pacific, covering over one-third of the planet, is 70 per cent of the earth's ocean.

Despite the new climate of diplomacy between the US and Russia, the Pentagon continues to upgrade its military involvement in the Pacific. While, in 1990, the Pentagon did agree with Russia to limit the numbers of cruise missiles that could be deployed on ocean vessels and to reduce the number of warships operating in the Pacific fleet, it maintained its nuclear Cruise and Trident II missile programs. Refusing Moscow's call for a nuclear freeze and a commitment to the total elimination of nuclear weapons at sea, the US responded by stating, through US Defence Secretary Cheney, that it had no intention of weakening its military presence in Asia and the Pacific (Jones, 1990: p. 8). Claiming that any withdrawal on their behalf would create a vacuum and destabilise the region, the US policy has been to "enhance deterrence" by restructuring and modernising its Pacific forces (McLellan, 1990: p. 8).

In 1991, announcements of nuclear disarmament continued on both sides. The US removed Sea-Launched Cruise Missiles from ships and submarines and stored them for possible redeployment (PCRC, October 1991: p. 8). Land-based tactical weapons were removed from South Korea, there was a 10–12 per cent cut in US troops in foreign bases, and the US Air Force was no longer kept on 24-hour alert (PCRC, October 1991: p. 8). With the Pentagon intending to destroy at least 7,000 warheads, it seemed that tension was easing. But, hand-in-hand with these developments, President Bush declared that his purpose was to "accelerate the retirement of some of the Soviet Union's most advanced military programs while protecting the key elements of the USA's 'strategic modernisation'" (PCRC, October 1991: p. 8). The Pentagon had merely shifted its emphasis to focus on weapons systems that could be rapidly deployed with maximum efficiency. Of prime importance were the B2 Stealth Bombers, the Trident II submarine missiles, and a portable version of the Strategic Defence Initiative (SDI) that makes it deployable in, and against, Third World nations (PCRC, November 1991: p. 9).

In the late 1980s there were over 500 foreign installations in the Pacific Islands and Rim countries – 90 per cent of which were American (Hayes, 1986), but these began to close during the early 1990s. The Pentagon was forced to withdraw from Subic Naval Base and Clarke Airforce Base in the Philippines because of growing anti-US sentiment and the damaged caused by the eruption of Mount Pinatubo. This substantially disadvantaged Pentagon aspirations in the region, but the bases have been replaced by "access agreements" in over 50 countries. These agreements allow US troops to use regional facilities without the associated costs or problems of local protest (PCRC, July 1993: p. 8). The cutting of US troops stationed in the region is coupled with the demand that regional allies increase their military spending and intensify their military activity. Thus nations in the region – Japan, South Korea, Australia, France, and others – pick up the bill for the US military presence.

Although armed forces are banned under Japan's 1947 Constitution, imposed during US occupation, Japan has been encouraged by the Pentagon to restore and increase its military. It has also increased its contribution towards the cost of basing US forces in Japan and Okinawa. Japan, which has the fastest growing military budget amongst the US's allies, is now the world's third largest force. It extends its ocean patrolling up to 1,000 nautical miles from Tokyo, bringing its sphere of influence to the shores of Russia, Korea, and China.

Korea, Japan's nearest neighbour, is also caught in the Pentagon's plans. Nic McLellan (1994) writes:

> In the aftermath of the Korean revolution following the Second World War, and the Korean war of 1950–53, the US military has played a significant role in South Korea. The division of the Korean peninsula has meant a significant US military presence in South Korea, especially in the period of dictatorship from the 1950s to 1987. The US has based tactical nuclear weapons in the south, and has threatened to use them against North Korea on many occasions. Even after the fall of the Park and Chun regimes, nuclear tensions have not been reduced.

Many Koreans are actively working for human rights against the South Korean government, calling for reunification and the removal of US bases and military forces. Critics and US officials alike warn that the build-up of military forces in this area is so intense that nuclear war is a constant threat. The nuclear stakes were raised in 1993–94, when the US and South Korean governments began to pressure North Korea over nuclear proliferation questions.

Australia has been a regional power in the southern Pacific since the 1880s when the colonial British government unilaterally declared New Guinea a British protectorate and demanded the annexation of Fiji and Vanuatu (then the New Hebrides). As the largest economic power in the southern Pacific, it influences, and has proven itself prepared to intervene in, the internal affairs of any regional nation, should it deem that its "interests", or those of the US, are threatened. For example, it supported the Papua New Guinea government in its war against Bougainville, because the crisis threatened its mining interests. It is presently experiencing the largest peace-time military build-up in its history, an extension that will enable it to fight anywhere in the south west Pacific and South East Asia arena whether alone, as part of a larger US effort or with regional allies (Bolt, 1990). In 1992, under cover of a program aimed at assisting Pacific nations to control their fishing waters and customs, Australia presented southern Pacific nations with patrol boats and extended its series of military training exercises. This was part of an endeavour to establish a regional defence network, headed by the Australian military.

After the US, France has more bases in the region, and indeed around the world, than any other nation. Enforcing its will on the area by maintaining colonies in the southern Pacific, it has established strong allegiances with the US. The nations of Kanaky (New Caledonia), Wallis and Futuna and Tahiti-Polynesia are considered crucial to France's stature as a global military and economic power. Tahiti-Polynesia is particularly vital to the French military as a testing site for their nuclear weapons program, although President François Mitterand's 1992 decision for a moratorium on nuclear testing, opened a significant debate over the future of its Pacific colonies. Tahiti-Polynesia's capital, Papeete, which homeports part of the French Pacific Fleet, is littered with military installations, including a huge rest and recreation facility.

The Pentagon maintains bilateral agreements with other nations in the region. The Philippines remains inextricably bound to the Pentagon's blueprint for the Pacific, despite the removal of Subic Naval and Clarke Airforce bases. Military agreements have recently been reached with Indonesia, Malaysia, Singapore, Taiwan and Thailand. This array of individual alliances, rather than one regional accord as in Europe, gives the Pentagon the freedom to operate militaristically without elaborate consultations, as is required by Europe's NATO alliance. Whilst maintaining control over the region, the US encourages cooperation among its allies through massive military exercises. The ASEAN nations, with participation of the major Pacific Rim military powers, are now moving towards establishing a regional Security Forum for the western Pacific.

The apparent withdrawal of the US forces from the region has resulted in an unprecedented arms build-up in Asia. Indonesia, the Philippines, Singapore, South Korea, Taiwan, and Thailand, fearful that the US may abandon the region, thereby enabling hegemonic moves by Japan and/or China, are all increasing their military capabilities. China witnessed a 50 per cent arms build-up in the three years prior to 1993 (PCRC, July 1993: p. 8). Japan, with a military that consists predominantly of officer class (therefore with the ability to rapidly recruit and control soldiers drawn from the civilian population), has consistently maintained its ability to rearm. While military spending has been cut in most regions of the world by 20 per cent or more, in

Asia it has increased. In 1981, the Asian military bill was 15 per cent of the world's total (excluding the US and Russia); by 1991 that had increased 25 per cent, representing 35 per cent of all the world's major weapons systems (PCRC, July 1993: p. 8). This increase has been encouraged by arms merchants who, in the absence of the Cold War sales to the US, Russia and Europe, are seeking new markets (PCRC, July 1993: p. 8).

Even the small island nations are involved in the Pentagon's Pacific. While the US is closing bases elsewhere, it maintains its stranglehold on the Micronesian islands: Guam, the Marshall Islands, the Northern Marianas, and Belau. This is nothing new. Long before World War Two the US military, claiming that their strategic boundaries lay along the Asiatic coast, set about establishing forward bases stretching from Alaska and the Aleutian Islands through Japan, South Korea, the Philippines and Australia to the Antarctic. This was to be backed up by another line of bases stretching from Tinian in the Northern Marianas through Guam to Belau. The Pentagon remains determined to gain lasting influence over those nations, even as the Micronesian nations move to self-government.

These smaller nations, dependent upon US aid, are particularly susceptible to the pressure to allow military bases in their territories, often at the expense of their own needs, as Claire Slatter (1988), of Fiji, explains:

> Many of our governments have been convinced, or are persuaded to believe, that the US activities are for our own benefit, that it is for the security of the Pacific region. We who work with the Movement for a Nuclear Free and Independent Pacific know that this is not so.

Organised violence is not something simply imposed on the region from without. The Government of Papua New Guinea has fought against the people of Bougainville. While the struggle began as sabotage against the abuses of an Australian-owned copper-mining company, the armed response by the PNG government has escalated the situation into a demand for sovereignty. In 1987, military coups destabilised Fijian society amid the loss of human rights. Indonesia has invaded East Timor and West Papua and continues a war against their determination for freedom.

Nonetheless, as the twenty-first century dawns, the US military remains the greatest threat to Pacific security, a concern expressed by Claire Slatter (1988):

> We know that it is the presence of the US military, their strategic interests, which threatens the Pacific region. The US regards the Pacific as an "American Lake".

It is dangerous, and perhaps meaningless, to fall into the numbers game when comparing the nations militarising the Pacific. Who has how many weapons, of what potential? Does it really matter, when the nuclear weapons presently deployed are capable of destroying homes, villages, indeed whole islands, anywhere in the Pacific, in a matter of minutes?

The "Cold War" had been declared over; the US and Russia have become allies; in 1990, US President Bush announced a "New World Order", but nothing has changed, least of all for the Pacific. The economic, political, and military battles of European nations continue to be "fought" in the lands and waters of the Pacific Indigenous people. Indigenous people do not distinguish between militarisation and other forms of oppression when faced with the overall effects on their communities. Hilda Halkyard-Harawira of Aotearoa emphasises:

> An Indigenous person does not give up the struggle for land and culture and survival to be over-awed by the threat of a larger bomb (Magnall, 1987).

What has been done to my people will be remembered for a long time. Our children and their children will remember it. It will be a scar on the memory of the people.
Theresa Minitong. Bougainville. (Minitong, 1990)

Militarisation is an issue of direct importance to women in the region. Although women do enlist in the military forces, and play roles supportive of the men thus engaged (Enloe, 1988 & 1989), men account for over 90 per cent of the world's armed personnel. War is predominantly a male game – it is predominantly men who manufacture, trade, use and control the world's weapon systems – while women and children are the predominant victims. Women are raped, tortured and killed (rape is often used as a political weapon against opponents and is regarded as the booty of war). Children die of starvation, malnutrition and diseases because essential food and medical supplies have been cut off. Fleeing bombed villages and cities, women provide for their families and friends, defiant in the face of incredible odds. They watch as their men, some of them boys, go off to fight other women's loved men, and to rape and kill other women and children. Yet, if they dare to protest this futile destruction of life they are imprisoned, "salvaged", "disappeared", killed. Robbed of scarce fertile lands by the presence of military bases, local communities lose their self-sufficiency and become dependent on the foreign power. Resultant poverty often leads women and children into prostitution and other low-paid menial jobs. Sue Culling (1988) from Aotearoa is concerned about the cost to women and children:

> When the military comes in to set up a base they demand certain things – rest and recreation it's called … what that really means is prostitutes and bars. When you put that into a Third World context, with people who are already suffering from appalling poverty, prostitution is often the only way available for women to feed their families. And it's not just women who do it "voluntarily" – there's also the added problem of child prostitution, [and] the kidnapping of girls.

The effects of militarisation on a people is both profound and far-reaching. The existence of organised armed violence within a community militarises every aspect of that society. Fijian, Suliana Siwatibau reports:

> I do not need to itemise the manifestation of militarisation. What is of concern is the subtle militarisation of Pacific Islanders' way of life. The World Council of Churches defined militarisation: "as the process whereby military values, ideology and patterns of behaviour achieve a dominating influence on the political, social, economic and external life of the state and as a consequence the structural, ideological and behavioural patterns of both society and government are 'militarised'" (Siwatibau, 1989a: p. 7).

The impact of foreign military bases and the resultant influx of foreign service personnel aside, the co-option of Indigenous males into the local military has distorted traditional societies, undermining women's status, as Theresa Minitong (1990) from Bougainville explains:

> Bougainville is matrilineal, women control the land and the wealth. Men could not go out and fight if the women did not give the wealth to the chief so he could distribute it to the allies to help him fight. Without the women he could not fight. But the western way is changing that. It is the militarisation of the men that is the greatest problem. When the colonial masters came they brought their own way, and it was mainly men who came. And I think our men saw that and thought, you know, "A man has brought this to us, so we men should stand up and be like that". During the First and Second World Wars, when the men went away and were trained as soldiers, they were away from the influence of their own people, and the ideas of generations that men walk side by side with women that had always been accepted were replaced. Men got to thinking that they were more important, they forgot their place in the society.
>
> Fighting was something that was there in the old days. Men went out fighting and women were left to care for the village, but when men came back they were equal partners. They went from the community, they were community-centred, and the community went with them and they always came back to the women. By being in the house, or just doing ordinary work where women are involved, they tended to look at other people as equal. Today, when they are trained as soldiers they are taken away from the society. They go as individuals and are removed from society itself. They are in defence training for two and a half years all on their own and are not connected to the women. They get lost. They look down on women and say, "We men are up here!". Today, the equality has been shifted in a way that women may eventually lose their status.

The result has been the institutionalised oppression of women and, as this shift moves further into the civilian population, an increase in the more "private" male pursuits of wife bashing, rape, incest, pornography, and other crimes.

Women also suffer directly from war. Bertha Nare, from Kanaky (New Caledonia),[1] observes that "women are always the last victims of men's murderous madness" (Nare,

---

1. The Kanak people have resisted colonisation since the French arrival in 1853. The massacre in 1987, during French presidential elections, resulted in the Matignon Accord which promises a referendum on political status in 1997. Signed in June 1988 by the French government, Kanaks and Caldoches (French settlers), it does not guarantee independence.

1989: p. 9). She considers the impact on the women of Ouvea and Hienghene of the massacre of nineteen Kanak males by French forces in 1988:

> ... the women, widows of freedom fighters, mothers of children, are today on their own – charged with the entire responsibility of bringing up their families and none of them will receive any allowances to compensate for the loss of their husbands murdered by the colonial oppressor (Nare, 1989: p. 9).

Bougainvillean, Theresa Minitong (1990) describes some of the difficulties that women face:

> Many men joined the Bougainvillean Revolutionary Army [BRA], or if they did stay at home, they were always on alert. They stopped helping in the gardens to grow food, village life was neglected, children were disturbed. Many houses were burnt down, the BRA just moved off but the women, children and old people were left behind to suffer the force of the attack. Their gardens were destroyed, animals killed, and personal possessions looted. They had to flee into the bush and were left to shelter in caves or were taken into so-called "care centres" by the government. The only time they can look for food is at night, or helicopters supplied by the Australian army will shoot them. The mothers have to put the little kids to their breasts to keep them quiet or they will be shot. Women were being raped and shot.

It would be misleading to present women's role in the military as passive onlookers. Women have been involved in local fighting long before the arrival of the Europeans with their sophisticated weaponry. In the Marshall Islands, women traditionally played the role of "encouragers", beating the drums, singing and dancing to encourage their men. This is a common story throughout the region. Today, wherever Indigenous peoples have been forced to resort to armed struggle in their bid for freedom, women have been active both on the front lines and in social programs. Bertha Nare describes the involvement of Kanak women:

> The Kanak women have well understood how important it is that they take part in the struggle for liberation. They take part in the political struggle not only to defend the rights of the people, but also to defend their own rights and to [better] their situation. They did not stop at political discourse, but they have taken an active part in the field and on the front lines such as barricades against colonial military forces and guerilla tactics (Nare, 1989: p. 9).

But women not only act as freedom fighters. As carers for their communities they provide the services that support the armed struggle and maintain their communities, as Lola Reis (1989) of East Timor attests:

> Like in most cases of war it is women who are the ones who have to endure. The task of women is doubled because apart from participating in the struggle against the Indonesian Army they have to raise the children. We have the East Timorese Women's Organisation, that is organising in the liberated areas. Providing schools for children, shelter for orphans. We organise the first aid section of the strategic villages for wounded and sick people. And supporting the men. We also have our own female section of the armed forces.

This is not to imply that men are not also victims of war, they are often co-opted into the military under duress. Titewhai Harawira (1985) describes the impact of the Second World War on the Maori community:

> The First World War came, and a lot of our men refused to go to war. They were imprisoned and sent to the South Island, they were used to build roads and things. But when the Second World War came they were only too happy to go to war – they wanted to get out of the depression that the British had put our people into. And so they went to war to fight for God, King and Country, we were told, and the women were left behind to manage the farms. But there was no money and they were forced, with their children, to move to the cities to work for the war effort, to keep things going while the men were away. Our men were killed in large numbers fighting someone else's war. When the men came back, those who did come back, they found that the farms had been sold. And so, the big migration of my people to the cities in search of work began in earnest.

Women have been critically involved in supporting the military. This is a question that needs to be addressed by feminists who are concerned about militarisation.
Clare Slatter. Fiji. (Slatter, 1988)

So, while it is men who usually wear the uniforms and are trained to kill, militarisation affects all members of the community. Fijian, Claire Slatter stressed the significance of the role women played in the Fijian coup in 1987. Her remarks are pertinent not only to Fiji but to all women. She warns that women's role in military violence needs to be seriously examined (Slatter, 1988):

> I think that the role women played in the Fiji coup is an issue of major concern to feminists. It is a mistake, first of all, to consider the military as a male institution in which women play no part. Although it is true women do figure only marginally, if at all, in the military, and that women have not been centrally involved in creating the institutions, we have nonetheless seen women's and men's passive acceptance of this institution as a necessary aspect of political life.
>
> Women have always been supportive of the military in Fiji. They are always very visible at military parades. Always part of reproducing ideas about the military that glorified it. Moreover, women have accepted the glory bestowed on their fathers, husbands and sons, for service in war. Women have been carrying out fundraising and other supportive activities for the Royal Fiji Forces.
>
> Following the first coup in Fiji, women were amongst the most confused, and therefore most vulnerable to military propaganda about the reasons for the coup. They became bearers of inchoate and poorly understood falsehoods that formed the basis for the military explanations of the coup. Explanations, for instance, that alleged Libyan involvement with

the deposed government, and allegations to do with the deposed government's intentions to take Fiji away from their traditional allies. These were couched in the classic enemy images. It's curious because Libya means nothing to most people in the Pacific. Ninety percent of people in Fiji know very little about Libya. They had no direct contact with Libya. How could such a ridiculous claim be believed? But the way these stories were told, and the fact that prior to the coup a wave of Libyan scares (largely thanks to the Australian press), prepared the ground for people to develop an image of Libya as a very evil power. This made people feel, even if only momentarily, that there was something sinister about the deposed government, something disloyal and unpatriotic, particularly about its Indian members.

Women began participating in the military's informal surveillance activities. Women, in workplaces and on the streets, were as involved as men were in spying on conversation, watching the preparation of documents and petitions, and conveying this information back. Most of us were aware of the role of secretaries in this regard, and it was extremely disturbing. Many women began to assume the role of informal adjuncts to the military.

Women were also, as an extension of this, rallying to the fore after the first coup, bringing food to the barracks for the army. Many of them were, of course, military wives, but many were not, so they were playing right into the propaganda the military had prepared. In neighbourhoods, where there were military roadblocks, women began taking food out to the soldiers. This contributed to a show of support and boosted the morale of the military, and was an important thing in convincing those in the military who might have had doubts that they were doing the right thing.

The military has also began recruiting women to join its ranks as officers. This was an entirely new development, greeted with much concern by feminists and women opposed to the military regime.

A final development affecting women is the creation of a Ministry of Women's Affairs – by the military government, the first ever such ministry to be established in Fiji. This has some worrying aspects because, for one thing, it puts anyone working with feminist organisations in a dilemma. Many groups are beginning to regard the so-called "civilian" government as a normal government, and to imbue it with the same sort of respect as former governments, and are therefore being part of programs which the Ministry of Women's Affairs are attempting to set up. Other women's organisations are in a real dilemma, because some members are saying they should take what the state offers, while others are saying, "No, we cannot because this is an illegitimate government". There are also problems for external agencies concerned with women's development which usually would be directed to the women's office – some of these are continuing to relate to it as if it were a normal civilian state body.

She acknowledges that not all women succumbed to the pressure of the military, but asserts that those who were actively against it were a minority, and thus their work was made more difficult (Slatter, 1988):

Some positive things have occurred in Fiji which illustrate the role taken by women against militarism and for peace. Women's collusion with the system was not the entire picture. There were many women who were utterly appalled and shocked, and who immediately set about trying to do something about it.

An initial very strong movement, called the "Back to Early May" movement, had amongst its leading members key women in the community who had stood tall amongst the men, and within the nation. There were attempts by women to organise two peace rallies, but they were denied permits so they couldn't go ahead. So the women then organised demonstrations without permits. The first was held by a very small number of women, the second by a larger number, but in any case both were very brave public stances taken by women against the military coup. Women also participated in a book on the military coup assessing its impact and effects, which was brought out on the anniversary of the coup on May 14. There was also the less public stance taken by women who refused to be co-opted by the military state, or to have anything to do with the women's ministry.

As military bases and personnel spread across the region, women are becoming increasingly aware of what militarisation means to their lives, and to the future of their peoples. They know that, as Aotearoan, Sue Culling (1988) emphasises:

The legacy of colonisation is the loss of land, language and culture, a warped development and, worst of all, the colonisation of people's minds so that they no longer trust their own traditions and history but look to Europe for answers. And Europe has nothing to offer but death.

THE SPIRIT OF RESISTANCE

The spirit of resistance is strong. We have withstood the erosion of our culture, and we continue to yearn for the freedom and peace which was once our birthright. And, if all we can do in our lifetime is guarantee our children's survival in a nuclear free and independent Pacific, then we will have achieved something.

Hilda Halkyard-Harawira. Aotearoa. (Halkyard-Harawira, 1986a)

Colonisation has taken many forms in the Pacific and has had many effects. Perhaps the most universal impact has been the distortion of the traditional gender-power relationship. Women's power has been undermined under the impact of colonisation. Traditionally, even in the most patrilineal societies, women were respected, their contribution to their society acknowledged and sought after. Today, while they may still retain a strong voice in their immediate community, many are barred from involvement in decision making in the broader spheres. Women have been increasingly silenced. And yet there have always been voices that have refused to be muted. Indigenous women are moving back into their power, leading their people into a future of justice, and although their task will be difficult they have the determination to succeed.

Recognising cultural heritage as vital in ensuring their community's survival, Indigenous people are reclaiming their customs. Women, however, have learnt that they must be selective in this process if they are to guard against the use of tradition to hinder their development, as women, within their societies. Fijian, Suliana Siwatibau (1989b) analyses this problem:

Culture has often been used as an excuse to ensure the continued domination of men over the women of their societies. If you look at the role that women play, not their status – their role, it is very important. In the subsistence societies in the rural areas, the role of women is extremely important. They are the main providers of food, main providers of requirements of the house like mats and pots. They are the ones responsible to see that the family survives, to see that children go to school, that the family health is taken care of and all that. So they are extremely important.

But when we come to the modern sector, men usually assert that the women's position is in the home. This kind of assertion prevents women from participating more in the modern activities outside the home. They say that our culture places women as second to men. That they should be providing for and looking after the children, and therefore not participating in the modern sector, not participating in decision-making. And again, it is internalised by the women themselves, as well as being promoted by the men. All that helps to keep the women down. The situation in most of the countries for women is fairly similar. We are well behind men. We're not as highly educated as men. We're behind in the development process. Not only in participating in the decision-making, but in reaping the benefits like taking opportunities for jobs, opportunities for higher education. I think this is because the structures of society have prevented women from going as far as men, but also because these very structures and values have been internalised by women themselves.

Vanessa Griffen, also from Fiji, adds her voice:

Culture, or custom, is the commonest argument used against any call for a new image of women in the Pacific. Even aware women are confused about this question because in the postcolonial period, cultural identity is an important part of national rehabilitation and pride. We as women need to deal with this question and present a clear statement of custom and tradition in relation to the liberation of women (Griffen, 1985: p. 526).

Women are insisting that Pacific heritage does not, and should not, include the domination of women; that even where women's status had been limited by social practices of the past it is possible to strengthen women's position in the community while reclaiming their national heritage. Ni-Vanuatu women claim that:

The main reason for the subservient role in which women are cast is described by men who say it is the custom or the traditional way of things. Closer examination of it reveals that it is a glib and falsely attractive answer. Traditional practices are not unchanging. One need only look at the history of the Pacific over the past one hundred years to realise that custom practices have accommodated dramatic changes in the face of contact with Europeans. Blackbirding. Christianity. Colonialism. Self-government and Independence. Custom is being used as an instrument of oppression to deny women equality which is theirs as a moral right (Women of Vanuatu, 1973: p. 2).

The custom works hand-in-hand with the Church. The custom is corrupted by religion.
Susanna Ounei. Kanaky. (Ounei, 1990)

The Christian Church has been one of the main perpetrators of male dominance in the region. Every colonising nation brought its own missionaries, disrupting Indigenous beliefs and instilling their own values. They came, they claimed, to "protect" the Indigenous from the increasing numbers of traders, gun-runners, beachcombers and others flooding into the region and to save the souls of "heathens". No doubt they believed that they were acting in the best interests of the Indigenous people, but their distorted benevolence was displayed by their acts of violence. Perhaps a useful example would be the "War of Extermination" where the early Jesuits entered the Marianas Islands and within twenty-three years had all but wiped out the resisting Chamorro (Oliver, 1985: p. 337). Indigenous people have paid heavily for Christianity. For many, their sacred rites, icons and places have been destroyed.

Cathy Craigie, presents an Aboriginal perspective of the role of the missionaries in the colonising process. Her story resounds around the Pacific:

When the massacres and other atrocities stopped, the missionaries moved in around 1830. We were forbidden to speak our own language and practise our cultures. We were given English names and made to dress in attire that was unsuitable for our life-style. From the

1890s Aboriginal people were rounded up and moved onto missions and later reserves similar to the bantustans in South Africa (Craigie, 1986).

Susanna Ounei (1990), from Kanaky, describes how the missionaries deliberately undermined the dignity of women:

> Christianity has done a lot of destruction. In Ouvea where my people are the people of that land, when the missionaries came they held a meeting that was the first segregation between men and women. The missionaries placed the women on one hand and the men on the other, and every day they talked to them. They said that women should obey the man. My mum told me, she's seventy-eight years old, it was my grandmother who told her. It was never like that, that the women should obey the man. That was the beginning of indoctrination. The women would look at the ground, and whenever a woman would speak they would say, "Who will listen to that one?". Why does she react like that? It comes from the missionaries. They destroyed women's power. They destroyed many things.

Missionaries were, she claims, directly responsible for the increasing violence directed towards women:

> When I see how women are considered, I can't handle the missionaries, or Christianity. Women are easily beaten and injured seriously by the husband or the boyfriend. Young women are raped and beaten. It is difficult because the position of women has been prescribed by Christianity, which said men are more important. In my home in Ouvea, the missionaries have done a lot to destroy the status of women. I don't want to idealise our society, that it was perfect, but without the missionaries, women had some dignity. That's why it is important for us to organise, but it's really difficult, especially in our colonial country where religion and custom go hand in hand (Ounei, 1990).

Deliberate attempts to destroy the spiritual basis of people's attitudes towards themselves and their lands were universal in the Pacific. Cita Morei (1992) scans the history of Christianity in Belau:

> Historically, the Spanish brought religion, but it was the Germans who destroyed Belauan religion. The Spanish didn't have much influence in Belau. They just bring in priests. They establish the schools. The older people didn't go, only the children went. The Spanish changed the Belauan marriage, a loose marriage, where women leave their husbands for another person. But the Spanish were only here for 14 years, from 1886 to 1899. They didn't really come here – they were in Yap and travelled back and forth. We were kind of left behind. I think that was good. We weren't so exposed as Guam or the Marianas. So Christianity didn't penetrate our minds for that long.
>
> Then the Germans were here from 1899 to 1914. When they came, they destroyed the *Ulengang*, spirits' house. A house built for the spirits. We were not to believe in the spirits. And women healers, they were taken, they destroy their houses too. These women who talk to the spirits every day. The Germans told them to give the money [they were paid for their services in turtle shell and rare, ancient stones, still used today] back to the people. My mother talk about these stories. The spirit house was smaller than an actual house. The spirit

lives inside. They take food there, there is a place to put it, on the step, for the spirit to take.

Then we interpreted Christian values and saw that Belauan values are Christian values. We did not have to abandon one for the other, except for some practices of believing in the spirits and believing in magic. To use *Ollai*, is magic. Meaning if you want to make someone like you, you use Ollai; or if you want to kill the person. It is those kind of things. The Church says that you don't believe in magic, that it is superstition, that it doesn't really exist. But it didn't succeed. Ollai is still going on. There is still people who prepare betel nut and give it to someone so that they will like you, or preparing an Ollai, to heal some bad disease. People now, they take the oil and bring it to the church so that the priest will bless it. It is a "holy oil", so you can use it. I think that takes place of the Belauan magic. What the church does is magic too. The mystical use of the holy water, the holy oil, the candle. But it is one thing that they stop, use of Ollai to kill people – God is good, so you use it for doing good.

The anguish that results from this disinheritance is expressed by Maori, Hinewirangi Kohu (1987):

I'm not going to put down Christianity because I'm sure that Jesus Christ is there next to Papatuanuku and being beautiful. But when they came they sent Christianity first to destroy, to change, and then "civilise" the "barbaric and savage" peoples of Aotearoa. And I'm one of those and, in fact, I have become more savage than ever before. And they tried to tell us that what we believed and felt deep in our hearts was wrong, was evil. They tried to tell us that our brown skin was evil. They taught us that we were too brown, too ugly, and they claimed our bodies, put clothes on right up to the neck and down to the ankles. We were a people of the land! We melted into the land!

Despite this major attack, Indigenous peoples have maintained and nurtured a strong spiritual connection with the land. According to Bernie Keldermans, Belauan spiritual beliefs continue through to the present, influencing the practices of daily life:

Our traditional religion, *Motekgnei* (which means "community"), teaches respect for nature. If you arrive at a river in the night you first throw in a stone to warn the river of your presence, then you go in yourself. You pray before tilling the ground, and talk to the plants before picking them. The same respect extends to people (Caldecott, 1983: pp. 109–10).

Barbara Flick, a Gamalroi (Aboriginal) woman, puts Christianity into a historical perspective:

Maybe 70,000 years before Jesus was born we too had our own stories and religion. The stories tell us how the ancestors' spirits travelled across the country and made the mountains, the rivers, the valleys and the oceans. Some of those ancestors' spirits rested in places where the spirits now are, considered sacred sites by us (WWNFIP, 1987: pp. 27–8).

In the reclamation of their indigenous cultures many Pacific peoples are rejecting Christianity or, having adopted it, are making changes that bring it into tune with the "Pacific Way", as this statement from the Pacific Conference of Churches asserts:

> We of the Churches of the Pacific want to preserve our rich heritage, identity and unique way of living. By many we are seen as a "drop in the vast ocean"; we believe that God has given us the right to be what and who we are (Myers, 1983: p. 13).

Today's Pacific is a very Christian one. Across the Pacific Indigenous people have incorporated Christianity into the framework of their traditional beliefs. Local medicine and magic is being practised, and contact made and kept with the ancestors' spirits and animal totems, by people who would be considered devoutly Christian. Rongelap, Lijon Eknilang (1986) relates her people's compromise:

> We still believe in our medicine and spirits. The pastor reads in the Bible, that if you really believe in God then you will be against the spirit and against black magic, and all that. If you really believed in God. You can read that in the Bible. But sometime when our baby is sick, and we couldn't do nothing, and some night we see the spirit and he's talking to us, and say, "I want you to go get that medicine". Will you walk the other way? Right. You will go in the way that he will take you. You will go and grab the things and put them on [the baby]. And then you will wake up and they're there. And so we can cure our children and our friends and ourselves. That has happened to me and my mother, but not that many people. It happens from daughter to daughter.

The Christian Church is a main avenue for women's organisation and, having understood its history in the region, is actively making amends. Fijian, Suliana Siwatibau (1989b) suggests the delineation of Christianity from Indigenous culture is not so easy:

> It's hard to differentiate what is imposed by Christianity and what was there before Christianity came. A lot of us have had Christianity for a long time. We have absorbed their values so much into our own structure.

She acknowledges that Christianity has played a role in the distortion of women's status in the region but, she emphasises:

> Just how far the status of women has been influenced by Christianity, and how far it is inherent in our culture before Christianity, I can't say, but I do know that Christianity has had a lot of influence as to how women see themselves (Siwatibau, 1989b).

In traditional structures channels of communication existed so that everyone had the opportunity to participate in the decision making of the village. Imported decision making bodies have taken over . . . [and] make few allowances for traditional channels and so the voice of women is no longer heard when important issues are under discussion.
Women of Vanuatu. (Women of Vanuatu, 1973: p. 2)

The colonial process has affected not only belief systems, but also political and economic methods, as Indigenous people find themselves increasingly pressured and coerced into accepting the colonisers' values and behaviours. European, male hierarchical structures are replacing the more consensual forms of decision making. Still, Kokatha, Joan Wingfield (1988c) asserts many Indigenous peoples persist in their traditional ways:

> Decisions are made in the Aboriginal community by consensus. If it's men's business, all the men get together and talk. If it's women's business, all the women get together. If it's something that affects the whole tribe, then they all get together and sit down and talk it through. And no one will leave until they all come to the same decision. That's where White society doesn't fit in with our traditional ways. Governments and mining companies expect us to make decisions there and then on the spot, and we can't do that, it's not our way. We shouldn't be made to change our ways. They've got to recognise that it's our way, that we're not being uncooperative, that we are protecting our interests. We've got to make the right decisions for our children and their children.

In many places the colonisers have used local customs to their advantage, superimposing their own structures upon the traditional, but, according to Bernie Keldermans (1986), women are increasingly questioning the dominance of men in politics:

> In our culture we have male representatives, and I think we prolonged this with this system of election and democracy. We just assumed that [men] should lead the country. Maybe that was not the right idea. Now women are starting to ask themselves whether we should go into government. But I think there's a fear amongst men that women cannot do it. They say, "Now look at Aquino: she's getting weaker – and see Thatcher: she's not so great either!". They think we can't do it in Belau.

Women, more than half the world's population, were, in 1990, represented by only 9.7 per cent of the world's parliamentarians and occupied just 3.5 per cent of cabinet-level positions, this drops to 1.6 per cent in the Asia/Pacific region. The figure for key political and economic ministries was lower still. In ninety countries there were no women ministers at all (Jamieson, 1990: p. 15). The majority of the world's decision-making power is in the hands of a small male elite of the White community – which, in itself, totals only 10 per cent of the world's population. Women's opinions and guidance simply are not being heard.

Hilda Lini from Vanuatu, one of the few women parliamentarians in the region, insists "that women can do it!":

> Because of the new decision-making institutions that are foreign to the Pacific, women are just starting to enter into the political arena. But I do not agree with the idea that men can handle it better than women because I feel that the ideas are foreign to all of us. When the missionaries came in they took the men to be the ministers and church workers. It prepared them to be ahead of the women who remained in the background all the time. Today you will find that not many women are prepared to speak out in public. But because these systems are new to Pacific people, everyone – both women and men – can learn how to handle it (Johnson, G., 1983: p. 57).

But who sets the agenda for that development? The Pacific is a graveyard of inappropriate development projects.

Sue Culling. Aotearoa. (Culling, 1987)

As Pacific Island states have emerged from centuries of domination they have invariably maintained the structures imposed on them by their colonisers. They have been caught in a world order built on capital exploitation in which they have been unable to compete. Forced to invite financial "assistance" they have handed the control of their local development over to the money lenders who set the agenda for their own benefit. Foreign governments, and corporate elite, intent as they are on making a profit, are seldom interested in the well-being of the people. Projects are designed to satisfy the donor rather than the needs of the recipients and may be linked to future projects or military concerns. Inevitably, budget deficits widen and the recipients become increasingly dependent on metropolitan powers, losing control over their social and foreign affairs. They often find themselves enmeshed in international politics that are against their own interests and human rights diminish. Pacific Island nations are amongst the highest aid recipients per capita in the world.

Sue Culling reminds us that US President Richard Nixon was quoted as saying: "Let us remember that the main purpose of American aid is not to help other nations but to help ourselves" (Culling, 1987: p. 41). She argues that aid is invariably linked to efforts by the dominating country to maintain control over the internal socio-political issues of the smaller nations:

> Foreign aid is an extension of the colonial process whereby the wealthy and powerful seek to exercise undue influence over poorer and less powerful nations ... The reason that aid is pumped into the Pacific is to safeguard the strategic interests of the West. After all it is much cheaper and easier to organise aid deals etc than it would be to have a standing army occupying the islands of the Pacific. Aid from Australia and New Zealand Governments to the Pacific has been seen very much as playing our part in the Western Alliance and contributing to US objectives ... The US and France pump millions into their remaining colonies every year ... apart from them Australia is the largest donor to the "independent" states ... the EEC is a very large donor ... and also Japan ... Apart from safeguarding the strategic interests of the West, foreign aid has even more benefits for us in the donor countries – it subsidises our exports and provides us with markets ... it also stimulates the development of new markets for our companies and it makes sure that the receivers of aid stay within the capitalist world market.

What has been the effect of all those millions of aid dollars on the Pacific Island nations who have been at the receiving end? Their fragile subsistence economies have been made highly dependent on aid. They have stayed economically underdeveloped, and by that I mean the whole Pacific ... The people have lost control over their own affairs because the demands from outside have had to be listened to. Often governments have been kept in power because they have had access to aid dollars and, for many nations, their biggest export has been their people, going to get more of what the West has to offer (Culling, 1987: p. 41).

Aid, Aotearoan, Sue Culling stresses, is "being used as a weapon of foreign policy" (1987: p. 3):

For example, the US poured money into Belau since the War – the money has been for educating Belauan youths who now have expectations that stem from a different culture. And now they are leaving their island because Belau "has nothing and the US has everything!". This is what I mean by inappropriate development. The US has put no money into making Belau economically self-sufficient but they've pumped in money to support an administrative system of sixteen states for fifteen thousand people – the only employer is the Government. The US has made Belau dependent on it (Culling, 1988: p. 3).

Hilda Lini (1989) describes how foreign governments maintain control over the development programs of the region:

The Pacific has the largest per capita of aid, but it comes with very long strings and tentacles. Because our countries are very small, our Governments are sometimes subjected to having to accept conditions that are imposed on them. But there are countries who have decided to go their own way and make independent decisions, like, for example, Kiribati and Vanuatu, but they suffer heavily because of that. Vanuatu especially, for being the only non-aligned country in the Pacific. We don't want other people to dictate to us how we need to go about our own business.

The efforts of Vanuatu to remain a non-aligned nation illustrates this point. Hilda Lini (1989) describes the pressure put on the nation as a result of its foreign policies:

Before independence we were called "communists" because we had a liberation movement although its objectives were formulated by the people. Since independence, because we established relations with Cuba, we were called "the Cuba of the Pacific". And then, when we signed a fishing agreement with the Russians, we were called "the Russians of the Pacific". And since then, because we also established diplomatic relations with Libya, we were called "the Gaddafi of the Pacific". But we are a non-aligned country. We establish relations with Russia and the US. We establish relations with Taiwan and China. We establish relations with North Korea and South Korea. We don't want other people to dictate to us how we need to go about our own business. Of course, we have faced problems with this. Aid has been cut off because we have been outspoken.

Institutionalising economic control into the hands of foreign companies and the settler community has marginalised Indigenous peoples. Pacific nations are dependent on foreign investment, foreign aid and loans, and fluctuating export markets, to the detriment of their own local needs. A community's social structure is further distorted by the creation of an educated, urban male elite who, protective of its privileges of power and wealth, support the capitalist development at the expense of women and rural dwellers. This new dominating class has been educated in the United States, Europe, Australia and Aotearoa (New Zealand), where they've been well trained in the value systems of the dominant culture. Although some return to assist their people, and most don't return at all (resulting in a drain of skills away from the community), many return to pick up where the colonisers left off. They benefit from the continuation of the status quo.

The sociological effect of this economic dependence has been considerable. The need for monetary income and the desire for the opportunities and material goods of the colonising nation has, in the absence of similar opportunities at home, led to massive migrations in search of employment. For example, there are now twice as many American Samoans in the US than are in the islands themselves, and the flow of Micronesians into Guam is increasing daily. Local communities have been distorted as the population moves from smaller, outlying islands to larger ones, from rural villages to urban centres and from island nations to cities in rim countries. There are benefits arising from this shift. For example, people living in the metropolitan nations support local development initiatives through money sent to relatives at home, and their involvement away from their home islands lessens the impact on the local environment and restricted infrastructure.

However, there are also disadvantages. Urbanisation has lead increasingly to social problems – drug- and alcohol-related problems, organised crime, domestic and street violence, poverty and localised environmental damage. A substantial growth in birth rates, coupled by a lack of infrastructure, further exacerbates the difficulties. High unemployment is not helped by skilled Europeans arriving in the region to dominate professional jobs.

And then there are the military relocations: people have lost their ancestral lands due to nuclear tests and military bases, such as the Pitjantjatjara people of Australia and the Marshallese of Kwajalein Atoll. They have been drawn to the urban centres in search of military construction jobs, as in Tahiti-Polynesia and the Philippines. And they have been forced from their fertile lands by transmigration programs, as with Kanaky (New Caledonia) and West Papua.

The rapid replacement of local structures with those of the metropolitan states has wrought havoc in the region. Local communities are having difficulty adapting to, and then keeping up with, the new methods. Suliana Siwatibau illustrates:

> Amidst an interplay of colonial domination and big power interests, island countries of the Pacific are attempting to survive the transition from a subsistence and barter-based economy to the modern technological age of international trade, monetary exchange and cash-based economy. They have to grapple with difficult problems of lack of resources, skills and expertise and extreme isolation – in terms of international trade and communications as well as in terms of access to the centres of intellectual and technological creativity that propel modern economics (Siwatibau, 1988: p. 5).

This is deliberate. A colonial power does not institute systems that will enable the colonised to shift the burden of oppression. They were not created as a response to Indigenous needs, nor do they develop from the local situation. Under colonial structures only the coloniser is to benefit. Indigenous women are aware of the effects on their communities and, according to Louise Aitsi (1989) from the Pacific Women's Resource Bureau of the South Pacific Commission, they are far from happy:

> Women are concerned about the multinationals which are coming into the country introducing new technologies, new ideas, and new ways of life. Pacific peoples are trying to adjust. But we are not helped to adjust. We are just left to cope for ourselves. This is where we have a lot of social problems. Women are very, very concerned. Some of them are actually becoming very angry. They are becoming very vocal.

The development process is controlled by men, to the detriment of women, as Suliana Siwatibau identifies:

> Development plans are drawn up by men to meet goals set by men whose primary goal is economic development measurable by Gross National Product per capita. Pacific countries have yet to question how much their plans serve people's development. A people-centred development would require a re-definition. In no country in Pacific Oceania have women made a substantial input into, or been fully considered in, development planning to date (Siwatibau, 1988: p. 5).

The result is that communities then miss out on the skills and foresight of half of their population. Indigenous Pacific women are warning that:

> Without equal opportunities for women's participation, development is impossible, for what kind of developed country would it be that refused the benefits of development to one half of its population? It is such a society that will emerge in our countries if the role of women is not improved and their abilities and opinions brought to bear on the development process (Women of Vanuatu, 1973: p. 1).

Most countries have government agencies and churches which design and run programs directed at women but, while definitely beneficial, these are limited in scope, often reinforcing the traditional roles of cooking, sewing, hygiene and childcare. Binatia Iakobo (1989) describes the work of the Kiribati Women's Fellowship:

> It's a time for women to gather for worship, sharing ideas, fundraising. The fellowship also does other things like development of basic skills for women. We are trying to promote women's welfare and contribute to greater self-reliance in the community.

The National Council of Women attempts to assist women in identifying their problems and organising to alleviate them. Its success, however, is limited by lack of resources as women remain primarily ignored in development programs.

Although women tend to do most of the work in the production of food crops, programs aimed at improving food production are aimed at men. Traditional women's work in the food gardens, the main source of subsistence farming, has been largely ignored while development programs are directed towards cash crops. Recent improvements in the area of cash cropping and other male responsibilities (for example, land-clearing, house-building) has made "men's work" more efficient and less time-consuming and widened the division of labour between the sexes. Suliana Siwatibau (1989b) tells a story of Fijian women that highlights the imbalance:

> In Fiji an agricultural development aid project brought in tractors and machinery and ploughs and fertilizers. So who do you think benefited? The men. They drove the tractors, they ploughed the land. And the women? Their role is to plant, coming after the ploughing – that's traditional. There was no consideration for the planting so they continued to plant by hand. And they had to get the water to irrigate the areas but there was nothing provided for irrigation so they had to continue to get buckets of water. And because the men could plough a lot more land there was more land to plant and water. And on top of all that they had to do all the housework and look after the children. If women were involved in the planning they would have said, "Let's get a pump so we can get water and let's get help for the planting so that it doesn't hold up the works". But no. So the men go plough the land and there's a lot more land ploughed but the rate of work altogether is slow because the women have to do the planting and watering and they still have to do that by hand. And now they've got so much more to do.

Inappropriate development increases the burden on women who already have their regular tasks: food marketing, gathering wood, fetching water, cooking and other house-hold chores and caring for children. Women deserve a better deal, not least because subsistence farming is the principal food source of the region. Further, technological improvements in the fields of women's work would free more women to achieve an education that would benefit not only themselves but their nations.

Women often find themselves supporting both their families and the wider com-munity, as Suliana Siwatibau (1989b) explains:

> Not only do women play an important role in running and keeping the family together but they also play a very important role in community development. For example, in Pohnpei the women now go out and do the kind of work the government should be doing. Water supplies, toilets and general village development. They even have an appropriate technology section engaged in building schools for the government. But there's not even a National Council of Women there. Women are not given a say. And there are very few women in the civil service. And yet they have proved themselves.
>
> In Samoa they have the village committees which are run by women. The Director of the Department of Health himself told me that without them his public health service would collapse. The village committees do all the work in the villages and that's the most important function of primary health care.
>
> Women also come in to cater for the mistakes. You know, the government comes in and does all these big developments like putting in roads, big constructions around the place, and then the women have to deal with the mistakes that happen.

And:

> One small volcanic island in Fiji was the recipient of generous government aid – which the bureaucrats decided had to be spent on constructing a circuminsular road. The bulldozer and its driver came at the expense of thousands of dollars, two years running. First to build, then to maintain or regrade the road. Each time the road was left for weed infestation and as a land crab playground. No one on the island had any sort of vehicle. They did not ask for the road. They did not use it. Meanwhile they continued – particularly through women's groups – to raise funds for school buildings, library books, improved kitchens, water tanks, improved toilets and a community-owned tourist resort run largely by the youth groups (Siwatibau, 1989a:8).

Faced with the need for change, women are organising for a greater share of the benefits of the work they perform. Papuan women, for example, have established rural exchange groups known as "*wok meri*" (women's work) where women of a clan group combine labour and cash earnings, making loans to members and buying communal equipment and tools. This has the added effect of keeping "*meris mani*" (women's money) out of the reach of men who, they fear, would spend it on alcohol and gambling.

The massive extent of the problem, however, means that the solution women work towards is difficult to obtain. With limited resources and a large terrain to cover it is impossible to reach, let alone assist, even the majority of women. Until the sexual-power imbalance shifts there will always be isolated village women trying to survive in a community where women's needs are not met. Elizabeth Yamonson (1989), of Papua New Guinea, recalling her life, expresses the frustrations felt when confronted by such a formidable challenge:

> I'm a mother who lives in a village. I have no job. I've got eight children. My children went to school. My husband is a drunken fellow. He never looks after me. I was trying my best to earn my living to get my children brought up properly in a school. In a life where they supposed to be. I find it very hard but anyway I struggle along. My husband is too bossy. He doesn't want me to work. He like me to stay home and work in the garden but that doesn't help me. He doesn't give me any money. He let me alone for years and years. So I have to work hard until I brought my children up. I have to make gardens, struggle hard, make gardens, bringing crops to town to market. Get the money and pay the school. Still I brought my children up. Bringing them up and now they are wed. So where is my life now?

Until the negative aspects of aid are overcome women will continue to further the advancement of their communities unassisted. Ruth Lechte, of Fiji, examines the difficulties they face:

> Almost all funding agencies will give money for projects but not for administration. For women in Pacific villages this can mean all hope of power and knowledge is removed from them. There is no way we can find grass-roots workers who can stay long enough in one place to inculcate understanding of how things work unless we can find money to pay their (modest) salaries. I can teach three dozen animators to go out and build stoves – no problem. But they will need three dozen salaries for years into the future, not project funds

for cement and the pipes – the women will raise that themselves. Thus, after twenty-five years in so-called "development" one faces the future knowing that some good things have happened but that the powerful systems – male, western, elite, or whatever – are still winning. We are being kept in our place, a place not defined by us (Lechte, 1988).

In the determination to regain control of their destiny, Indigenous peoples across the Pacific are initiating programs which recognise the essential and dynamic link between culture and development. Puanani Burgess (1994b) explains their intention:

Economic development is a force of great creativity. "Economy" means to protect the hearth, the heart of the home. It is through economic development that a people may step beyond the control of imperialistic forces. Without that power they remain forever at the beck and call of someone else's wants. The modern process of development, which separates culture from economy, strips a community of its wealth. Real service is enabling people to recapture their economic development, taking control of their lives back into their own hands.

In Hawai'i, Puanani Burgess is involved in a project that takes 2,000 Kanaka Maoli children into the *kalo lo'i* (taro fields) in the belief that taro, honoured throughout the Pacific as an ancestor, together with children hold the key to the survival of the culture. In Ka'ala Valley, the "womb" centre of O'ahu, children are being educated in their own people's spiritual, social and political values within a context aimed at re-establishing an economic basis to the community.

People come and go – the land, the mountains, night and day stay the same. One may fall in battle but another rushes in to fill the place.
Hilda Halkyard-Harawira. Aotearoa. (Halkyard-Harawira, 1990b)

At the cutting edge of change is the Nuclear Free and Independent Pacific (NFIP) movement, a pan-Pacific network that unites village-based organisations, provincial governments, newly independent nations, and supporters, in the common goal of reasserting the inalienable rights of Indigenous peoples to their lands, cultures, languages, religions, and the protection of their heritage.

Women, ever prominent in the movement, have been instrumental in challenging the colonisers' structures in a way that connects issues, as Fijian, Vanessa Griffen (1988a) explains:

Women's involvement in pressuring for a nuclear free and independent Pacific has been very much part of the Pacific women's movement. We are used to working regionally, but we are not a continent. We are very many island nations. And there's a particular problem and a particular strength that we gain from actually bridging the ocean that divides us, and meeting as small countries, often with very little money, but getting together to discuss the issues that concern us.

We had two very important meetings in the 1970s, particularly in 1975, that was the ATOM [Against Testing on Moruroa] conference. It was the first time that we were able to get together people from all over the Pacific countries, not just peace groups but independence groups. People came from Micronesia we had never met before: we had never heard of the experience of Bikini from anyone from Micronesia. People came from the French territories, Australia and Aotearoa.

That meeting changed how we approached the nuclear testing and environmental issues, because the Micronesians forced us to understand more about their political status under the US, as well as the continuing effects of US testing. And the people of the French colonial territories also explained to us the degree of repression they had in the French territories. And the Indigenous people of Australia and Aotearoa taught us about their struggles. So the connections between political status and nuclear issues was made. As we have had continuing meetings in the Pacific there has been a genuine understanding that these things cannot be separated.

And there's also been a question of social justice. That, if we are for peace, we cannot ignore what has happened to Pacific people's land. And so our movement came to be for a Nuclear Free and Independent Pacific. We were against nuclear testing, we were against colonial domination and we were for the struggles of Indigenous peoples in White dominated societies, for their culture, language and land rights to be recognised.

When we have had women's conferences we have constantly had that perspective. So this changes our idea of women's issues. In our first conference women came just wanting to discuss "women's issues" separately. But we learnt to see the connection between nuclear testing and colonialism and discussed economic exploitation and financial and other dependence of Pacific countries on the first world.

This meant that whenever we were in international forums we brought up the nuclear issue. It is an issue where we can bridge gaps between ourselves as women. It has been one issue that we have always understood, particularly the effects on women personally, in that they bear children. Women, once they hear about nuclear testing, the genetic effects, have always understood. Pacific women in different countries have been involved in specific local actions against nuclear testing or for a nuclear free Pacific. Women are very much part of the anti-nuclear organisations, and are very much part of the network that keeps the nuclear free and independent movements going.

Hilda Halkyard-Harawira (1990b), who has been involved in the NFIP since its beginnings, stresses the potential that the movement has to bring substantial change not only to the Pacific, but to the world:

Our movement encompasses many issues. We are united by the threats to the well-being of the Pacific. For me the NFIP movement is a liberation movement, a survival movement. It is a people's struggle, a grassroots movement. It encompasses all social, political, cultural, and economic considerations for Pacific peoples. It is each country working on its own issues in their regions and networking with each other. That is the NFIP movement. The NFIP movement will go where we take it. It will be what we make it. We can make NFIP go forward into new, uncharted areas.

Pacific peoples, with women in a prominent role, have maintained their culture, sustained their land, organised their people – all against incredible odds. They are survivors. They have endured. They are rising now from the chaos and confusion, the havoc wreaked by the greedy, and their passion ensures that their visions of justice for their peoples, and their ocean, will prosper.

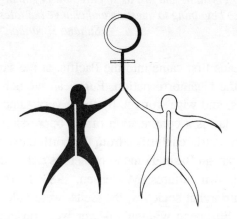

TAKE UP THE CHALLENGE

Pacific women are losing their status because we have inherited the modern civilization from your society. In your society men have specific roles, or had specific roles – you're changing too – and women had specific roles. So, along with civilization, we have adopted the roles that went along with it. And just as you are now beginning to question and change the roles, so we are also beginning to question and change the roles.

Suliana Siwatibau. Fiji. (Siwatibau, 1989b)

At the time that Europeans first came into the Pacific, at the same time of the War of Extermination against the Chamorro nation, European women were being burnt for being healers, midwives, and wise women, by those very same powers. What is happening in the Pacific today is a continuation of the oppression that began in Europe 5,000 to 8,000 years ago. Patriarchal tribes from the north moved through the continent and far into the Mediterranean Basin, home to numerous rich and flourishing matrifocal cultures, imposing their own cultures (Mortensen, 1983; Starhawk, 1987). Although the last of Europe's matriarchal societies, the Celts, were colonised 1,500 years ago, the last semblances of European women's power were pushed underground during the sixteenth and seventeenth centuries. These were the Burning Times. Called "the Renaissance", and regarded in male history as a time of discovery and enlightenment, it was a time of terror. While the exact number cannot be calculated with certainty, at least 100,000–200,000 people and possibly many jmore thousands, 80 per cent of them women, were tortured and burnt at the stake or died in prison, their murder condoned by the Christian Church (Dworkin, 1974 & 1976; Monter, 1977; van Vuuren, 1973). Monter notes that, "absolutely no part of Europe escaped the witch mania (1977: p. 130). Their daughters, many who must have witnessed their mothers' deaths, were silenced through fear, and succumbed to the tyranny of patriarchal rule. European women became the property of men and the old European religions that revered the Earth went into hiding.

The Pacific experience parallels that colonisation of Old Europe: the people subdued through massacres and bloodshed; the land stolen and violated; women raped and devalued; the spiritual belief of the Earth as a dynamic force denigrated; a foreign culture imposed; the language, oral traditions and cultural practices banned; and many men seduced by the promises of male domination.

Jean Florence (1989: p. 4), a member of the British network, Women Working for a Nuclear Free and Independent Pacific, wrote:

I have come to see Micronesia as a microcosm. All the threads of White, Western patriarchal history are tangled there. From the Jesuit persecution which reduced the people of the Marianas from 40,000 to 4,000; to the struggle of the matriarchs of Belau to protect their land from their own puppet "democratic" government; from the breaking of Marshallese women's matrilineal bonds with the land; to the uprooting of whole peoples from their lands and herding them into urban slums. Sexism. racism, religious bigotry, colonialism, militarism and, finally, nuclearism – it's all there right up to and including the big bang!

The male dominance of the female has been carried out on a global scale: male Europe has invaded a female Pacific; a male-dominated culture overruns cultures that are traditionally egalitarian and often matrilineal; a culture alienated from the Earth has attempted to vanquish a people who remember, in every way, their source – remember that they are *Tangata O Moana*: People of the Ocean.

Today, the world's last matrilineal societies are being violated by the acculturated male desire for power. This point is so important that I'll repeat it: the last matrilineal communities on our planet, communities where women are respected and honoured, are being attacked by the patriarchal pestilence.

European women can no longer continue to think of "matriarchy" (inappropriately named I think, for it implies female rule, male subjection) as an old story belonging to our ancient past. It is necessary for us to forsake the relative safety of distance and time and realise that the past we yearn for and the future we envisage is under attack – now – in the Pacific. In our efforts to reclaim a world where women have power, where women have a respected and honoured role in gender-balanced societies, we do well to stand beside our sisters who are living the reality of our dream. In striving to protect their lands and people, to restore their heritage, these women are guardians of a world in which women are free.

As women, we share a common heritage that stretches across our different histories and lifestyles. We are bound by common histories, albeit with different experiences and responsibilities. European women of the region are the daughters, the descendants, of the colonisers, and as such have benefited from the invasions. European women who have never visited the region have a responsibility that comes through the histories of their people – Dutch, Portuguese, Spanish, English, Irish, Scottish, Welsh, German, French, North American, Canadian . . . the list goes on. Across our different communities we share common concerns – peace, justice, self-determination, unemployment, health, a productive Earth. These are the things that can unite us.

But the onus lies with those of us who are part of the dominant culture. European women can do a lot to change the patriarchal power imbalance – not only in our individual lives but in our own communities and in the Pacific. We cannot nurture our dreams of a "matriarchal world" and not add our efforts to the moves to protect the last surviving strands of that same reality. If we are to be free then we must work, now, for the freedom of the Pacific. For as our histories are intertwined with those of Indigenous women, so certainly our futures can also be connected.

Learn to love the land and the people, and then you will know what you are fighting for.
Roman Bedor. Belau. (Bedor, 1986)

Those of us who are European are being called to take up the challenge given to us by Indigenous women: to find the courage to step beyond the confines of our internalised oppression and name the lies that bind us. It is time for us to unlearn our powerlessness, to refind our fury.

Over the years, as I have watched women listening to the stories told by Indigenous women, or have "talked story" myself, I have seen one woman after another take the pain into her heart. I have seen women crippled by their sorrow who then went deeper still, travelling through despair to the other side, the place of pure rage. I have also known women who turned away from their despair unable to cope, waiting for another time; and others who would not allow themselves to feel. And then, of course, there are the millions that just don't want to know, who have chosen to hide from even the most blatant truths. But those who reached the place of anger have been transformed.

I encourage you also to turn the pain you have felt reading these stories into positive, creative anger. Anger is empowering. I have witnessed women who had not believed in their own power become dynamic forces for change. Concerned for the Pacific, not because it was "over there" and removed from their own reality, but precisely because the stories had connected somewhere deep inside their soul. They had responded to the pain of Pacific women by finding its reflection inside themselves. In moving to work against the violations so apparent in the Pacific they were vanquishing their own oppression. Empowered, enraged, they will let nothing stop them from changing the world.

It's time to cry out for the blood spilled on this planet, the women raped, the children born deformed, the animals facing extinction, the ever-present threat that there may be no future to hand to our children. And that cry will be a cry of passion that rises from the base of our guts exploding into the world as unremitted fury.

Our rage gives us the courage to resist the colonial claim on our minds and bodies. In our rage we refuse to wait any longer. Already it has been too long. We remember the pain of our mothers who came before us, and of our sisters around the Earth today, and promise that for the daughters of tomorrow it will be different.

The anger I speak of is not violence. I am not advocating that we women lose our centre of purpose. The world we desire to build must be lived today. Anger is our pathway. It empowers us to act and through action comes hope – the power source of those who strive for justice. As we act, we reach out to others who are also responding and we meet in very power-filled ways. Through uniting in common struggle, sharing visions and giving each other strength, we become aware that we are not alone – that we are in fact bonded together with other women all around the planet.

We are all women ... we share a common oppressor, but we are rich in our differences.
Our woman knowledge, our woman strength, comes from different cultural and visionary
sources ...

Ngahuia Te Awekotuku and Marilyn Waring. Aotearoa.
(Te Awekotuku and Waring, 1985: p. 486)

The call is to work together. But how? As we work in solidarity we meet different
peoples, different individuals, and it is not always easy to remember that as women we
share a common oppression: all of us are oppressed, to some extent, by men. Yes,
European women are benefactors of the European male system, but they are also victims.
Yes, Black men are oppressed by that same system, but they are also the oppressors of
Black, and sometimes European, women. So, as women we share the experience of
being oppressed by men. This is the link that can bind us. Although our experiences
are different we share a common heritage of oppression: we are, all of us, women. It is
in the recognition of this that, as women, we can meet. Our task is nothing less than
bringing down patriarchal culture.

While we have, in the past, allowed our differences to separate us, we can use our
diversity as a strength. We can learn to stand side-by-side, strongly supportive of each
other, knowing that we are not alone in this world. Knowing that we are surrounded by
sisters – Black, Brown, Red, Yellow, White – sisters with different visions, needs and
struggles, all sharing a common heritage as women.

For this union to be possible, however, it's necessary for European women to take
on the perspectives of our Indigenous sisters, incorporating them into the parameters
of our own lives. Take, for example, the concept we define as "feminism". Feminism,
in its essence, comprehends the sacredness of life and aims towards the liberation of
all people. It is obvious from the stories contained in this book that this respect for life,
both individual and collective, is the motivating force and underlies the methods of our
Indigenous sisters. And yet "feminism", as a concept, is met with great hesitancy in
Pacific circles.

Gender inequality is often seen as essentially a product of European culture and
therefore inevitably a concern of European women. Bwgcolman (Aboriginal), Rachael
Cummins (1989) reflected:

I feel sorry for White women, I think they've got a harder battle than Black women with
their men. White women, from as far back, were always put on a pedestal, were always,
you know, "delicate little porcelain ladies". The male "I'll protect my family at all costs,
don't you worry your pretty little face about it" sort of mentality. And at the same time
there were these women, "the scum of the earth", that the husbands were having these

affairs with – the whores. White women weren't able to, weren't allowed to, develop in their community. Or to develop their own community. And White women today have to work against this background. Whereas the Black woman – she was always recognised, always respected. She knew her rights. She was free.

But there is a distinct Pacific feminism, as Vanessa Griffen (1988a) has observed:

There is no single perspective on feminism. Early on I found it very hard to talk to western feminists, to understand what they were on about. I couldn't understand how they could be concerned with sometimes very narrow issues when for us what was happening in our communities could not be ignored. Fortunately I have been involved in meetings between women from the "north" and the "south" where we have arrived at a feminist perspective that is more international. The definition of feminism has been broadened to take into account the economic, the political and the social, and then women's place in the world.

Suliana Siwatibau (1989b), from Fiji, outlines a Pacific woman's perspective of "feminism":

A lot of Pacific women say that feminism is an imported concept. I think what they refer to is probably the concept of women dominating men. I think it is a misinterpretation. To me, feminism means the liberation of women so that they can become equal with men in every way in society. It means breaking the barriers of attitudes that are so hard in both men and women so that they have a different concept of women. Feminism is the liberation of society.

European women have tended to assume that we are the vanguard of the feminist movement. This is an extremely ethnocentric perspective. Feminism has long been strong in the Pacific, as the lives of Indigenous women attest. In our ignorance we have too often ignored, or,at best, misunderstood the needs and aspirations of women of other cultures. And until this changes, "feminism" will continue to be seen by many to be just another oppressive "ism". True feminism, which strives for a world where all peoples are free, has been present in every culture in the world and in every period of history since the suppression of women began. Only when European women come to really understand this, and act upon that understanding, will union between our cultures be possible.

Sexist attitudes did not wipe out whole tribes of our people, sexist attitudes are not slowly killing our people – racism did, and continues to do so.
Pat O'Shane. Australia. (O'Shane, 1976)

It should not be assumed that all Indigenous women see "feminism" as their major priority. For many Indigenous women, particularly those coming traditionally from more egalitarian societies than the European patriarchal model, racism is seen as the main issue. European women are, therefore, left with the challenge of incorporating the question of racism into our concept of "feminism".

That requires European women taking on the issues facing Indigenous women – like an end to the racism that results in Indigenous people having the highest infant mortality rate, the highest prison populations, the highest suicide rates, malnutrition of their children because they don't have access to the land that once fed them, premature aging because of nuclear testing, the loss of their ancestral lands because of the military and tourist industries – and actively assisting them in bringing an end to these violations. In a world where over one billion women are totally occupied with meeting basic survival needs, feminism becomes far more than issues like equal pay. In Australia, it means realising that an Aboriginal woman, whether she lives in the city or the desert, does not have access to the same resources as European women. It means speaking out against the situation in the Marshalls, where women are afraid to give birth because of the risk of deformities. And it means actively supporting women in Papua New Guinea in their campaign against wife-beating.

Basically, it means sharing the resources that we can gain by means of being European in this world – tools, money, media. But it particularly means incorporating Indigenous women's visions and needs into our own. Committing ourselves to change means changing ourselves. It requires us to stop acting as if we alone have the gift that will save humanity, or that Indigenous women need us, or indeed even assuming that they will want to give anything to us. It means acting on the realisation that in an equal partnership we both have contributions to make to each other. This means, as Hawai'ian, Ho'oipo De Cambra (1986) suggests, taking responsibility for our actions and our history:

> We need to take responsibility for the oppression in order to take the foot of the oppressor off our belly, and to stand up. And, at the same time, you have a responsibility. As I have looked and found what my responsibility is, I beg you to look and find what your responsibility is in this world. It may be a world problem, yes, but we live in neighbourhoods. We live on islands. We can make change. The world's a small place. So it may be a global problem, but I really think we have local solutions and we need to discover what they are. And we must check out if we are not part of the problem.
>
> For a long time I was part of the problem. I cooperated with the assimilation and the oppression. I refuse to do that any more because I take responsibility to liberate myself, my people, my family. I think what we are about here is to discover what our responsibilities are for the time we are alive. It's a short time. We cannot dilly-dally once we discover and we know more. And you know more today than you ever did in your lifetime, and because you know more you have a greater responsibility and calling. And you should allow Indigenous peoples to speak the truth of their experience. It's always good to combat a problem from the point of view of the person who is experiencing the problem. I think that it's easier to get at the solutions. And to trust that those people are right. And that's the hardest thing for people to do – to trust that the oppressed can liberate themselves.

One of the responsibilities European women face is to deal with our racism. Racism is the imposition of political, social and economic systems by one group over another in the belief that one group is naturally superior. True feminism and racism, therefore, cannot co-exist. If we, as women, are intent on creating an alternative to this patriarchal world where the norm is power over others then we must deal with our own failings, and as European women that means challenging our racism.

We've got to accept the responsibility that comes when we realise that the European world was built on the backs of Indigenous and other peoples of the exploited world. Little has changed since the days when the empire-builders swarmed into the Pacific, or Africa, Asia and the Americas, taking lands and resources, destroying culture and identity. The attitude has always been that Indigenous people, Black people – and particularly women – are expendable. How else could weapons systems, a direct product of rival tensions between European males in the northern hemisphere, be constructed with so much pain to Pacific peoples? The Kokatha people are a prime example: uranium mined from their sacred sites was made into bombs and tested upon the same people! What attitude allows that? Racism.

Until each one of us actually stands up and actively works to stop that exploitation then we perpetuate that lie – our silence condones and allows it, as Bwgcolman, Rachael Cummins (1989) explains:

> The ignorance of White Australia! They really don't know. It's all been hidden away. I'm not talking about the outright racists. I'm talking about the person who might care if they knew. Multinationals who have their interests in keeping the general public ignorant are helping to keep the truth from being told and are drumming up racism. They are saying, "If you give these people their land they're going to snatch away your one-acre block. They're going to be claiming land rights all over the place". The Land Rights issue is just not being told properly. So the people who would if they knew support Aboriginal people are being kept ignorant. Out-and-out racists always believed that Aboriginals weren't up to scratch. And Whites won't listen to us, because we're Aboriginals. White people have got to find out what's happening, and then tell others. That's their responsibility as White people in Australia.

Until we rid ourselves of our racism we limit our potential. If we wish to create a world without racism then we must eradicate racism in our own selves. We must accept the challenge given by Maori, Titewhai Harawira (1985):

> I don't believe that we can grow in strength, or do anything that's going to be of any real importance for change, if we don't deal with the whole question of racism. I don't believe that Whites can afford the luxury any more of just concerning themselves with the nuclear issue because unless you deal with the cause of it you're just doing a lot of head trips. Racism is at the base of the whole nuclear issue – you wouldn't be testing in the Pacific if it was populated by Whites. And who makes those bombs? It's White men!

Dealing with our racism isn't easy or comfortable. It means giving room to Indigenous peoples, learning when to be quiet and watch and when to participate, and being willing to withdraw completely if that's appropriate. It means learning how it feels to be "other", and to know that the pain of that is only a fraction of the pain inflicted over the years. It means realising that you don't necessarily have all the answers. It means finding pride in yourself – and your culture – and knowing where your boundaries are, knowing what you're prepared to do and not do. It means being honest and being prepared to make mistakes. It means responding to challenges without getting caught up in guilt. It means going out on a limb in your own community, taking a risk. It means being lonely – and sometimes frightened. Dealing with our own racism means all of this and more – and it isn't easy. But it's got to be done. The history of oppression is, to a large extent, the history of European racism. Sue Culling, from Aotearoa, reminds us:

> Colonisation is a disease that has been killing people for years. The peace movement is supposed to be against violence and yet colonisation is probably the most violent process happening to people around the world. If the peace movement is about peace then the whole thing must be about fighting colonialism. They must look at justice (and not just getting rid of the bomb and the visible "arms") and how White racism has killed millions of the world's people. There's the mining for uranium on Aboriginal lands, the testing in the Marshalls and Australia, Tahiti, Christmas Island, waste dumping, relocations like Rongelap and Bikini, or in the case of Kwajalein and Belau it's military bases. That's all tied up with colonisation and White racism (1988: p. 3).

Racism is rife through all strata of life. Maori women – Lenis Davidson (1990) , from the Ngati Maru, and Mona Lisa Johnson (1990), from the Ngati Porou and Ngati Kahungunu (Rongomai-Wahine), tribes relate their perspective from the other side of racism.

Lenis Davidson:

> The Pakeha see the Maori in a particular way because of the media. It gives them certain sorts of ideas: that we're lazy or low achievers, that we can't possibly grasp certain concepts in the Pakeha world, can't operate as well as a Pakeha. Fundamental imaginings really. You are confronted with a double burden: sexism says women can't do things, racism says Maoris can't do things.

Mona Lisa Johnson:

> We have a close connection with Pakeha women who are on board – it's a real sister thing – but some Pakeha women just go so far on the *kaupapa* for the ride. Instead of supporting they come up and take the positions, the leading roles. And we're accused of racism because we say, "Hey, hold on a minute!". This is the damage Pakeha women can do once we let them in the door. They take power instead of being supportive. They get on this trip that we're all one people. I keep saying, "We are not one people!". That is the beauty of us – the differences. It's easier to cope with one people because that way they don't have to recognise any culture bar the White because that's the one people. They're the people that have to be in control and it's the easiest way to control people by telling them they're one people.

Lenis Davidson:

> Look, if tomorrow we could put dye into our water and everybody would instantly be brown, Pakehas would still be Pakeha on the inside. You see? Even though they're brown

on the outside, the way they think, the way they are, their concepts of the world would still be Pakeha – even though their skins are dyed brown. So, you see, it's the concept of where they come from, how they operate, their culture that makes us what we are. Even though the Pakeha might not think they have a culture we as Maoris see it clearly.

One of the most important questions facing humanity is to find out where Indigenous people and European people can meet, to find that common ground upon which we can move together towards a just society. And only when Europeans learn to honour the cultures of Indigenous people in the absence of racism will we succeed.

Everybody's got a culture. You White people have got a culture. What is it? Where is it? Do you know? Because it's important to know who you are. It's important if you're doing solidarity work with Indigenous women to know where you are coming from.
                                    Joan Wingfield. Kokatha. (Wingfield, 1988a)

Pride in culture strengthens resistance, Joan Wingfield (1988a) claims:

We're proud. That's our resistance. The resistance has always been going on. That's why we call ourselves "Black" people because we're proud of our colour, proud of our culture and that's our resistance. And that's why a lot of us don't want to learn how to be like Whites. That resistance is still going on – the resistance to keep our culture alive and strong.

With these words she challenged me to find my own identity. Yes, I was Australian – but what else was I? I had a history. I came from a family and a people, all of whom shared a common background. I had ancestors. Who were they? What were their stories? Where did they come from? Where were their lands? Land, it kept coming down to land. A people came from a land. Land is an essential part of identity – it tells you, as I had heard so often during the Pacific journey, who you are.

It was in search of the answers that I went to Ireland. Although I had been brought up on stories of Eire I knew I was a "real" Australian and that they were "only stories". But as I sailed across the Irish Sea I was filled with an emotion that surfaced from the very depths of my being – a deep sadness and a fierce pride – feelings impossible to deny. I was the first of two generations to be "going home". I was returning to the land of my grandparents. I felt the pain of the land lost. Like most European-Australian children I had grown up ignorant of the Aboriginal community, but as I had grown older I had begun to learn the true story of the Australian nation. So, I knew that the land had been stolen with massacres and sinful arrogance, but it was there, on that ship, that

I began to understand in my heart, began to really understand, what that meant. The spiritual wrenching, the pain – and the joy and pride of returning. Finally, as I connected with my own ancestral land, I had begun to understand what as an Irish woman I had always known but never quite comprehended: the centuries of colonisation, the stolen land, the loss of language and culture, the enforced assimilation into the dominant race, the everlasting defiance and striving to be free. Even in Australia, where the Irish have been part of the colonising force, they were considered by the English to be "so benighted ... that, in their eyes, there was nothing but the shade of a Catholic's skin to distinguish [them] from an aborigine" (Dixson, 1976: p. 155). My mother's siblings had difficulty getting a job because they carried a Catholic name.

So, the story of my people tells me that I am Irish-Australian. But my identity is greater than that. I am a woman and a Lesbian. And it's important that I claim pride in both. As a woman I am joined with all other women by the common legacy of subjection, and refusal, to male rule. As a Lesbian I know what it is to be ostracised, silenced, abused, denied and threatened for being what I am. It is here that I know what Jaya Graves means when she says:

> Black to me is a political identity. It is not to the colour of my skin that I am committed but to all those countless people, then and now, who have suffered, and still do, because they share that colour skin. I grew up thinking that I was a human being. As I got older I decided I had to be a Black Woman. Why? Because we wish to be recognised, confronted, acknowledged. We will not be assimilated. We will keep our specificity until we come to that place where Black and White can meet with understanding and without pretense (Graves, 1986: p. 7).

It is in being Lesbian that I come closest to understanding the oppression that my Indigenous and Black sisters suffer. We too are murdered by governments and our blood spilled in city streets, we are hounded and harassed and rarely have equal legal rights even in the most "enlightened" countries. It is for this reason that you will find a high level of Lesbian involvement in just about any struggle for justice for women. Lesbians, because of our outsider role, have a unique potential to understand oppression. This is not to imply that we always tap into that potential, simply that our experiences in a heterosexist world makes that possible. This experience of oppression does not deny the sheer joy of being Lesbian. Being Lesbian brings me a sense of strength and freedom, that I had not known in my earlier life. Being Lesbian empowers me in a way I never thought possible. I am defiant, rebellious and proud. I am now who I have always been.

The process of learning pride in my own identity has gone hand in hand with my work with Indigenous women. I realised early on that I could not assist other women to protect and reclaim their heritage if I could not find the ability to do the same for myself. I know that, as the saying goes, "while any of us is oppressed then we are all oppressed". The history of oppression of Lesbians parallels the oppression of other peoples. We died in the gas ovens of the German Reich along with our Jewish sisters.

We died in the flames of the Inquisition at the same time that the Spanish decimated the Chamorro nation. What is more, there are those of us who are also Jewish, also Indigenous. If, when pressured by heterosexism, I deny my own Lesbianism then I dishonour my heritage, my sisters, myself. Hence, I speak out. I will not be silenced, made invisible, assimilated, and I wait eagerly for that day when we, Lesbian and heterosexual women, can, as Jaya says, "meet with understanding and without pretense". If we are to do solidarity work, if we are to unite in our diversity, then we must know what those differences are. We must boldly speak of them with each other. Taking risks. Trusting.

But identity is more than knowing who you are – it's reclaiming your connection with the land. Indigenous women have always known that – European women are remembering it.

Indigenous people know that they are caretakers of the Earth. They share an understanding of the Earth as a living entity and the source of all life. They know that, as custodians, it is their profound duty to honour the Earth. Indigenous people nurture the sacred places and the Dreaming tracks, the webs of energy that cradle our planet. They know that this physical world is not the only reality – that we are wrapped in realms of spirits, some with whom we can connect. These are the places of our ancestors.

As I travelled through the Pacific I witnessed and shared in life-sustaining rituals to nurture the Earth. From the *hula* ceremony on Kaho'olawe calling on Lono to protect the land, to walking with spirits on Mejatto in the dead of night with only my feet to guide me. I have visited Elabaob, the Rock Islands of Belau where visitors are encouraged to put their food scraps on the limestone ledges away from the water or risk having stones thrown at them by displeased spirits. I am privileged to have been taken deep into the Guam jungle by Chamoru *Chetlu* (brothers and sisters), to the ruins of ancient villages, witnessing a sacred ceremony that connected the people of today with their ancestors. I have been taken into the Australian desert by Kukatja Law women and given a glimpse of their vast knowledge.

The veils that hang between the worlds are thin in these places. But where the land has been violated and the "Dreaming" forgotten, the Earth is heavy and needs healing.

Native American, Tawna Sanchez (1987) calls on European women to reclaim our spiritual link with the Earth:

> I believe that if Europeans would search back into their own lives and their own land for their true religion and way of life they could find out who they really are. Europeans have to refind their true religion. I've been to Europe, you can feel it's there, but the land is dying because no one thinks about it any more, no one gives thanks for that land, or to the Earth Mother that it is. European people do not give thanks for the land. They pray to a god that they fear. And that they think is male! Who told them that lie? You know, who is the real giver of life? It's the Earth. Without the Earth nothing could live.

Many European women, realising their loss, are reclaiming the Old Religions banished during the centuries of male rule, are finding a new way that arises from this time, from our historical experience and from the hidden traditions. In places like Australia, where historically we come from European backgrounds but now have an undeniable connection for the land with which we live, the challenge is different. We must find a way that honours our own experience without taking from the peoples in whose lands we live.

The knowledge of our heritage provides a meeting place of pride where we can come together, aware of our own unique qualities and thus able to respect others for their contribution to the struggle. We need that sense of perspective. It is only in knowing our own history that we no longer fall into the trap of denigrating or romanticising someone else's culture. When we romanticise Indigenous people we deny their reality.

Pacific peoples are as different in opinion and desires as any community. For example, not all Indigenous people want to live in a Pacific free from nuclear warships; not all Belauans want independence from the US. When we create a stereotype of Indigenous Pacific women we assume, indeed insist, that they have all the answers to changing this world, or even their own people's dilemma. We set up an unequal situation making it impossible to connect.

The support we give each other as women must be mutual. By recognising our different but connected struggles we can allow space for each other and respect our different needs, aspirations and methods of working. As we learn to come together there must be both room to make mistakes and room to challenge each other. That requires each one of us, European and Indigenous/Black women alike, to make an honest inventory of our own internalised oppressions and prejudices. If the world that we want to create is a world without oppression then there is no place for racism, sexism, heterosexism, or any of the other "isms", inside our own minds.

Solidarity must be a two-way exchange. Unless we can stand side-by-side together we create a hierarchy where one has power-over and the other gives away her power. This results in a denial of the inherent value of both women – neither can be who they really are. It would be a mere repetition of the power imbalance that we are attempting to dissolve – only the players are changed. Women have a greater responsibility to each other than to duplicate the same old patriarchal mistakes. We must create a situation that empowers all of us. Each woman must be honoured for who she is. She must be respected for her contribution to our one shared struggle. We owe this to ourselves, to each other, to the Earth.

There are some who believe that the custom says women's position is below the man. There is nothing says that: that in the custom women should be beaten or raped, or she should shut her mouth when her husband is around. There is nothing in the custom says that. That is a big lie. It is just to protect themselves, their power.

Susanna Ounei. Kanaky. (Ounei, 1990)

This is a time when women need each other. Wherever we look violence is being perpetrated against us. But men respond to our unity as if they fear our power. Certainly they fear an end to their privileged position. Possibly for those men who are engaged in their own struggle for justice it is easier, but sometimes even they betray their own sisters. Susanna Ounei (1990), from Kanaky, tells of the difficulty she has faced as a woman working within her people's struggle:

We started the fight for independence in 1969 with the Red Scarf, led by the son of the chief of Maré. But there were not many women at that time. Only one who came back from France in the 1970s who could express herself around the meetings. She was my best friend. We were sent together to jail in 1974 for political reasons. In jail we decided to create something for women, and started it when we got out. In 1987, there was a big dispute between the women's group and some members of the movement that disagreed with us who did everything they could to humiliate women. Every time women tried to talk, they would say it was against the custom or that it was a waste of time. We were not getting support from the men. We were discouraged. We were badly viewed, not only by men but by a few women, because we were talking about contraception and things like that. There were very few who had the courage to stand and talk against the exploitation of women.

I don't want to divide my brothers from us women because we have a common struggle. It is very important, our struggle. It is not easy. But the situation of women is something that is in my heart. I feel so sorry for the sisters: that they are beaten, raped, exploited. Without the real liberation of women there is no independence. Independence for one is liberation of all people – not only men but women as well. Otherwise the men will have the power – and what about the women? It is important for us to raise, through our action, the role of women in a free Kanaky. Our struggle is a struggle in the long term. Things are really slow. We have to fight hard to make men understand that a free Kanaky is for everyone. Not only independence for men but independence for everyone. I try to change the attitudes of my brothers but I can't hate them. I know that when they get shot my heart cries. The nineteen brothers I lost in Ouvea [massacre, 1987]. It was heavy. They are my nephews, my brothers, my cousins. But it is their responsibility also to encourage us because when we work for liberation it is the liberation of everyone.

This is not an isolated incident, as the stories contained in this book attest. And yet, men have little to lose and their own liberation to gain as women move for their freedom, but they must unburden themselves of the patriarchal myths – as we all must. This challenge goes first and foremost to European men. They are being called to shed the privileges they gain by virtue of being European and male in this lopsided world. Maori, Titewhai Harawira challenges:

As First Nation women, as White women, women are strong and they move to stop this nuclear madness. What are white men doing about it? There needs to be a commitment to challenge the structures that keep this whole cycle going, and that power and those structures belong to White men (WWNFIP, 1987: p. 37).

Men are being challenged to join in the dismantling of their own power systems. They are being challenged to stand beside their sisters and become actively involved in the downfall of the patriarchal regime. We can no longer afford to run the world by the games men have played.

It is time to raise the awareness of people who are non-Pacific to the Pacific women and to our experience.

Kiri Potaka-Dewes. Aotearoa. (Potaka-Dewes, 1989)

Often, as I have retold stories given to me by Indigenous women, I am asked, "What can I do?". Women want to act: we know that in action is empowerment. But it's not always easy to know what to do, especially when the problem seems so huge and all-encompassing.

Bridget Roberts (1987), with whom I initiated the British network Women Working for a Nuclear Free and Independent Pacific (WWNFIP), writes reassuringly:

Sometimes, for women just beginning or wanting to do something for the Pacific peoples, the problems just seem far too huge, or too complicated, and the network [WWNFIP] seems too elusive and full of "experts". But we probably all felt like that once. There was a time, not so long ago either, when none of us knew anything about the Pacific – and then, in different ways, we heard and it hurt – it all seemed too painful, too big, and we felt over-whelmed – but we also felt very, very angry and we wanted to do something about it – and then we found other women who felt the same way – and so WWNFIP was born. We found that we had different pieces of information about different nation/issues, that we had different interests. We learnt, and are still learning, that we complement and need each other.

Louise Aitsi (1989), assisting women's development programs in nineteen countries for the Pacific Women's Resource Bureau of the South Pacific Commission, offers an answer to our question: "what can we as European women do?":

What role can women from outside the region or non-indigenous women have? Well, in terms of providing resource materials, giving us seed money for projects for health, nutrition, water supply and self-employment programs for women. And sharing their experiences, their ideas and skills because most of our women have to learn new techniques in order to turn around and help their own women in their own country. It's a big job. We really don't have the resources. I find myself overcome at times because we're expected to work miracles and, of course, I can't work miracles, especially when money becomes the tool to reach people nowadays. In the Pacific the major problem is transport, how to get from one island to the next, and that consumes most of the money. Because governments prioritise economic development and women's priority is social welfare we have difficulty getting support from the governments. It's just not their priority. So the women's programs don't have much money. It's quite a difficult task. But women are hard workers and practical planners.

Pacific women are, according to Kiri Potaka-Dewes (1989) of Aotearoa, requesting programs that will give them the skills for survival:

> The issue that keeps repeating is the need for Pacific women to have access to training, to awareness-raising, to politicisation, in order to cope with the demands and needs of living in the modern arena of the Pacific.

Ruth Lechte (1988) who works for the Young Women's Christian Association in development projects, alerts us that this need for information and training is urgent:

> Working in village and communities with women and village groups brings one very rapidly to the conclusion that the main thing to be passed on to our sisters is knowledge. Knowledge leads to understanding and that leads to constructive action. I once wrote something called "Knowledge + Loving = Power". Women need that Power for care of their environment, protection of cultures, for using and conserving what the earth and seas give. They need new ideas to cope with the new structures of their lives: children are now in schools not doing the fishing. Vegetables are for sale, not for eating. There are many challenges to be faced and new ways to be learned. Yet women perceive themselves as being without Power. In some of our cultures they have a role in decision making. But it is minimal in areas that affect their future: environmental destruction, energy use, research and development priorities, technology options. Anyone working at the grass roots can do good service by discussing these and other issues, indicating how to lobby for change, how to get a waste system that is safe, or decent transport, finance or credit.

Pacific women's resources may be limited but their spirit is fighting fit, despite the obstacles weighed against them they are determined to improve the position of their people. There is a place in this for European women – we are the ones who have greatest access to the resources Indigenous women require.

But, in becoming involved with Indigenous women in their campaigns to improve the lives of their peoples, European women must recognise that, as Chamorro, Chailang Palacios (1985) reminds us:

> We as Pacific women must decide for ourselves what needs to be done, but you can help us by finding the funds to finance our work and by using your media to publicise what is happening in the Pacific.

And we must acknowledge that, as Chailang Palacios (1985) declares, they will do it with or without our support:

> But, you know, whether European women want to help us or not we are still strong as people, as women. We will keep on fighting because one day there will be justice for all of us.

European women, and men, around the world have begun to work beside their Indigenous neighbours. There are individuals, networks and organisations in the majority of European countries, as well as in Asian countries such as Japan, Malaysia, Indonesia and the Philippines, and also non-Indigenous people living in the Pacific nations, including Australia, Aotearoa and Great Turtle Island (the North Americas), who have lent their efforts to the struggle. Bridget Roberts (1987) expresses the spirit of the British network:

> Women Working for a Nuclear Free and Independent Pacific (WWNFIP) is not an organisation. We are a network. There is no membership and no leaders. We are simply a national gathering of women who feel strongly about what's going on in the Pacific and have been so inspired by the strength of our Indigenous Pacific sisters that we want to do something about it – no matter how small. We come together to give each other support and we do what we can where we are: in the home; with our children; in other peace and justice groups; alone – everywhere.

This network began around the fires of Greenham Common, at a women's peace camp outside a US Air force base in southern England. After exhausting days of creative actions or dealing with bailiffs, police and soldiers, women would gather for the evening meal and then sit around the fires late into the night. There were a few of us there from Australia and Aotearoa who would tell tales of the Pacific – sometimes stories of strength, sometimes of pain – and the women who listened would hurt, find their anger, and take the stories on to the next gathering of women. These were women who themselves lived on a frontline but we knew that, compared to the Pacific women, living there was a choice – albeit an essential one. All women live on the frontline, there are only different degrees of intensity.

Women came to Greenham from all over the world – sometimes for a few hours, sometimes staying for years – and each brought with her her own concerns and issues, and shared them with other women. Increasingly women ceased to focus their energy on the base and turned around to look out into the world and link with other women. We began to work on issues from Central America, Africa, Ireland, different situations in Britain and, of course, the Pacific. From there the Pacific network flourished. We organised meetings and raised funds, sending money into the Pacific, and bringing Indigenous women to tour Britain and Europe.

It was the stories these women told that drew women in Britain together into a network that continues to work with Indigenous Pacific women today. Bridget Roberts (1987) writes about the power of the women's stories:

Pacific women are the backbone of the movement to be nuclear free and independent. Their stories have inspired us, touched our hearts. We have been moved to act – not only in support of them, but for ourselves and our own communities. There are many powerful women out in the Pacific. Their words reach people's souls in a way missed by even the "best" analysis of the facts and figures of Pacific history. We see that the Pacific her-story has to be known and reciprocated if we are really going to build a worldwide movement for a nuclear free and independent Pacific, and a nuclear free and independent world.

Jean Florence (1989: p. 4) was one woman who was so moved by the stories that it changed her life. She wrote about her experience:

I was eight years old on the Day of Two Suns when Bravo was dropped on Bikini and the children of Rongelap played in the radioactive dust. Years later, when the people of Rongelap had returned from their first exile to their poisoned island, and the "jelly-fish" babies were beginning to be born, I was doing 0-Level Geography. An image which is often in my mind, when I am thinking of the Pacific, is those neat little diagrams in my geography book showing how coral atolls are formed: tiny polyps shedding their shells over thousands of years to make a necklace of islands round a lagoon. Nobody told me that these islands were inhabited. Nobody told me they were irradiated. Nobody told me how many had already been blown off the face of the planet . . .

Lijon told me that, twenty-seven years later, sitting with Lorenza from Belau and a small group of women in St Werburgh's Community Centre, Bristol. I cried then. But as Lijon said, "I didn't come all the way for you to cry for me. I have come for you to see yourself through me". I cried, but I also began to feel the rage which is on the other side of grief. Rage at my own ignorance; rage at my White racist education; rage at the power of imperialist nations which can write whole peoples out of our "history" books. It is the ignorance which gives the power, which gave Henry Kissinger permission to make his often quoted remark about Micronesia: "There are only ninety thousand people out there, who gives a damn?". If the US are allowed to get away with using a whole people as nuclear guinea pigs what can they not do?

We are being called urgently to educate our own people. For over 400 years the Pacific experience has been allowed to proceed under the cover of our ignorance. We must break the conspiracy of silence that keeps the Pacific on the edges of our maps, and the far corners of our minds. European women must learn the true story of the Pacific. Too many lies have been told for too long. Indigenous peoples have been silenced and their experiences erased. Cita Morei (1992), from Belau, asserts:

History is written by the outsiders. But what they have written is their perspective – it is not the Belauan perspective. The history of Belau should be rewritten. We should write our own history.

Europeans dominate the processes of knowledge through the imposition of our own cultural reliance on the written word, and, as a result, the knowledge contained within oral traditions is silenced. Native American, Tawna Sanchez (1987) explains:

I'm Indian and that means my word, my religion and my history is not the truth because it's not written down. But everything you say in your history, in your religion, has been written down. Whether it's a lie or not, it has been written down, so therefore it is the truth. For us there is no written language, we never wanted to have one. We know that it is more important to keep our religion, our ways, our history oral, so that our minds would never become weak, and we would never forget. And I cannot ever forget what has happened to my people, or to the people of the Pacific.

Maori, Hilda Halkyard-Harawira challenges European women to learn the true stories:

You can't make changes if you don't understand what went on beforehand – and what caused it. We have a saying that our past is our present and our future. But colonial mentality has an amnesia of the past (Hanly, 1986).

Lorenza Pedro (1986), from Belau, asks us to break that amnesia:

First know that we exist: we are not on your maps of the world. Then tell other people.

The stories of Indigenous women must be heard. The silence must be broken. And we European women have a role in this: it is after all our people who have forgotten how to listen.

Native American woman, Tawna Sanchez (1987), demands that we hear, and speak:

You know, every now and then I get the feeling that people aren't really listening when we tell you what is happening in the Pacific. You go, "Oh, my god! It's so awful?". But you're not listening! Well, you've got to wake up. It's urgent and you've got to wake up, now! It's necessary for you to learn what is going on, going on in your name. And it's important for you to tell other people. Think about what you can do. And if you don't think you can do something about it teach someone else, maybe someone else can do something about it. Keep the movement going. It's most important that all of you learn about what is happening and then do something about it! We're not going to live much longer on the Earth if we keep trying to kill her.

This is the purpose of this book. It is a book of and for story tellers. We need to listen to, learn and retell the stories, of our Indigenous sisters. We need to learn and tell our own stories. We need to listen to the stories of all our sisters around the world. We need to tell ourselves stories of our shared visions and of our strengths. It is through our stories, our songs and our murmurings late at night that we will formulate the words that will pass our experience on to each other and the generations to come. We need to tell our stories until all women of all cultures are free of oppression.

That time is coming. Women are coming into our power. It is time to band together, supporting each other, giving each other strength. Trusting that our vision will survive.

Listen to, and hear with your hearts, the voices of the women. Take up the Challenge.

ANCESTORS, ANCIENT MOTHERS

Hinewirangi Kohu. Ngati Kahungungu,
Ngati Ranginui (Maori). Aotearoa. 1994

Ancestors, Ancient Mothers
Today we come to the sacred circle
winds come from all oceans
and we remember you.
remembering the stories, songs, chants
drums beating, haunting flutes singing
the heart rhythms of
Ancestor memories.

Circles of life – spiralling visions
across indigenous lands, oceans, forests.
Mountain peaks kissing the rising sun
pride, dignity echoed
in men, women and children.
Elders crouched around morning fires
In sacred sweat lodges
cleansing rituals, preparations.
Elders birthing our future
Our histories, rich and free
four colours, four nations, four winds
once all gathered at that sacred circle

Ancestors, Ancient Mothers
Today we sit
at the circle of the ocean people
washing rituals of pain
and remember the songs
colonization – genocide
spiritual, cultural, mental, physical, family
all raped.
relocation songs – residential schools
stolen children to white ways
the Bible, bullet, bullshit
Anger, pain, hate of the Western barbaric's
colonization – neo colonization
multi nationals – trans nationals
governments – systems
all part of our destruction.

Ancestors, Ancient Mothers.
　　We sit at the crossroads
Where the sacred circle has brought us
from all winds, all corners,
knowing – that some are still not
at the gathering.
Some still hold the power.
　　power over
　　　　power ego
　　　　　　powerlessness
afraid to let go
　　afraid to accept our power
　　spiritual power
our power to protect, to care, to share
our power to love with no conditions.

Sitting at the crossroads
waiting, learning of patience
　　loving our healing
songs of resistances are sung
　　no longer afraid
no longer victims
　　Survivors
　　not afraid to hear
the sounds of a longest time
remembering suppression, oppression
depression.

Sitting at the crossroads
in the light of men, women and children
　　with elders
　　　　chanting healing songs
waiting, waiting for YOU
privileged few
　　who dare to deliberate
in fear, maintaining your fears
of release, maybe liberation from
your own atrocities.

Sitting at the crossroads
　　Still, the drum beats
　　Still the koauau – flute sings
　　Still Indigenous peoples sing
　　Still we wait in love.
Waiting at the Crossroads for YOU.

References

Aitsi, Louise. (1989). Interview by Zohl dé Ishtar at Twenty-Fifth Congress of the Women's International League for Peace and Freedom, Sydney, July 1989.

Albertini, Jim, Nelson Foster, Wally Inglis and Gil Roeder. (1980). *The Dark Side of Paradise. Hawaii in a Nuclear World.* Honolulu: Catholic Action of Hawaii, Peace Education Project.

Ali, Shamima. (1986). Interviewed by Zohl dé Ishtar and Bridget Roberts, Suva, Fiji, September 1986.

Aluli, Noa Emmett. (1986). Speech recorded by Zohl dé Ishtar and Bridget Roberts, Kaho'olawe Island, Hawai'i, May 1986.

Aluli, Noa Emmett. (1987, April–May). "Aloha 'Aina: Without Land We Are Nothing." *Pacific News Bulletin*, 2(2), 6–7. Sydney: Pacific Concerns Resource Centre.

Anjain, Renam. (1986). Interview by Zohl dé Ishtar and Bridget Roberts, Mejatto, Republic of the Marshall Islands, June 1986.

Aweau, Sharkal. (1986). Interview by Zohl dé Ishtar and Bridget Roberts, Wai'anae, Hawai'i, May 1986.

Beckett, Jeremy. (1987). *Torres Strait Islanders. Custom and Colonialism.* Cambridge: Cambridge University Press.

Bedor, Roman. (1986). Interview by Zohl dé Ishtar and Bridget Roberts, Koror, Republic of Belau, August 1986.

Bertell, Rosalie. (1985). *No Immediate Danger. Prognosis for a Radioactive Earth.* London: The Women's Press.

Bolt, Richard. (1990). "The New Australian Militarism." In Graeme Cheeseman and St John Kettle (Eds.) *The New Australian Militarism. Undermining Our Future Security.* Sydney: Pluto Press. 25–73.

Buretini, Rusula. (1989). Interview by Zohl dé Ishtar at The Grail's Women of the Pacific Conference, Townsville, Queensland, July 3–9, 1989.

Burgess, Hayden (aka Poka Laenui). (1982). "A Nation Betrayed". *Te Hui Oranga O Te Moana Nui A Kiwa.* Aotearoa/New Zealand: Pacific People's Anti-Nuclear Action Committee and Te Reo Oranga O Te Moana Nui a Kiwa. 22–23.

Burgess, Puanani. (1986a). Interview by Zohl dé Ishtar and Bridget Roberts, Wai'anae, Hawai'i, May 1986.

Burgess, Puanani. (1986b). Hear Us, Sisters. Poem written as "The Liturgy" for Celebratory Mass, 1986. Hawai'i.

Burgess, Puanani. (1994a). "Hawai'i Pono'I. Unpublished poem.

Burgess, Puanani. (1994b). Phone conversation with Zohl dé Ishtar, May 1994.

Caldecott, Leonie. (1983). "The Land is Our Life. A Pacific Experience." In Leonie Caldecott and Stephanie Leland (Eds.) *Reclaim the Earth. Women Speak for Life on Earth.* London: The Women's Press. 107–110.

Carter, John. (1984). *Pacific Islands Year Book.* Edited by John Carter. Fifteenth edition. Sydney & New York: Pacific Publications.

Chin, Sue. (1983, January 1). "'We are sick and tired of being guinea pigs.'" *International Examiner*. Seattle, USA.

Ching, Charlie. (1988). "The Fight for Independence – Tahiti Polynesia." Unpublished paper based on Charlie Ching's May 1988 tour of Britain, produced by Women Working for a Nuclear Free, Britain.

Clifton, Joan. (1989). Interviewed by Zohl dé Ishtar, Port Augusta, November 1989.

Collier, Sylvia. (1988, February 29). *Paradise Lost*. London: Channel 4. Television Documentary. Shown on Australian *Four Corners* as *Palau and the United States: Compact of Free Association or Part of a Nuclear Strategy?*.

Connelly, Frances, Joan Grant, Susie Cohn and Fran Willard. (1987). *Pacific Paradise. Nuclear Nightmare*. Written for Women Working for a Nuclear Free and Independent Pacific. London: Campaign for Nuclear Disarmament.

Corbett, Helen. (1987a). Paper to United Nations Working Group on Indigenous Populations, Geneva.

Corbett, Helen. (1987b). Speech recorded by Zohl dé Ishtar at European Nuclear Disarmament Conference, Britain, June 1987.

Cox, Sarah. (1983, August 10–17). "Nuclear Testing. Coral Islands Vapourized in Radio-active Pacific." *The Ubyssey*. II(7), 1–2. Vancouver, British Columbia, Canada.

Craigie, Cathy. (1986). "We Fight Together – Aboriginal Women in Australia." *Third World Women's News*, 1(1), 28–29. London.

Cristobal, Hope. (1986). Interview by Zohl dé Ishtar and Bridget Roberts, Guam, July 1986.

Crocombe, Ron. (1976). *The Pacific Way. An Emerging Identity*. Suva, Fiji: Lotu Pasifika Productions.

Culling, Sue. (1987). "Foreign Aid: Whose Needs and Priorities?" *Report from the Pacific Concerns Resource Centre Fifth International Conference: For the Advancement of the Pacific Peoples' Struggles for Self-Determination and Peace*. Sydney: Pacific Concerns Resource Centre. 40–43.

Culling, Sue. (1988). "A Black Women's Korero on Militarisation in the Pacific." *Be Active for a Nuclear Free and Independent Pacific*, 13, 3. Britain: Women Working for a Nuclear Free and Independent Pacific. Based on interview by Zohl dé Ishtar at European Nuclear Disarmament Conference, Britain, June 1987.

Cummins, Rachael. (1989). Speech recorded by Zohl dé Ishtar at The Grail's Women of the Pacific Conference, Townsville, Queensland, July 3–9, 1989.

Danielsson, Marie-Therese. (1985). "The Ultimate Polynesian Islands." Unpublished paper presented to the NGO Women's Conference in Rarotonga, Cook Islands, March 19–24, 1985, on behalf of the Women's International League for Peace and Freedom, Polynesian Section.

Danielsson, Marie-Therese. (1987). Interview by Zohl dé Ishtar and Bridget Roberts, Paea, Tahiti Polynesia, March 1987.

Davidson, Lenis. (1990). Interview by Zohl dé Ishtar, Christchurch, Aotearoa/New Zealand, November 1990.

De Cambra, Ho'oipo. (1986). Speech recorded by Zohl dé Ishtar at Ninth World Futures Studies Federation Conference, University of Hawai'i, May 26–28, 1986.

Denaro, Judith. (1987, August). "Letter from Fiji." *Sanity. Voice of CND*. London: Campaign for Nuclear Disarmament.

Department of Aboriginal Affairs. (1988, August). *The Torres Strait Islanders*. Canberra: Australian Government Publishing Service.

Dibblin, Jane. (1985a, April). "De Nuke the Pacific." *Outwrite*. London.

Dibblin, Jane. (1985b, September 20). "Britain is in the Dock." *New Statesman*. London.

Dibblin, Jane. (1988). *Day of Two Suns. US Nuclear Testing and the Pacific Islanders*. London: Virago.

Dixson, Miriam. (1976). *The Real Matilda. Woman and Identity in Australia. 1788 to 1975*. Ringwood, Victoria, Australia: Penguin Books.

Dworkin, Andrea. (1974). *Women-Hating*. New York: E. P. Dutton and Co.

Dworkin, Andrea. (1976). *Our Blood. Prophecies and Discourses on Sexual Politics*. New York: Harper and Row.

Edmond, Betty. (1986). Interview by Zohl dé Ishtar and Bridget Roberts, Majuro, Republic of the Marshall Islands, June 1986.

Eknilang, Lijon. (1986). Interview by Zohl dé Ishtar and Bridget Roberts, Ebeye and Mejatto, Republic of the Marshall Islands, June 1986.

Elder, Bruce. (1988). *Blood on the Wattle. Massacres and Maltreatment of Australian Aboriginals since 1788*. Frenchs Forest, NSW: Child and Associates.

Enloe, Cynthia. (1988). *Does Khaki Become You? The Militarisation of Women's Lives*. London: Pandora.

Enloe, Cynthia. (1989). *Bananas, Beaches and Bases. Making Feminist Sense of International Politics*. London: Pandora.

Evatt Memorial Foundation. (1989, June). *A Submission to the Commonwealth Government on Behalf of the Australian South Sea Islanders*. Unpublished paper. Sydney: H. V. Evatt Memorial Foundation.

Flick, Karen. (1987). Interview by Zohl dé Ishtar and Bridget Roberts at New South Wales Lands Rights Council, Sydney, October 1986.

Florence, Jean. (1989, May). "Talking About Rongelap." *Be Active for a Nuclear Free and Independent Pacific*, 16, 4–5. Britain: Women Working for a Nuclear Free and Independent Pacific.

Fox, Charles E.. (1967). *The Story of the Solomons*. Sydney: Pacific Publications.

Francke, Lizzie. (1985, May). "The Pacific Need for Peace." *Sanity. Voice of CND*, 5, 28–31. London: Campaign for Nuclear Disarmament.

Friends of Micronesia. (1972). *Micronesia for the People*. Berkeley, CA: Friends of Micronesia.

Gomez, Ku'umea'aloha. (1982). "Hawai'ian Women in Struggle Parallels Across the Pacific." *Te Hui Oranga O Te Moana Nui A Kiwa*, 1982. Te Hui Oranga O Te Moana Nui A Kiwa and Pacific Peoples Anti-Nuclear Action Committee. 20–21.

Gomez, Ku'umea'aloha. (1986). Interview by Zohl dé Ishtar and Bridget Roberts, O'ahu, Hawai'i, May 1986.

Gordon, Pauline. (1990). Speech recorded by Zohl dé Ishtar at Pacific Women's Conference, hosted by Regional Pacific Women's Seminars and Resources Development Association, at New South Wales Museum, Sydney, Australia, July 1990.

Grassby, Al, and Marji Hill. (1988). *Six Australian Battlefields. The Black Resistance to Invasion and the White Struggle Against Colonial Oppression*. Sydney: Angus and Robertson.

Graves, Jaya. (1986, June 6). "Racism is everyone's problem." *Peace News*, 7, 9. London.

Greco, Robyn. (1986). "The Marshall Islands. A Report." Unpublished internal report for the Nuclear Free and Independent Pacific network. Melbourne, Australia.

Greenpeace International and Toimata. (1990). Edited by Stephanie Mills, Julie Miles, Madaleen Helmer and Saskia Kouwenberg. "'My baby became rigid, like wood'". *Testimonies. Witnesses of French Nuclear Testing in the South Pacific*. 63.

Griffen, Vanessa. (1985). "All It Requires Is Ourselves." In Robin Morgan (Ed.) *Sisterhood is Global. The International Women's Movement Anthology*. Harmondsworth: Penguin Books. 520–527.

Griffen, Vanessa. (1988a). Speech recorded by Zohl dé Ishtar at European Nuclear Disarmament Conference, Sweden.

Griffen, Vanessa. (1988b). Interview by Stephanie Mills, on behalf of Zohl dé Ishtar, Sydney, Australia.

Halkyard-Harawira, Hilda. (1986a). "Spirit of Kiwa." *Be Active for a Nuclear Free and Independent Pacific*, 6, 23. Britain: Women Working for a Nuclear Free and Independent Pacific.

Halkyard-Harawira, Hilda. (1986b, July). "Pacific guinea pigs." *Sanity. The Voice of CND*. London: Campaign for Nuclear Disarmament. 32.

Halkyard-Harawira, Hilda. (1990a). Ed. *He Kuaka Marangaranga*. Aotearoa/New Zealand.

Halkyard-Harawira, Hilda. (1990b). Opening speech recorded by Zohl dé Ishtar at 1990 Nuclear Free and Independent Pacific Conference, Aotearoa.

Halkyard-Harawira, Hilda and Katie Boanas with Zohl dé Ishtar. (1992). "Pacific Connections: Women and the Peace Movement in Aotearoa." In Rosemary Du Plessis with Phillida Bunkle, Kathie Irwin, Alison Laurie and Sue Middleton (Eds.), *Feminist Voices. Women's Studies Texts for Aotearoa/New Zealand*. Auckland: Oxford University Press. 317–337.

Hanly, Gil. (1986). *Peace is More than the Absence of War*. Auckland: New Women's Press.

Harawira, Titewhai. (1985). Speech recorded by Zohl dé Ishtar during First Pacific Women's Tour of Britain, hosted by Women Working for a Nuclear Free and Independent Pacific, Britain, March 1985.

Hawke, Sharon and Louise Rafkin. (1984). "Hawai'ian Women in Struggle. Parallels Across the Pacific." *Te Hui Oranga O Te Moananui A Kiwa*. Conference Report.

Hayes, Peter, Lyuba Zarsky and Walden Bello. (1986). *American Lake: Nuclear Peril In The Pacific*. Harmondsworth, Britain: Penguin Books.

Hill, Lenora. (1987). Speech recorded by Zohl dé Ishtar at University of California, Los Angeles, May 1987.

Hutton, Barbara. (1988, January 22). "A Grief Too Great to Join the Party." *The Age*. Melbourne, Australia. 13.

Iakobo, Binatia. (1989). Interview by Zohl dé Ishtar at The Grail's Women of the Pacific Conference, Townsville, Queensland, July 3–9, 1989.

Jacklick, Alvin. (1986). Interview by Zohl dé Ishtar and Bridget Roberts, Ebeye, Republic of the Marshall Islands, June 1986.

Jackson, Syd. (1990). "Indigenous Rights." In Hilda Halkyard-Harawira (Ed.) *He Kuaka Marangaranga*. Aotearoa. 10–12.

Jamieson, Annie. (1990, March 8). "The Wasted Talent Lost in the Women's Chorus Line. Women in Parliament." *The Australian*. Sydney, Australia. 15.

Jelij, Katrine. (1986). Interview by Zohl dé Ishtar and Bridget Roberts interpreted by Lijon Eknilang, Mejatto, Republic of the Marshall Islands, June 1986.

Johnson, Giff. (1983, May–June). "Hilda Lini, Pacific Women's Resource Bureau." *Pacific Magazine*. 55–57.

Johnson, Giff. (1984). *Collision Course at Kwajalein. Marshall Islanders in the Shadow of the Bomb*. Hawai'i: Pacific Concerns Resource Centre.

Johnson, Giff. (1990, January–February). "Special Report: 'The Reconstruction of Ebeye'. Ebeye: From Pacific Slum to Isle Showcase." *Pacific Magazine*. 30–32, 34, 39, 41–42, 44–50, 61.

Johnson, Mona Lisa. (1990). Interview by Zohl dé Ishtar, Christchurch, Aotearoa/New Zealand, in November 1990.

Jones, Peter. (1990). "Reduced Tensions in Europe … What do they mean for the Pacific?". *Pacific News Bulletin*, 5(3), 8–9. Sydney: Pacific Concerns Resource Centre.

Keju-Johnson, Darlene. (1983). Statement to the World Council of Churches, Vancouver Assembly. July 30.

Keldermans, Bernie. (1986). Interview by Zohl dé Ishtar and Bridget Roberts, Koror, Republic of Belau, August 1986.

Keldermans, Bernie. (1987). Interview by Zohl dé Ishtar and Bridget Roberts, Manchester, Britain.

Kohu, Hinewirangi. (1986). Speech recorded by Zohl dé Ishtar, Hawai'i, May 1986.

Kohu, Hinewirangi. (1987). Speech recorded by Zohl dé Ishtar at University of California, Los Angeles, USA.

Kohu, Hinewirangi. (1994). "Ancestors, Ancient Mothers." Unpublished poem. Aotearoa.

Kohu, Moana. (1990). Interview by Zohl dé Ishtar, Christchurch, Aotearoa/New Zealand, November 1990.

Koon, Admini. (1986). Interview by Zohl dé Ishtar and Bridget Roberts with interpreting assistance by Lijon Eknilang, Mejatto, Republic of the Marshall Islands, June 1986.

Kyle, Erica. (1989). Interview by Zohl dé Ishtar at The Grail's Women of the Pacific Conference, Townsville, Queensland, July 3–9, 1989.

Laninvelik, Roko. (1986). Interview by Zohl dé Ishtar and Bridget Roberts with interpreting assistance by Xavier Maech, Majuro, Republic of the Marshall Islands, June 1986.

Lechte, Ruth. (1988, January). "No Woman is an Island. South Pacific Women Find Knowledge is the Key to Power." *Be Active for a Nuclear Free and Independent Pacific*, 11, 3. Britain: Women Working for a Nuclear Free and Independent Pacific.

Lewis, David. (1977). *From Maui to Cook. The Discovery and Settlement of the Pacific*. Sydney: Doubleday.

Magnall, Karen. (1987, June). *New Zealand Herald*, excerpts reprinted by Women Working for a Nuclear Free and Independent Pacific. *Be Active for a Nuclear Free and Independent Pacific*, Bulletin. Late Summer, 9, 11. Britain: Women Working for a Nuclear Free and Independent Pacific.

Makanani, Alohawaina. (1986). Recorded speech by Zohl dé Ishtar, O'ahu, Hawai'i, May 1986.

Marfil, Ernestine. (1986). Interview by Zohl dé Ishtar and Bridget Roberts, Wai'anae, Hawai'i, May 1986.

Marianas Visitors Bureau. (1991). *1991 Annual Report*. Saipan, Northern Marianas: Northern Marianas Visitors Bureau.

Marshall Islands Journal. 1985. Vol. 16, No. 17. April. 1, 5.

Maude, H. E. (1986). *Slavers in Paradise. The Peruvian Labour Trade in Polynesia 1862–1864*. Suva, Fiji: University of the South Pacific. (Third edition.)

McAnany, Sister Anna. (1986). Interview by Zohl dé Ishtar and Bridget Roberts, Nanakuli, Hawai'i, May 1986.

McArdell, Pania. (1992). "Whanaupani." In Rosemary Du Plessis with Phillida Bunkle, Kathie Irwin, Alison Laurie and Sue Middleton (Eds.) *Feminist Voices. Women's Studies Texts for Aotearoa/New Zealand*. Auckland: Oxford University Press. 74–90.

McClelland, J. R. (1985). *The Report of the Royal Commission into British Nuclear Tests in Australia. Conclusions and Recommendations*. Parliamentary Paper No. 484/November.

McLellan, Nic. (1989, September). "Liberty, Equality, Fraternity? French military forces in the Pacific." *Sea Change*, 2.

McLellan, Nic. (1990). "Military Changes in the North Pacific: 'No fanfare for naval nuclear disarmament'." *Pacific News Bulletin*, 5(7), 8–9. Sydney: Pacific Concerns Resource Centre.

McLellan, Nic. (1994). Personal correspondence with Zohl dé Ishtar.

McWomynus, Theresa. (1985, April 5). "'Let them dump in their own backyard.' The Struggle for a Nuclear Free and Independent Pacific." *Peace News*. London

Micronesian Support Committee. (1982a, Spring and Summer). "TINIAN: An Island for Uncle Sam?" *Micronesian Support Committee's 7th Anniversary Special Issue. Bulletin*, 7(1&2), 36–38. Honolulu, Hawai'i: Micronesian Support Committee.

Micronesian Support Committee. (1982b, August 1). "Tinian – An Island for Uncle Sam." *Win*. Honolulu, Hawai'i: Micronesian Support Committee. 22.

Minhinnick, Nganeko. (1988). Statement to the United Nations Committee on Human Rights. March 7.

Minhinnick, Nganeko. (1989). Speech recorded by Zohl dé Ishtar at Twenty-Fifth Congress of Women's International League for Peace and Freedom, July 1989.

Minitong, Theresa. (1990). Speech recorded by Zohl dé Ishtar at Pacific Women's Conference, hosted by Regional Pacific Women's Seminars and Resources Development Association, at New South Wales Museum, Sydney, Australia, July 1990.

Monter, E. William. (1977). "The Pedestal and the Stake: Courtly Love and Witchcraft." In Renate Bridenthal and Claudia Koonz (Eds.) *Becoming Visible. Women in European History*. Boston: Houghton Mifflin Company. 119–136.

Morei, Cita. (1992). Interview by Zohl dé Ishtar, Koror, Belau, February 1992.

Mortensen, Annette. (1983, July–August). "Theory: Maori Sovereignty and Matriarchy." *Broadsheet*. Aotearoa/New Zealand. 38–39.

Myers, Ched. (1983, August). "The Wind that Diverts the Storm. The Gospel and the Nuclear Free and Independent Pacific Movement." *Sojourners*, 12(7), 10–13. Washington, DC. USA.

Naidu, Vijay. (1987). Interview by Zohl dé Ishtar and Bridget Roberts, London, England, July 1987.

Napanangka, Tjama. (1994). Interview by Zohl dé Ishtar, Wirrumanu (aka Balgo) Western Australia, January 1994.

Nare, Bertha. (1990, January). "Kanaky: the Life of a Woman." *Be Active for a Nuclear Free and Independent Pacific*, 18, 8–9. Britain: Women Working for a Nuclear Free and Independent Pacific. (Excerpts from speech at Women's International League for Peace and Freedom Congress, Sydney, 1989. July.)

Ngirakedrang, Maech. (1986). Interview by Zohl dé Ishtar and Bridget Roberts, with interpreting assistance by Xavier Ngirakedrang, Koror, Republic of Belau, August 1986.

Ngirmang, Gabriela. (1986). Interview by Zohl dé Ishtar and Bridget Roberts, with interpreting assistance by Lorenza Pedro, Koror, Republic of Belau, August 1986.

Ngirmang, Gabriela. (1988). Unpublished statement to US Senate Energy Committee, January 26, 1988.

Ngirmang, Gabriela. (1992). Interview by Zohl dé Ishtar, with interpreting assistance by Cita Morei and Isabella Sumang, Koror, Republic of Belau. February 1992.

Oliver, Douglas L. (1985). *The Pacific Islands*. Honolulu: University of Hawaii Press. (Fifth edition.)

O'Shane, Pat. (1976). "Is There Any Relevance in the Women's Movement for Aboriginal Women?" *Refractory Girl*. 12/31–34.

OPIR (Organization of People for Indigenous Rights). (nd). *Hunggan!! Chamorro Self-Determination. Mantieni i Direchota. A message for the Organization of People for Indigenous Rights*. Leaflet. Guam.

Ounei, Susanna. (1990). Interview by Zohl dé Ishtar, Christchurch, Aotearoa/New Zealand, November 1990.

Pacific Concerns Resource Centre (PCRC). (1991, February). "Guam Spells Out Its Concerns." *Pacific News Bulletin*, 6(2), 7. Sydney: Pacific Concerns Resource Centre.

Pacific Concerns Resource Centre (PCRC). (1991, October). "The New World Order . . . What does it mean for the Pacific?" *Pacific News Bulletin*, 6(10), 8–9. Sydney: Pacific Concerns Resource Centre.

Pacific Concerns Resource Centre. (1991, November). "Star Wars reborn . . . a 'shield' against Third World 'threats'." Pacific News Bulletin, 6(11), 8–9. Sydney: Pacific Concerns Resource Centre.

Pacific Concerns Resource Centre. (1992, January). "Patterns of Militarisation: some changes in the region." *Pacific News Bulletin*, 7(1), 8–10. Sydney: Pacific Concerns Resource Centre.

Pacific Concerns Resource Centre. (1992, June). "Tahiti: imagining life after the CEP." *Pacific News Bulletin*, 7(6), 6–7. Sydney: Pacific Concerns Resource Centre.

Pacific Concerns Resource Centre. (1993, June). "Regional Security Dialogue amidst an unprecedented arms buildup." *Pacific News Bulletin*, 8(7), 8–9. Sydney: Pacific Concerns Resource Centre.

Pacific Concerns Resource Centre (PCRC). (1993, December). "Nuke Tests Shock." *Pacific News Bulletin*, 8(12), 4. Sydney: Pacific Concerns Resource Centre.

Palacios, Chailang. (1985). Interview by Zohl dé Ishtar and Bridget Roberts, during First Pacific Women's Tour of Britain, hosted by Women Working for a Nuclear Free and Independent Pacific, Britain. March 1985.

Palacios, Chailang. (1986). Interview by Zohl dé Ishtar and Bridget Roberts, Saipan, Commonwealth of the Northern Marianas, July 1986.

Palacios, Chailang. (1992). Interview by Zohl dé Ishtar, Saipan, Commonwealth of the Northern Marianas, February 1992.

Pedro, Balerio. (1986). Interview by Zohl dé Ishtar and Bridget Roberts, Ngeaur (Angaur), Republic of Belau, August 1986.

Pedro, Lorenza. (1986). Interview by Zohl dé Ishtar, Belau, August 1986.

Pomaré Brothers (1987). Interviewed by Zohyl dé Ishtar and Bridget Roberts. Translated by Bridget Roberts. Tahiti, Polynesia, March 1987.

Potaka-Dewes, Kiri. (1989). Speech recorded by Zohl dé Ishtar at Twenty-Fifth Congress of the Women's International League for Peace and Freedom, Sydney.

Pro-Hawai'ian Sovereignty Working Group. (1990, May). "What is Sovereignty?" *Ka Mana O Ka 'Aina. Bulletin of the Pro-Hawai'ian Sovereignty Working Group*, 2(1), 1. Hawai'i.

Rathman, Gwen. (1989). Interviewed by Zohl dé Ishtar, Port Augusta, November 1989.

Rehetaoch, Ubad. (1986). Interview by Zohl dé Ishtar and Bridget Roberts, with interpreting assistance by Xavier Ngirakedrang, Koror, Republic of Belau, August 1986.

Reis, Lola. (1989). Interview by Zohl dé Ishtar at Twenty-Fifth Congress of the Women's International League for Peace and Freedom, Sydney, July 1989.

Reynolds, Henry. (1988). White Man Came Took Everything. In Verity Burgmann and Jenny Lee (Eds.) *A Most Valuable Acquisition. A People's History of Australia Since 1788.* Sydney: Penguin. 1–12.

Riklon, Julian. (1986). Interview by Zohl dé Ishtar and Bridget Roberts, Ebeye, Republic of the Marshall Islands, June 1986.

Roberts, Bridget. (1986, 1987). Excerpts from Bridget Roberts' unpublished journal of the 1986–1987 Pacific Journey.

Roberts, Janine. (1978). *From Massacres to Mining. The Colonisation of Aboriginal Australia.* London: CIMRA and War on Want.

Robertson, Robert T. and Akosita Tamanisau. (1988). *Fiji. Shattered Coops.* Pluto Press in association with Australian Council for Overseas Aid and the Fiji Independent News Service.

Robie, David. (1980, November). "Tahitian Women Protest." *The Nation.* Aotearoa/New Zealand.

Santos, Angel. (1992). Interview by Zohl dé Ishtar, Guam, February 1992.

Sanchez, Tawna. (1987). Speech recorded by Zohl dé Ishtar at Conference University of California, Los Angeles, May 1987.

Sarapao, Margarita Omar. (1992). Interview by Zohl dé Ishtar, Saipan, Commonwealth of the Northern Marianas, February 1992.

Sau Chee Low. (1985, September). "Pacific Human Rights." *Broadsheet.* Aotearoa/New Zealand. 21.

Seman, Jacoba. (1985). Interviewed by Zohl dé Ishtar, Britain, October 1985.

Seman, Jacoba. (1987, May). "Military in Saipan: 'Waltzing Around'." *Pacific News Bulletin*,

2(2), 5, 10. Sydney: Pacific Concerns Resource Centre.

Siwatibau, Suliana and B. David Williams. (1982). *A Call to a New Exodus. An Anti-Nuclear Primer for Pacific People*. Suva, Fiji: Lotu Pasifika Productions, Pacific Council of Churches.

Siwatibau, Suliana. (1988). "Women, Development and Peace in the South Pacific Region." Unpublished paper presented at the Fourth Annual Conference of World Women Parliamentarians for Peace, Canberra, Australia, September 28, 1988.

Siwatibau, Suliana. (1989a). "The Main Issues and Problems in the Pacific and how they affect Women." Unpublished paper presented at the opening of One World or None at Nuclear Free and Independent Pacific dinner, Sydney, September 2 1989.

Siwatibau, Suliana. (1989b). Interview by Zohl dé Ishtar, Sydney, September 1989.

Slatter, Claire. (1988). Speech recorded by Zohl dé Ishtar at European Nuclear Disarmament Conference, Sweden.

Smith, Jude. (1983, February). "Islanders Speak on Nuclear Damage." *Pacific Peacemaker*, 2. Seattle, USA: Pacific Peacemaker.

Solang. (1986). Interview by Zohl dé Ishtar and Bridget Roberts at Museum of the Marshall Islands, Majuro, Republic of the Marshall Islands. Last name withheld.

Souder, Laura. (1989, March). "Self Determination." *The Grail Newsletter*, 21(3), 4–7. North Sydney, Australia: The Grail.

Souder, Laura. (1990). "Guam Update: Chamorro Self-determination and Militarisation of Guam: 'US Violates Spirit and Intent of United Nations Declaration'", *Pacific News Bulletin*, Vol. 5, No. 6. 8–10. Sydney: Pacific Concerns Recource Centre.

Starhawk. (1987). *Truth or Dare. Encounters with Power, Authority, and Mystery*. San Francisco: Harper and Row.

Sumang, Isabella. (1992). Interview by Zohl dé Ishtar, Koror, Republic of Belau, February 1992.

Suzuki, Manami. (1987). Interview by Zohl dé Ishtar, Manchester, England, July 1987.

Taitano, Melissa. (1989). Speech recorded by Zohl dé Ishtar at Twenty-fifth Congress of the Women's International League for Peace and Freedom, Sydney.

Tcheng, William. (1987). Interview by Zohl dé Ishtar and Bridget Roberts, Raiatea, Tahiti Polynesia, March 1987.

Te Awekotuku, Ngahuia, and Marilyn J. Waring. (1985). "Foreigners in Our Own Land." In Robin Morgan (Ed.) *Sisterhood is Global. The International Women's Movement Anthology*. Harmondsworth: Penguin Books. 483–487.

Temaru, Oscar. (1987). Interview by Zohl dé Ishtar and Bridget Roberts in Faa'a, Tahiti, Tahiti Polynesia, March 1987.

Tematua, Maea. (1991). Interview arranged by Marie-Therese Danielsson for Zohl dé Ishtar, and translated and transcribed by Bronwyn Winters.

Tighe, Ruth. (1985). "What Price Tourism?" *Northern Marianas Women's Association Newsletter*. Northern Marianas. 4.

Tima, Aisen. (1986). Interview by Zohl dé Ishtar and Bridget Roberts, Mejatto, Republic of the Marshall Islands, June 1986.

Toyosaki, Hiromitsu. (1986). *Good-bye Rongelap!* Tokyo, Japan: Tsukiji Shokan Publishing

Co. (Photographic essay, with text in Japanese and English.)

Uregei, Louis. (1987). Speech recorded by Zohl dé Ishtar at Bikini Day Ceremony, Papeete, Tahiti-Polynesia. March 1987.

van Vuuren, Nancy. (1973). *The Subversion of Women as Practiced by Churches, Witch-hunters and Other Sexists*. Philadelphia: The Westminster Press.

Vercoe, Rt Reverend Whakahuihui. (1990). "The Treaty and the Bishop." In Hilda Halkyard-Harawira (Ed.) *He Kuaka Marangaranga*. Aotearoa/New Zealand. 6. (Text of speech given at Waitangi, February 6 1990.)

Wai'anae Women's Association. (1982). *A Time for Sharing. Women's Stories from the Wai'anae Coast*. Hawai'i: Wai'anae Women's Association.

Wenkam, Robert and Byron Baker. (1971). *Micronesia – the Breadfruit Revolution. The Marshalls, the Carolinians, and the Marianas. A Photographic Rediscovery*. Hawai'i: East-West Center Press, University of Hawai'i. (Photo-essay by Wenkam, text by Baker.)

Wingfield, Joan. (1988a). Interview by Zohl dé Ishtar, London.

Wingfield, Joan. (1988b). Speech recorded by Zohl dé Ishtar at Greenham Common Women's Peace Camp, Britain.

Wingfield, Joan. (1988c). Speech recorded by Zohl dé Ishtar at Gathering of Women Working for a Nuclear Free and Independent Pacific, Britain.

Wingfield, Joan. (1988d). Speech recorded by Zohl dé Ishtar at European Nuclear Disarmament Conference, Sweden.

Women of Vanuatu. (1973). "Integration of Women in the Development Process." *Pacific Perspectives*, II(2), 1–4.

Women Working for a Nuclear Free and Independent Pacific. (1987). *Pacific Women Speak. Why Haven't You Known?* Oxford: Greenline. (Includes stories told by: Darlene Keju-Johnson, Chailang Palacios, Lijon Eknilang, Lorenza Pedro, Jacoba Seman, Maria Pangelinan, Barbara Flick, Joan Wingfield, and Titewhai Harawira.)

Women Working for a Nuclear Free and Independent Pacific. (1989, February). *Be Active for a Nuclear Free and Independent Pacific*. Bulletin, 15, Cover. Britain.

Women Working for a Nuclear Free and Independent Pacific. (1989, August). "France in the Pacific." *Be Active for a Nuclear Free and Independent Pacific*. Bulletin, 17, 11–17. Britain.

Women Working for a Nuclear Free and Independent Pacific. (1990, March–April). "Aotearoa. Land and Language." *Be Active for a Nuclear Free and Independent Pacific*. Bulletin, 19, 15. Britain.

Yamonson, Elizabeth. (1989). Speech recorded by Zohl dé Ishtar at Grail's Women of the Pacific Conference, Townsville, Queensland, July 3–9, 1989.

Yasseril, Elaine. (1989). Interviewed by Zohl dé Ishtar. Port Augusta, November 1989.

Further Reading

Aldridge, Robert, C. (1989). *Nuclear Empire*. Vancouver, Canada: New Star Books.

Aldridge, Bob and Ched Myers. (1990). *Resisting the Serpent: Palau's Struggle for Self-Determination*. McLean, VA, USA: Fortkamp Publishing Co.

Anti-Slavery Society. (1990). *West Papua: Plunder in Paradise*. London: Anti-Slavery Society.

Awatere, Donna. *Maori Sovereignty*. (1984). Auckland, Aotearoa/New Zealand: *Broadsheet* Magazine Ltd.

Babbage, Ross (Ed.). (1989). *The Soviets in the Pacific in the 1990's*. Canberra: Strategic and Defence Studies Centre, Australian National University.

Bandler, Faith. (1989). *Turning the Tide: A Personal History of the Federal Council for the Advancement of Aborigines and Torres Strait Islanders*. Sydney: Aboriginal Studies Press for the Australian Institute of Aboriginal Studies.

Bell, Diane. (1984). *Daughters of the Dreaming*. Melbourne, Australia: McPhee Gribble/George Allen & Unwin.

Bell, Ian, Glenda Lasslett, George Preston and George Tieman. (1989). *East Timor. The Hidden War. The struggle for justice at home and abroad*. Melbourne: Australia-East Timor Association.

Berger, Julian. (1990). *The Gaia Atlas of First Peoples: A Future for the Indigenous World*. Sydney: Penguin Books.

Biddlecomb, Cindy. (1981). *Pacific Tourism. Contrasts in Values and Expectations*. Suva, Fiji: Pacific Conference of Churches.

Bolger, Audrey. (1991). *Aboriginal Women and Violence*. Casuarina, Northern Territory, Australia: Australian National University.

Chambers, Barbara and Jan Pettman. (1986). *Anti-Racism: A Handbook for Adult Educators*. Human Rights Commission Education Series No. 1. Canberra: Australian Government Publishing Service.

Cheeseman, Graeme and St John Kettle (Eds.). (1990). *The New Australian Militarism. Undermining Our Future Security*. Sydney, Australia: Pluto Press.

Connell, John and Grant McCall. (1989). *South Pacific Islanders in Australia*. Sydney: Research Institute for Asia and the Pacific, University of Sydney.

Connell, John and Richard Howitt. (1991). *Mining and Indigenous People in Australasia*. Melbourne: Sydney University Press in association with Oxford University Press.

Crocombe, Ron and Kushnam Patel. (1985). *Tahiti. The Other Side*. Suva, Fiji: University of the South Pacific. (Oral histories.)

Danielsson, Bengt. (1977). *Moruroa, mon amour: the French Nuclear Tests in the Pacific*. Harmondsworth, Britain: Penguin Books.

Danielsson, Bengt. (1986). *Poisoned Reign: French Nuclear Colonialism in the Pacific*. Ringwood, Australia: Penguin Books. (2nd edition.)

Edwards, Carol and Peter Read (Eds.). (1989). *Lost Children: Thirteen Australians taken from their Aboriginal families tell of the struggle to find their natural parents*. Sydney: Doubleday.

Firth, Stewart. (1987). *Nuclear Playground.* Sydney: Allen & Unwin.

Fyfe, Judith. (1990). *Matriarchs. A Generation of New Zealand Women talk to Judith Fyfe.* Auckland, Aotearoa: Penguin Books. (Life histories of ten matriarchs of Aotearoa.)

Gale, Fay (Ed.). (1983). *We Are Bosses Ourselves. The Status and Role of Aboriginal Women Today.* Canberra, Australia: Australian Institute of Aboriginal Studies.

Gerson, Joseph and Bruce Birchard (Eds.). (1991). *The Sun Never Sets: Confronting the Network of Foreign US Military Bases.* Philadelphia, PA, USA: South End Press.

Goodman, Madeleine J. (1985). "Matrilineal Heritage: A Look at the Power of Contemporary Micronesian Women". Edited by Madeleine Goodman in *Women in Asia and the Pacific. Towards East-West Dialogue.* University of Hawai'i, Hawai'i. 129–52.

Greene, Gracie, Joe Tramacchi and Lucille Gill. (1993). *Tjarany: Roughtail. The Dreaming of the Roughtail Lizard and other stories told by the Kukatja.* Broome, Australia: Magabala Books.

Hinewirangi. (1990). *kanohi ki te kanohi.* Wellington, Aotearoa: Moana Press.

Jones, Peter. (1988). *From Bikini to Belau: the Nuclear Colonisation of the Pacific.* London, England: War Resisters' International.

Kim, Marion Kennedy (Ed. and trans.). (1992). "Once I had a dream . . ." *Stories told by Korean women minjung.* Hong Kong: Documentation for Action Groups in Asia (DAGA).

Knight, Gerald. (1982). *Man This Reef.* Marshall Islands, a Micronitor book published with arrangement with the author. Marshall Islands Museum. (Oral stories as told by male Marshallese elder La Bedbedin.)

Kotovam blong Vanuatu. (1980). *Vanuatu. Twenti wan tingting long team blong independens.* Vanuatu: Institute of Pacific Studies, the University of the South Pacific and the South Pacific Social Sciences Association.

Langton, Marcia. (1990). "Aboriginals: the phantoms of the northern militarisation". In Graeme Cheeseman, Graeme and St John Kettle (Eds.) *The New Australian Militarism. Undermining Our Future Security.* Sydney, Australia: Pluto Press. 169–174.

Mackay, David. (1985). *In the Wake of Cook: Exploration, Science and Empire.* London: London & Wellington.

Macy, Joanna Rogers. (1983). *Despair and Personal Power in the Nuclear Age.* Philadelphia: New Society Publishers.

McIntosh, Malcolm. (1987). *Arms Across the Pacific. Security and Trade Issues across the Pacific.* London: Pinter Publishers.

Micronesian Support Committee and Pacific Concerns Resource Center. (1982, 2nd edition). *From Trusteeship to …? Micronesia And Its Future.* Hawai'i: Pacific Concerns Resource Centre.

Miles, Julie and Elaine Shaw. (1990). *Chronology. The French Presence in the South Pacific 1838–1990.* Auckland, Aotearoa/New Zealand: Greenpeace International.

Moorhead, Alan. (1987). *The Fatal Impact. The brutal and tragic story of how the South Pacific was "civilized" 1767–1840.* Harmondsworth, Britain: Penguin.

Morgan, Robin. (1983). *The Anatomy of Freedom. Feminism, Physics and Global Politics.* Oxford: Robertson.

Neidjie, Bill. (1989). *Story About Feeling*. Edited by Keith Taylor. Broome, Australia: Magabala Books. (Oral history by Bill Neidjie, Bunitj Elder, Northern Territory.)

Pring, Adele (Ed.) (1990). *Women of the Centre*. Apollo Bay, Victoria, Australia: Pascoe Publishing. (Oral histories of eight Aboriginal women.)

Read, Peter. (1982). "The Stolen Generations: The Removal of Aboriginal Children in NSW. 1883–1969." NSW Ministry of Aboriginal Affairs. Sydney: Australian Government Printer.

Reynolds, Henry. (1982). *The Other Side of the Frontier: Aboriginal Resistance to the European Invasion of Australia*. Ringwood, Australia: Penguin Books.

Reynolds, Henry. (1987). *Frontier: Aborigines, Settlers and Land*. Sydney: Allen & Unwin.

Reynolds, Henry. (1989). *Dispossession: Black Australians and White Invaders*. Sydney: Allen & Unwin.

Robertson, Robert T. and Akosita Tamanisau. (1988). *Fiji. Shattered Coups*. Sydney: Pluto Press in association with the Australian Council For Overseas Aid and the Fiji Independent News Service.

Robie, David. (1986). *Eyes of Fire. The Last Voyage of the Rainbow Warrior*. Auckland: Lindon Publishers.

Robie, David. (1989). *Blood on Their Banner. Nationalist Struggles in the South Pacific*. Sydney: Pluto Press.

Robie, David (ed.) (1992). *Tu Galala: Change in the Pacific*. Wellington, Aotearoa/New Zealand and Annandale, NSW, Australia: Bridget Williams and Pluto Press.

Roff, Sue. (1991, January). *Overreaching in Paradise: United States Policy in Palau since 1945*. Alaska: Denali Press.

Rokotuivuna, Amelia. (1988). *Working With Women: A Community Development Handbook for Pacific Women*. New Caledonia: South Pacific Commission.

Santos, Aida F. (1991). *Pangarap at Hinagpis: Mga Awit ng Kababaihang Maralita. Dreams and Woes: Songs of Poor Women*. Quezon City, Philippines: Gabriela, Institute of Women's Studies. (Poetry.)

Sharp, Andrew. (1964). *Ancient Voyagers in the Polynesia*. San Francisco: University of California Press.

Smith, Gary. (1991). *Micronesia: Decolonisation and US Military Interests in the Trust Territories of the Pacific Islands*. Canberra, Australia: Peace Research Centre, Research School of Pacific Studies, Australian National University.

Smith, Joan. (1985). *Clouds of Deceit: The Deadly Legacy of Britain's Bomb Tests*. London: Faber & Faber.

TAPOL. (1983). *West Papua: The Obliteration of a People*. London: TAPOL.

Te Awekotuku, Ngahuia. (1992). *Mana Wahine Maori*. Auckland, Aotearoa/New Zealand: New Women's Press.

Tongamoa, Taiamoni. (1988). *Pacific Women. Roles and Status of Women in Pacific Societies*. Suva, Fiji: Institute of Pacific Studies, University of the South Pacific.

Van Trease, Howard, Barrie MacDonald, and Students at the University of the South Pacific, Kiribati. (1979). *Kiribati. Aspects of History*. Kiribati: Institute of Pacific Studies and Extension Services, University of the South Pacific and the Ministry of Education, Training and Culture, Kiribati Government.

Verhelst, Thierry G. (1990). *No Life Without Roots. Culture and Development.* Translated by Bob Cummings. London, Britain: Zed Books. (First published in French by Editions Duculot, Paris-Gembloux, in 1987.)

Waldman, Carl and Alan Wexler. (1992). *Who Was Who in World Exploration.* New York & Oxford: Facts On File.

Wilks, Judy. (1981). *Fields of Thunder: The Maralinga Story.* Sydney: Friends of the Earth.

Glossary

MARSHALL ISLANDS
Alab. clan leader
biro. cake made from breadfruit
boum boum. small motor boat
Dri Jerbal. traditional landowner
Iroij. paramount chief/public servant
keno. wood
komolo. welcoming custom involving the giving of gifts including food
ribelli. foreigners/white person
wu'u. head garland of flowers
yew. coconut sprout

HEAR US SISTERS
aloha. love
kai. ocean
Ke Anuenue. rainbow
wai. inland water (e.g. rivers, lakes)

BELAU
abai. men's meeting house
Bilung. highest ranking woman of western Koror
Ibedul. paramount chief/public servant
kenpo. constitution
Machas. women elders
Mirair. highest ranking woman of eastern Koror
Motekgnei. traditional religion ("community")
Ollai. magic (now holy oil)
Rubak. male elders
Ulengang. spirits' house

GUAM
aire. air
chelus. brothers and sisters
hanom. water
hinnenghe. spirituality
kottura. culture
linguahe. language
tano. land

NORTHERN MARIANAS
ainang. clans (Carolinian)
gunammwey. peace/abundance (Carolinian)
Ineferri. female Carolinian ancestor who established the clans
Unn. name of Margarita Sarapao's father's clan
utt. man house/boat house (Carolinian)
uu. fishing trap (Carolinian)
Wite. name of Margarita Sarapao's mother's clan

HAWAI'I

'aina. land

akua. gods and goddesses, ancestor spirits

aloha 'aina. love the land

aloha. love

'aumakua. gods and goddesses

halau. longhouse

Haole. foreigner/white person

ho'okupu. offerings to the gods and goddesses

hula. sacred dance

kahu. stewards, carers of the land

kalo. taro

kalo lo'i. taro field

Kanaka Maoli. Indigenous Hawai'ian

kapu. sacred/taboo

kupuna. elder

limu. seaweed

maka'aina. commoner

malama. the sacred obligation to care

mana. sacred power/dignity

'ohana. extended family

po'e. people

Po'e Hawai'i. Kanaka Maoli/Indigenous Hawai'ian

pono. justice, righteousness, hope

FIJI

mataqali. clans (Melanesian Fijian)

narak. hell (Indian Fijian)

taukei. indigenous

Taukei movement. name of the movement that overthrew the elected Government of Bavadra in 1987.

AUSTRALIA

gin. racist term used to refer to Aboriginal woman (British)

Gulda. sleepy lizard – ancestral being of the Kokatha people (Kokatha)

Kanaka. derogatory term to describe indentured labourers/South Sea Islanders. (Br)

karnti. yam (Kukatja)

Kartiya. white/European person (Kukatja)

lipi. white (colour, originally white person)

Mina Mina. a Dreaming track (Kukatja)

Nakarra Nakarra. a Dreaming track (Kukatja)

terra nullius. empty land, uninhabited (British)

tiiwa. long way, far (Kukatja)

Tjakamarra. skin name in kinship structure (one of eight "skins": female Nakamarra)

Tjapanangka. skin name (female: Napanangka)

Tjipari. a Dreaming track (Kukatja)

Tjukurrpa. Dreaming (Kukatja)

yawulyu. women's Dreaming (Kukatja)

AOTEAROA

ariki. leaders, gods

haka. sacred singing

hapu. clan, village

hikoi. the march, struggle

hui. meeting, gathering

hui wahine. women's movement

iwi. tribe/people

kai awhina. carers

kaupapa. philosophy

kohanga reo. language nests

Kohu. sky clan

kura kaupapa Maori. primary school based on Maori philosophy

mana. power, dignity

marae. tribal meeting grounds

nei. no

paepae. welcome bench at entrance to marae

Pakeha. White/European people

powhiri. welcome ceremony

rangatira. leaders

reo. language

reo Maori. Maori language

take. mandate

tamariki. children

tane. man

tangata tiriti. people of the treaty, by virtue of the treaty

tangata whenua. people of the land, Indigenous, Maori

taonga. cultural treasures eg. language

tapu. sacred

Te Ao. the Light

Te Ika a Maui. the great fish of Maui = the North Island

te kawanantanga. governorship

Te Kore. the Darkness, Creative Void

Te Tiriti o Waitangi. the Treaty of Waitangi

Te Waipounamu. the South Island

te whare tangata. the people of the home

tino rangatiratanga. absolute sovereignty

tupuna. ancestor

wahine. women

waiata. sacred song

waiora. medicine

wairua. soul

whakapapa. genealogy

whanau. family

whare waranga. house of higher learning, university

whenua. land

TAHITI POLYNESIA
bébé martyre d'atomique. baby martyrs of the bomb
independantistes. people for independence
Tavini Hurratira. Polynesian Liberation Front
Te Ao Maohi. people of the land
Te Taata Tahiti Tiama. Free Tahiti Party
vahine. women

THE SPIRIT OF RESISTANCE
meri. women (PNG)
meris mani. women's money
Motekgnei. traditional Belauan religion, translates as "community"
ollai. magic/oil (Belau)
ulengang. spirit house (Belau)
wok meri. women's working co-operative based on kinship lines (PNG)

Some Useful Addresses

GENERAL OFFICES FOR THE PACIFIC REGION

Pacific Concerns Resource Centre
83 Amy St, Toorak, Private Mail Bag, Suva, Fiji.
Tel: (679) 304649 Fax: (679) 304755

For more information, subscribe to: Pacific News Bulletin
PO Box 489, Petersham, NSW, 2049, Australia.
Tel: (61) (2) 5526022 Fax: (61) (2) 5524583

Pacific Campaign to Disarm the Seas
Hiro Umebayashi, 3-3-1 Minowa-cho, Kohoku-ku, Yokahama-shi, 223 Japan.
Fax: (81) (45) 5639907

Pacific Council of Churches
PO Box 208, Suva, Fiji.

PACIFIC RIM COUNTRIES

BRITAIN

Women for a Nuclear Free and Independent Pacific,
c/- 89 Great Russell St,
London WC1B 3PS. Britain.

CANADA

South Pacific Peoples' Foundation
415–620 View St, Victoria. British Columbia. V8W 1J6. Canada.
Tel: (1) (604) 3814131

EUROPE

Europe-Pacific Network
PO Box 151, 3700 Ad Zeist. The Netherlands.
Tel: (31) 3404 24844 Fax: (31) 3404 25614

JAPAN

Nuclear Free Pacific Centre Tokyo
c/- Jishu-Koza, 1-3-7, Mukogaoka, Bunkyo-ku, Tokyo. Japan, 113
Tel: (81) (3) 8151648 Fax: (81) (3) 8159325

UNITED STATES

International Indian Treaty Council Pacific Desk
123 Townsend St. 575 San Francisco. CA 94107 – 1907 United States.
Tel: (1) (415) 5121501 Fax: (1) (415) 5121507 Email: Peace Net: IITC

Storytellers

Abbreviations

A Aotearoa	Fr France	J Japan	S Solomon Islands
Au Australia	FSM Federated States	K Kiribati	TP Tahiti Polynesia
B Belau	of Micronesia	Ka Kanaky	TSI Torres Strait Islands
Bo Bougainville	G Guam	MI Marshall Islands	US United States
Br Britain	GT Great Turtle Island/	NM Northern Marianas	of America
ET East Timor	North America	P Philippines	V Vanuatu
F Fiji	H Hawai'i	PNG Papua New Guinea	

Index